PARTISANS OF ALLAH

PARTISANS

OF ALLAH

JIHAD IN SOUTH ASIA

Ayesha Jalal

HARVARD UNIVERSITY PRESS

Cambridge, Massachusetts
London, England
2008

B+T 29.95 4/08

Library of Congress Cataloging-in-Publication Data

Jalal, Ayesha.
Partisans of Allah : jihad in South Asia / Ayesha Jalal.
    p.   cm.
Includes bibliographical references and index.
ISBN-13: 978-0-674-02801-2 (alk. paper)
1. Jihad.   2. Martydom—Islam.   3. Muslim martyrs—South Asia.
4. Islam and politics—Asia.   I. Title.

297.7'20954—dc22   2007040881

For my mother Zakia Hamid Jalal on her eightieth birthday—
celebrating a life exemplifying the struggle to be human

Contents

Maps

Preface

The call to prayer at the break of dawn has a special spiritual significance for Muslims, even if few actually manage to stir from the depths of slumber to give proof of their faith. Not willing to leave the decision to the individual believer, mullahs at the ever-increasing number of mosques dotting the urban landscapes of Pakistan have in recent years taken to forcibly rousing the faithful from bed. Only the deepest sleepers escape the cries every morning of an army of rival muezzins, one more raucous than the last. On recent visits to my home city of Lahore I have been struck by the lack of any elementary spirituality in the half hour cacophony caused by scores of different calls to prayer. Some observers see this as a sign of growing religiosity. Others frown at the excess, which they attribute to the temporal rivalries between as well as within different Muslim sects. Once a simple, beautiful, and melodious invocation of the divine, the *azan* is in danger of becoming nothing but a shrill and strident display of human arrogance.

In my last book, *Self and Sovereignty,* I drew a distinction between religion as faith and religion as a demarcator of difference. The need persists for a disaggregation and contextualization of the elements of religious experience, but it was in the desire to gain a deeper understanding of religion as faith *(iman)* that I launched my research for this book. My exploration of the literature on the subject immediately brought home to me the intrinsic connection between the concept of jihad as endeavor and the Muslim faith. Far from being a passive and mindless activity, submission *(islam)* assumes dynamic effort and reasoned self-control against the personal inclinations and social tendencies preventing a believer from heeding God's commands, and thereby destroying any internal or external sense of balance and proportion. As Frithjof Schuon put it succinctly in *Understanding Islam,* "The practice of Islam at whatever level means to be at rest in effort; Islam is the way of equilibrium and of light resting on that equilibrium." If the purpose of spiritual life and morality in Christianity is the upward flight toward perfection as exemplified by Christ, in Islam it inheres in the realization of an equilibrium without which there can be no center from which to launch the ascent toward union with the divine Creator.

In the unitary Islamic worldview, faith in one God is balanced by an ethical conception of life. The Quranic emphasis on egalitarianism promotes a God-centered humanism, as distinct from the anthropocentric standard of the secular West. How far were these normative ideals upheld in actual historical practice? It is a commonplace to assert that the sacred and the temporal in Islam are inextricably intertwined; however, the interplay of ethics and politics in the unfolding of Muslim history has not been subjected to critical scrutiny. One way of remedying that oversight is to train the spotlight on the much-contested idea of jihad and its practice. To what extent was a concept that is at the heart of Islamic ethics transformed in shifting historical contexts as a consequence of temporal imperatives? Far too often Islam is simplistically associated with a specific geographical location, what is today called the Middle East. Yet some of the key innovations in early modern and modern Islamic thought have taken place in the South Asian subcontinent, which is home to more than a third of the world's Muslims. In particular, the idea and practice of jihad have followed a trajectory in the subcontinent that illuminates the tension between faith and identity that has characterized Islam throughout its history.

The ethical meanings of jihad may well have been often swept aside by legal and political tendencies privileging its connotations as "holy war" against infidels. This propensity makes it all the more important to investigate the historical forces that powered the process leading many Muslims to emphasize the outer husk of their religion more than its inner core. Yet the notion of jihad was never wholly dislodged from its place at the center of Islamic ethics. My own scholarly effort in writing this book has over the past few years been an intellectual jihad, in the sense of a constant struggle based on the rigorous exercise of *ijtihad,* or independent reasoning. It has been an endeavor that has received the support of many institutions and individuals. The moment has come for me to record my gratitude to them.

Grappling with the concept of jihad in South Asian history would have been inconceivable without knowledge of Islamic thought and practice. The John D. and Catherine T. MacArthur Foundation, through five generous years of support, made it possible for me to train myself to read and interpret texts in Islamic theology, law, and philosophy. It was an enriching experience, which has broadened my intellectual horizons and allowed me to connect the separate worlds of religious studies and South Asian history in ways that have significantly influenced this project, as well as my teaching at both the undergraduate and graduate level. I received unstinting support from Tufts University throughout the period of researching and writing this work. I was granted leave for four spring semesters during my time as a MacArthur Fellow to conduct research in archives and libraries in Britain and

South Asia. I owe a special thanks to the provost of Tufts, Jamshed Barucha, for nominating me for a fellowship from the Carnegie Foundation at a most opportune time. To the Carnegie Foundation, I owe an important debt—a yearlong fellowship during 2005–2006, when I most needed the peace of mind to bring my work to fruition.

I have presented parts of this book at several institutions, including Harvard University, Yale University, the State University of New York at Buffalo, Duke University, Ryukoko University in Japan, and University of Brunswick Law School in Fredericton, Canada. My interactions with audiences in these places have helped me better elucidate and fine-tune my arguments. Classroom exchanges with both undergraduate and graduate students at Tufts have played a considerable role in fashioning some of the main arguments in *Partisans of Allah.* My graduate students at the history department and those who took my class on Islam and the West at Fletcher heard my initial arguments and forced me to clarify complex issues. I was fortunate to have capable research assistants in Neeti Nair, Neilesh Bose, Maliha Masud, and Lata Parwani, who procured materials for me from the Tufts and Harvard libraries. In Lahore, Afzaal Ahmad at Sang-e-Meel went beyond the call of duty as my publisher in Pakistan to find me rare books and pamphlets without which my research would have been incomplete. Khwaja Mujeeb Ahmad was also resourceful in obtaining access for me to the publications of different militant groups.

Conversations with many individuals in the United States, Britain, and South Asia have provided valuable insights that hours of solitary research could not. I have gained much from discussing aspects of the research with a number of people, especially Khaled Ahmed, C. A. Bayly, Homi Bhabha, Mridu Rai, and Amartya Sen. I appreciate their support and critical interest in my work. My colleagues at the History Department and the

Fletcher School of Law and Diplomacy have been accommodating and have not begrudged my absences from Tufts. Leila Fawaz has been a caring friend, and she played a pivotal role in convincing me to place my findings in a comparative perspective at conferences organized by the Fares Center, which she directs. Jeanne Penvenne has been a warm and supportive colleague. Shruti Kapila went out of her way to get photocopies of relevant materials from the India Office Library. Annette Lazzara, the history department administrator, has been a model of efficiency and a major factor in keeping life at Tufts on an even keel.

The two anonymous readers for Harvard University Press provided much food for thought and enabled me to improve the overall quality of the work. I was lucky to have found a meticulous editor in Joyce Seltzer. An exacting taskmaster, she gave the text a careful reading. Her suggestions guided me through the final revision and made me conscious of the need to make the book accessible to a larger, nonspecialist audience. Rukun Advani, my publisher in India, spurred me on with his encouraging comments to complete the manuscript for publication.

My family has been as warm and accommodating as always. I am, as ever, deeply indebted to my mother, whose confidence in my abilities is both reassuring and inspiring. I am grateful to my siblings and their families for giving me the time and space to pursue my preoccupation with research and writing. Friends on three different continents have sustained me emotionally by helping me keep things in perspective. Although it is impossible to name them all, I would like to register my thanks to Durre Ahmed, Naazish Ataullah, Nuscie Jamil, and Nita Nazir for their friendship and understanding. When it has come to cheering me along through the occasional highs and more frequent lows of my personal jihad, Sugata Bose has been exemplary in the patience and indulgence he has shown over the years that this project has been on the drawing board. He scrupulously read my innumerable drafts and provided invaluable criticisms, while constantly reminding me that the purpose of this work will be achieved only if it breaches the artificial walls separating an academic and a general readership. If I succeed in reaching out, he deserves the credit in large measure. But if I fail to do so, the blame must rest with me alone.

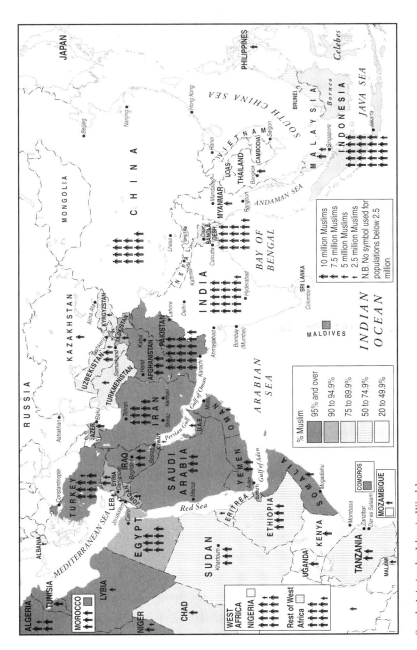

South Asia in the Islamic World

PARTISANS OF ALLAH

⟪ I ⟫

Jihad as Ethics, Jihad as War

B ALAKOT is in many ways the epicenter of jihad in South Asia. Blanketed by green, terraced fields and thick, dark forests, this beautiful town is situated about eighteen miles from the city of Mansehra in the North West Frontier Province (NWFP) of Pakistan. Situated on the banks of the river Kunhar, it serves as a gateway to the picturesque Kaghan Valley, which is bounded on the east and the south by Kashmir. It is also a point of entry into the history of jihad, struggle in the way of Allah, in the subcontinent. It was here that Sayyid Ahmad of Rai Bareilly (1786–1831) and Shah Ismail (1779–1831), quintessential Islamic warriors in South Asian Muslim consciousness, fell in battle against the Sikhs on 6 May 1831. Considered to be the only real jihad ever fought in the subcontinent to establish the supremacy of the Islamic faith, it ended in dismal failure, owing to the treachery of some of the Pathan tribesmen, who had initially rallied to the cause with alacrity. Instead of pursuing the high ethical ideals for which the jihad had been launched, the movement became embroiled in a series of temporal compromises that led to an internecine war among Muslims.

Legends about the Islamic warriors' courageous stand against a vastly superior army of infidels have overshadowed the history of betrayal at the hands of fellow Muslims. The jihad came to be remembered in the early twentieth century as a prelude to anticolonial resistance against the British. With the cry "Allahu Akbar" ("God is Great") on his lips, Sayyid Ahmad had charged out of the mosque where he had said his final prayers, and then bravely faced death on the battlefield. It matters little to his devotees that he achieved his spiritual goal of martyrdom after his temporal ambitions had been shattered by fellow Muslims. For several decades, many believed that Sayyid Ahmad had miraculously escaped from Balakot and would return at the appointed time as their savior. To this day, pilgrims pour into the town to pay homage to the two martyrs, Sayyid Ahmad and Shah Ismail, whose graves have acquired the status of sacred sites. Balakot's association with the idea and practice of jihad in South Asia was reinforced in the 1990s, when militant groups set up training camps in its environs to prepare for their campaign against Indian security forces stationed in predominantly Muslim Kashmir. For these militants, Sayyid Ahmad and Shah Ismail are great heroes, whose jihad their admirers wish to emulate, to redress what they perceive as current injustices.

Almost 175 years after the momentous battle of Balakot, a catastrophic earthquake hit northern Pakistan on the fateful morning of 8 October 2005 and flattened the mountainous town in a flash, adding thousands of martyrs to the few that had given it prominence in the history of Islam in the subcontinent. (The victims of natural disasters like earthquakes are considered martyrs in the Islamic tradition.) Before the Pakistani state's relief operations got under way, young men belonging to radical Islamic groups like the Lashkar-i-Tayyiba (Army of the Righteous) rushed to assist men, women, and children trapped under the rubble. The Lashkar, which appeared on the American list of banned terrorist organizations, has assumed the name Jamaat-ud-Dawa (Party That Propagates the Faith). Instead of the guns and grenades they had learned to use in training camps in and around Balakot to achieve martyrdom in the killing fields of Kashmir, they showed their mettle in the wake of the earthquake, with their bare hands saving the lives of hundreds of people and digging out scores of decomposing bodies and severed limbs. If not for the zealous work done by these young men, the fatalities might have been higher, the despair of Balakot's hapless residents more hellish. Acknowledging the efficacy of their relief efforts, foreign aid agencies joined forces with militant organizations to extend a helping hand to the unfortunates living out under the open sky in what had once been a town of legendary beauty.

Where men had failed, could an act of God change the form of jihad in Pakistan? Had these young radicals found a new way to struggle in the way of Allah? The Lashkar-i-Tayyiba leader, Hafiz Mohammed Saeed, did not see this as waging jihad, but rather as doing relief work. Working to alleviate human suffering might be construed as *jihd-o-jihad,* a derivative of *jihad* used in speaking of everyday struggles. Saeed allowed as much, but in his view the results could not compare with the benefits of the military jihad he and his men were waging in Afghanistan and Kashmir.[1]

An attempt to unravel the multiple meanings of *jihad* in shifting historical contexts is long overdue. Few concepts have been subjected to more consistent distortion than the Arabic word *jihad*—whose literal meaning is "striving for a worthy and ennobling cause" but which is commonly thought today to mean "holy war" against non-Muslims. It is paradoxical that Islam, whose very meaning is *salam,* or peace, has come to be seen as a belligerent religion with fanatical adherents determined to wage perpetual war against unbelievers. This enduring perception stems from an insistence on defining jihad as ideological warfare against non-Muslims, a hopeless distortion of a concept that is the core principle of Islamic faith and ethics. People have lost sight of the ethical connotations of *jihad* in the turmoil of political battles within the Muslim community, as well as the historical imperatives of conquest that temporal rulers have pursued in the name of Islam. A critical analysis of the theory and practice of jihad over the centuries in South Asia can help retrieve its ethical meanings by throwing light on how Muslims interpreted this essential idea as they negotiated relations with members of other religious communities.

Often overlooked in discussions about Islam, South Asia is home to one out of every three of the 1.8 billion Muslims in the world. The region has played a crucial role, politically, economically, culturally, and intellectually, in the history of Islam for over a millennium. Only by identifying some of the key dynamics in Muslim interactions with predominantly non-Muslim populations is it possible to see how legal concepts of jihad in South Asia departed from their West Asian and Central Asian roots to lend fresh nuance to its meaning within the religious framework of Islam. These adaptations over time continue to inform the ideological disputes among Muslims in South Asia. This is true not only of militant groups in contemporary Pakistan but also of anticolonial nationalists who waged jihad against the British.

> Alas, not all things in life are easy;
> Even man struggles to be human.[2]

This deceptively simple couplet by the great Urdu poet of north India Mirza Asadullah Khan Ghalib (1797–1869) on the face of it bears no relation to jihad, popularly construed as holy war. But it lends itself well to a discussion of jihad as a spiritual and ethical struggle that is meaningless without faith *(iman)*. The assertion that nothing is achievable in life without concerted effort is based on the observation that while being human comes

Mirza Asadullah Khan Ghalib, poet of the struggle to be human.

naturally enough, most people do not live up to the ethical standards of true humanity. What troubles the poet are not the hardships of life, but man's unfitness to be the greatest creation of God. It follows that what is deemed to be easy is actually difficult to achieve, and nothing more so than the struggle to be human.

Ghalib's extensive corpus in both Urdu and Persian is imbued with a humanistic sensibility transcending religious distinctions. This great poet was ensconced in the cultural milieu of Hindustan—India, if one gives the term its most expansive spatial interpretation; or in its more restrictive sense, northern India with Delhi as its center. At the same time, he identified himself with the Muslim community and within it, despite his Sunni background, with the Shia sect. Wary of all forms of religious orthodoxy, Ghalib defied social conventions and rejected cultural rituals that set one community apart from the other. True faith for him was not about mundane controversies over belief but about commitment to the unity of God. Never a stickler for external religious rituals, he confessed:

> I know the virtues of devotion and prayer,
> But my temperament leads me to neither.
> . . .
> With what face will you go to the *Kaaba,* Ghalib?
> But then, you are quite shameless.[3]

His poetic evocation of the struggle to be human points to the complexity of ethical issues in the history of Islam in South Asia. Without a heightened awareness of Islamic ethics and of the distinction between the temporal and the sacred aspects of jihad, there can be little understanding of jihad as a key correlate of Islamic faith. Most works on jihad, while nodding in the direction of its spiritual significance, have treated it as the Muslim practice of war, whether of the aggressive or the defensive kind. Relying on historical, legal, and literary sources, this book instead focuses on the development of the idea and practice of jihad over several centuries and across the space that connects West Asia to South Asia. The Indian social and political scene before, during, and after British colonial rule forms the main locus for the unfolding of the history of Islam.

Ghalib's conception of the struggle to be human drew on

the original meaning of *jihad* in the Quran. The word *jihad* is derived etymologically from the Arabic root meaning to strive against an undesirable opponent—an external enemy, Satan, or the base inner self. Pre-Islamic Arab society interpreted it as any endeavor in the service of a worthy cause; other words were more commonly used for warfare. The opening sentence of the Prophet's agreement with the different tribes and religious communities of Medina after the migration *(hijrat)* from Mecca mentions *jahada* as striving for the collective well-being of the whole community consisting of believers and nonbelievers. Fighting for God was incumbent upon all Muslims, whereas the defense of Medina was the responsibility of all signatories to the document.[4] Semantically, *jahada* cannot be interpreted as armed struggle, much less holy war, without twisting its Quranic meaning.

The root word appears forty-one times in eighteen chapters of the Quran—and not always in the sense of sacred war—while prohibitions against warring occur more than seventy times.[5] Apart from verses specifically linking *jahada* to fighting on behalf of God, all its derivative terms are most often used in relation to striving in the cause of faith.[6] The preferred word for fighting in general is *qital* or *harb*,[7] though there are instances of verses prescribing fighting for God.[8] The only form of *jahada* mentioned in the Quran as legitimate armed struggle is *jihad fi sabil allah*—that is, jihad in the way of God. But even verses employing that term are typically followed by exhortations to patience in adversity and leniency in strength, the essence of being of gentle disposition.

If the Quran does not lend itself well to the notion of jihad as holy war, and far less to the idea of continuous warfare against infidels, how did the discrepancy between the text and the later, legally based interpretations of the concept arise? To understand why jihad was effectively stripped of its role as the moving principle of Muslim faith and ethics, we need to broaden the scope of our enquiry from the specific question of warfare to other equally important political and intellectual debates that vexed the early community of Islam. In the first century of Islam, the extremist Kharajite sect defined jihad as legitimate violence against the enemies of Islam, both internal and external, and declared it a pillar of the faith. In the Kharajite view, Muslims deviating from the Quran and practice as prescribed by the Prophet could not remain part of the community. A jihad had to be waged against nonbelievers and those associating other beings with God. Such a radical solution to the problem of true faith met with stiff resistance from those who later assumed the mantle of Sunni orthodoxy. The Kharajites were roundly rejected and none of the early Muslim legal schools endorsed their position.[9]

Although the Kharajite challenge had been thwarted, the debate it had unleashed on the relationship between ethical actions and faith would continue to preoccupy the leading minds of the Muslim community.[10] With the exception of the Kharajites, none of the other participants in the debate considered evidence of moral wrong to be justification for excommunication. Immorality was to be checked through preaching good and forbidding wrong. Some considered this to be jihad of the tongue instead of the sword.[11] Pragmatic accommodation to the problem of immorality left the domain of inner conscience to the individual, while the guardians of the community, religious or lay, concentrated on monitoring external actions. An emphasis on Islamic ritual gave believers a formal unity and served the cause of an expanding religious community. But it was a unity achieved by obfuscating faith *(iman)* and virtuous conduct *(ihsan)* as substantive elements of *islam* and making the performance of ritual practices the primary focus of religious life. The suspension of moral judgment by the Muslim community had grave consequences for an ethics based on the Quran.[12]

In counteracting the extremist Kharajite position, the more influential among the spokesmen of the Muslim community tended to sideline ethics as an intrinsic element of the Muslim faith. The implications of this became even more pronounced once Islamic law *(fiqh)*—the main source of both the Muslim and the Western understanding of jihad—detached itself from the ethical considerations spelled out in the Quran. The expansive Quranic conception of jihad was lost, and it assumed a reductive meaning in the Islamic legal tradition. What had given Islamic law its distinctive character and dynamism during the lifetimes of the Prophet and the first four caliphs was precisely the incorporation of ethical motivations into legal norms based on interpretations of the revelation.[13]

The need for an ideology to legitimate the wars of conquest fought by the Umayyad (661–750) and Abbasid (750–1258) dynasties induced Muslim legists to define jihad as armed struggle and to divorce law from ethics. Classical juridical texts skirted around the moral and spiritual meanings of jihad to concentrate on the material facets of warfare—the division of spoils, the treatment of non-Muslims, and the rules of conduct for the Muslim army. Such stipulations were matched by the invention of traditions (hadith) extolling jihad as armed struggle. Some Muslims questioned the application of the concept of jihad to wars fought by temporal rulers that had nothing to do with struggle for the cause of God. One popular tradition justified the reservation. Upon returning from one of the early wars in defense of the newly established community, the Prophet Muhammad is said to have told his companions that they had come back from waging *jihad al-asghar,* or the lesser war, to fight the *jihad al-akbar,* or the greater war, against those base inner forces which prevent man from becoming human in accordance with his primordial and God-given nature.[14] This tradition was not included in any of the authoritative collections of hadith during the Umayyad and Abbasid caliphates, an omission that in itself reveals the mindset of the compilers and the political climate of the times.

Proclamations of jihad against dissenting co-religionists elicited skepticism from many Muslims. Those with a mystical bent deplored the overemphasis on legal and external aspects of religion, deeming it to be an inadequate expression of the spirit of Islam, which required a jihad to purify the heart, in order to make human conduct truly moral. They contested the reduction of the notion of jihad to armed struggle alone. The Quran itself defines jihad in terms that are much broader than the political uses made of it in response to the exigencies attendant on Arab expansion. What was spread by the sword was not the religion of Islam but "the *political dominion* of Islam."[15] Instead of paving the way for an egalitarian and just order, the expansion of Islam was a secular process that, even when drawing upon religious ideology, rarely managed to achieve the ideals prescribed in the Quran and underscored in the practice of the Prophet.

Notwithstanding changes in Islamic jurisprudence and theology in response to political developments from the end of the seventh century on, mystical, ethical, poetic, and philosophical Muslim literature attest to the indissoluble connection between jihad and the quality of a believer's faith and actions. Sufism in particular contributed in important measure to the development of a humanistic ethics in Islam. Indeed, Muslim ethics has been described as an "ethics of mysticism" because of its inherent spirituality and asceticism.[16] The prominence that the ethical writings of Ibn Miskawayh (d. 1030) and Abu Hamid al-Ghazali (1058–1111) achieved, to say nothing of the widespread appeal of the mystical poetry of Jalaluddin Rumi (1207–1273), make it plain that members of the community never quite lost sight of the ideal of a balance between inner conscience and external adherence to Islamic rituals.[17] By the eleventh century, Muslim writings on ethics *(akhlaq)* bore the imprint of creative borrowings from Greek philosophy. Miskawayh's *Tehzib-ul-Akhlaq,* which is marked by Platonic and Neoplatonic influences, has served as a model for all subsequent Muslim writings on ethics. Significantly enough, it begins with the author's description of his ongoing personal struggle for restraint, courage, and discernment.[18] Writing against the backdrop of the Crusades, Ghazali in his magnum opus does not take a glorified view of jihad against infidels. Like the Sufis, he focuses on the inner spiritual jihad, which he likens to a battle between the armies of good and evil. Good conduct based on self-control and sincere effort in the way of God is described as constituting half of religion, and being of greater merit than ritual worship. In addition to including the famous tradition in which the Prophet makes a distinction between the greater and the lesser jihad, Ghazali quotes him as saying: "Fight your passion with hunger and thirst. Its merits are equal to those gained by Jihad in the way of God."[19] In similar vein, Rumi noted that not everyone killed in battle was a martyr.[20]

The prominence given to legal and theological writings in modern scholarship have had the result that jihad is unquestioningly linked with ideological warfare against the enemies of Islam. In more recent times, it has on the one hand been described as an article of Muslim faith, and on the other equated with terrorism. Shorn of its inner dimensions and reduced to perpetual holy war against non-Muslims, jihad is a recipe for disequilibrium and an inversion of a key concept in Islam. Having uncovered textual evidence of the Muslim preoccupation in the early centuries of Islam with war, a strand of Orientalist scholarship has done much to lend credence to simplistic divisions between the Islamic and the non-Islamic traditions.[21] As in any of the other great religious traditions—Christianity, Judaism, or Hinduism—in Islam the ultimate goal for political and moral philosophy is to create a just and equitable social order. Not only did Islam build on preexisting tribal traditions of kingship in the Arabian peninsula, but it also borrowed from those of the ancient Near East and the Indian subcontinent, as well as the Hellenistic and Roman world.[22] The concept of a just war in Hinduism, as well as in the Judeo-Christian tradition, echoes the interpretation by Muslims of jihad as armed struggle.[23]

An exclusive reliance on the works of legal scholars and theologians would be far too limited to provide a measured view of jihad in Muslim history.[24] Legists and theologians with ties to state power tailored the concept of jihad to fit the shifting requirements of temporal rulers, who even while paying lip service to Islamic law (sharia) administered their domains on the basis of secular law. Not a creed or religion in the narrow sense of the word, Islam is often deemed to be an all-encompassing way of life *(din)* whose precepts are unchanging in nature. This has become a pretext for drawing an unjustified stark distinction between Islam and concepts of the secular.[25] Ignoring the passage of time and a constantly changing tradition has skewed understanding of Islam, to the detriment of Muslims and non-Muslims alike. Notions of the religious and the secular borrowed from historical experience of other religious traditions cannot explain the subtle overlap between the spiritual and the secular in Islam. In Christendom, the clash between the authority of the church and that of the state established the contours of so-called religious and secular space. In the absence of a church in Islam, secular state authority had no need to separate itself from the religious.

The word *secular* has a dual meaning, for it refers to both location and time. Secularization is an historical process through which human beings abandon otherworldly concerns and focus on the here and now. During the European Enlightenment, religion came to be seen as an impersonal system of beliefs and practices, rather than a matter of personal faith. Without denying the existence of a Creator, Enlightenment thought rejected the notion of the cruel and punishing God who threatened mankind with eternal damnation. It was the consolidation of the modern nation-state in the nineteenth century that established the separation between religion on the one hand and law, science, rationality, and politics on the other. According to the confident assumptions of this particular brand of modernism, the increasing secularization of daily life would ultimately marginalize religion or relegate it to the private sphere. The long historical process of secularization had been an open-ended one, in which values and worldviews were subject to revision. The secularism of the modern nation-state, by contrast, became a closed ideology, which projected its values as absolute, superior, and final. The certitude underpinning the secularism of modern states must not be confused with the relativity of values and vibrant debates that marked the more ecumenical process of secularization.[26]

Despite widespread unease among Muslims with what is perceived as the hubris of secularism in modern nation-states, the history of Islam could not have escaped the process of secularization. Islamic theocentricism, on the face of it, is antithetical to secularization based on human assumption of the responsibility to reformulate ethical values. Yet Muslims throughout history have resorted to the right of rational interpretation *(ijtihad)* to question values not strictly embodied in the Quran. This questioning is in keeping with the Islamic aim of effecting a revolutionary change in human consciousness through ethical social development. The Islamic conception of religion has been explained by stressing: submission *(islam),* or obedience relating to external acts, faith *(iman)* pertaining to the believer's inner thoughts, and virtuous intentions *(ihsan)* aimed at doing what is beneficial for the individual and the community.[27] In the hierarchy of importance spelled out in the Quran, faith in one God and the unity of creation *(tawhid)* precedes submission, whether individual or collective. Virtuous intentions expand and deepen faith, so that it becomes a lived certitude, thereby ensuring that *islam,* instead of being restricted to specific rituals and attitudes, touches every aspect of a believer's life.[28] Living according to the teachings of the Quran and the Prophet requires not only submission but also faith and good intentions. If the triad of submission, faith, and good conduct is constitutive of Islam, its moving principle is the notion of jihad as a spiritual, intellectual, and moral struggle. To isolate jihad from faith and virtuous intentions is to lose sight of the high ethical standards that distinguish mere mortals from human beings, and to reduce the sacred to the profane and the transcendental to the purely worldly.

Intrinsic to faith in the unity of creation, and to the moving principle of Islamic ethics in political, economic, and social activity, jihad has been susceptible to consistent misunderstanding and misuse. Confusing God's will with the practical and logistical imperatives of an expanding Muslim community, and conflating the sacred and the profane, Muslim exegetes, legists, theologians, and historians in different times and places have distorted the meaning of jihad in the Quran. Without restoring the historical dimension and the distinction between the temporal and the sacred, there can be no understanding of jihad as a key correlate of Islamic faith and ethics. A multilayered concept like jihad is best understood with reference to the historical evolution of the idea in response to the shifting requirements of the Muslim community, especially in the South Asian context.

The relation between the normative theory of jihad and its actual historical practice followed a somewhat different trajectory in the South Asian subcontinent than it did in West Asia. In the Arab lands tensions between Islamic law *(fiqh)* and religion in the broadest sense *(din)* that were caused by the imperatives of the wars of conquest had made the extrinsic features of being a Muslim more important than the spiritual and ethical struggle to be human. Some of the debates between legists *(fuquha)* and philosophers *(falsuf)* in West and Central Asia were replicated in South Asia. But there was a crucial difference. The subcontinent, where the Islamic faithful are in the minority, is an interesting laboratory for a study of the multiple, less reductive meanings of jihad. India under Muslim rule was deemed to be a *Dar-ul-Islam,* an abode of peace. According to the jurists, jihad could only be waged against a *Dar-ul-Harb,* an abode of war. The legal discourse on jihad and *aman,* or the granting of peace to non-Muslims, developed by the dominant Sunni school of Hanafi law in the subcontinent, featured pragmatic adjustments to the Indian environment. Sufis and freethinking philosophers contested the narrow interpretations of the Arab and Arab-influenced legists and theologians throughout India's precolonial history. The accommodative tendencies were in the ascendant during much of the Sultanate and the Mughal era stretching from the thirteenth to the seventeenth centuries. These attitudes gained their fullest expression during the reign of the Mughal emperor Akbar (1556–1605), who enunciated a policy of peace for all. Akbar's attempts to build bridges with non-Muslims in his empire did, however, provoke a withering critique from the Muslim theologian Sheikh Ahmad Sirhandi (1564–1624). War and peace, faith and ethics were matters of constant debate in precolonial India.

Many of the key innovations in modern Islamic thought were fashioned in South Asia rather than West Asia. Muslim rulers in the subcontinent were not indifferent to the sharia, as is best illustrated by the *Fatawa-i-Alamgiri,* a late seventeenth-century compendium of Hanafi law, commissioned by Akbar's great-grandson Aurangzeb. Yet it was not until the eighteenth century that fears about the loss of Muslim sovereignty triggered a redefinition of jihad as the obverse of *aman.* The writings of the redoubtable Delhi-based scholar Shah Waliullah (1703–1762), known for his enunciation of the most systematic theory of jihad in South Asia, must be read in this historical context. His career bridged the precolonial and colonial eras of South Asian history. Hailed as being at once a Muslim modernist and the architect of Sunni orthodoxy, Waliullah left an intellectual legacy that casts a long shadow over all subsequent explications of jihad in theory and attempts to translate it into practice.

It was Waliullah's theory that Sayyid Ahmad of Rai Bareilly sought to implement between 1826 and 1831. His endeavor illustrates how the high ethical values associated with jihad were diluted by the confusion between religion as faith and religion as a demarcator of difference as well as of pragmatic compromise. The geographic focal point of the jihad of 1826 to 1831 on the northwest frontier of the subcontinent corresponds to the nerve center of the current confrontation between Islamic radicals and the West. The jihad movement directed primarily against the Sikhs was transmuted in the course of the war into a conflict pitting Muslim against Muslim. This feature of intrafaith conflict in a jihad as armed struggle has not diminished its appeal for contemporary militants, who evidence many of the same failings that undermined Sayyid Ahmad's high ideals. The martyrdom of those who fell at Balakot continues to weave its spell, making it imperative to investigate the myth in its making.

If Sayyid Ahmad of Rai Bareilly's early nineteenth-century jihad was seen as a precursor to an anticolonial war, his namesake Sayyid Ahmad Khan (1817–1898) of Aligarh tried in the late nineteenth century to reinterpret jihad in terms other than those of armed struggle. He and other Muslim modernists like Maulvi Chiragh Ali (1844–1895) and Mirza Ghulam Ahmad (ca. 1839–1908)—the controversial founder of the heterodox Ahmadi community—made concerted attempts to rethink jihad in the light of British colonial rule. The historical context of the decisive suppression of the great rebellion in 1857 is of great importance for understanding the reformulation of the idea of jihad. Yet the texts need to be read on their own terms, not least because of the intellectual caliber of those who were responding to colonial strictures on Islam as a religion of the sword and perceptions of Muslim disloyalty. Variously dismissed as apologists of Islam and colonial collaborators, these men tried in their different ways to bring the concept of jihad closer to the expansive, spiritual meanings it has in the Quran. They also played a major role in constructing a communitarian view in late nineteenth-century India of a distinctive Muslim identity. It is thus useful to trace the extent to which efforts to revive the role of jihad, both in theory and in practice, as a core principle of Islamic ethics reflected their notion of jihad as defensive warfare.

With the start of a new Western offensive against the Muslim world in the late nineteenth century, jihad entered another historical era, one that created the conditions for articulating an Islamic universalism that could be squared with the competing ideal of territorial nationalism. The universalist dreams of Sayyid Jamaluddin al-Afghani (1839–1897), the magnetic Iranian who initiated the campaign against Western imperialism in the Muslim world, may have been somewhat ahead of his time. But his ideas found a welcoming niche in the thought and politics of such pro–Indian National Congress Muslims as Maulana Abul Kalam Azad (1888–1958) and Obaidullah Sindhi (1872–1944). Even as they espoused their own versions of Islamic humanism and sought common ground with non-Muslims, these two anticolonial nationalists saw jihad as a legitimate means to wage a transnational struggle against British imperialism. Azad, a key voice in the field of Islamic law and ethics, was the preeminent Muslim leader of the Congress, not just in preindependence India but also in the first decade after independence. Paradoxically, he is best remembered today as a "secular nationalist," having served as education minister in India's first independent government led by Jawaharlal Nehru. Azad's less successful contemporary, Obaidullah Sindhi, was a Sikh convert to Islam who tried giving practical shape to Waliullah's ideas by starting a transnational jihad during World War I with the help of Afghans, Germans, Russians, and Turks. His own writings and the memoirs of some of his close associates offer a welter of insights into the complex mindset of anticolonial nationalists, for whom jihad was a powerful weapon against the British as well as a means to combat injustices in their own society. Even the great poet and philosopher Muhammad Iqbal (1877–1938), not an anticolonial radical by any stretch of the imagination, dwelled at length on the virtues of jihad as struggle against Western imperialism. His poem "Jihad" lamented that Muslims in the face of colonial subjugation had lost all delight in death.

The history of jihad in postcolonial South Asia spotlights the relationship between the modern nation-state and the ulema, or religious scholars trained in madrassas. The end of British colonial rule brought the partition of the subcontinent, ostensibly along religious lines, and the transfer of power to two nation-states—one avowedly secular, the other created as a Muslim homeland. Contrary to the perception that modernity had eclipsed the role of religious scholars, managers of modern states like Pakistan gave the ulema greater prominence, by letting them pose as guardians of public morality, if not Islamic ethics, so long as they did not undermine state authority. The thought of Islamic ideologues like Abul Ala Mawdudi (1903–1979) and the politics of contemporary self-styled "jihadis" need to be studied in this context. The renewed interest in jihad by Mawdudi and, through him, by such West Asian radicals as Sayyid Qutb—the two authors most frequently cited by Western "experts" on so-called Islamic fundamentalism and terrorism—had more to do with the internal dynamics of Muslim society than with an outright rejection of modernity under Western colonialism. In a sense, jihad in the postcolonial era has been a more effective instrument of political opposition to the secular modernity promoted by Muslim nation-states than of resistance to Western domination. Mawdudi advocated waging jihad against faithless and unethical Muslims as a means toward achieving an Islamic society as he conceived it. The irony in proclaiming jihad against co-religionists has been lost on those who adopted Mawdudi's reformulation of the concept. Yet with the exception of Saudi Arabia and Iran, Muslim nation-states have desisted from formally declaring a jihad, even as they have selectively implemented parts of the sharia that do not undermine their claims to temporal power. This is a judicious response, to be sure, which in such states as Pakistan has resulted on the one hand in efforts to enforce punitive aspects of the sharia, in the guise of Islamization, and on the other in support for so-called jihadis waging war to liberate co-religionists in Afghanistan and Kashmir.

Muslim nation-states have been more eager to manipulate and control religion than to correct the acts of omission and commission committed during the early centuries of Islam. These, in separating law from the ethical teachings of the Quran, led to external rituals' replacing virtuous actions as the predominant concern of the community. The result has been not just the secularization of Islamic law but the diminishment of the ideal of jihad from the spiritual to the profane. Armed struggle in the way of God is a contradiction in terms, without reference to the ethical values outlined in the Quran. Jihad today is a pliable instrument in the hands of a few who are more politically motivated than ethically grounded. Their version of jihad has in turn nourished ill-informed denunciations of Islam, most notably among commentators and policy makers in the West. The bias and suspicion pervading these administrative circles have historical roots in the age of modern imperialism, when the theme of jihad was interwoven with the anticolonial struggle. By teasing out the shifting interpretations of jihad in different historical phases, I aim to restore its essential meaning as an ethical struggle to be human and thereby more effectively combat the forces of disequilibrium that plague the contemporary world.

⟪ 2 ⟫

Jihad in Precolonial South Asia

Sᴏᴜᴛʜ ᴀsɪᴀ furnishes rich historical evidence of the multiple meanings and symbolisms of jihad in Muslim consciousness. From court chroniclers seeking to legitimate wars fought by their patrons against non-Muslim and Muslim rivals to Muslim legists and theologians articulating theories that later reappeared in symbolic form in Persian and Urdu poetry and prose (to say nothing of popular myths and legends), advocates of jihad have been many—testimony to the potency of the idea and its pivotal place in the Muslim imagination. Representing in all their variety the manifold meanings of jihad in Muslim society, these expressions undermine any notion that the idea is associated exclusively with armed struggle. The Urdu phrase *jihd-o-jihad,* denoting effort and exertion in a positive endeavor, finds widespread use in everyday life. At the same time, collective myths and legends about jihad based on selective representations of history have been part and parcel of popular consciousness—none more so than the jihad launched by Sayyid Ahmad of Rai Bareilly in the early nineteenth century. Widely cited and variously remembered, it serves as a trope whose psychological and mythological meanings and symbolism continue to inform political and ideological disagreements among Muslims in South Asia.

Deciphering both the sacred and secular symbolism of jihad in South Asia illustrates how the politics of religious identity shaped the idea, in combination with Muslim conceptions of faith *(iman)* and ethics—both as *akhlaq* and *adab* (literally, correct social behavior). This region, where the Muslim faithful are in the minority, constitutes a particularly interesting case study for jihad against non-Muslims. Often downplayed in discussions about Muslims, South Asia is crucial to the historical evolution of the idea and practice of jihad. Jihad had multiple meanings in precolonial India, tensions between law *(fiqh)* and religion *(din)* making the external facets of being Muslim more important than the inner spiritual and ethical struggle to be human. Muslims in precolonial India had constantly to face the challenge of balancing the inner dimensions of faith with the external manifestations of their identity in new and ever-changing circumstances.

Jihad or Temporal Warfare?

A spate of conquests by Muslim warlords from the beginning of the second millennium on is often described as the "coming of Islam to India." An emphasis on the militaristic aspects of the Muslim expansion overlooks how Islam in South Asia, far from being a signed and sealed product exported from West Asia, was fashioned by the Indian environment. Muslim rulers' recourse to an ideology of jihad for purposes of legitimacy was counterbalanced by the practical need to govern non-Muslim subjects. Despite the demographics, India under Muslim rule was considered a *Dar-ul-Islam* (an abode of peace). According to the jurists, jihad could only be waged against a *Dar-ul-Harb* (an abode of war). This perception made the Indian subcontinent a fascinating testing ground for the historical application of the Islamic principles of war and peace.

The layered meanings of jihad in South Asia can be best grasped by analyzing the different worldviews underlying the written historical sources—by identifying their strengths and weaknesses and juxtaposing their claims. Although Islamic law was initially developed by Central Asian ulema that flocked to Delhi during the period of the sultanate, Muslim efforts to seek accommodation with non-Muslims lent fresh nuance to Islam as both a faith *(iman)* and a culture *(adab)*. Insofar as faith has been key to the articulation of religiously informed cultural differences,[1] it is useful to explore how Islamic law dealt with the problem of Muslim rule over non-Muslims. The commentary of two Hanafi scholars—Abu Yusuf and Muhammad ash-Shaybani—on the twelfth-century Central Asian jurist Ali ibn Abi Bakr Marginani's *Al-Hedaya* provided the blueprint for Islamic jurisprudence in the subcontinent.[2] Islamic legal theory does not recognize custom as an independent source of law. In the absence of textual sources, *Al-Hedaya* accorded customary practices a role in legal theory, thereby facilitating the adaptation of Islamic principles to preexisting social customs in newly conquered territories.

The application of Hanafi law in a context where Muslims were in a minority had important implications for the concept of jihad. Legal interpretations of jihad in South Asia, though based on those developed in Western and Central Asia, also departed from them, while remaining within the religious framework of Islam. Under classical jurisprudence, a non-Muslim refusing to accept Islam or pay the *jizya,* or poll tax, could legitimately be put to the sword. There had been disagreement among classical jurists whether *jizya* could be collected from non-Arab polytheists. But as early as Muhammad bin Qasim's conquest of Sind in A.D. 712, safe-conduct was extended to non-Muslims who agreed to pay *jizya,* in acknowledgment of their protected status under Muslim suzerainty.[3] The elasticity of Muslim jurisprudence, despite its perceived hidebound character, can be deduced from the treatment of jihad and its obverse, *aman* (peace), in legal discourse and practice.

Elaborated by jurists hailing in the main from commercial backgrounds,[4] Hanafi law marks the triumph of the material over the spiritual in Islamic law. Ownership of property was the defining feature of the legal personality, or *zimma,* defined as an individual who can claim rights and incur obligations. From *zamm,* "to blame,"[5] *zimma* means the capacity to incur contractual obligation and resembles *aman,* in that it guarantees the security of life and property. The Islamic concept of *zimmi,* a non-Muslim granted peace by a Muslim authority, was a substantial improvement over slavery. *Zimmis* were given equal legal status if they were owners of property. As a human being, a slave is a legal person. But as the property of other people, a slave cannot own property and is therefore not a full legal person.[6] Without erasing all differences between Muslims and non-Muslims, discrimination in matters to do with religion did not extend to the secular sphere of socioeconomic interactions. Such liberality of vision made Hanafi classics like *Al-Hedaya* essential reading for the more erudite among India's Muslim rulers.

In addition to authors of works on jurisprudence, court chroniclers employed the trope of jihad, along with its concomitants *ghazi* (warrior of the faith) and *shaheed* (martyr), to shower praise on royal patrons. Since these works were uncritically taken as source materials for later histories, jihad as a war against infidels had become part of popular imagination long before colonial historians appeared on the scene. A succession of Muslim writers commenting on Mahmud of Ghazni's raids into India between 997 and 1030 defined it as a jihad against *kafirs.*[7] A *kafir* is one who denies the truth of the one and only God. Its transference to entire groups of people, by blurring the distinction between the temporal and the sacred, fuels the belief that Muslims are enjoined by their religion to subjugate, convert, or, failing that, kill infidels. Like all half-truths, this charge has resonated in inverse proportion to its historical credibility. Muslim warlords no doubt had a sense of their religious identity and sought legitimacy in Islamic law whenever it suited their purpose. But when temporal necessity proved incompatible with sacred law, Muslim warlords and dynasts had no qualms about skirting around the injunctions of the sharia. Throughout the long period of Muslim rule in the subcontinent, the sharia remained subordinate to the laws decreed by temporal rulers, displaying varying degrees of faith and piety.

Some of the Indian ulema were always ready to castigate rulers for departing from the norms of the sharia in their efforts to govern a predominantly non-Muslim population. Often religious exclusionists for whom Islam served more as a determinant of identity than a faith, they were loudest in showering praises on the valor of Muslim rulers who were described as *ghazis* or *shaheeds.* Any sort of cross-fertilization of ideas was frowned upon and declared heretical. Among the more important statements of their ideological position was the *Din Panha,* the doctrine for the protection of religion, enunciated by Nuruddin Mubarik Ghaznavi at the court of Shamsuddin Iltutmish in the thirteenth century.[8] Its rank bigotry toward Hindus made it politically inexpedient to implement. But its spirit continued to influence the politics of a segment of the Muslim ulema in its battles for power and prestige.

A succession of Delhi sultans kept opponents of accommodation with non-Muslims at an arm's length. It was a delicate balancing act, since alienating the ulema could undermine claims to Islamic legitimacy, not something any Muslim ruler was prepared to countenance. So a Faustian bargain was struck between temporal and religious authorities. Throughout the period of Muslim rule in India, the ulema occupied most of the non-military positions in the state administration. The rulers could bypass the sharia in the interests of statecraft but by the same token could not aspire to be guardians of the faith—a status the ulema claimed for themselves by spreading specious traditions about their inherent superiority in matters having to do with religion. In classical Islamic political theory, the Muslim ruler (imam) was the vice-regent of God, and the ulema were the heirs of the Prophet. The Quran condemns remuneration for propagating the divine message and rejects the institution of professional priesthood. This categorical commandment made it difficult for products of Muslim religious seminaries to eke out a living. By the eleventh century, Muslim legists had found ways to justify the existence of a professional class of salaried religious officials responsible for giving the call to prayer and performing other rituals in public and private mosques. *Al-Hedaya* upholds the legitimacy of payment for religious duties.[9] The ulema associated with private mosques and madrassas continued to enjoy a measure of autonomy from temporal authority. Those dependent on state employment had no choice but to refrain from attacking policies that contravened the sharia.

It is tempting to see this as evidence of the secular triumphing over the religious. A closer analysis of the historical evolution of the sharia in South Asia, however, militates against a clear-cut separation of the religious and the secular. With the dissociation of ethics from law after the third century of Islam, the content of the sharia, if not its form, was subject to secularization through constant interpretation and change. Hanafi *fiqh* became the dominant school of jurisprudence in the subcontinent as early as the reign of Qutb-ud-din Aibek. All manner of court cases were decided by judges *(qazis),* however, using the principle of equity *(itisihan)* to privilege customary laws *(urf)* over the sharia.

Known as *qanun-i-shahi* or *zawabit,* these contained both religious and secular elements and applied to both Muslims and
non-Muslims in varying measure.[10]

While Muslim rulers made a point of paying lip service to the
sharia as defined by jurists and theologians, secular works on
ethics like Khwajah Nasir ud Din Tusi's *Akhlaq-i-Nasiri* and Muhammad bin Asad Dawani's *Akhlaq-i-Jalali* are known to have influenced notions of good governance in India under both the sultanate and the Mughals.[11] A deep concern with legitimacy and an
ability to divide temporal sovereignty acted as safeguards against
any tendency toward absolutism. Under the norms of Muslim
rule, absolute sovereignty was vested in Allah. As his vice-regent—or the "shadow of God on earth"—the ruler had ultimate
responsibility to Allah, which served as a check on the ruler's secular role as lord and master of his subjects. The administration of
law and order, intrinsic to legitimacy, was vital to fulfilling that
responsibility, given the Quranic emphasis on justice and equity,
or *adl.* Integrating Greek thought with Islam and borrowing
heavily from Miskawayh's *Tehzib-ul-Akhlaq,* Tusi's thirteenth-
century text interpreted justice as social balance among conflicting interests. This has led to a flawed historical argument that
although religion was a part of the ideal state, it was not religion
(din) as defined by the jurists and the theologians. The sharia was
important, in this view, but it was not sharia in the strict juridical
sense. Justice, the cornerstone of the sharia, was seen to be defined in terms of secular ethics.[12]

The merits of such an argument are marred by the separation it assumes between the secular and the religious. This can be
quite misleading if "secular" implies the capacity to respond to
temporal change and "religious" refers to unchanging divine
principles. Even though no one would deny the importance of
akhlaq literature—a sort of mirror for princes—in defining Muslim norms of governance, the sharia was not in fact wholly dis-

tinct from a secular ethics. Muslim rulers, it is generally accepted, were not indifferent to the sharia. Several Delhi sultans and the Mughal emperor Aurangzeb actively cultivated the ulema, the legists among them in particular. A recognition by temporal rulers of the juristic authority exercised by the legal scholars afforded madrassa-educated Muslims opportunities for state employment. This created the basis for lucrative collaboration between state power and the ulema. But there were also important points of contention. Rulers consulted the jurists when administrative requirements made it necessary to refer to the sharia. The most popular form of juristic literature was the fatwa, which took the shape of questions and answers to key legal issues. While adhering to the broad principles outlined by earlier works of jurisprudence, the muftis or the givers of fatwas in their responses took account of the changing socioeconomic and political context in India. Typically, the muftis were expected to take ethical considerations into account when delivering an opinion. But the judge *(qazi)* was under no obligation to give greater weight to an opinion simply because it ranked higher on the ethical scale. In principle a judge schooled in the methods of Islamic jurisprudence could use his independent judgment *(ijtihad)* when there was disagreement among the jurists on any particular issue. If he was not a qualified *mujtahid* (one who has the legal training to exercise independent reasoning), he was expected to hand down a ruling based on the fatwa of a learned jurist.[13] Disagreements were widespread, and later generations of legists frequently departed from decisions rendered by their mentors. This practice ensured that even though the broad outlines of the sharia were observed, jurists had considerable scope to accommodate temporal change when doing so was politically expedient.[14]

Underscoring the constant overlap between the religious and the secular in precolonial India is the distinction in Hanafite law between the private rights of individuals *(huquq al-abad)* and the rights of God *(huquq al-allah),* the latter of which comprise the public rights of the state in connection with the welfare of the community. The rights assigned to human beings, including the right to life and property, are covered by the law of transactions and the rules governing marriage, the family, inheritance, and parts of penal law. All acts of religious devotion, including jihad, are subsumed under the rights of God, which in Islamic law cover adultery *(zina),* the consumption of alcohol, and theft or banditry.[15] Punishments for infringing the rights of God *(hud)* are specified in the sharia and can be imposed on Muslims and non-Muslims alike, except in the case of the consumption of alcohol, punishment for which is exclusively applicable to believers. Penalties relating to the violation of the rights of man *(tazir)* are not mentioned in the sharia and can be enforced on Muslims only with the sanction of a Muslim ruler. The Islamic law on homicide, *qisas* (just retaliation), has two facets. One relates to the rights of man, in that it deals with compensation to the kin of the murdered victim. The other stems from the rights of God, in that it aims to keep the world free of conflict and sedition. The second resembles the Islamic idea of waging jihad to establish peace and harmony. With the exception of punishment for certain *hud* offences that is imposed for the well-being of the community, the rights of man have primacy over the rights of God because, unlike human beings, God is all-powerful.[16] This reasoning partly explains why discussions of jihad as armed struggle in the legal literature deal more with the secular than with the divine.

Given that the procedural aspects of the law were more important than the ethical content of the ruling, the activity of the legists could hardly avoid the stamp of expediency. The issues commonly referred to legal scholars had to do with the legal status of non-Muslims; the ruler's share in the spoils of war and other proceeds of the state treasury; imposition of taxes; and punishments to be meted out to leaders of heretical sects and political offenders.[17] In the event of a clash between a sharia ruling and the needs of the emerging state, it was never in doubt that temporal power would take precedence. The struggle between state power and the legists reflected the broader contest between temporal rulers and the ulema for the mantle of Islamic authority. In executing God's will, the ruler and his selected law officers, like *qazis* and muftis, had to appear to be doing what was just and right. And even though rulers often made light of the legal niceties in asserting their temporal authority, certain honest and courageous Muslim judges dared to question the excesses of a sultan. A high value was placed on a judge's moral and ethical qualities. The personal erudition and local stature of the judge were more important than his role as an appointee of the sultan in determining the relative quality of the administration of justice.

When the great Moroccan traveler Abu Abdallah ibn Battuta (d. 1368) visited India in the early 1330s, he ended up spending nearly eight years as magistrate of Delhi in the administration of Muhammad bin Tughluq. Battuta belonged to the Maliki school of Islamic jurisprudence, whereas the overwhelming majority of Indian Muslims followed the Hanafi school. Tughluq could afford to overlook the discrepancy. While formally respecting the sharia—he is said to have memorized *Al-Hedaya*[18]—Tughluq kept a tight lid on the ulema and on Sufis and curtailed the independence of judges to formulate legal opinions. He gave the position to Battuta as a royal sinecure. As was the wont of the nobility, Battuta showered gifts on the sultan to retain his favor. The duration of his stay in India was marked by excessive expenditure. His indebtedness made him even more dependent on the sultan. The only known ruling Battuta gave as a judge imposed in full the specified sharia punishment *(hud)* for drinking wine—eighty lashes![19] If he had cared to consult the Hanafi canons, Battuta might have been more lenient. Although a transgression of the

limits set by God, the consumption of alcohol often went un-
punished, owing to the conditions defined by jurists for the detection and reporting of the crime. According to the popular dic-
tum, it was better for the judge to forgive in error than to punish
in error. Typically a drinker was liable to be punished while he
smelled of alcohol. There was always room for doubt, the possibility of denial on the part of the accused, or repentance leading
to forgiveness. A Hanafi judge might very well have let off the
transgressor Battuta punished, because he had confessed to con-
suming alcohol eight years earlier![20]

Sentences for *hud* offences were not intended to eliminate sedition and sin from *Dar-ul-Islam*. They could be rooted out only
by means of repentance *(tawba)*—and not through the enforcement of *hudood*—literally, transgressions of set limits. Anything
residing in the inner sanctum of individual consciousness lay beyond the scope of a law geared to monitoring external actions.
Hud was enforced by the imam or someone deputed by him. Offenders were punished only in extreme situations, and even then
the accused was given ample opportunity to deny or repent. In a
glaring example of utter disregard of the ethical values spelled out
in the Quran, Hanafi jurisprudence held that an imam, who had
no superior authority over him, was not liable to be punished if
he drank, stole, or accused someone of adultery. This made nonsense of the normative view that as the slave of God, the imam
was no more immune to punishment than his subjects. Indian
legists, using their power of interpretation to make politically expedient rulings, took the secularization of Islamic law to new
lengths. Since power was a key determinant of change, later
Hanafi jurists overlooked Abu Hanifa's view that force was legitimate only when used by the ruler. Indian *fuqaha* conformed to
the opinion of later jurists, in holding that the use of force by any
man powerful enough to enforce his will was legitimate.[21]

Letting Muslims rulers off the hook in plain violation of God's rights was the kiss of death for any sort of Islamic ethics. The limited Quranic basis for the Muslim administration of justice did not, however, signify that jurists lacked influence over the broader community to which they belonged. Their monopoly on interpreting law and implementing the sharia gave them an advantage over temporal rulers in shaping the popular conception of religion. A certain degree of ambiguity continued to characterize the relationship between the ulema and temporal authority. While judicial officials endorsed state actions that contributed to the public interest, equity, and necessity, the ulema jealously guarded their own domain of expertise and reserved the right to critique rulers for transgressing Islamic norms.[22]

Under weaker rulers, the ulema flourished through political intrigue, issuing fatwas against heresy as well as against unacceptable innovation *(bidat)*. But as a corporate interest, they never managed to reverse state policies, for some within their own brotherhood were only too eager to come to the aid of a ruler accused of transgressing Islamic law. The ulema met their nemesis in the Mughal emperor Akbar, during whose reign they were kept firmly in control. Depicted as a *ghazi* by court chroniclers detailing his military exploits, Akbar often invoked divine dispensation to legitimate his rule. His personal correspondence is laced with Islamic idioms and reflects an awareness of the high ideals that ethicists expected of a just ruler.[23] Akbar's rejection of all forms of orthodoxy and policies of religious reconciliation earned him the stinging abuse of a segment of the ulema led by Sheikh Ahmad Sirhandi who accused him of being an infidel.[24] In Akbar's India, according to Sirhandi, things had "come to such a pass that the *kafirs* openly ridicule Islam and abuse the Muslims." He was particularly irked by "the ceremonies of the *kufr* in every street and bazaar," not least because "such liberty was denied to the followers of Islam," who were "reviled for obeying the *Shariat*."[25] A firm believer in the need to use state power to enforce Islam, Sirhandi coined the slogan "*Shariat* can be fostered through the sword."[26] But even when the ruler was renowned for his faith and piety, as in the case of Aurangzeb, the temporal concerns of government *(dawla)* outweighed those of religion *(din)*. Contests between the wielders of state authority and the ulema were not about secular and religious power, as is commonly conceived, but over the monopoly claimed by the divines on interpretations of what was Islamic and un-Islamic.

The common misconception that the sharia is divinely ordained and unreceptive to change has prevented a systematic analysis of the concept in historical context. The *Fatawa-i-Alamgiri,* which superseded the *Fatawa-i-Firuz Shahi,* was commissioned by Aurangzeb to lend coherence to Hanafi jurisprudence in India.[27] Its *Kitab al-Siyar* provides many useful insights into legal opinions on jihad that technically come under that aspect of retaliation *(qisas)* which relates to the rights of God. Yet the jurists were expected to give more weight to the rights of man if these conflicted with the rights of God. Since the legal validity of a ruling is more important than its judiciousness in establishing the truth in Islamic law, it is no cause for surprise that what passes for jihad bears little if any resemblance to its Quranic source. The *Kitab al-Siyar* does not refer to jihad as a spiritual and ethical struggle. In treating jihad as armed struggle, it avoids the issue of intentionality and concentrates on delineating precise rules for the division of spoils, the treatment of defeated enemies, and the norms of behavior expected of Muslim soldiers. More like a manual of commercial behavior and fair exchange, the *Kitab al-Siyar*'s reduction of jihad to the norms of temporal warfare is manifestly "secular" in orientation.

There is a fascinating case about two fictional characters, Zayd and Umro. Zayd gives Umro money and materials to wage jihad. The legal question testing the jurists' grounding in the Quran and hadith is whether Umro can use the money and materials for himself and his family. The variation in responses allowed a good deal of scope to the judge to exercise independent judgment.[28] According to one view, if Zayd asked Umro to use the money and materials to wage jihad on his behalf, then Umro cannot use it himself. But if Zayd said, this is yours, go and wage jihad with it, Umro can use it for himself and his family. If he cannot go to fight the jihad, he can give the remaining money and materials to someone else to wage jihad. He can also give the money to the state treasury and avoid jihad. Alternatively, he can decide to keep the money for his personal use and not go on a jihad at all![29]

The willingness to divorce ethical considerations from the norms of waging war in the name of God makes a parody of the Quranic idea of jihad. The *Fatawa-i-Alamgiri* makes plain that what is otherwise considered sinful is acceptable if it furthers the temporal aims of warfare. Soldiers are expected to obey the orders of the Muslim commander even if they entail committing a sin. But at the same time, soldiers can disobey the orders of the commander and commit sins if doing so furthers the cause of the Muslim community. Although it is preferable for the imam to appoint a sagacious, pious, and courageous man to lead the Muslim forces, the ruler is at liberty to appoint the best available man, even if he is an egregious sinner![30] When it came to jihad as a means of consolidating Muslim temporal power, most Hanafi jurists preferred to take the course of pragmatism.

A preoccupation with external conformity to Islam, understandable in a context where many of the faithful were new converts, is borne out by legal rulings on waging jihad and the extension of peace *(aman)*. Since jihad can be waged only against a non-Muslim who refuses to accept Islam or pay the *jizya,* the jurists spilled considerable ink arguing over when an infidel's conversion was legitimate. Their rulings betray a concern with drawing community boundaries. There is a striking lack of concern with the soundness of faith *(iman)* or the performance of virtuous actions *(ihsan)* on the part of the new adherents. A non-Muslim who declares himself a Muslim is not considered one unless he publicly renounces his earlier faith. If he changes his mind, he will be killed, even if he recites the first part of the Islamic creed: "There is no God but God." In the event that the new convert does not recant publicly but says his prayers with the Muslim congregation, he will be considered a Muslim. The jurists disagreed whether a new convert who says his prayers in private can be deemed a Muslim. Abu Hanifa thought that private prayers were insufficient to bring the new convert into the Muslim fold. Later jurists held that a new convert could not be killed if he was seen offering prayers in a mosque. According to one juristic opinion, a non-Muslim could be forcibly converted. Another jurist asserted that a non-Muslim who accepts Islam while intoxicated will be considered a Muslim. If he renounces his decision once he is sober, he will be considered an apostate and punished accordingly.[31]

At the same time, Hanafi jurisprudence was relatively broadminded when it came to providing protection to non-Muslims—a vital issue in governing mainly Hindu India. Even if a Muslim granting peace *(aman)* to a non-Muslim is no more than a peasant, the offer is binding on the entire community. Any Muslim killing a non-Muslim who has been granted safe conduct faces the same punishment based on retaliation *(qisas)* as for slaying a Muslim. A non-Muslim living under Muslim rule *(zimmi)* who has participated in jihad can extend a promise of security if asked to do so by the commander of the Muslim forces; however, the ruler can, after conveying the decision to the concerned party, withdraw the protection if it is considered detrimental to Muslim interests. In principle, non-Muslim women cannot be granted *aman,* because they are war booty in the same way as jewels and other forms of liquid capital. Under certain conditions, an enemy can request that the *aman* also cover his womenfolk. Jurists invoking the principle of equity *(istishan)* can extend *aman* to his dependents. Such gestures toward peace and accommodation with non-Muslims, however, were overshadowed by juristic pre-occupations with the status of the material goods owned by the man seeking protection. In principle, everything a man brings with him when he asks for protection belongs to him and is not included in the war booty. Since this meant denying Muslims their due share of the spoils of war, the jurists ruled that if the seeker of *aman* came overladen with goods, these would not be considered protected, on account of the evident excess.[32]

An emphasis on the material rather than the spiritual aspects of jihad was symptomatic of a much broader collusion between secular authority and the would-be guardians of the sharia. It did not go uncontested. Sufis, philosophers, and free thinkers roundly opposed the worldly men of religion who were prepared to dance to the tune of a temporal ruler. They were derogatively called worldly clerics—ulema-*i-duniya* or ulema-*i-suh*—in order to differentiate them from the ulema-*i-akhirat* or the ulema-*i-rabbani*—literally, those concerned with the hereafter and spiritualism. The distinction attempted to spare the pious and the virtuous from the ignominy of association with those who compromised faith for practical advantage. But it was a slippery one to uphold and served merely as a weapon to discredit opponents.[33] Such internal divisions among the ulema gave rulers considerable latitude to assert temporal power without renouncing their own claims to religious authority.

Early Debates on Indian Muslim Identity

Not only are misplaced notions rife about the relation between the secular and the religious, but too much has also been made of the clash between Sufis and the would-be guardians of the sharia. The differences were really more about temperamental preferences, esoteric or exoteric, than about doctrinal differences. Spiritually minded ulema were also Sufis, just as many learned mystics were religious scholars *(alims)*. In the subcontinent there are more instances of warrior saints' combining their mystical leanings with the tradition of chivalry *(futawa)* to fight jihad than of the worldly clerics' taking up arms in the cause of Islam.[34] Few Muslim mystics rejected the sharia. Most deemed it to be the external manifestation of the inner spiritual struggle through strict adherence to the correct path *(tariqah)* toward the one and only truth *(haqiqah)*. Believers of a mystical orientation see concordance between religious traditions and view them as expressions of the same ultimate truth.[35] Sufism in its efforts to accommodate Islam to the Indian environment did make compromises with regional cultural traditions. This was hardly a novel development. Islam had, since its first appearance on the Arabian peninsula, permitted the incorporation of customary practices, so long as these did not violate the basic tenets of the faith. If mystical excesses contributed to the vulgarization of the tenets of Islam, "orthodox" exponents of Sunnism put forth a welter of ideological myths that distorted the teachings of the Quran and the Prophet.

More serious than the clashes between Sufis and the ulema were disputes originating in the cultural orientation of proponents of one Islamic point of view or the other. The most significant cultural cleavage was between the Arabized and the Persianized *(Ajami)* forms of Islam. Culturally, the Persian imprint was more widespread and remains so to this day. It elicited opposition from those who drew upon Arab influences, which took the form of puritanical movements.[36] Crusaders for the Arabized form of Islam were incensed by the willingness of Sufis—especially those who did not adhere strictly to the sharia—to accommodate popular practices associated with Hinduism. The critique of polytheistic practices covered the gamut of activities, from attacks on such popular superstitious practices as worshipping at the graves of saints to calls for the remarriage of widows to disdain for those who failed to perform the hajj. At the intellectual level the criticism manifested itself in disagreement, starting in the early fifteenth century, between those who followed Ibn al-ʿArabi (d. 1240) and those who adhered to Ahmad Sirhandi's interpretation of the ideas of the Central Asian mystic Ala'ud-Daula Simnani (1261–1336).[37]

Ibn al-ʿArabi upbraided Sufis, especially al-Ghazali, for suggesting that God could be known without any reference to the temporal world. Ignoring Ibn al-ʿArabi's subtle but crucial distinction between the affirmation of God's transcendence *(tanzih)* and his likeness in created beings *(tashbih),* Ghazali accused al-ʿArabi of conflating God's essence and his attributes. The charge of pantheism coming from varied quarters to this day is based on a misreading of Ibn al-ʿArabi.[38] He never denied the difference between God and his creation. But he did note that the sacred was immanent in the world, an attitude of mind that inculcates respect for other human beings irrespective of their specific religious traditions. He likened the synthesis of the two aspects to perceiving the "Many as One and the One as Many." According to Ibn al-ʿArabi, only the Prophet Muhammad and the Quran embodied real harmony and synthesis between the transcendence of God and his likeness to created beings.[39]

Though Ibn al-ʿArabi never used the term, his followers popularized his main ideas under the name *wahdut al-wujud*—literally, the unity of creation. Opponents of the concept, like Sirhandi, saw in it elements of pantheism and posited the alternative of the *wahdut al-shuhud,* or the unity of appearances. Despite tensions at the level of terminology, the two concepts overlapped in historical practice. Reduced to the slogans of *hama ust* (All is God; *wahdut al-wujud*) or *hama az ust* (All is from God; *wahdut al-shuhud*), it pitted Sufis as well as the ulema against one another. In his highly intellectualized notion of the unity of all creation, incomprehensible to the vast majority of Muslims, Ibn al-'Arabi rejected the difference between Islam and infidelity *(kufr)* as a merely superficial phenomenon. Instead of probing the deeper implications of his line of reasoning, his detractors seized upon it—most notably Taqi al-Din Ibn Taymiyya (1263–1328), who charged the Andalusian theosophist of association *(shirk)* with God.[40] This line of critique was promising for Muslims living in historical contexts where they felt politically threatened as a minority. Sirhandi attacked Ibn al-'Arabi for supposedly suggesting that the status of the infidel might be good and salutary, and that evil was relative only to true faith and righteousness. This suggestion was tantamount to sanctioning misguidedness. In Sirhandi's opinion, Islam and unbelief are incompatible, and the strengthening of one can only come at the expense of the other. Sirhandi fulminated against keeping company with infidels, who should be "kept at arm's length like dogs"; and he asserted that "no relationship should be established with *kafirs*."[41]

Adherents of Ibn al-'Arabi's ideas, who were known as *wujudis,* tended to be more open-minded than other Muslims about the cultural practices of other religious communities.[42] In principle, Sufis of all schools subscribed to the popular maxim "Those who die before they die, they are not dead when they die." This was not a celebration of martyrdom on the field of battle but of spiritual triumph over the lower self, which through annihilation *(fana)* attains to salvation *(baqa)* in the unity of creation. Mystical writings regularly invoke the dagger of *la,* signifying the Arabic letters *lam* and *alif* which constitute the first word of the Muslim creed, *la ilaha ilallah.*[43] Waging war against infidels tended to be a natural corollary of this inner purification for those influenced by Sirhandi, who were referred to as *shuhudis.* By contrast, the *wujudis* preached universal humanity and put a premium on *jihad al-akbar,* the greater jihad against the lower self which the Prophet had said was "man's greatest enemy."

The leading fourteenth-century proponent of Ibn al-'Arabi's thought in the subcontinent, Sheikh Sharf ud-Din Ahmad bin Yahya Manyari, ridiculed those who wanted to annihilate non-believers with the sword.[44] He placed a premium on the inner battle against self-conceit, which was the source of infidelity and polytheism. The well-being of Muslims was more important than prayers and fasting, and there should be no question of compelling anyone to perform actions against his will. He was dismayed by hypocrisy parading as religion. Faith was rare, and the faithful as precious as the philosopher's stone. The greatest obstacle to religion was government office, which Manyari likened to an idol and a Brahmanical thread of steel. "What type of Muslims are these," he lamented, "who are neither true to the people nor to God?" This was "mere confusion, not Islam"; "a self-conceited one cannot worship God at all."[45] Faith was nothing but release from self-conceit—a highly ethical concept, to say the least.

Not only does blanket condemnation of Ibn al-'Arabi's followers as pantheistic denigrate their liberal stance on social and cultural accommodations, but it is symptomatic of the failure to come to grips with the mystical orientation.[46] In declaring that all is God, the *wujudis* never implied that God is in the material world, as their detractors maintained, but only that the world itself is inexplicably immersed in God.[47] An equally powerful charge against this strand of Islamic thought has been its alleged erasure of the distinction between faith and unbelief. Ibn al-'Arabi's followers cultivated a temperament that saw only good in the world, and no evil. To suggest that such a worldview cannot arrive at "a genuinely ethical plane," as Fazlur Rahman has argued, confuses an intellectual stance with a moral world view.[48] Like Ibn al-'Arabi, Manyari saw no difference between infidelity and faith because God had no need of either. What mattered was piety and virtuous actions. This was the essence of the ethical life lived by the Prophet, and it required struggle against oneself, the greater jihad without which religion was a mirage.

In the power struggles that characterized the precolonial and early colonial Indian social and political landscape, people lost sight of these subtle but significant points. With the sense of community fractured by ideological and sectarian divisions, the intellectual standoff between *wujudis* and *shuhudis* bred opposing attitudes of mind, accommodative or closed, open-minded or plainly bigoted. Historically, the *wujudi* view predominated and flourished. Through creative interactions with yogis and Hindu saints, it gave rise to the devotional *bhakti* movement and aided Islam's adaptation to the Indian environment.[49] Sirhandi deplored these accommodations. He hated the Sufis for not differentiating between faith and infidelity but held the worldly ulema responsible for all the ills Muslims had suffered. They had misled the rulers and contributed to the division of the community into seventy-two squabbling sects. As a result, the "entire world appear[ed] like a vast ocean of darkness" on account of innovation, and the Islamic tradition had been reduced to "a mere glow-worm."[50]

Yet long before Akbar's religious policy of peace for all and his great grandson Dara Shikoh's exertions to assimilate Sufism and Hindu mysticism, Sufis studying the *Advaita Vedanta* found it entirely compatible with Islam.[51] It was the efforts at mutual dialogue and knowledge about each other's religious traditions that rankled with the *shuhudis,* for whom the exclusionary attitudes of a Sirhandi were a more effective means of combating the sense of insecurity that flowed from residing in a sea of infidels.

Shah Waliullah's Intellectual Legacy

The eighteenth-century sage Shah Waliullah (1703–1762), credited with explicating the most systematic theory of jihad in South

Asia, made a concerted attempt to harmonize all points of contention between the *wujudis* and the *shuhudis,* as well as between scholars of the Sufi *tariqah* and of the sharia. He compared knowledge of the unity of creation *(wahdut-ul-wujud)* to the waters of the Nile, which are water to adherents and a curse for opponents. Since ordinary Muslims were incapable of understanding the issues involved, it was best for them to stick to blind imitation *(taqlid)* on questions of the sharia and ignore the writings of the theologians.[52] His widely acknowledged intellectual feats in reconciling the *wujudi-shuhudi* rift and bridging the gulf between the upholders of the *tariqah* and those of the sharia*,* however, were tainted by inherited as well as acquired beliefs and biases. In Waliullah's own words:

> I hail from a foreign country. My forebears came to India as emigrants. I am proud of my Arab origin and my knowledge of Arabic, for both of these bring a person close to "the *sayyid* (master) of the Ancients and the Moderns," "the most excellent of the prophets sent by God" and "the pride of the whole creation." In gratitude for this great favour I ought to conform to the habits and customs of the early Arabs and the Prophet himself as much as I can, and to abstain from the customs of the Turks *('ajam)* and the habits of the Indians.[53]

As he explains in his magnum opus *Hujjut Allah al-Baligha* (literally, the conclusive argument from God), "loving the Arab is a way to taking on their style" and "a means for inclining one to join the monotheistic (Hanafi) religion since it was instantiated through their customs and determined by the command of the divine law brought by Muhammad."[54]

Waliullah's pro-Arab bias flowed from his antipathy toward the Persian and Hindu influences on the Mughal state. Waliullah deplored the decadent lifestyle of the nobility and attributed Delhi's steady drift toward anarchy after Aurangzeb's death in 1707 to a Shia and Hindu conspiracy to weaken Muslim state power. At the same time, he was aware of the internal reasons for the ethical degeneration of the Indian Muslim community. The scion of a noted scholarly family of Delhi, Waliullah spent his formative years under the tutelage of his father, Shah Abdul Rahman, who had briefly joined the group of ulema invited by Aurangzeb to help compile the *Fatawa-i-Alamgiri*. An accomplished scholar with a deep understanding of the Islamic intellectual and mystical tradition, the elder Shah did not take long to realize the futility of the exercise. Reforming the ethical values of Indian Muslim society was no mean undertaking.

Aurangzeb's imposition of Hanafi law made a mockery of the administration of justice. Zealous attempts by the department of accountability *(ihtisab)* to act as a moral police encroached on similar duties previously assigned to Muslim law officers. The accountability department's agenda for establishing Islamic morality was the prohibition of consumption of wine and cannabis *(bhang)*, destruction of temples, and supervision of weights and measures in the market. It failed to eradicate the smoking of cannabis—even the *muezzins* of Delhi mosques allegedly smoked it. The department tried compensating by enforcing prescribed lengths for trousers and beards, making a laughing stock of its officials and further undermining its own credibility. Instead of spreading morality, the promotion of sharia laws allowed criminals and corrupt revenue officials to expiate their crimes by embracing Islam. Unscrupulous debtors sought refuge in Islam to evade creditors, by accusing them of reviling the Prophet. The result was complete degeneracy and, worse still, utter disarray and confusion in the administration of justice.[55]

A firm believer in the Islamic principles of justice *(adl)* and balance *(tawazun),* Waliullah tried revitalizing Sunni orthodoxy with a frontal attack on the spread of polytheistic and heretic practices among Indian Muslims.[56] In his opinion, while Islam was a universal religion and open to all, a distinction had to be made between those who accepted the message of the Prophet and those who did not. Contact with infidels undermined faith; he advised Muslims to live so far from Hindu towns that they could not see the light of the fires in Hindu houses.[57] If the circumstances pertaining in the first half of the eighteenth century led Waliullah to emphasize religion as a demarcator of difference, he also wrote prolifically on religion as faith. The pen of the heart, he once wrote, was purer and more eloquent than the pen of the tongue, for "God does not look at your faces and actions but keeps an eye on your hearts."[58] One of the leading originators of orthodox Sunni Muslim thought in modern South Asia, Waliullah handed down writings that elucidate the relation between jihad and *iman* at the normative level, in addition to affording opportunities for seeing the practical outcome of that understanding.

A prolific theologian and sensitive mystic, Waliullah was a master of Islamic jurisprudence *(fiqh)* and a keen observer of human history, who aimed at providing a complete political, social, and ethical framework for the regeneration of Sunni Islam in India. A Hanafi of the Maturdite persuasion who admired al-Shafi for privileging independent reasoning and hadith, he considered renouncing affiliation to any particular school of jurisprudence. Upon receiving a divine vision, he decided to concentrate on harmonizing the four schools of Sunni jurisprudence as a first step toward unifying a divided community. Like Sirhandi, he gave more weight to the sharia than to the Sufi *tariqah* and tried reconciling the two by bringing about a synthesis in the grand Hegelian mode.

Waliullah has been described as the "bridge between medieval and modern Islam in India." Others have called him "the founder of Muslim Modernism."[59] If his championing of the hadith gave rise to puritanical reform movements in Islam, his equally emphatic endorsement of independent reasoning inspired Muslim modernists to try to craft an Islamic response to colonialism and Western modernity. They were encouraged by his apparent familiarity with new forms of knowledge in the West.[60] Like so many Muslim modernists after him, Waliullah stated that the resurgent West merely reflected back the knowledge it had borrowed from the Islamic sciences. In the preface to the *Hujjat,* he claims that God inspired him to write the book because the time had come to elucidate the laws of the sharia on the basis of scientific reasoning.[61] But for all his rich intellectual contributions, particularly in the domain of Islamic ethics, this doyen of Sunni orthodoxy was also responsible for providing the intellectual justification for a stark distinction between the internal and the external facets of the community.

This feat is all the more remarkable given that Waliullah distinguished between the outer husk of religion and its inner kernel, which he likened to the pearl concealed in the oyster shell. The entire thrust of his philosophy was to tease out the inner meaning of Islamic symbols and practices. He did so by integrating mystical, intellectual, and scriptural sources with rational argument, knowledge of history, and empirical observation. His undeniably ambitious enterprise was informed by a worldview based on an internal dialectic of conflict between different stages of consciousness and the struggle to balance and harmonize them, in order to attain a higher purpose. As such, the Quranic concept of jihad as a constant inner spiritual struggle aimed at achieving an ethical way of life pervades Waliullah's syncretic and theocentric philosophy.[62] "Our battle," he once wrote to a close friend and associate, "is also one of the branches of peace." A true believer was one who used his rational faculties to investigate the matter in a balanced manner, to avoid dictums of Hanafi law that were contrary to the hadith.[63]

This effort was especially urgent in an "age of *fitna* (social discord)," which was how Waliullah viewed the political situation in eighteenth-century India.[64] With his keen interest in human psychology and history combined with contextually specific interpretations of the Islamic tradition, he proposed stiff measures to counteract non-Muslim influences. Valuing action above intellectual insight, he stressed the external over the internal dimensions of Muslim identity and called for renewed interest in jihad as armed struggle. This tactical rather than a strategic position never entailed a denial of jihad's broader meaning as permanent effort for balance in all spheres of life. The only logical *hikmat-i-amali,* or practical wisdom for Muslim rulers, was to strengthen community boundaries by conducting jihad against opponents and promoting the cultural practices *(adab)* that differentiated the faithful from non-Muslims. Jihad's quality as a generative virtue made it an ideal ideological aim for Muslim state power in India.

Islam was the most perfect of all revealed religions, according to Waliullah, because it enjoined jihad. Like a bitter medicine to be administered to the patient, jihad was a self-correcting principle preventing dispersion, and the cornerstone of sociopolitical equilibrium.[65] It was because of the jihad carried out by the Prophet and his companions that Muslims conquered territories and established the Islamic way of life as the only logical course for humanity. This proved that jihad as armed struggle was vital for the political glory of the community.[66] A critic of dynastic rule, Waliullah recognized the need to deploy state power to create an Islamic social order in the subcontinent, so he made a virtue out of pragmatic necessity. He matched an incisive intellectual critique of hereditary rule with practical efforts to strengthen Muslim power. A strong Muslim state was needed to wage jihad against social practices that in his opinion ran counter to the tenets of Islam. The contrived nature of the reconciliation underlined the gap between intention and result in Waliullah's advocacy of jihad as an instrument of state power. Equally significantly, the outcome reflected the ambiguity that had always characterized relations between the ulema and the wielders of temporal power.

Waliullah may have been "radical" by the standards of Sunni orthodoxy;[67] yet for all his willingness to engage with the wider world and his affirmation of the universal validity of human values, he upheld many strictures of mainstream Sunnism and did much to consolidate its precepts in the light of his own times. Anything short of a complete transformation of the Mughal state, in his opinion, would result in divine chastisement:

> When wrong doing, conflict, disorder . . . overindulgence in pastimes, profligacy, pursuit of charming things . . . , use of instruments of music become widespread, and every socioeconomic development becomes a burden on man and every earning changes into suffering carrying no benefit whatsoever and the ruling authority resorts to oppression, then will await man a suitable punishment in some countries which then will be dominated by the most powerful persons who will violate the honour of their inhabitants. I find Delhi heading towards that punishment.

The only hope for the inhabitants of the city was to "take recourse with a learned man who may straighten their crookedness and guide them to the right path."[68]

Waliullah was staking a bid for the intellectual and ethical leadership of the Muslim community, not simply as a learned man but as a spiritual leader. An adherent, like Sirhandi, of the Naqshandiya order, he too claimed to be a *qutb* (literally, a pole or axis)—a medium through whom God and the Prophet Muhammad communicated in dreams and visions. *Qutb* signifies the axis or support where the transcendent intersects with the temporal. Waliullah justified his claims on the grounds that an individual who had striven to acquire true spirituality and then balanced it with reason could become the recipient of God-given knowledge. Such a person could discover beneficial elements in the sharia of which other people were unaware, and use them to buttress civilization.[69] This is what the prophets had done by combining divine revelation with the customary practices of the people among whom they lived. While certain acts are deemed to be inherently good or bad by all people no matter what their cultural and ideological differences, others are specifically prescribed or prohibited by God. Demonstrating the capacity of Islamic thinkers to incorporate the temporal and the secular within the their religious framework, Waliullah maintained that it was possible for the select to have knowledge about things on which the sharia was silent.[70] Together with his insistence on independent reasoning, this point allowed sufficient scope for the development of a theory in which human life on earth evolves, so that it increasingly converges with divinely revealed moral law.

Waliullah saw the historical development of human societies as leading to religious life suited to the ideal form of humanity. According to this view, when humankind attains the highest stage of religious consciousness *(irtiqadat),* social relations will mirror spirituality. Waliullah uses the term *irtifaqat* for the different stages of civilization, which he defines as balanced socioeconomic and political life based on an understanding of the salutary purposes of the sharia. The term is derived from the Arabic root *rfq,* which means gentle, soft, gracious, and civil, and the eighth form of the Arabic verb from this root conveys the idea of resting on a support. He identified four stages of *irtifaqat:* 1) the elemental aspects of collective life based on natural and instinctual laws; 2) the integration of family life and social transactions according to just principles; 3) the establishment of a local political order, as in the governance of a city *(madinah);* and 4) the extension of this order to the international level, in the form of a universal Islamic sovereignty or caliphate *(khilafat),* which he considered the ultimate stage of human development.[71] The various stages are a reflection of the different levels of spiritual proximity to God *(irtiqadat).* Each stage is an elaboration of the preceding stage.[72] The first stage of *irtifaqat* provides for the basic needs of human beings. The second stage adds the knowledge of experiment and ethics. Aesthetics *(zarafat)* is added at the third stage, the initial political form of the Islamic state that is attained only with the realization of universal caliphate in the fourth stage of *irtifaqat.* The ideal Islamic state is the result of a balanced pursuit of sociocultural aims, as dictated by natural disposition. By the same token, the foundations of civilization are undermined when people adopt forms of governance or lifestyles that run contrary to their natural disposition or belong to a stage of development attained prematurely, before the requirements of the earlier stage have been fulfilled. As he states in the *Al-Budur-Al-Bazigah,* when human beings internalize the different stages of *irtifaqat,* the rules of natural religion (Islam) are revealed to them accordingly.[73]

In the *Hujjut,* Waliullah delineates the various aspects of faith *(iman).* He identifies four personal virtues—piety, humility, magnanimity, and just social dealings—that together help the individual attain the equilibrium between the inner and outer self that is explicitly decreed in the Quran and epitomized by the Prophet. An individual possessing these four virtues would attain intellectual and practical perfection by conforming to his or her original nature *(fitrat).*[74] Waliullah explains in the *Al-Budur-Al-Bazigah* that the higher stages of a spiritual relationship with God *(irtiqadat)* require seven virtues: wisdom *(hikmat),* virtue or piety *(iffat),* magnanimity *(samahat),* courage *(shujaat),* eloquence *(fasahat),* honesty *(diyanat),* and good conduct *(samt salah).*[75] Most people, being dominated by the lower passions and satanic temptations, have to be prevented from spreading corruption in the world. To subject such sinners to compulsion, so that faith finds its way into their hearts and minds is an act of divine mercy. But for compulsion to work, those causing the greatest harm have to be killed, their power broken, and their riches captured, so that they pose no further threat. It is only then that their followers and progeny can embrace faith freely, through conscious submission.[76]

Waliullah declared that the "actual intention of the providence behind the divine legislation" was "not the condition of the individual but rather the condition of the collectivity."[77] It followed that a person of exceptional spiritual merit had to be appointed imam to promulgate the faith and ensure its ascendancy over other faiths. The imam had to use "great compulsion" in enforcing the external rituals of the faith, for the religious duties of the majority of people can be fulfilled only by establishing times, guidelines, conditions, rules, and punishments. Ordinary Muslims have no choice in matters to do with the sharia. The imam

> should keep hidden the knowledge of the inner meanings of the divine laws . . . because most of those on whom the laws are imposed do not recognize the beneficial purposes, nor are they able to recognize them unless they are precisely determined by regulating devices . . . For if he permitted them to omit some of them, and explained that the basic goal is something other than these outer forms, he would widen for them the avenues of unqualified discussion and they would disagree excessively, and what God wanted for them would not be achieved.[78]

In focusing on regulating the outward behavior of Muslims rather than on the quality of faith, Waliullah was not going against the grain of the sharia. Actions have an inherent connection with inner conscience; human beings are what they do. All the revealed laws (sharia), he held, were in accordance with the habits and customs *(adat)* of ordinary people. Whichever of their habits are harmful are prohibited, while good habits are left undisturbed.[79]

Waliullah's conception of good and bad habits offers crucial insights into the orthodox mentality. His discussion of gender relations at the second stage of development *(irtifaqat)* shows him to be the quintessential patriarch. He considered men intelligent, but not women, who have to be obedient to their husbands. This difference he assigns to the fact that human beings are either masters or slaves.[80] He derided the dominance of women over men in his own time but was equally against men's violation of the natural rights of women. These natural rights evidently did not extend to the equality of faith between men and women explicitly granted in the Quran. In Waliullah's opinion, women were inferior in both intelligence and religion. He quoted an alleged hadith of the Prophet in which women are held to be deficient in religion because they do not pray and fast during their monthly menstruation cycle. Women were not alone in bearing the brunt of his conservatism. He reserved his sharpest criticism for effeminate men who were inclined to dress like women and had to be prevented from doing so in the general social interest. There was no room for gender equality, much less sexual deviancy, in Waliullah's social ethics.[81]

Distressed by the political turmoil and socioeconomic crises in Mughal India, Waliullah favored the emergence of a strong Muslim authority capable of waging a jihad to purge Sunni Islam of polytheistic accretions, particularly the excesses of certain variants of a resurgent Shi'ism. The internal struggle within Islam could not prosper without a successful jihad against Maratha and Jat warlords who were flouting Mughal state authority with impunity. According to his evolutionary scheme, India in the first half of the eighteenth century represented the third stage of *irtifaqat.* In his assessment, the two primary causes for ethical and political degeneration of cities were the depletion of the treasury and the state's nurturing of parasitical retainers.[82] The failings of the Mughals he attributed to an imbalance between socioeconomic realities and the lifestyle of the ruling strata. He criticized the Mughal state for levying heavy taxes on farmers, merchants, and professionals and spending extravagantly on architectural projects, instead of meeting the basic needs of the populace. In adopting the ways of a higher stage of *irtifaqat* without fulfilling the requirements of their own stage of development, the Mughals had destroyed the social and human cultural underpinnings of civilization. Unless the state created an infrastructure capable of meeting the socioeconomic needs of the people, prospects for their moral and spiritual development would remain dim.[83]

Walilullah based his theory of human development on empirical observation and inductive reasoning, rather than on the authority of the Quran and the practice of the Prophet (sunna). This approach allowed him to accommodate the material, secular world into his religious framework. The secularization of the idea of jihad in his writings followed as a natural consequence. In keeping with Sunni juristic opinion, he considered it illegitimate to rebel against a government which had Muslim support, even if the leader was not qualified for office. Muslims are obliged to struggle for the deposition of a ruler only if he undermines the essential postulates of Islam. In that case, the attempt to overthrow him would be the highest form of jihad.[84] The removal of a corrupt person, a scourge to humanity, is commendable in the eyes of God because it is for the universal welfare. In the face of despotism, "inspiration manifests itself in the heart of a righteous man to kill him." Upon feeling extreme anger, he is "effaced from his own will and subsists through the will of God, and is absorbed in the mercy of God and His light, and humanity and countries benefit from that." At times God decrees the end of the rule of tyrannical states and prompts his prophets to fight against them. The desire to wage war is inculcated in the hearts of the Prophet's people, and they become "a people brought out for mankind" and are blessed with divine mercy. In another instance, a group realizes "through the comprehensive outlook of the goodness of saving the oppressed ones from the predatory ones and undertaking the punishment of the disobedient ones and forbidding evil, so that this becomes a cause of the peace and contentment of the people and thus God rewards them for their action."[85]

Waliullah held that jihad can be waged successfully only when there is a Muslim caliph with requisite military power at his disposal. Once the war had been won, it was imperative for the caliph to follow strictly the example set by the Prophet and his companions for a just and equitable division of the war booty. Waliullah conceded that the spoils of war could potentially detract from the objectives of jihad in the way of God *(jihad fi sabil allah)*. But since human beings by nature and habit were not conditioned to endanger their lives without hope of extracting some benefit, God made war booty legitimate for Muslims.[86] Departing from his argument about the need to fulfill earlier stages of development, Waliullah advocated waging jihad to counteract the weakening of Muslim political power in the subcontinent.

In keeping with his belief in jihad as the paramount duty of an Islamic state, Waliullah wrote several letters to Muslim rulers and notables in eighteenth-century India. His calls for harsh measures against Hindus and Shias display his political naïveté even more than they do his biases.[87] He recommended avoiding the company of "non-Muslims of devilish disposition" who were superficial and devoid of any concern for religion.[88] Ignoring the potential for a backlash and overestimating Muslim political power, he proposed banning *holi* and *muharram* festivals and confiscating Hindu wealth. This proposal has been attributed to his desire to restore the supremacy of Islam in India rather than to an inherently exclusionary attitude.[89] It is difficult to discern the difference between the two, given Waliullah's bigoted statements about Hindus and Shias. The most that can be done is to place these utterances in the historical context of eighteenth-century India.

Commenting on the reduction of Mughal power to a shadow of its former self and the rise of Maratha, Jat, and Sikh power, Waliullah noted that Muslim sovereignty existed only in name. After Nadir Shah's devastating raid of 1739, the "sultanate of Delhi had become a child's game." Shias were the real power behind the Mughal throne, and Hindus held important positions in the Mughal administration. While Hindus had amassed wealth, the majority of the Muslims were living in destitution and despair. It was necessary to break the power of the Hindus and curb the Shias. Unless this was done, Waliullah thought, Muslims would be tempted to abandon Islam and there would no longer be any distinction between Muslims and non-Muslims. In the name of God and the Prophet, he urged Muslim rulers and military commanders to take up arms against non-Muslims, thereby adding their names to the list of fighters in the way of Allah *(mujahidin fi sabil allah)*.[90] With this in view, Waliullah in his letters to the Rohilla Afghan military commander Najib-ud-Dawla exhorted him to engage in jihad to strengthen Muslim power in India. Waliullah had received spiritual communications from the angelic world in his dreams that the power of the Marathas and the Jats was destined to be destroyed shortly. All that was needed was for Muslims with military means at their disposal to raise the standard of Islam. This was of the essence, for the dagger of insurrection had pierced through to the bone of Muslim power in India.[91]

His letter inviting Ahmad Shah Abdali to invade India has been the subject of considerable controversy. Some scholars have questioned the authenticity of the letter, while others have discounted its importance in the overall context of Waliullah's religious thought.[92] Given his firm belief in the need to wage jihad to stem the decay in eighteenth-century India, the letter to Abdali seems to be genuine. Flattering the Durrani Afghan warlord by praising his manliness, courage, and foresight, Waliullah reminded him of his obligation to embark on a jihad against polytheism. If he did so, great rewards would accrue to him. Not only would he be assured God's recompense in the hereafter, but "as far as worldly gains are concerned, incalculable booty would fall into the hands of the Islamic *ghazis* and the Muslims would be liberated from their bonds."[93] It seems incongruous to find Waliullah, who had bitterly rued the destruction that Nadir Shah had left in his wake, asking for help from someone who had been part of the army that had brought death and despoliation to Delhi.

Hujjat al-Baligha underscores the discrepancy between Waliullah's understanding of jihad as a sacred duty and the political uses he made of it in response to temporal exigencies. Jihad is the "greatest of all deeds"; not to perform it "during such times as the present" would deprive Muslims of "tremendous good." Waliullah cited a tradition in which someone asked the Prophet whether a man fighting to display his courage and another who did it out of "sheer fury" would be seen as fighting in the path of God. The Prophet's reply was that only the one who fought to exalt the divine word would be considered to be struggling in the way of God. Jihad is a means to establish "the paramountcy of the symbolic commands of God and His Religion and for the popularization of all those virtues that please God." It was "an exercise in which every part depends on the other . . . like a structure in which the wall rests on the foundation and the roof rests over the wall."[94] The heart of a true warrior of the faith is so inspired by jihad that he develops the attitude of an angel. According to Waliullah, "the one[s] most worthy of this perfection among all humans are those who are farthest from the evils of animality and in whose minds and hearts Religion is deeply seated" and is "indicative of one's purity of heart." An angelic disposition of this sort is inconceivable without piety, for the "human soul attains its bliss through utmost concentration on the proximity of God."[95]

In exhorting Abdali to fight the Marathas and the Jats to eradicate polytheism, Waliullah let his own high standards of jihad fall by the wayside. At the theoretical level, he had argued that only a struggle aimed at establishing universal truth, human dignity, and high ethical values qualified as jihad. But he was prepared to compromise to rein in the foes of Islam. His political and ethical framework called for an imam whose foremost responsibility was keeping the *Dar-ul-Islam*—the territories of Islam—free of infidel forces and waging jihad for the supremacy of Islam. Within his own domains, the imam was expected to forcibly regulate the outward behavior of Muslims, by ensuring the removal of polytheistic accretions, preaching good, and forbidding evil. In giving more importance to religion as a demarcator of Muslim identity than to religion as faith, Waliullah was responding to his own situation in predominantly non-Muslim India rather than to anything remotely connected with the spirit of the Quranic message. In his words, because mere conquest "cannot remove the thick veils over their hearts," the truth of faith has to be established through forceful rhetoric, so that all distortions of Islam are corrected in the public eye.[96]

Waliullah thus had no illusions about Abdali and his capacity to wreak destruction on the people of Delhi. This would be the fatal blow after the grievous injury inflicted by Nadir Shah. His letters make plain that he was afraid of becoming a victim in any violence against ordinary citizens following an invasion by the Durrani tribesman.[97] This understandable human reaction was accompanied by pleas to Najib-ud-Dawla to ensure that no harm was done to the people of Delhi, either Muslims or non-Muslims who had protected *(zimmi)* status. Despite Waliullah's advice on how the "Islamic army" (described as "that paragon of bounty"[98]) should conduct itself on arrival, Abdali's sack of Delhi in January 1761 was a calamitous event. Mir Taqi Mir (1722–1810), has left a chilling account of the atrocities committed by the soldiers of Abdali and Najib-ud-Dawla:

> They stole and plundered, and obscenely enriched themselves. They laid hands upon women. They waved their swords and snatched away wealth . . . In every lane there was a reign of terror, and every marketplace was a field of combat . . . The poor were drained bloodless, while tyrants wallowed in their blood . . . wherever one looked one saw heads and limbs and torsos.

"The cries of the devastated people reached the seventh heaven," Mir exclaimed, "but they went unheard by the Shah [Abdali], who remained engrossed in his own thoughts since he regarded himself [as] a dervish."[99] Another poet gave a graphic description of the misery afflicting Delhi's citizens: "How can I describe the desolation of Delhi?" wrote Mirza Muhammad Rafi Sauda (1713–1781). There was not a house in the city from where the jackals' cry could not be heard. The mosques were deserted: "No one cares for Islam these days." The lovely buildings and magnificent gardens that had adorned the city lay in ruins. In the villages surrounding Delhi, young women were no longer seen drawing water from the wells, which were now full of corpses.[100]

Waliullah died in 1762, leaving behind no record of his reactions to the inhuman treatment unleashed on the inhabitants of Delhi by the self-styled *ghazis* of Islam. But even for a man who propounded the theory of *fuq kul nizam,* variously defined as anarchy or complete revolution, the destruction of Delhi was the last thing he could possibly have wanted. His shortsightedness in deeming Abdali to be a savior of Sunni Islam, the product of miscalculation, points up the problems inherent in translating into practice the theory of jihad as a sacred duty. Far from paving the way for the triumph of Islamic power, as Waliullah, on the basis of his spiritual visions, had confidently predicted in various epistles to Najib-ud-Dawla, Abdali's incursion dealt a serious blow to Muslim political power in northern India. It contributed to the strengthening of Sikh power, thereby leading one author to comment wryly that Abdali was the "greatest benefactor" of the Sikhs.[101] After an interlude of wildly fluctuating political fortunes, Delhi fell into the hands of the English East India Company by 1803.

Abdali's sack of Delhi has never been claimed as a jihad; but neither has the gulf between the intention and the outcome of Waliullah's foray into the political maelstrom of eighteenth-century India been subjected to rigorous critical scrutiny. Instead, his idea of jihad has been seized on to serve a variety of political agendas. In the process, the difficulties involved in squaring sacred precepts with temporal practice have been conveniently overlooked. It is widely believed, albeit not without dispute, that the only real jihad movement ever to be launched in the subcontinent was directly inspired by Waliullah's teachings.[102] This is the jihad waged against the Sikhs between 1826 and 1831 by his grandson, Shah Ismail, under the leadership of Sayyid Ahmad of Rai Bareilly, a disciple of Waliullah's son, the equally illustrious religious scholar Shah Abdul Aziz (1745–1824). A favorite among anticolonial nationalists and modern-day militants, Sayyid Ahmad—and his movement and martyrdom—help distinguish the intertwined threads of the sacred and the temporal, the ethical and the politically expedient, that have characterized the historical meanings of jihad in modern South Asia.

◖◖ 3 ◗◗

The Martyrs of Balakot

THIS IS how Hakim Momin Khan Momin (1801–1852) expressed his desire for martyrdom, as he prodded himself to prove
his faith by engaging in jihad:

> Momin, if you have any respect for faith,
> Jihad means battle: so go there now;
> Be fair, more than God you love that life
> Which you used to sacrifice for idols![1]

Anything short of that was infidelity *(kufr)*. A devotee of Sayyid
Ahmad of Rai Bareilly, to whom he had given an oath of allegiance, Momin wrote poetry that pulsates with passion for the
cause to which his mentor had devoted his life. Despite his frail
health, he yearned to join Sayyid Ahmad's forces:

> The army of Islam has congregated.
> Heed the imam of the times—
> Sacrifice your life for the sake of God.

Oh God, make me worthy of martyrdom too.
Make me worthy of this highest of all forms of worship.[2]

Momin had grown up in an environment permeated with the teachings of Waliullah, who had popularized a hadith in which jihad was described as better than fasting and praying for a whole month. Momin had been given his name at the instance of his father's spiritual guide, Shah Abdul Aziz, under whom he received his early education. The scion of a family of Muslim physicians associated with the Mughal court, Momin is described as a pleasure seeker during his youth, who was "far too human to sink into [being] a dour puritan."[3] But the influence of the Waliullah clan on his thinking is evident. He resented the British lording it over Delhi, while the Mughal emperor remained a virtual prisoner in the Red Fort. Momin has recorded the effects of his conversion to Sayyid Ahmad's struggle in several of his poems, the *Masnavi-i-Jihadiyya* in particular. Overlooked as a recruit on account of his ill health, Momin wrote about the hardships of an endeavor that demanded piety and extreme physical exertion, lamenting: "Kafir hua mein din key adab dekh kar" (I became an infidel upon seeing the ethics of Islam).[4]

Momin's sympathy with Sayyid Ahmad's jihad is well known. More intriguing is Khawaja Manzoor Hosain's discovery of the all-pervasive presence of jihad in the verses of nineteenth-century poets as different in temperament and disposition as Khawaja Haider Ali Aatish (1767–1847), Sheikh Muhammad Ibrahim Zauq (1788/9–1854), Mustafa Khan Shefta (d. 1869), Sheikh Imam Baksh Nasikh (d. 1838), and Ghalib. In Hosain's view, the jihad fought by Sayyid Ahmad on the northwest frontier and in the Punjab vies with the tragedy of Karbala as an explanation for the appeal the theme of martyrdom has had for Persian and Urdu poets and writers, both Shia and Sunni, in the subconti-

Hakim Momin Khan, *Portrait of the Poet* (verso), attributed to Jivan Ram, c. 1835, black ink and opaque watercolor on off-white paper. Harvard University Art Museums, Arthur M. Sackler Museum, Promised Gift of Stuart Cary Welch, Jr., 253.1983. Photo: Allan Macintyre © President and Fellows of Harvard College.

nent. Noted for his liberality of vision and his humanistic poetry, Aatish extolled jihad as a deed that absolves sins and makes the life of the fighters in God's cause meaningful.[5] He likens the sword wound on the face of the warrior to a piece of jewelry.[6] Zauq and Nasikh savor their association with Sayyid Ahmad's circle, even though neither took up arms. Ghalib's alleged infatuation with Shah Ismail and because of him with Sayyid Ahmad and his jihad is a more complex issue, whose explanation must await a fuller research into the movement. For now, it is sufficient to note that where fact takes a backseat to sentiment, as in hagiographies and eulogistic poetry about the jihad movement, the historian has the opportunity to investigate the meanings and symbolism of an important element in Indian Muslim consciousness.

The Making of a Myth

Sayyid Ahmad's war against the Sikh kingdom of Ranjit Singh in the Punjab took place at a time when sovereignty had to all intents and purposes passed into British hands. The historical significance of the war lies in the indelible imprint it has left on the subcontinental Muslim psyche. Whatever the literary critic's verdict on Manzoor Hosain's interpretation of certain verses, the most gifted Muslims thinkers and poets of India were evidently influenced by the movement and wrote feelingly about Sayyid Ahmad's martyrdom, along with that of Shah Ismail in Balakot on 6 May 1831.[7] To this day, Balakot, where the sayyid lies buried, is a spot that has been greatly revered, not only by militants in contemporary Pakistan, some of whom have set up training camps near Balakot, but also by anticolonial nationalists, who interpreted the movement as a prelude to a jihad against the British in India.[8]

The *Shahnamah-i-Balakot* is an extended laudatory poem on

the movement by a Pakistani poet. Writing across the great divide of 1947, Maulana Husain Ahmad Nadwi notes in his foreword that the hallowed blood shed on that famous battlefield still runs in the veins of the Muslim community *(millat)*. This is because Sayyid Ahmad Shaheed and Maulana Ismail Shaheed's movement blended Ahmad Sirhandi's ideas on Sunni reform and the elimination of *bidat* (innovation) with Shah Waliullah's jihad movement. The party of six hundred or so selfless Muslim mujahideen who fought in the rugged terrain of the northwest frontier along with tens of thousands of Pathan tribesmen ushered in the spring of Islamic culture and civilization. It is their deeds that have kept alive the spirit of jihad in Muslim society to this day in the shape of various Muslim organizations and movements.[9] The poet Alim Nasiri, for his part, extols Balakot and its beautiful peaks, the envy of the Himalayas because they are colored with the blood of the mujahideen. He venerates the martyrs' blood that has sanctified the *millat* and their supreme sacrifice, which has strengthened the faith.[10] Another modern writer spells out the symbolism of Balakot:

> Even today the mountains and valleys of Balakot tell the visitor stories of the mujahideen's deeds. Those with sensitivity can feel the spirituality still emanating from the place. Upon seeing the landscape of Balakot, a discerning mind can see that while nature had provided for all the possible needs of the Islamic mujahideen, Muslims by their own treachery and animosity tried extinguishing the light of Islam. Muslims, or rather those Muslims in name who separate themselves from Islam, can perish, but Islam, God's eternal message, can never perish. Keeping the message alive is the party of the mujahideen who raise the name of Islam by perishing themselves. It is one such pious *mujahid* who lies buried in Balakot. Blessed are those people who upon seeing this pi-

ous soil can obtain grace, and lucky are those Muslims who take from the lives of the martyrs in the path of truth some useful lesson for their own lives.[11]

Accolades showered on the martyrs of Balakot and reverential accounts of the movement written by Sayyid Ahmad's followers and admirers have since 1831 assumed such proportions that separating the myth from its history is a difficult enterprise. Biographies by close relatives and ardent disciples give a larger-than-life picture of Sayyid Ahmad.[12] An Urdu biography by Maulvi Muhammad Jafar Thanesari presents him as a man with supernatural powers, able to work miracles. Possessing the characteristics of the Prophet Muhammad, he is believed to have received divine commands. A *mujaddid* or renovator of the faith in the thirteenth century of the Islamic calendar, the sayyid is likened to the middle Mahdi, or messiah before the return of Christ. Thanesari held that Sayyid Ahmad had mysteriously disappeared from Balakot and would return to complete the task of subduing the enemies of Islam.[13] The legend acquired a life of its own, and elaborate rituals came to be constructed around it. During a British expedition against the sayyids of Kaghan, allies of Sayyid Ahmad, "an inflated hide . . . [was] dressed up as one of the holy family, and placed in a cave before a Koran to [im]personate the deceased saint."[14] The British, who had to contend with the jihad movement from 1853 to 1863, noted that there was disagreement over Sayyid Ahmad's spiritual status. In Bengal, the Faraizis led by Haji Shariatullah (1781–1840) and his son Dudu Mian (1819–1860) simply considered him to be a "good man," whereas his followers in northern India thought he was an imam, who had temporarily disappeared and would return after some years. This was the belief of the illiterate and, "though denied by the more educated Wahabee Moulvies, appears to have been fostered indirectly by them with a view to excite the religious zeal of their disciples in expectation of victory over infidels and worldly dominion and power, general spread of the pure Mahomedan faith, and ultimate enjoyment of Paradise."[15]

The eighteenth-century Arab reformer Muhammad Abdul Wahab shared some teachers with Shah Waliullah during the latter's extended sojourn in the Hejaz.[16] And though there is no evidence of their coming into direct contact with one another, their followers have been linked together as "Wahabis." In the early nineteenth century the Arabian Wahabis were anathema to orthodox Sunnis, bitter over Wahabi destruction of historic Muslim shrines in Medina, including that of the Prophet, on the grounds that they invited polytheism *(shirk)*. By the time the Arabian Wahabis were put down, Indian Muslims who felt an emotional association with the holy places of Islam had ample reason to hate Wahabis. But insofar as Wahabism represented an ideological stance, the term *Wahabi* was used for those who deplored the accommodations most South Asian Muslims had made with their Indian surroundings. After Sayyid Ahmad's death, his followers called themselves Ahl-i-Hadith or adherents of the Tariqah-i-Muhammadi—the Path of Muhammad—founded by him.

The appellation Wahabi, however, stuck in the colonial mind after the military confrontation with Arabian Wahabis in the early nineteenth century. An eighteenth century diplomatic memoir by Sir Harford Jones, which would have been read by British officials who dealt with the remnants of Sayyid Ahmad's jihad movement, lists four beliefs held by Arabian Wahabis: 1) to invoke Muhammad or any of the imams for help is to make them partners with God and is tantamount to blasphemy; 2) any Muslim deviating from the literal injunctions of the Quran was as much an infidel as a Christian or a Jew, and fighting such Muslims is a positive duty incumbent upon every Wahabi and true Muslim; 3) bestowing titles and honors on men is odious; God alone deserves magnificent titles; and 4) all true Muslims are obliged by the Quran to wage continuous war on unbelievers until they convert or become hapless tributaries. If this was not already too severe a regime for Indian Muslims to accept, Wahab's followers thought that the construction of a magnificent tomb in anyone's memory was idol worship. In alliance with the Saud, they wanted to destroy all Muslim tombs in Arabia and Persia and to put their valuable ornaments to "better and more worldly purposes." Jones rounded off his memoir by noting the "less consequential" opinions held by these "Puritans." Among these was a firm belief that "everyone of their sect who falls in warring against infidels . . . [is] immediately permitted to enjoy the delights of Paradise." They "not only regard a regular War against their brother Musalmans of a different sect as incumbent on them but each individual Whabee esteems it a meritorious act to plunder, rob and murder any other individual Arab, he may meet and in consequence of this opinion the Whabees have lately been a terrible annoyance to the caravans in passing the desert."[17]

Jones may be guilty of exaggerating, if not misrepresenting, Abdul Wahab's ideas. But the Wahabi creed was crafted more by zealous followers than by the relatively more circumspect founder. The puritanism they aspired to was matched by a focus on temporal rewards, a heady doctrine that eventually led to the establishment of the Kingdom of Saudi Arabia. Sayyid Ahmad of Rai Bareilly made the attempt to win state power on the northwest frontier of the subcontinent, which, although it ended in a complete fiasco, inspired a few hundred of his followers based in Patna to continue the jihad. Perseverance was made possible only by perpetuation of the legend of his return. Forced to snuff out the threat posed by the armed Patna rebels in 1863, the British associated them with the Arabian Wahabis and inflated the military menace.[18] Despite the nuisance the Patna rebels represented for the colonial state seeking to impose its authority on a lawless tribal frontier, even at their strongest they were hardly a match for the British Indian army. After the suppression of the 1857 revolt they were forced to beat a retreat into the tribal areas on the northwestern frontier, where other fleeing rebels, not all of them Muslim, joined the insurgency. The British would have liked to nip it in the bud, but it was only when some of the tribal chiefs went back on their word not to support the rebel forces that the British carried out the Ambala campaign, in 1863, to quash the rebellion.

Compared with the myths, memories, and meanings attached to it, the actual jihad movement was relatively inconsequential in the annals of the subcontinent's colonial history. Tracing the dialectic between the event and its recollection reveals how the trope of Sayyid Ahmad's jihad has been socially constructed and imagined by individuals with different ideological leanings and political agendas. Described as India's first Islamic movement with a universal message, Sayyid Ahmad's jihad has to be placed in the social and political context of the early nineteenth century before we can assess its debt to either Waliullah's or Shah Abdul Aziz's teachings. Those who have interpreted the jihad against the Sikhs as the implementation of the ideas of the two Delhi scholars have portrayed it as a dress rehearsal for the ultimate battle with the British.[19] Waliullah had nothing to say about the English, who were making inroads in Bengal; rather, he was primarily concerned with the threat posed by the Marathas and the Jats. Shah Abdul Aziz, for his part, was distressed by the assertion of Sikh power:

> May God sweep them away from this country
> They are our greatest enemies, they are like bands of demons.
> My own fate and those of others I entrust to God;
> I hope He will protect us.[20]

This was a prayer to God, not a declaration of intent to wage war on the Sikhs, or far less against the English, who had established a firm foothold in eastern India by the late eighteenth century.

A fatwa by Shah Abdul Aziz sometime after the fall of Delhi in 1803, declaring India an abode of war *(Dar-ul-Harb),* has been at the center of a controversy. Widespread disagreement existed, even among his most fervent admirers, about the precise implications of the fatwa. Nationalist writers, like Maulana Husain Ahmad Madni (1879–1957), made much of the fact that the fatwa was addressed to both Muslims and non-Muslims. Maulana Syed Muhammad Mian, a follower of Madni, argued that the fatwa was political rather than religious in meaning. According to Shah Abdul Aziz, India had become a *Dar-ul-Harb* because Muslims had lost sovereignty and the infidels were administering the affairs of the country. Muslims no longer had freedom of conscience and political liberty. It was immaterial that the Christian rulers allowed the observance of Islamic rites like the Friday prayer, the daily calls to prayer, and the sacrifice of cows, "because these things do not hold any value in their eyes." They had no qualms about razing mosques, and no one could enter the city without their permission.[21] Legally speaking, Muslims living in hostile territory are obliged to perform *hijrat* to another Muslim country or to fight a jihad to wrest political control from the infidels.

Shah Abdul Aziz did not explicitly call for a jihad or a *hijrat,* however. He instead demonstrated a remarkable degree of pragmatism in the face of altered circumstances. The ambiguity of his position gave rise to the story that he had constituted a central revolutionary organization to implement his father's principles.[22] The claim is uncorroborated. Sayyid Ahmad is also said to have joined the forces of the Pindari leader Nawab Amir Khan of Tonk with the permission of his spiritual mentor, to acquire military training to launch a jihad.[23] Yet Shah Abdul Aziz's measured attitude toward the English East India Company's newly formed administration in Delhi was far removed from jihad as armed struggle. In 1807 his brother Shah Rafiuddin, known for his translation of the Quran into Urdu, was implicated in the first public disturbance in the city after the company's takeover. It led to several deaths, after enraged Muslims attacked a Hindu procession transporting an idol to a local temple. Colonial officials attributed the troubles to the "mistaken bigotry" of Muslims. But Alexander Seton, the resident of Delhi, who was full of praise and admiration for Shah Abdul Aziz's piety and learning, noted that his attitude throughout the disturbances "was no less marked by mildness and moderation, than regulated by sound judgment."[24] The high estimation in which he was held by the British and the restoration of rights to land taken away from the Waliullah family hint at why Shah Abdul Aziz might have preferred the path of least resistance.[25]

Indeed, it is debatable whether the fatwa was legally binding on Indian Muslims. As he himself admitted, there was no agreement among the ulema on the matter. Shah Abdul Aziz is not known to have consulted with anyone else on the subject. Questions about India's becoming a *Dar-ul-Harb* were raised not because Muslims were concerned about the obligation of jihad or *hijrat,* or even about ways of strengthening their religion. Those who sent him queries on the subject wanted to know whether taking interest in commercial transactions was permissible under non-Muslim rule. Shah Abdul Aziz's response was that under Islamic law interest on money invested for profitable purposes was legitimate for Muslims living in a *Dar-ul-Harb.* Such flexibility was accompanied by a series of other judgments underscoring how Islamic doctrines, instead of being impervious to change, were liable to continual modification, often at the expense of stretching logic to the utmost. Having asserted, for example, that the continuation of normal Islamic rituals in the absence of a Muslim imam could not prevent a *Dar-ul-Islam* from becoming a *Dar-ul-Harb,* Shah Abdul Aziz argued that Muslims need not migrate from an abode of war, so long as they were allowed by the infidel power to practice their religious rites in public.[26] He also declared it legitimate for Muslims to seek employment in the company's administration, so long as it did not undermine the cause of Islam.[27] As someone who believed that "bigotry against infidels and innovatory sects *(shias)*" was "a virtue and an act of worship," he had no objections to Muslims wearing European dress if the reason was practical comfort rather than a bid to win the approval of infidels.[28]

Shah Abdul Aziz was elaborating on his father's ideas on jihad in response to the temporal imperatives of life under non-Muslim rule. He identified three kinds of jihad. The first was carried out verbally *(jihad-i-zabani)* through writings, sermons, and preaching with a view to explaining God's commands and inviting people to embrace Islam. Then there was jihad geared to preparations for fighting so that opponents would be frightened by the Muslim show of strength. Finally, there was jihad involving physical combat against the enemies of Islam. He noted that the Prophet Muhammad had engaged only in the first two types of jihad, a fact proving their superior status by comparison with the third form, *jihad al-asghar*, the lesser jihad.[29] Instead of taking into account the different meanings and categories of jihad, most nationalist writers have interpreted it as fighting *(qital)*. The fact that Sayyid Ahmad did not embark upon the third kind of jihad until well after Shah Abdul Aziz's death in 1824 has generally been discounted on the grounds that the earlier two types of jihad were merely preparation for jihad as armed struggle.

According to Obaidullah Sindhi, Shah Abdul Aziz intended his fatwa to translate Waliullah's revolutionary ideas into practice. The aim was to revive the Quranic revolution by setting up a national government pledged to introducing the ethical values practiced by the holy Prophet back into the economy and society. Without offering anything substantial in support of the claim, some people present the jihad against the Sikhs as a first step to ousting the British from India. Sayyid Ahmad is said to have been chosen because he belonged to a family long associated with the chivalric tradition *(futawa)* in Sufism. His genealogy was expected to make him more acceptable to the Pathan tribesman.[30] Ghulam Rasul Mehr, who has written the most extensively on the movement, agrees that the main objective was the expulsion of the British from India. But he dismisses Sindhi's efforts to trace the jihad to Waliullah and Shah Abdul Aziz. Thoroughly impressed with Sayyid Ahmad of Rai Bareilly, Mehr maintains that he was committed to fighting a jihad to establish an Islamic government in India long before he joined Shah Abdul Aziz's circle.[31]

Critics of neat, linear views of history have correctly noted that such a nationalist construction is more revealing of the exigencies of the colonial and postcolonial contexts in which the authors wrote than of the subject of their study. Missing from works of this kind is a systematic attempt to decipher the meanings of jihad, especially its relationship with faith, on the basis of a critical assessment of the actions of Sayyid Ahmad and his valiant warriors. The potency of the popular myths that have grown up around Sayyid Ahmad's jihad has not been diluted by the skepticism of scholars. Many people still regard it as the first step toward restoring the glory of Islam in the subcontinent after the onset of colonial rule, a view reinforced by works like W. W. Hunter's *Indian Musalmans.* Published in 1871 to examine whether Muslims were bound by their religion to rebel against the queen, the book drew on the writings of Sayyid Ahmad's followers. It has served as a point of departure for several accounts of the jihad movement since the late nineteenth century. Displaying the myth in the process of its making, and proving that it is not purely a Muslim construct, Hunter contended that Sayyid Ahmad did not openly advocate jihad before leaving for a hajj in 1820 but returned to India "a fanatical disciple" of Muhammad Abdul Wahab. Although several Muslim writers vociferously denied that assessment, anticolonial nationalists educated in religious seminaries seized upon it because it suited their particular value systems and orientations.[32] Modern-day militants have found in it a perfect mixture of religious belief and strong Arab overtones. This has provided them with an ideology of warfare to assert the political supremacy of a variant of Islam that is outwardly puritanical and inwardly liable to serious doctrinal and ethical breaches.

The common puritanical thread running through two reform movements, separated in both time and space, should not detract attention from key differences. Unlike their Arabian counterparts, the militants categorized as Wahabis in India never rejected the mystical tradition in Islam. Although the focus on practical morality rather than matters of doctrine among Indian Wahabis points to certain similarities between them and Abdul Wahab's followers, Sayyid Ahmad's main attraction for ordinary people was precisely the aura of mystical spirituality that built up around him. Arabian Wahabis, with their insistence on literalism, would have been horrified by Sayyid Ahmad's dreams and visions, in which the Prophet Muhammad and God invested him with the badge of prophecy! He even dreamed of Ali giving him a bath and Fatima dressing him up in the finest clothes.[33] Such dreams and visions, however difficult for non-Sufis to accept, are not uncommon among Sufi mystics.

Hunter, who dismisses Sayyid Ahmad's spiritual trances as epileptic fits, defines his movement as a "fanatical war" between Indian Muslim Wahabis and "Hindu Sikhs." He vividly describes Sayyid Ahmad as a Pindari bandit-turned-prophet, above middle height and with a flowing beard falling over his chest. Ahmad was prone to religious ecstasy and mystical trances. Though unlearned in Islamic law, he started his "apostolic career" at the age of thirty-four, preaching the message of God's unity and the equality of all men. Hunter notes that his first two converts, Shah Ismail and Maulana Abdul Hayee, the nephew and son-in-law of Abdul Aziz, respectively, were men of "profound scholarship." Like Sayyid Ahmad, they had studied at the feet of Shah Abdul Aziz, the "Sun of India" and worthy successor to "the greatest Muhammadan Doctor of the age." The respect shown by Shah Ismail and Abdul Hayee for the "ignorant horse-soldier" with his "smattering of Arabic" helped establish his credentials as a "prophet."[34]

Hunter would have known that ascribing the status of prophet to anyone after Muhammad undermines a key tenet of Islam. But instead of underscoring this point, he focuses on the seditious activities of Sayyid Ahmad's followers. These centered on the activities of two brothers, Maulanas Wilayat Ali (1790–1852) and Inayat Ali (d. 1858), of the Sadiqpur family of Azimabad, Patna. They popularized the legend of Sayyid Ahmad's miraculous disappearance from the battlefield of Balakot and his anticipated return as the imam Mahdi, to lead his followers to victory over all infidels.[35] Wilayat Ali fought the Sikhs until he was defeated in 1847 by Gulab Singh, a key British ally following the annexation of the Punjab in 1846. From his base on the frontier, Wilayat Ali tried inciting the Muslim soldiers of the company's Fourth Native Infantry in Rawalpindi to rebellion. After his death, Inayat Ali assumed control of the movement and made Sittana his base. Impetuous as well as zealous, he was eager to start a jihad against the Christians without waiting for Sayyid Ahmad's return. He fought skirmishes against the British on the northwest frontier from 1853 until his death in 1858. Inayat Ali's efforts to goad Muslim soldiers to rebel made him the archvillain in the British demonization of Indian "Wahabis."[36] Remnants of the Patna rebel forces, recruited in the main from Eastern Bengal, continued to defy British authority even after their defeat in 1863.[37]

State trials interpreted the jihad as political treason. While claiming that "the Government had no possible wish or intention of interference with the religious opinions of any portion of the community," British officials had no illusions about the political factors that had sustained the movement. The commissioner of Patna was of the opinion that without the supply of money to the rebel center in Sadiqpur through an elaborate network stretching from Bengal and the Deccan to the Mulka-Sittana Hills on the frontier, "the priestly character of these Moulvies will cease to exercise much influence." The British had already inflicted heavy losses on the border tribes during the Ambala campaign. It was imperative, therefore, to "get rid of this center of disaffection and intrigue" and to spare no means "to secure the expulsion of the Moulvies from the Hills."[38] In the event, the British were more successful in destroying the Sadiqpur center than in cleansing the frontier of anticolonial rebels.

T. E. Ravenshaw, the magistrate of Patna, noted some two years after the Ambala campaign that the British had "not yet succeeded in driving out the Hindustanee and Bengalee fanatics from their position in the Hills." Furthermore, "as long as these men remain," he warned, "so long will the minds of their fellows and followers in Bengal be unsettled." An alliance between the frontier rebels and the Faraizis would test the British, for the "influence" these itinerant maulvis "exert[ed was] extraordinary." The only difference he could detect between the "Wahabee" and the "Ferazie" was that the former was "an ultra-Ferazie . . . on the subject of *Jehad.*" But he had no doubt that the real object of the Faraizis was "subverting the British Government" and "the restoration of the Mahomedan power." The government had "to keep an eye on the sect," whether it went under the "appellation of Wahabees, Ferazies, Hidayeties, Mahomeddies or Nya [new] Mussulmans." With their "blind adherence to their Moulvies, teachers and leaders, and the pertinacity with which they adhere to their belief in the duty of *Jehad,*" Ravenshaw thought, "Ere many years . . . elapsed they will be again heard of and may cause trouble."[39]

It is tempting to see the trouble being caused today by Osama bin Laden's followers in the hills as a fulfillment of Ravenshaw's prophecy. But the twists and turns in the jihad Sayyid Ahmad and the Patna rebels waged against the Sikhs and the British militate against seeing an unbroken link between them and Waliullah, or still less with the self-styled jihadis of today. It is intellectually more fruitful to examine the evolution of the idea in Indian Muslim history. Disentangling the meanings assigned to Sayyid Ahmad's movement illustrates how Muslims, in their feverish effort to establish their distinctness both from other Muslim sects and from other religious communities, lost sight of the high ethical values associated with jihad. Sayyid Ahmad's struggle, occurring at a time of deep political, social, and psychological turmoil during the transition to colonial rule, captures the formation of a mindset, which in emphasizing the outer husk of religion in order to establish the boundary with the "other," eroded the inner kernel of the faith.

The Jihad in Theory

When Sayyid Ahmad launched his reform movement, mystical elements pervaded his practical teachings on morality; however, unlike the Sufis, with their otherworldly outlook, he made his focus the affairs of this world. This was not unusual for a man who, though not illiterate, as some of his followers have suggested, had no interest in acquiring the knowledge of the Islamic sciences for which the Waliullah clan is deservedly renowned. Endowed with greater than normal physical strength, he held that someone devoted to intense spiritual exercises could not become a *mujahid,* for one must remain constantly alert in order to take on the infidels. More a warrior-saint than a stickler for religious niceties, Sayyid Ahmad stressed the importance of the sharia only in terms of observing the five pillars of Islam. He told those joining his

Tariqah-i-Muhammadi that the relationship of this Sufi *tariqah* with the Prophet was exoteric, involving the performance of external rituals in conformity with the sharia. But he was mostly silent on the sharia as it related to matters of law and avoided issues linked with doctrine.

Evidence of Waliullah's moral positivism in the sayyid's teachings against idolatrous, superstitious, and innovative practices is apparent in the refrain that not only were these un-Islamic, but they brought economic ruin. He impressed upon those who gave him their oath of allegiance that devotion to God and the Prophet is sufficient for a Muslim. Discipleship would be meaningless if believers told lies or deceived others. If disciples were truthful and trustworthy, they needed no spiritual mentor other than God. He prescribed no new ritual or special oath for the Tariqah-i-Muhammadi and asked his followers to heed all four schools of jurisprudence. But if they came across an authentic hadith of the Prophet, they should not seek out any legal scholar's decision. Sayyid Ahmad's rejection of the authority of earlier jurists has led to his classification as a *ghair muqallid* (one who does not adhere to any school of jurisprudence). This has led to speculations about his links with the Yemeni scholar Muhammad bin Ali al-Shawkani (1760–1834), who emphasized independent reasoning *(ijtihad)*. Others have attributed the approach to Ibn Taymiyya's writings, which were well known in India.[40] Whatever the intellectual antecedents, Sayyid Ahmad's insistence on *ijtihad* was to make him popular among modernist thinkers, writers, and politicians. But he also instructed his followers to look upon the Ahl-i-Hadith as imams and to place their honour above themselves.[41]

There is a contradiction between rejecting blind adherence *(taqlid)* to the schools of Sunni jurisprudence and calling the Ahl-i-Hadith imams. Apart from dividing the Muslim community between the Ahl-i-Hadith and the Hanafis, this contradiction was to split the Tariqah-i-Muhammadi after Sayyid Ahmad's death. It is worth probing into why Sayyid Ahmad upheld independent reasoning and at the same time claimed to be an imam created in the likeness of the Prophet Muhammad. The *Sirat-i-Mustaqim,* a compilation of his religious discourses written down by Shah Ismail and Maulana Abdul Hayee prior to the hajj, gives a complicated line of reasoning on the subject. It says not that Sayyid Ahmad was equal in status to the Prophet Muhammad, but that he was "born to the path of prophethood," which any truly spiritual man can attain through self-abnegation and absolute servitude to God. The path of prophethood was contrasted with the path of sainthood. The two were linked, respectively, to the concepts of *hubb-i-imani*—literally, love of the faith, but closer to steadfastness in belief—and *hubb-i-ishqi,* or passion for the self in relation to God. Although the two are not mutually exclusive, the path of prophethood has a higher status, for it is based on knowledge of God's attributes, whereas the path of sainthood leads toward union with God.[42]

Using terminology slightly different from Ahmad Sirhandi's, Sayyid Ahmad rejected Ibn al-'Arabi's notion that sainthood was superior to prophethood. While conceding that the two paths are not mutually exclusive, he claimed that he was not merely a saint but one on the path of prophethood. He blamed Sufis, who violated the sharia, for the social and moral degradation of Muslims in India. They were exemplars of *hubb-i-ishqi* whose manifestation was the "neglect of knowledge and external acts of worship" and a failure to understand the relation between the external and the hidden aspects of the sharia. By contrast, *hubb-i-imani* represented a strong determination to follow the sharia in its outward forms. Unlike *hubb-i-ishqi,* which Sayyid Ahmad likened to a mere roadside inn, *hubb-i-imani* was compared to a royal horse awaiting the warrior—the *hujutullah*—the proof of God armed with sword and spear to reform society.[43] This reformation required a conscious revival of the sunna based on the hadith, thereby purging Sunni Islam of such Shia innovations as the *taziya* processions taken out during *muharram* and polytheistic practices like visitations to the graves of dead saints. Sayyid Ahmad identified illiteracy among lower-class Muslims as the primary factor in the success "heretic Sufis" had in popularizing economically wasteful polytheistic and innovative practices.[44]

Insofar as Sayyid Ahmad was translating Waliullah's philosophy of moral positivism and social welfare into practice, the attack on polytheism and innovation was motivated by both religious and secular reasons. He extolled piety, equity, and social service and condemned un-Islamic practices. The degree to which he was successful in eradicating polytheism and innovation can be gleaned from the fantastical narratives of his followers. Jafar Thanesari depicts him as an *ummi,* or unlettered person, like the Prophet Muhammad and makes much of the fact that Sayyid Ahmad was born on the first day of the thirteenth century of the Islamic era. Miracles are attributed to Sayyid Ahmad, who allegedly performed a *miraj* to Syria to meet the *qutb al-aqtab,* the living "axis" or spiritual master of the age.[45] The axis is said to be in direct contact with God through the intermediary of the spiritual world *(alam-i-malukat).* Both Sirhandi and Waliullah claimed to be living axes of their time. If Sayyid Ahmad himself made no similar claim, then certainly his followers did, some going so far as to accord him the status of a prophet, without actually putting him on par with Muhammad, who is the seal of the prophets. Taken literally to mean the finality of prophethood in Muhammad, the term has a deeper significance.[46] This is the belief that the essence of Muhammad's prophethood was already present in the previous prophets.[47] The *Sirat-i-Mustaqim,* in introducing the novel idea of the path of prophethood, as superior to the path of sainthood, strains orthodox Muslim belief in the uniqueness of Muhammad's prophethood.

In distinguishing between the two, Sayyid Ahmad affirmed Sirhandi's and Waliullah's ideas, while creating the leeway to make a bid for his own leadership of the Muslim community. Like his predecessors, he too was defining the outer limits of Muslim identity. What he calls *hubb-i-imani* is a firm belief in the observance of outward rituals. Admirers of the movement have portrayed the mujahideen as models of Islamic piety and correct ethical behavior.[48] Even if this portrayal is taken at face value, much greater emphasis was placed on Islamic rituals as a demarcator of identity than on the universal ethical values enshrined in the concept of *iman* in Islam. And this despite the fact that Sayyid Ahmad in his own dealings treated Muslims and non-Muslims with equal courtesy. He sought help from Hindu rulers and showed no pangs of conscience about paying hefty interest on money delivered to him by Hindu financiers for the military campaign against the Sikhs. Such pragmatic adjustments to India's social and religious diversity, however, stood in some contrast to his strident teachings of exclusiveness. These targeted Sunni Muslims (known as *tafdilis,* who gave primacy to Ali over the other caliphs) as much as Shias and non-Muslims.

As Shah Ismail explained in the *Taqwiyat-ul-Iman,* written during and after Sayyid Ahmad's return from hajj, "good faith" constitutes belief in the one and only God *(tawhid)* and the way of the Prophet Muhammad (sunna). This means rejecting associationism (associating anyone or anything with God) and innovation; "all other sins," by comparison, are less significant, for "they corrupt the morals only." Once a believer is purified of the evils of polytheism and innovation, "whatever transgressions he may be guilty of, may be ascribed to the frailty of human nature, or to error." The sins of a "perfect Unitarian" are a "hundredfold better" than the good deeds of "a pious Polytheist" because God forgives a repentant believer, whereas a "rebellious sycophant . . . is proud of his hypocrisy."[49]

This was a response to the sociological context of early nineteenth-century India, rather than a strict application of Islamic teachings. The privileging of form over substance was to have far-reaching consequences for the Muslim understanding of jihad and faith in the subsequent history of the subcontinent—all the more so because that attitude was predicated on a critical assumption which has been the bane of most Muslim intellectual endeavors since the tenth century—namely, that rational thought undermines faith, albeit faith defined by human interpretation of beliefs about what constitutes the essence of the Quranic message disseminated by the Prophet Muhammad.[50] The Quran repeatedly makes plain that faith *(iman)* in Islam is inextricably linked to the human capacity for reason *(al-aql)* based on intuition or intelligence and is a precondition for knowledge *(ilm)*. Faith has meaning only if it is in accordance with what one knows to be reasonable, something that stands the test of a universal human morality. It is belief, rather than faith in this sense of the term, that has determined the positions taken by Muslim thinkers on several issues. Alluding to the age-old conflict between the Mutazilites and the Asharites over human free will and predestination, Shah Ismail categorically endorsed the Asharites. He based his reasoning on a hadith in which the Prophet denigrated people who indulge in their own theories instead of relying on God. Some of them end up becoming atheists, others heretics and polytheists. In Shah Ismail's words:

He alone who reposes his sole reliance on God, and does not pursue any other course, is liked by Him, and is guided in the right path; thereby he derives that comfort and ease of mind which never falls to the lot of a freethinker. Of course every one experiences in the world so much as has already been written in his fate, but the whole career of the life of a rationalist is nothing but misery and distress while that of the other is incessant comfort and happiness.[51]

An antirationalist stance, along with an intemperate view of everyday social practices among Muslims, provoked virulent opposition to Sayyid Ahmad's cause. The *Sirat-i-Mustaqim* deplores the financial and emotional excesses of *muharram* observances. Muslims are instead asked to feed the sayyids who were starving. The truest expression of love for the great Shia martyr Imam Husayn was the sacrifice of life and property for Islam, following the sharia, and "carrying on open hostilities against infidels, sinners and innovators." Such customary Indian Muslim practices as circumcision ceremonies, weddings, and funerals were written off as a waste of scarce resources. Some concessions were made to human frailty. Muslims were not condemned for failing to say their prayers. The giving of food and recitation of the opening verse of the Quran *(fatiha)* were permitted, but the emphasis was on simplicity. Muslims were urged to follow the Prophet's example by limiting wedding festivities to the *walima,* the marriage feast whose costs are borne by the bridegroom's family. In short, all ceremonies and customs that had originated in Hindustan, Sind, Persia, or the Byzantine Empire had to be done away with. The ban on remarriage of widows was the most repugnant of all customs. Those who prevented widows from remarrying were threatened with social boycott. Descendants of sayyid and saintly *(pir)* families expecting intercession on the day of judgment were declared sinners.[52]

The most stringent critic of the movement was Maulana Fazl-i-Haq Khairabadi (1797–1861), a senior disciple of Shah Abdul Aziz who served the English East India Company in various capacities before becoming chief justice of Delhi in 1855. He came from a family that extended cooperation to the British after the fall of Delhi and promoted secular learning.[53] A philosopher of logic and a rationalist, Fazl-i-Haq Khairabadi used his official position to try to curb Shah Ismail's "Wahabai" activities, even before the start of the jihad movement. Like other Hanafi ulema, he was incensed by the *Taqwiyat-ul-Iman*'s charge that the majority of Muslims were steeped in polytheism. Instead Fazl-i-Haq stoutly defended the concept of intercession. He was perturbed by Shah Ismail's suggestion that God had the power to create another human being like Muhammad but did not, since doing so would negate the concept of the seal of the prophets. Not only was the argument thoroughly irrational, but it represented a subterfuge to credit Sayyid Ahmad with the holy qualities of the Prophet Muhammad. He berated Shah Ismail for not having the first idea about logic and rational perceptions. To maintain that God cannot create a second Muhammad is not quite the same as saying that God does not have the power to do so. Fazl-i-Haq enlisted the help of Ghalib, his close friend and disciple, in exposing Shah Ismail's fallacy. Showing his independence of mind, Ghalib did not fully endorse his mentor and certainly refrained from saying that God did not have the power to create another Muhammad. When taken to task for the lapse, he simply added verses stating that God had the power to create many new worlds and therefore as many Muhammads.[54] A fatwa signed by Fazl-i-Haq and other leading ulema denounced Shah Ismail as an infidel who deserved to be executed for apostasy. Anyone supporting him was also an infidel, guilty of insulting the holy Prophet.[55]

Ideological controversies sparked by Sayyid Ahmad's and Shah Ismail's teachings persisted even after the commencement of the jihad against the Sikhs. Hated for their attacks on long-cherished religious beliefs, the "Indian Wahabis" were, as Hunter discovered, "a menace to all classes" whose "hand [had] fallen heavily" on any Muslim "so criminal as to differ from their views." Operating as reformers—not on the order of Luther or Cromwell, but "as destroyers" in the spirit of Robespierre—they were, Hunter pointed out, "revolutionists alike in politics and religion." Not surprisingly, their doctrines were "hateful to the well-to-do classes" of Muslims, who considered them a "scourge." The strength of the Wahabis lay in the practical morality they preached to the poorer class of Muslims, suitably adapted to their hopes and aspirations. Hunter considered most of Sayyid Ahmad's teachings, as propagated by his vice-regents, to be "faultless," insofar as they aimed at "stir[ring] up thousands of their countrymen to purer life, and a truer conception of the Almighty." But an overemphasis on the regulation of outward behavior was not without its drawbacks. Since "a mere system of morality can never hold together a great sect," the religious dimension of the movement "began to lose its power," and the sayyid's agents placed more emphasis on "their hearers' detestation of the Infidel." By capitalizing on the "permanent hatred" Indian Muslims felt for the English, the reformers "transferred the basis of their teachings from the noblest capabilities of the Musalman heart to the fanatical fury of the populace."[56]

Such an interpretation of the movement's development implies a shift away from an emphasis on practical morality to an open declaration of war against infidels by Sayyid Ahmad's followers centered in Patna well after his martyrdom in 1831. A jihad was fought because merely preaching practical morality did not guarantee continued success for the movement. The religious sanctions that Sikhs imposed on Muslims in the Punjab made it obligatory for Sayyid Ahmad to undertake the jihad to prove the sincerity of what he preached. Hunter maintains that Sayyid Ahmad, until his pilgrimage to Mecca, had not formulated a coherent system of beliefs and that his peripatetic preaching went largely unheeded by the British authorities. W. Connor, the honorary magistrate of Aligarh, recalled observing Sayyid Ahmad's and Shah Ismail's activities in the district fifty years earlier. They did "not touch any subject having tendency towards the Christians" but invited Muslims to join their "doctrine for the Conversion of Sikhs." The two did "not preach any Jehad at all, nor was such a thing as Jehad known in those times."[57]

These views are belied by the fact that the *Sirat-i-Mustaqim,* described by Hunter as the Quran of the movement, was put together at least four years before Sayyid Ahmad's departure for a hajj in 1820.[58] The book compared jihad to rainfall that brings down heavenly grace on all created beings and makes believers sound in prayer, thus facilitating the spread of divine mercy and the light of faith, so that justice prevails and the "munificence of liberal people improves the economic conditions of the people." Jihad was a boon even for non-Muslims, for it might inspire them to enter the fold of Islam.[59] India's conversion into a *Dar-ul-Harb* had deprived it of heavenly blessings, such as just rulers, learned ulema, and pious saints of the kind that had existed a few centuries ago.[60] Highlighting the worldly benefits of jihad, rather than the rewards that would accrue to the martyrs in the hereafter, was intended to broaden the movement's appeal. It also explains the reason for claiming that Sayyid Ahmad had been in the path of prophethood or, more accurately, in the likeness of the Prophet. Ascribing a high spiritual status to Sayyid Ahmad gave him the authority to motivate the mujahideen to undergo the rigors of self-discipline, thereby assuring staunch commitment to the leader and the cause. Jihad, Sayyid Ahmad stated, was meaningful only when the wielders of the sword had correct intentions, honorable principles, and training in ethical reform. Since there was no assured method of keeping a check on the intentions of the mujahideen, belief in the imam's status and an emphasis on external conformity became the main focus of attention.

In the *Mansab-i-Imamate,* Shah Ismail likened the imam to the son of the Prophet. An imam who raises the standard of jihad is described as a *sahib-i-dawat* (literally, one who invites). His actions and achievements replicate those of the Prophet, and it is through him that divine commandments are revealed. In a departure from the classical Sunni theory of *imamate,* Shah Ismail maintained that the imam is the vice-regent of the Prophet and one closest to God. Muslims are obliged to obey his commands; disobedience to them is an act of faithlessness, analogous to disobeying the Prophet himself. Though the sharia does not prohibit nationalistic wars, these are not *jihad fi sabil allah*. A *sahib-i-dawat* fights only for the sake of God, whereas wars fought by temporal rulers against infidels and idolaters are imperialistic ventures.[61]

The ideological justification for making a subtle distinction between temporal rulership and *imamate* set the stage for the armed struggle. Care had been taken to establish a sophisticated network of deputies extending from northern India to the Deccan. Apart from disseminating the sayyid's teachings, their main responsibility was to recruit men and collect funds for the campaign. On 17 January 1826, optimistic about swaying Muslim rulers and Pathan tribal chiefs to join the cause, Sayyid Ahmad and some six hundred of his carefully selected Hindustani disciples embarked upon a *hijrat* from Rai Bareilly to the frontier with the explicit aim of waging jihad.

The Business of Jihad

A sense of spectacle surrounded the long and winding journey to the frontier, which took some ten months to complete.[62] Hundreds jostled to catch a glimpse of Sayyid Ahmad's sacred personage and offer him their oath of allegiance. Although many were moved by his sermons on jihad as a means to restore the lost glory of Islam, others harbored doubts about the ability of his poorly armed warriors to vanquish the Sikhs. Few ventured to join the ranks as the party snaked through the towns and countryside of northern India. Amid all the pageantry of the occasion, Sayyid Ahmad was aware of the need to impress onlookers with something more than pious words. Needing allies, recruits, and

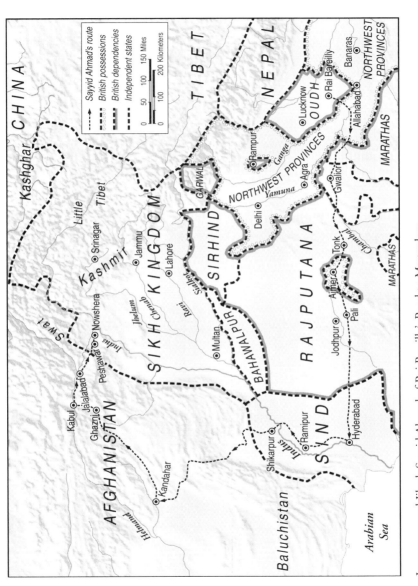

Journey toward Jihad: Sayyid Ahmad of Rai Bareilly's Road to Martyrdom

war materials, he made two strategic stops, in Gwalior and Tonk, whose rulers held him in high esteem on account of his spirituality and physical courage. In Gwalior, he and his followers were royally entertained by Hindu Rao, the brother-in-law of the ruler Maharaja Daulat Rao, and had presents lavished on them. In Tonk Sayyid Ahmad was given a royal welcome by his old employer, Nawab Amir Khan, and his son, Nawab Wazir-ud-Dullah. The sayyid stayed here for over a month, during which he received generous gifts in money and war materials, indicating that Sayyid Ahmad had remained on good terms with Amir Khan even after the latter had struck a deal with the British.[63] The willingness to rub shoulders with a Hindu infidel and a former patron who turned British ally hints at the political pragmatism that was to prove to be Sayyid Ahmad's greatest strength and also his principal weakness in his efforts to translate the theory of jihad into practice.

As the jihadis passed through different parts of Sind and Baluchistan to reach Peshawar, curiosity interspersed with awe and suspicion greeted the soldiers. On entering Sind with high hopes of securing the support of the Talpur Mirs, Sayyid Ahmad was taken aback to learn that some people thought he and his men were British spies. At the same time several took an oath of allegiance to him and graciously extended their hospitality. Invitations to the rulers of Sind and Bahawalpur to support the jihad failed to elicit a positive response. Only the Hur leader, the Pir of Pagara Sibgatullah Shah, in his desire to parry the threat posed by the Sikhs, showed an inclination to join the party. But he postponed his decision until the sayyid had established a central command on the frontier and, more important, had secured military victories. Recognizing Pir Sibgatullah as a friend and potential ally, Sayyid Ahmad left his family in the protection of the Hurs and proceeded to Baluchistan, where he delivered the call to jihad to the reigning Mehran, Mehrab Khan. The Mehran declined, as the Baluch were facing a threat from Abdullah Khan Durrani's Kandahari army. Vowing to mediate the dispute between his co-religionists, Sayyid Ahmad left for Peshawar on 22 August 1826 via Kandahar and Kabul.[64]

Before leaving for the frontier, Sayyid Ahmad had written to different tribal chiefs asking them to heed his call to jihad. So there was great anticipation among the Pathans, who saw in his movement a means to unite their warring clans, in order to make a concerted attempt to be rid of the Sikh menace. But by the time he reached Peshawar, the sayyid had gained firsthand experience of the intensity of the infighting among the frontier tribesmen and realized the difficulty of the task ahead. A relatively cold welcome from the Durrani chieftains of Peshawar, who paid an annual tribute to the Sikhs in return for relative peace, persuaded Sayyid Ahmad to move on quickly toward Yusufzai territory. Sworn enemies of the Sikhs, who plundered their property at will, the Yusufzai received him cordially. Several hundred tribesmen offered to fight alongside two hundred Kandahari volunteers and the Hindustanis. Capturing the goods of conquered foes for one's personal aggrandizement was customary practice on the frontier. The tribesmen joined the sayyid's men in the expectation of collecting loot, not demonstrating religious virtue. Convinced of the righteousness of his cause, Sayyid Ahmad welcomed the new recruits. The stage was set for the first military encounter on 20 December 1826 in Okara near Nowshera with a ten-thousand-strong Sikh army under the command of General Budh Singh. A surprise nocturnal attack ended in disaster: the local recruits thought the success of the attack entitled them to engage in wholesale looting, but as the tribesmen concentrated on collecting goods and disappeared to their homes, the Sikhs were able to regroup and inflict losses on Sayyid Ahmad's men and the Kandaharis who did fight.[65]

This was an ill-fated beginning to the jihad. The battle of

Okara nevertheless had a marked effect. Reports of the war booty collected raised the status of Sayyid Ahmad's warriors in the eyes of the local Pathans. Many more tribal chiefs now came forward to swear loyalty. Khade Khan, the chief of Hund, offered his territory as the command center for the movement. Once bitten but not twice shy, Sayyid Ahmad accepted the invitation, only to discover that his new ally was primarily interested in amassing booty. Unable to succumb to such lowly temptations, the sayyid refused to have anything to do with Khade Khan's plot to raid the Sikh commercial center of Hazru. He then relented and agreed, on the unenforceable condition that no Muslim be put in harm's way during the course of the attack. Sayyid Ahmad watched as the tribesmen and a few Kandaharis crossed the river to take the Sikhs by surprise. As in Okara, the raid was initially a success. But then the looting started, giving the Sikhs time to stage a counterattack on the tribesmen crossing the river. Many of them, laden with goods, drowned in the process. The Kandaharis meanwhile made a desperate attempt to defend the fleeing Pathans. Sayyid Ahmad had to set aside his noble ideals and send in reinforcements, thereby becoming party to a raid carried out with the clear intent to acquire material goods. Once the Sikhs had been beaten back, the war booty proved to be a problem. When Khade Khan ordered his men to let Sayyid Ahmad decide on the distribution, a general uproar and a certain amount of verbal abuse ensued. Fearing an uprising, Sayyid Ahmad had to let the quarrelsome tribesmen keep what they had collected, in contravention of principles outlined in the sharia for dividing the spoils of war.[66]

The first two battles had made painfully clear that the local tribesmen lacked organization and had no understanding of the basic principles of Islamic law concerning jihad, much less its spiritual and ethical dimensions. Shah Ismail was deputed to lift the spiritual sights of the Pathan tribesmen, so that jihad in the way of God *(jihad fi sabil allah)* was not reduced to the crass business of accumulating war booty. Even more important for the future of the campaign was the need to bring the tribesmen under the aegis of a single central authority, for the local chiefs were hopelessly divided. In keeping with the sharia, it was decided to appoint Sayyid Ahmad imam. On 11 January 1827 near the lake at Hund, various Pathan notables, mystics, and common people pledged themselves to jihad under Sayyid Ahmad's leadership. The *ghazis* from India referred to him as *amir-ul-momineen* (the commander of the faithful). The local Pathans called him Sayyid Badshah, or Sayyid the king, and in his correspondence with the Sikhs he used the appellation Khalifa (Caliph) Sahib. Under the terms of the agreement, Sayyid Ahmad's duties as imam were confined to the business of jihad, while day-to-day administration remained the responsibility of the tribal chiefs.[67]

This was hardly an optimal solution to the problem of disciplining the Pathans. The indeterminate boundary between Sayyid Ahmad's spiritual powers as an imam and the temporal authority he exercised in attempting to enforce the sharia brought him into conflict with the tribal chiefs, who considered the oath of allegiance to be limited to fighting. There was increasing criticism of Sayyid Ahmad's activities on the frontier. Needing to keep up the morale of his troops, Sayyid Ahmad sent out another flurry of letters urging Pathan tribal chiefs and the rulers of Chitral, Kashmir, and Bukhara to wage jihad. Mingling pious exhortations and pretensions to spiritual eminence, the epistles served only to arouse further suspicions about his ultimate aims. Those who came forward to take the oath of allegiance were the Durrani chiefs of Peshawar, Yar Muhammad Khan and Pir Muhammad Khan, who had betrayed their own brothers in the quest for power. Wary of the sayyid's rising stock among Pathan tribesmen, the Durrani brothers calculated that joining the assemblage carried fewer dangers than outright opposition. Within two months of Sayyid Ahmad's becoming imam, an estimated eighty thousand Pathans are said to have pledged allegiance. Sayyid Ahmad was warned that Yar Muhammad Khan and Pir Muhammad Khan were untrustworthy; but he left the matter to Allah, who could turn betrayers into firm believers. The arrival of the Durranis added another twenty thousand men to the sayyid's army; but numerical strength did not make for a more effective fighting force. Most of the men lacked proper military training and were poorly equipped. Worse still, they all followed the orders of their own chiefs, each of whom had his own insignia. A conservative estimate put the number of large military flags as high as a thousand! Whether out of naïveté, a sense of opportunity, or both, Sayyid Ahmad thought he had a chance to strike at the heart of Budh Singh's army, consisting of around thirty thousand disciplined and well-armed men.[68]

The British traveler Charles Masson, who was in the region at the time of the mobilization, remarked that Sayyid Ahmad, "joined by adventurers and crusaders from all parts of Afghanistan," intended "to take possession of the Panjab, Hindostan and China." "Hope and exultation" in the Muslim camp were running high, and the imam was vowing to "compel Ranjit Singh to turn Mussulman or cut off his head." Confidence in their numerical advantage over the Sikhs, and "the presumed favour of heaven, permitted none to doubt of success." The dividing up of Sikh towns and villages was done before a shot had been fired. In a telling observation that contradicts hagiographical representations of Sayyid Ahmad as a paragon of humility, Masson alleged that the imam's "soul . . . [had] dilated" so much that "in his pride of feeling, he used expressions implying that he considered himself the master of Peshawer, and the Sirdars [tribal chiefs] as his vassals."[69]

Even if Masson exaggerated, there is no doubt that the Durrani chiefs harbored grave suspicions about Sayyid Ahmad. It was not long before they entered into an intrigue with Budh Singh, who promised them amnesty if they avoided taking part in military action. A crafty operator, Yar Muhammad Khan not only switched sides but poisoned Sayyid Ahmad the night before the battle of Shaidu. Barely able to stay conscious, Sayyid Ahmad had to sit it out, while his forces took on the Sikhs. Despite early gains, the mujahideen were doomed once the Durranis refused to fight. Their treachery cleared the way for a Sikh victory. Sayyid Ahmad escaped capture after determined resistance by his Hindustani followers allowed time for his elephant to be taken across the river. Among the innumerable casualties, an estimated six thousand mujahideen are said to have perished in the battle.[70]

Feeling defeated, and physically debilitated by the poisoning, Sayyid Ahmad married a third time, after securing the approval of his first two wives. The new wife, Sayyida Fatima, was from the Ismaili sect and had to be given instruction on how to conform to his view of Islam. As he slowly began to regain his strength, Sayyid Ahmad made a public show of repentance, declaring that the military debacle was God's retribution for mistakes that he and his men had committed. He prayed for forgiveness and guidance. But spiritual repentance alone could not assure him success with his unruly Pathan allies. Unless he found a way of managing internal feuds among the Pathan tribal chiefs, victory against the Sikhs would continue to elude him. So Shah Ismail was delegated to try to paper over the disagreements among the tribal leaders around Hazara and in the surrounding areas. Urgent requests were circulated for provision of funds and recruits from Hindustan. Following a decisive defeat, such requests were not without peril. The Durranis in Peshawar, even as they paid for their treachery by coughing up a hefty annual tribute to the Sikh court, obstructed the flow of monies and men.

Just how badly things were progressing was apparent once Maulvi Mahboob Ali arrived with a group of recruits from Delhi.

Harassed by the Durranis on the way, he had written a charged letter to Sayyid Ahmad, saying it was necessary to leave the Sikhs alone and focus instead on fighting Muslim "infidels." By the time the maulvi reached Sayyid Ahmad's camp in Panjtar, he was in a petulant mood; he exploded on seeing a horse with a heavily ornate cloth on its back prepared for the imam. Mahboob Ali accused the sayyid of adopting a conciliatory attitude towards the Durrani sardars, living an unconscionably ostentatious life, and leaving the mujahideen to starve. Sayyid Ahmad tried placating the irate maulvi by offering him the imamate. The difficulties in reconciling high ideals with the more mundane requirements of waging a jihad were plain. Instead of taking the bait, Mahboob Ali began telling the mujahideen to return to India, because no jihad was taking place. They had killed no infidels and acquired no land. Their only concern was with cooking food. Shah Ismail, who was away in Pakhli at the time, urged him to wait in Panjtar until his return. But he had seen enough and left for Delhi without bothering to inform anyone.[71]

Mahboob Ali's account of what was happening on the frontier was disappointing to the circles in Delhi that had been supporting Sayyid Ahmad. They suspended the flow of recruits as well as money and forced Sayyid Ahmad to offer men salaries to enlist. Paying soldiers to wage jihad was consistent with neither the practice of the Prophet nor the sharia. In a sermon Sayyid Ahmad skirted this technical difficulty, on the grounds that a man waging jihad for a salary also demonstrated virtue, albeit not to the same degree as one who did so for the sake of Allah. After recruiting two hundred men as paid soldiers for two months, he had to abandon the practice because of a shortage of funds. This was not the only instance in which expediency resulted in stretching the logic of jihad in the way of God. Since Shah Ishaq and Shah Yaqub remained unreconciled to his methods and the Durrani chiefs were interfering in efforts to raise money in Peshawar,

Sayyid Ahmad ignored the Islamic injunction on the payment of interest and entered into an agreement with Hindu moneylenders in Manara, a large commercial center near Hund on the western side of the river Indus. There, two brothers, Moti and Santo, had agreed to honor letters of credit arriving from other parts of India. They charged twelve rupees interest for every hundred rupees sent.[72]

The arrangement replenished the kitty to the tune of thirty-five thousand rupees. Sayyid Ahmad was consequently in a position to heed the advice of the council of Usmanzai tribal elders: they recommended putting down the Peshawar sardars, who were rebelling against his authority as imam, in violation of their oath of allegiance. But for the war to be successful, it was important to win the support of the tribal chiefs of Khyber. A delegation carrying Sayyid Ahmad's message informed them that jihad had become impossible unless they dealt with those who were spreading sedition.[73] This amounted to a declaration of war against their co-religionists—just what Maulvi Mahboob Ali had prescribed. Building an effective alliance to crush the Durrani chiefs, however, meant cutting through a web of intrigues and counter-intrigues. After agreeing to fight alongside Sayyid Ahmad's men, the Khyber chiefs went back on their word, once again converting a possible victory into certain defeat. The jihad campaign had by now become a war between Muslims. Sayyid Ahmad even praised a Hindu named Rajaram for fighting courageously alongside the mujahideen.[74]

The abortive campaign against the Durranis in Peshawar forced Sayyid Ahmad to reconsider the logic of confining his power to spiritual matters alone. It was now decided that together with the *imamate-i-jihad* he should assume the secular authority to implement the sharia. The problem of funding would be solved once Sayyid Ahmad could collect the *ushr* (tithe), a tenth of the yield of the land. On 6 February 1829 at a special meeting in Panjtar, the ulema and certain tribal chiefs agreed to let Sayyid Ahmad enforce the sharia. The scope of the laws was broadly defined to include the compulsory enforcement of Islamic injunctions relating to prayers and fasting, as well as a ban on usury, polygamy, consumption of wine, distribution of a deceased man's wife and children among his brothers, and involvement in family feuds.[75] Anyone transgressing the sharia after swearing allegiance to Sayyid Ahmad was to be treated as a sinner and rebel. Any breach was punishable by death, and Muslims were prohibited from saying prayers at the funerals of such people. Two weeks later, after another meeting of tribesmen, Sayyid Ahmad began appointing judges in different parts of the frontier. Maulvi Sayyid Muhammad Haban was selected as the chief judge *(qazi-ul-qaza)*.[76] The moves, which had been justified on the grounds that a judicial administration was needed to implement the sharia, infringed on the temporal powers of the tribal chiefs and seriously undermined the prerogatives of local religious leaders.

Even as the inner core of mujahideen from northern India remained devoted and willing to sacrifice themselves for the cause, the new measures met with stiff resistance from the Pathan tribal chiefs and religious leaders. Those like Khade Khan who had initially rallied to the support of Sayyid Ahmad drew back in horror once the implications of the policies dawned upon them. Defections now came thick and fast. From the front Khade Khan took the lead by striking a deal with the Sikhs. His dissension was endorsed by two other powerful Pathan clans, the Ismailzai and Daulatzai, who had not been present at the meeting where the decision to enforce the sharia was taken. The ulema of these two tribes were resolute in opposing the sharia laws, because by custom they were entitled to proceeds from the *ushr* tax. Facing an outright revolt among the very people he had come to rally for a jihad against the Sikhs, Sayyid Ahmad, for all his high ethical ideals and spiritual resolve, was in need of a divine reprieve. After the plan to attack Attock Fort with five hundred of his men was leaked to Khade Khan, the sayyid was left to bemoan the treachery of the Pathan chiefs who had made a sham of his jihad. Unwilling to fight Khade Khan, Sayyid Ahmad met with him, only to be told that the Pathan chiefs would ignore the decision to enforce the sharia: the local ulema had made the ruling, and the rulers felt no need to adhere to it. "We are Pakhtuns [Pathans, or Pashtuns]," Khade Khan bluntly declared, "and these ulema are dependent on our beneficence and have no say in matters to do with the running of government." If the advice given by the ulema was useful, it was accepted; if not, it was simply ignored.[77]

The statement was categorical. As the chief notable in the area, Khade Khan considered the sayyid of Rai Bareilly a cleric dependent on his patronage. There was no common ground here. At Panjtar, Khade Khan joined forces with the Sikhs led by the Italian mercenary commander Colonel Jean-Baptiste Ventura. Sayyid Ahmad, seeing that his men were heavily outnumbered, told them to recite verses from the Quran. Miraculously, Ventura recalled his troops. This withdrawal emboldened the *ghazis* to join with the residents of Manari to overpower Khade Khan's men, who had occupied their territory. The Pathan tribesmen were sufficiently impressed by the mujahideen's success in averting a battle that some of them offered to assist in expelling the Sikhs from the area. Promises of this sort had been made before, with disastrous results. Facing the Durranis in the northwest and Khade Khan in the south, Sayyid Ahmad had little choice but to accept whatever assistance he could secure. After intense deliberations on the wisdom of fighting fellow Muslims, a decision was taken to attack Khade Khan's fort at Hund. Heaven was smiling on the mujahideen. Before an armed exchange could take place, a *ghazi* shot Khade Khan dead. His brothers, incensed by the murder, began mobilizing the tribes, including the Durranis, to wreak vengeance on the mujahideen.[78]

The elimination of a key foe like Khade Khan and the acquisition of his property made the financial and military position of Sayyid Ahmad stronger than ever. His sights were now set on the Durrani camp at Topi near Zaida and, more ambitiously, on Kashmir, which he wanted to "liberate" and use as a permanent base for his jihad.[79] In September 1829, after a brief exchange at Zaida during which elements of the Durrani forces conspired with the mujahideen, Yar Mohammed Khan was killed and his men put to flight. The war booty included six guns, an elephant, over sixty camels, and three hundred horses, not to mention a huge cache of arms and ammunition. It gave Sayyid Ahmad an aura of "almost regal power."[80] Sensing an opportunity to expand his influence into Kashmir, he demanded access through Amb from its ruler, Painda Khan, known to be a sworn enemy of the Sikhs. Located on the western bank of the Indus, Amb was strategically vital as an approach to Kashmir, which was under Sikh control. Though he had earlier expressed his support for Sayyid Ahmad, Painda Khan refused to let the *ghazis* move through his territory. Sayyid Ahmad defeated him and forced him to cede territory on the western bank of the Indus. But he allowed Painda Khan to retain control of the eastern area, so long as he did not obstruct the movement of the *ghazis*. In testimony of future goodwill, the sayyid promised Painda Khan grants of land in Kashmir and Peshawar—once these had been taken.

Encouraged by successive victories and by offers of assistance from the rulers of Chitral and Kawai in the Khagan Valley, Sayyid Ahmad decided to try to conquer Kashmir. This was a tactical error: Painda Khan was still not reconciled to accepting the dictates of the *amir-ul-momineen*. Time was of the essence. The Sikh governor of Kashmir, Diwan Ram Diyal, had been recalled by the Lahore court for alleged misdemeanors. Ram Singh, the keeper of the Qadirabad fort north of Nowshera on the eastern bank of the Indus River, was a former resident of Rai Bareilly. He had the highest regard for Sayyid Ahmad and his family and offered useful advice and assistance to the mujahideen. As a consequence, Sayyid Ahmad, now confident of victory, sent a detachment led by his nephew, Sayyid Ahmad Ali, to attack Phulera, ten miles from Mansehra in the Hazara district. Painda Khan, fearing that he would be caught in a pincer movement, sent a missive to Hari Singh, the Sikh commander stationed near Manshera, to solicit assistance. This led to a surprise attack by the Sikhs and the rout of the mujahideen. Among those killed in the battle of Phulera was Sayyid Ahmad Ali.

Sayyid Ahmad found his ambition to take Kashmir thwarted, and the Durranis a thorn in his side. He turned his attention to consolidating his forces and forming a government to administer the conquered areas from Panjtar to Amb. But his narrowly punitive conception of the sharia was at odds with the customary practices of the frontier tribesmen, who did not take at all kindly to the new laws. In a departure from the leniency shown in the *Sirat-i-Mustaqim* on the matter, those who did not say their prayers were punished. Women found violating the sharia came in for special treatment. Upon hearing that one Pathan woman had lied about the death of her husband, who was still alive, Sayyid Ahmad had her tied to the stairs and lashed. He went to the women's quarters himself to watch the punishment being carried out. The local custom of bathing naked in the river was strictly prohibited; people caught doing so were initially fined eight annas and later subjected to lashing. Various fines were also levied and punishments inflicted on those who allowed their animals to graze on cultivated fields.[81] In response to a shortage of food, Sayyid Ahmad issued a decree: those who had fled Amb were to come back to take charge of their fields; the lands of any residents who failed to return would be handed over to the *ghazis*. Watermelons were to be planted in the fields that were lying fallow.

To counter his growing unpopularity, stories were circulated about Sayyid Ahmad's miraculous powers. Mehr recounts one, the parable of a barren mango tree that had formerly borne fruit, in times when the rulers were honest. The sayyid prayed near the tree and ordered the *ghazis* to receive their Quran lessons under it. In time the tree once again bore fruit! Similar stories were propagated with an eye to restoring the spiritual status of an imam who was implementing unpalatable laws. While ritualizing religious practices among the Pathans by force, Sayyid Ahmad continued to inculcate ethical values among his men, who were constantly exhorted to be self-effacing and to sacrifice everything for God.[82]

A revealing exchange between Ventura and Sayyid Ahmad's emissary, Maulvi Khairuddin, in May 1830 suggests that such stories were generating heightened curiosity about the sayyid's modus operandi. The Italian mercenary asked searching questions about jihad. How could someone who had neither men nor materials, Ventura inquired, decide to take on such a powerful force as the Sikhs? Khairuddin gave him a long lecture on the religious obligation of jihad, which was mandatory even for earlier prophets. Sayyid Ahmad had come to the frontier because the Yusufzai needed to fight the Sikhs. Khairuddin took care to add that jihad was not only about waging war but about exercising one's strength in the cause of God. Conquest was merely a by-product of efforts to promote the faith. Ventura, expressing deep admiration for Sayyid Ahmad, revealed that he (Ventura) was being accused by his Sikh employers of disloyalty. Ventura wanted to send Sayyid Ahmad a horse as a token of his appreciation but also asked for a gift in exchange. Khairuddin dismissed the request. Far from having a horse at his disposal, Sayyid Ahmad did not have a donkey to give; he expected Ventura to pay not only the tax imposed on recent converts to Islam *(khairaj)* but also the *jizya* levied on non-Muslims.[83]

Arrogance cloaked in piety may have been a good strategy

when it came to dealing with the enemy. But it was beginning to backfire, as Sayyid Ahmad's chief judicial officer, Qazi Sayyid Muhammad Haban, was discovering to his cost. The local mullahs continued to resist efforts to collect *ushr* for the mujahideen, and some mullahs began preparing for an uprising. Backed by Shah Ismail, Haban (quoting various law books) argued that any *ushr* that was collected rightly belonged to the imam and not to them. The mullah of Kotah brusquely told him that he was quite wrong in thinking that preaching could make the Pathans abandon their customs. Instead of heeding the advice, Haban set up a network of local councilors *(nizams)* to collect *ushr*. Regularly, people who disobeyed the laws were subjected to lashing, often for insignificant reasons. These coercive measures served only to keep Pathan tempers at the boil. While withholding the payment of *ushr,* the ruler of Mardan entered into talks with the Durranis with the purpose of getting rid of the new revenue officers. On hearing of this plan, Haban decided to attack Mardan. It proved to be a fatal decision. Although the mujahideen prevailed, Haban himself perished in the fray.[84]

Recognizing that several local khans and mullahs were eager to join the struggle, Sultan Muhammad Durrani saw this as an opportune moment to avenge the death of his brother Yar Muhammad Khan. On the eve of the battle, Sayyid Ahmad lamented:

Look at the works of Allah! We migrated from Hindustan to unite Muslims in a war against infidels. It is regrettable that let alone the infidels, Muslims themselves are thirsting for our blood and we have prepared to fight them. We never wanted to fight them. Consequently we repeatedly tried to persuade Sultan Muhammad. But alas, Satan has gained such complete control over his soul that he understands nothing. Well, if this is what has to be, we are helpless and whatever happens we will deal with it.[85]

Sayyid Ahmad, resigned to his fate, donned his finest clothes and looking every bit the king, as the local epithet Sayyid Badshah implied, went into battle carrying an array of weapons, including two English rifles. Whether out of strategic considerations or a sense of quiet confidence, he chose not to transport the cannons back from Amb, which had fallen into the hands of the mujahideen after the battle of Zaida. When the battle lines were drawn at Mayar, some two miles north of Mardan, three thousand of Sayyid Ahmad's men faced a Durrani force estimated at twelve thousand strong and backed by six cannons. Before firing a shot, both sides summoned religion to their side. As was by now established practice among them, the *ghazis* said prayers and recited verses from the Quran, in addition to chanting songs and poetry praising Sayyid Ahmad and declaring jihad to be the passport to paradise. For their part, the Durrani soldiers had to pass under a hastily constructed doorway from which a Quran dangled: this gesture was intended as symbolic of their oath not to desert in the heat of battle.[86]

The Durrani attempts to bribe providence were in vain. Negotiations between the two sides, mediated by Faizullah Khan Hazarkhani, allowed Sayyid Ahmad to advance to Peshawar in October 1830. Faizullah Khan reached a spoken agreement with Sultan Mohammad, leader of the Durranis, whereby the mujahideen were to enter the city as "guests," and not conquerors. They were to refrain from looting and to accept food only if they paid for it. These concessions to wounded Durrani pride underscored Sayyid Ahmad's continuing concern with winning over to his side this troublesome clan. But the Durranis were slippery customers, as Faizullah Khan himself admitted. According to the terms of the formal treaty, the Durranis were to pay forty thousand rupees: twenty thousand in Peshawar, and the rest once the mujahideen had retreated to Charsada. As a further condition, the Durranis had to agree to participate in jihad. Sultan Muhammad, when he came to meet Sayyid Ahmad, showed him a fatwa addressed to the Pathan chiefs, which alleged that the sayyid was an impostor and his jihad a ruse to take over their country. It accused him of starting a new religion and of being a British spy. Sayyid Ahmad asked Shah Ismail not to mention the fatwa to the mujahideen, who might in their anger do something irrational. Seeing the sense in cutting his losses, Sultan Muhammad accepted the terms, despite rumblings of dissent in his camp. Faizullah Khan warned Sayyid Ahmad that the Durranis might attack his men as soon as they began the retreat. There was a wave of criticism from within his rank and file.[87] Sayyid Ahmad appointed Maulvi Mazhar Ali Khan as his deputy in Peshawar, to take responsibility for collecting the money from the Durranis and keeping watch on their activities.

It was a tenuous arrangement, given the mounting opposition to Sayyid Ahmad's sharia laws. No one really knew "how long this priestly rule and anomalous power of the Sayad" could succeed in "holding in restraint a wild, brave and independent people." The manifest ease with which Sayyid Ahmad's "undisciplined hordes" had prevailed over the regular armies of ruling chieftains had "give[n] some colour to the popular superstition that he possessed the faculty of silencing guns and rendering bullets harmless." Instead of using this reputation for spiritual prowess to good advantage, the sayyid had, "in the pride of his success, forgotten to be moderate, and ventured to impose upon his subjects a strict and oppressive *regime* from which even their superstitious reverence revolted."[88] The ulema in Peshawar attacked him for being a *ghair muqallid* and a Wahabi. Taking refuge in his family prestige, Sayyid Ahmad declared himself a staunch Hanafi.[89] He denied being vindictive or cruel and justified his fighting against Muslim chiefs, by asserting that he had not struck even a dog unnecessarily, but punishing and killing hypocrites and apostates was "a divine blessing." In fact, "enthusiasm for strengthening the faith and the contemptuous treatment of its enemies were basic elements of faith." If he had committed any mistakes, the ulema ought to "warn him personally and not spread scandals in the assemblies." He appealed to the Pathans not to desert him because of his personal failings during the jihad against the Sikhs.[90]

His pleas fell on deaf ears. Outraged by the imposition of the sharia at the expense of customary law, the Pathans openly defied his authority. They were particularly riled by Sayyid Ahmad's distribution of newly acquired lands to the mujahideen and the levying of Islamic taxes. But the final straw, the offense that exhausted the patience of Pathan patriarchal society, was the sayyid's attempt at reforming marriage customs. Under the customary law prevalent on the northwest frontier, daughters were "sold" in wedlock to the highest bidder. Sayyid Ahmad abolished the practice and decreed that all Pathans should give their daughters in marriage at an early age without receiving money. Girls who were not married could be claimed by their nearest relatives.[91] Hunter has alleged that another edict was issued, according to which any girl unmarried for twelve days would become the property of the mujahideen.[92] If his allegation is true, the sayyid's zeal in finding wives for his men backfired badly. As if the imposition of onerous taxes were not enough, tinkering with marriage laws represented even more egregious interference in the domestic affairs of the Pathans. The Yusufzai tribesmen rose in revolt. A secret council met and appointed a day for the slaughter of Sayyid Ahmad's soldiers and agents. The popular code word for the mission was *threshing* (of corn), and the chosen signal for its commencement the lighting of a bonfire.[93] On the designated Friday, no sooner had the fire been lit than the Durranis, who either were privy to the plot or were apprised of it by word of mouth, brutally murdered Maulvi Mazhar Ali and Faizulah Khan Hazarkhani, along with all those who had been left behind in

Peshawar to oversee the interests of the mujahideen. One British traveler, likening it to the insurrection of the Sicilian Vespers, recorded that as "the fiery cross was passed round the hills as the signal for the massacre of his agents . . . in one hour,—the hour of evening prayer—they were murdered by the tribesmen almost to a man."[94] Not content with the blood they had already shed, the Yusufzai threatened to march to Panjtar to eradicate what remained of the warriors of Allah. Sayyid Ahmad managed to evade the attack and, taking care to bury en route the cache of guns he had seized from the Durranis, crossed the Indus to take refuge in Pakli.[95]

The scale of the carnage shook the mujahideen to the core. Before Sayyid Ahmad could repair the damage and affirm the Islamic basis of his fledgling government, his stint at the helm of power was over. Instead of uniting Muslims in a jihad, his policies had sharpened the rifts between his own men and the Pathan tribesmen, some of whom connived with the Sikhs to pave the way for his decisive defeat at Balakot. Deeming the area to be impregnable because of its topography, Sayyid Ahmad reckoned that the Sikh forces under the command of Sher Singh would not be able to attack. A battle could take place only if the mujahideen came forward to confront the enemy. In his last letter, written on 25 April 1831, he even expressed the solemn hope that a victory would ensure that the mujahideen held control all the way to Kashmir. What upset his calculations yet again was betrayal on the part of some local Pathans, who disclosed to the Sikhs the narrow winding pathways leading to the place where the mujahideen were holding out.

The attack on his forward positions came as a shock to Sayyid Ahmad. All the precautions, piety, and prayers in the world had not prevented the enemy from breaching his defenses. Yet upon learning of a massive Sikh advance, he chose not to look for an escape route. Most significantly, on the fateful morning of 6 May

1831, he scrapped the battle plan, pronounced the *takbir*—God is great—and lunged out of the mosque where he had finished saying his prayers to attack the Sikhs, rather than wait for them to congregate on the plain below. A ferocious battle ensued, in which several hundred mujahideen and Sikhs are said to have perished. Sayyid Ahmad and Shah Ismail fought with exemplary courage, until they were felled by Sikh bullets. Both had realized their ultimate spiritual aim of martyrdom, without attaining any of their temporal objectives. It was, as Sayyid Ahmad might have said, one more example of the mysterious ways in which Allah worked his will!

The precise circumstances of Sayyid Ahmad's death remain shrouded in controversy, for no eyewitness survived to relate the details of his final moments. Some of his loyal followers held that although wounded, he escaped from the battlefield with the help of some Gujar cattle herders. This report fueled the legend of his disappearance and imminent return to revitalize the jihad movement. Other sources suggest that Nawab Khan Tanaoli found and identified his headless body in the presence of Sher Singh and gave it an Islamic burial.[96] What transpired after Sher Singh departed from the scene is clouded by myth to such an extent that even the burial ground of the revered martyr remains subject to wild speculation. Mehr discounts the theory that the Gujars carried Sayyid Ahmad off the battlefield, but he is less emphatic in rejecting the story that Sayyid Ahmad's body was exhumed by some Nihangs, thrown into the river, and, on reaching the shore, hacked to pieces. He thinks that if this did take place, it was at the behest of Sardars Mahan Singh and Lakhmir Singh, who feared that Sayyid Ahmad's grave would become a popular center of Muslim devotion.[97] In a slight variation on the theme, a local landlord is said to have rescued one of Sayyid Ahmad's thighs and buried it at Pallikot.[98] Mehr relates that an old woman found the sayyid's severed head, which was later buried in the place considered to be his tomb.[99] Whatever the factual truth, Sayyid Ahmad in death was a more potent symbol in Muslim consciousness than he had been during his lifetime—a just reward for his tireless, if ultimately tragic, efforts to strive in the way of Allah!

Postmortem of a Jihad

The irony that the jihad ended in a dismal failure through the machinations of co-religionists has scarred Muslim consciousness in South Asia, inviting bitter controversy over religious belief *(aqida)* at the expense of faith *(iman)*. But it has not dampened the enthusiasm of the segment of Muslims who, having imbibed tales of the piety and valor of the mujahideen, still believe in the possibility of an Islamic revival using Sayyid Ahmad's methods. Few have paused to consider whether the gap between the high ideals of the movement and its tragic end affords any lessons that might have been overlooked in the eulogistic and nostalgic fog enveloping the martyrs of Balakot. Fewer still have pondered over the disjunction between a commitment to Islam's high ethical values and a teaching that not only stressed the killing of infidels and Muslim apostates but differentiated itself from the beliefs of the rest of the Muslim community. Even those who have discerned a modern positivist attitude in Sayyid Ahmad's teachings on morality and religion have been hard pressed to deny its divisive effect on the Muslim community.[100] The use of religious symbols and the insistence on reforming social rituals in the light of new exigencies—or the rationalization of the mythical that has been identified as a key characteristic of modern-day "fundamentalists"—point to the temporal considerations that led Sayyid Ahmad and Shah Ismail to focus more on religion as an identity than on religion as faith.

This assertion might enrage Muslims who idolize the two men as pious and selfless martyrs. The point is not to question their intentions, much less cast aspersions on the pious lives they are said to have led. Rather, it is to assess the impact of their words and actions at each step in the development of the jihad movement. The important tactical shift from verbal jihad to armed struggle seems to have resulted in a much harsher stance towards the performance of religious rituals, such as daily prayers. Anyone found guilty of not praying was liable to be punished with whiplashing. The second significant shift after the battle of Balakot was shaped far more by the reality of colonialism than by the ethical teachings of Sayyid Ahmad. In Hunter's words: "Starting with an admirable system of morality, they by degrees abandoned the spiritual element in their teaching, and strengthened their declining cause by appealing to the worst passions of the human heart."[101]

None of Sayyid Ahmad's star-studded gallery of admirers has offered a satisfactory answer to these stinging charges. On the contrary, by emphasizing the singular importance of jihad and martyrdom, they have merely confirmed the worst fears of non-Muslims. Reducing the concept of martyrdom to the fighting of wars against non-Muslims, as we have seen, is a gross misreading of the concept. According to a famous hadith, the Prophet Muhammad said that there were seven types of martyrdom, in addition to being killed in Allah's cause: one who dies of plague is a martyr; one who is drowned is a martyr; one who dies of pleurisy is a martyr; one who dies of an internal complaint is a martyr; one who is burned to death is a martyr; one killed by a building falling on him is a martyr; and a woman who dies in childbirth is a martyr.[102] The number seven signifies "many" in the Arabic idiom used in the Prophet's time. Thus, martyrdom in the path of God is so varied as to encompass death from any kind of exertion—physical, intellectual, or spiritual.

Conscious of the intrinsic relation between jihad and faith, Sayyid Ahmad constantly laid stress on ethical virtues without which armed struggle would have no meaning. The *Sirat-i-Mustaqim* condemns envy, jealousy, avarice, presumption, backbiting, malevolence, hypocrisy, lying, and cupidity. Those who can banish those defects are assured untold rewards. A believer's satisfaction with God's will and the cleansing of the heart through self-negation is a precondition for courage, contentment, generosity, and purity. Along with these general ethical principles, Muslims are urged to abide by the five pillars of Islam and give special attention to jihad because it occupies a central place in the religious life of a believer. Tyranny is unacceptable because it breeds pride and insurrection. The latter can take several forms, but insurrection against the living imam is forcefully condemned. Interestingly enough for a movement centered on preaching good and forbidding evil, an undue interest in finding fault in others is likened to homicide. Muslims are directed to be kind and merciful to all created beings, but this does not mean pleasing everyone. Muslims should pray that guidance will be given to Muslims and non-Muslims, but seek Allah's special mercies only for the faithful.[103]

Unbending determination to maintain a sharp distinction between Muslims and non-Muslims blunted the effect of Sayyid Ahmad's ethical teachings. Together with the practical adjustments he had to make while establishing his authority on the frontier, this exclusionary attitude eroded the spiritual and ethical dimensions of his reformist efforts, reducing them to a political movement that became increasingly more secular as it struggled against old and emergent challenges. What remained sacred was Sayyid Ahmad's and Shah Ismail's *shahadat* (martyrdom) and their courageous stand against a more disciplined Sikh army in the treacherous terrain of India's northwestern frontier. But even at that time people of different sensibilities differed in their interpretations of the jihad movement.

Contemporaries who met with Sayyid Ahmad felt the magnetic pull of his personality, which radiated spirituality. Yet no single factor can fully explain why his teachings appealed to Muslims. Those who already subscribed to the ideological worldview of the Waliullah clan had no difficulty accepting the doctrine of jihad as a way of resisting religious infidelity. Some were drawn to him because of their distaste for infidel rule and alien cultural influences. Others joined out of frustration at their dramatic loss of social and political stature. Not all Muslims were culturally insular, even if it is possible to discern a broad correlation between a sense of difference informed by religion and the proclivity to participate in the jihad.

A strong element of anticolonialism was also present in literary circles. The Delhi-based Urdu poet Hakim Khan Momin believed that infidels and rebels had usurped Muslim power. Although forced to accept a pension from the company to compensate for the loss of his family estate, Momin found life under English rule unbearable.[104] He thought even less of Fazl-i-Haq Khairabadi for advising him to come to terms with the new dispensation. Vowing to die rather than submit to Christ, Momin preferred to embrace the ideals of Sayyid Ahmad's movement. Taunted by Fazl-i-Haq, he tried shunning his company. When this tactic proved socially impractical, Momin relented, going so far as to accept Fazl-i-Haq's contention that those preparing for jihad were just envious of Christian power. What was the use of building mosques, Momin asked rhetorically, when they could be razed at the drop of a hat. Everything in Delhi had changed; neither the land nor the sky was the same. Burning with sadness, he longed, he said, for the cool breath of the sword.[105]

Aatish was cut to the quick by the effects of the company's dominance of the social and political life of Awadh. Thoroughly enthralled by Waliullah's family, he wrote complimentary verses on their piety and bravery, describing all of them as beautiful men of steel. Shah Ismail was inimitable; there was no idol so pure as he in the Brahman's house. To find another Shah Ismail among a thousand men, Aatish declared, would be like discovering a heavenly seed in a pomegranate.[106] Zauq, the poet laureate at Bahadur Shah's court, composed verses regretting Amir Khan's decision to give up military struggle against the company in return for the rulership of Tonk. Zauq too was taken by Sayyid Ahmad's determination to fight the infidels.[107] For one like Ghalib, tempted by unbelief but held back by faith, the rough-and-ready strictures of the Tariqah-i-Muhammadi were utterly alien to his temperament. Fiercely independent in his thinking and corresponding worldview, he could not suffer the narrow-mindedness that characterized the movement. Ghalib had read Waliullah; he is said to have been a close friend and admirer of Shah Ismail, who introduced him to Sayyid Ahmad and his circle.

Manzoor Hosain finds symbolic references to Sayyid Ahmad's jihad in Ghalib's poetry, although this view has not been endorsed by most literary scholars. Though Ghalib frequently alludes to Karbala, he makes no direct reference to Sayyid Ahmad's jihad. Even Ghulam Rasul Mehr, an ardent admirer of Sayyid Ahmad, does not refer in his strictly literary interpretations of Ghalib to the movement. Rejecting the notion that Urdu poetry is devoid of historical concerns, Hosain claims that Ghalib and other poets of the period masked references to Sayyid Ahmad's jihad through the use of traditional poetic devices. In this view, Ghalib deployed familiar poetic terms to convey his skepticism about the movement, as well as his awe for the supreme sacrifice of martyrdom. In a couplet interpreted by Hosain as an allusion to Sayyid Ahmad's jihad, Ghalib is astonished by the intensity of his desire for martyrdom and the nonchalance with which he placed his head under the beloved's sword. Mehr notes that in terms of literary conventions, martyrdom here is a metaphor for exertion in the cause of love, whether for a beloved here on earth or for God.[108] By speaking of *shahadat* in the cause of love, either temporal or transcendental, Ghalib draws on the meaning of martyrdom in the Islamic context, while also lending it ethical significance. Self-abnegation and a willingness to sacrifice all for the cause of God or for love is the ultimate test of a believer's faith.

Ghalib's poetry is replete with references to *shamshir* and *tegh*, meaning sword, as well as *khun* or blood, not all of which are attributable to the influence of Sayyid Ahmad's jihad. In one couplet he declares that nothing is more delightful for the lover than to arrive at the place of his own death and see the beloved's naked sword.[109] A literal reader might marvel at the morbidity of the poet. But Ghalib is referring to the joy a believer feels on attaining an objective after concerted effort. In the Islamic mystical tradition this is described as the moment of annihilation *(fana)*, which he likens to Eid, the Muslim religious festival. Part of the same *ghazal* whose opening verse provided the point of departure for considering jihad as an ethical and spiritual quest to be human, which cannot be divorced from faith *(iman)*, the couplet invokes the ecstasy that grips one nearing the completion of a struggle. To suggest that the poet is referring to exertions against the base inner self to achieve higher moral purposes in life is no more far-fetched than to discover the trope of Sayyid Ahmad's jihad in Ghalib's poetry.

Ghalib found it impossible to fulfill the conditions of membership in Sayyid Ahmad's circle, and even more so to engage in the jihad movement. Giving up habits like drinking wine proved to be impossible. At first he tried blaming Sayyid Ahmad, but then turned to regretting his own failure, which he continued to do for the rest of his life.[110] The anguish he felt found expression in innumerable verses:

> That endearing congregation is something else, Ghalib;
> We too went there and came away crying over your fate.[111]

Ghalib considered Shah Ismail a paragon of intellectual beauty and majesty and dearly missed his presence in Delhi. His close friendship with Maulana Fazl-i-Haq, who thought that Shah Ismail and Sayyid Ahmad were leading their followers up the garden path, occasionally led Ghalib to express his skepticism. But he could not forget the experience of having had a friend like Shah Ismail and, because of him, was mesmerized by Sayyid Ahmad's personality.[112]

Regardless of the attraction Ghalib felt toward Shah Ismail's intellect and Sayyid Ahmad's spirituality, what is significant is that when presented with the possibility of engaging in armed struggle, he chose the struggle of the pen.[113] According to his self-confident pronouncement, he had mastered self-abnegation and annihilation while Majnun, the forlorn lover of the popular Arabic folktale *Laila-Majnun,* was still learning how to write *lam* (ل) and *alif* (ا) on the school walls. In invoking the imagery of the sword in the word *la* (لا), composed of the Arabic letters *alif* (ا) and *lam* (ل),[114] this colossus of Urdu literature in the subcontinent conveys the essence of the relation between jihad and *iman* with a stroke of the pen. Signifying the sword of negation in the word *la,* the same letters in a different configuration, *alif, lam,* and *alif,* become "Allah" (الله). The initial negation followed by absolute affirmation is the essence of the Muslim confession *la ilaha ilalla*—There is no God but God. This statement reaffirms the link between knowledge and faith. Those who rush to promote jihad as a duty incumbent on Muslims, without understanding the reasons for its intrinsic importance to the religious life of the community, have lost sight of that link.

Ghalib used the theme of struggle and martyrdom in ways that are diametrically at odds with the limited meaning assigned to jihad as holy war. For him it remained a struggle to achieve the elementary virtues of humanity *(insaniyat).* As he mourned:

> He died of threats who was not a courageous warrior
> Love calls for a man whose profession is warfare.[115]

For Ghalib, to die for love was the ultimate form of martyrdom, and he understood this in terms consistent with Sufi spiritualism. According to Muslim mystics, one who sheds blood for God is at peace with him—the ultimate ethical ideal in Islam. Only a man capable of suffering severe hardships could tread the path of love, along which thousands of human limbs adorn the thornbushes, like red roses.[116] Ghalib follows this with a verse that Hosain chalks up to the poet's regret at not joining the jihad movement:

> The thought of death was such a worry in life,
> My face was pale before I could even fly.[117]

The last verse of the same *ghazal* finds Ghalib taking his pathos to an extreme, declaring:

> This coffinless corpse is of that hapless soul, Asad;
> God have mercy: he was a uniquely independent man.[118]

Using similar imagery in another couplet, Ghalib declares that the coffin has hidden the blemishes of his naked body.[119] Otherwise, whatever clothing he wore, his body remained naked, a source of embarrassment to himself and humanity because he lacked virtue. Ghalib deploys the imagery of the naked body and its blemishes to return to the theme of man's struggle to be human. What he means is that in addition to the physical characteristics of the body, God has provided human beings with the virtues of piety and abstinence. Stripped of these virtues, man is naked in relation to life and humanity; only death brings this state to an end. To die in the struggle to be human, then, is of far greater importance than to achieve physical martyrdom on the field of battle. Even if Ghalib felt remorse at not participating in the jihad, it was not a feeling he ever shared with anyone.

In the opening verse of one of his greatest *ghazals,* Ghalib congratulates himself for enduring pain without becoming indebted to anyone; suffering has made him neither commendable nor worthy of condemnation.[120] The penultimate verse in this *ghazal* is seen as symbolizing Ghalib's musings about Shah Ismail's and Sayyid Ahmad's jihad, years after their death:

> Was this a robbery or a teasing of the heart?
> In taking away the heart, the teaser never left.[121]

In the verses preceding these, Ghalib complains that he has gone to state his grievances to his beloved, only to find his rivals there. There was such commotion that he could not convey his feelings. Where is he to go to try his fortune, now that his beloved has withheld the dagger? And then at his poignant best, Ghalib asks:

> Was Nimrod the reigning God,
> That nothing good came of my devotion?[122]

This is a comment on unrequited love, which the poet compares with Pharaoh's injustice. In the next verse, Ghalib makes plain that in his view life lost on the path toward God is a poor recompense for the unbounded gifts bestowed on man by the Creator:

> Gave up life, but it was given by him;
> Truth is that what was owed was not repaid.[123]

4

Jihad in Colonial India

Ghalib made his definitive statement on jihad in the way of Allah while Muslims were debating the implications of Shah Abdul Aziz's fatwa declaring India a *Dar-ul-Harb.* Giving one's life for Allah, he asserted, is insufficient recompense for what one owes God. In invoking the idea of human indebtedness, the essence of the Islamic concept of *din,* Ghalib once again alluded to jihad as a struggle to be human. The poignancy of the comment was not lost on Muslims conscious of the broader ethical meanings of the term. Preoccupation with the political and legal ramifications of the loss of sovereignty, however, ensured that the reality of British colonial rule framed the discourse on jihad during the second half of the nineteenth century. Amid suspicion about Muslim loyalty to a non-Muslim government, each side tried to harness Islamic theology and law for its own purposes in the debate.

During the 1857 uprising, the ulema could not agree whether to declare a jihad. Once the colonial state reestablished authority, sustaining the passion for jihad became a more perilous exercise. The risk did not deter a succession of rebels from making their way to the frontier, inspired by anticolonial feelings and the myth of Sayyid Ahmad's return. The Ambala campaign of 1863 was a success for the British in terms of immediate military objectives. But insofar as sedition was a symptom of disenchantment with colonial dominance, the campaign did not stop the flow of rebels to the northwestern frontier. The raw justice meted out to the defeated rebels led to further acts of sedition, while the targeting of Muslims as the principal conspirators increased insecurity and disaffection.

As the Patna rebels kept the standard of revolt afloat on the frontier, colonial officials made much of "Wahabi" conspiracies among their Muslim subjects. Alarmed by the prospect of British hostility, Muslims representing a broad spectrum of ideological orientations ventured to state their opinions on whether or not they were religiously bound to wage war against the queen. Those with the "vested interests of the Musalman clergy to back them" repudiated the doctrine of jihad propounded by Sayyid Ahmad Barelvi and his followers.[1] The impetus of the so-called Wahabi trials led to the transportation and exile of the rebel leaders in 1864 and 1865 and the harassment of Muslims accused of harboring pro-jihadi sentiments. A spate of fatwas questioned the validity of a jihad, arguing that so long as Muslims were allowed to practice their religious rituals without hindrance as protected people *(mustamin),* India was an abode of peace *(Dar-ul-Aman).*

With some variations, this was the view of Sayyid Ahmad Khan (1817–1898), Nawab Abdul Latif Khan (1828–1893), Maulana Karamat Ali of Jaunpur (1800–1873), a follower of Sayyid Ahmad of Rai Bareilly who engineered a split in the Tariqah-i-Muhammadi, and a student of Karamat Ali, Syed Ameer Ali (1829–1928). A broad spectrum of Muslim intellectuals questioned the equation of jihad and warfare in the late nineteenth century. Mirza Ghulam Ahmad (1836–1908), founder of the heterodox Ahmadi movement in the Punjab, rejected armed jihad as anachronistic. In an atmosphere where loyalty to the raj was at a premium, even such influential members of the Ahl-i-Hadith as Maulana Sayyid Nazir Husain Dehalvi (d. 1902) advocated political quietism, despite their adherence to the Waliullah school.[2] The debate within the Muslim community demonstrates how religious principles in combination with emerging secular requirements could alter the terms of the debate on jihad. If the remnants of Sayyid Ahmad's movement offered an outlet to those who considered an armed jihad obligatory in the face of foreign rule, others denied its very significance and reached an accommodation with the colonial state. Temporal factors affected spiritual and ideological considerations in both instances, albeit with qualitatively different results for Muslim conceptions of religiously informed cultural identities.

An analysis of the intellectual discourse on the appropriateness of fighting infidel rule challenges the common misconception that Muslims have always understood jihad as armed struggle. Modernist Indian Muslims, denying that jihad was an aggressive endeavor, pointed to its defensive and ethical aspects. The Orientalist dismissal of this argument as a mere apologia is in need of critical reexamination. In attempting to correct the colonial view of Islam as a religion of conquerors, some Muslims may have been overly defensive. It remains to be seen how far this attitude was a function of the strength of the attack on Islam by British scholars and former officials, rather than a deliberate attempt to misrepresent the concept of jihad. If we are to assess the balance between the religious and the secular in the rebellion of 1857, modernist Muslim thought must be reclaimed from the dismissive stigma of apologia. This aim can be achieved specifically by analyzing the thought of a representative group of Muslims with different ideological and sectarian affiliations. In repudiating the notion of jihad as armed struggle, did Muslims in late nineteenth-century India succeed in reconceptualizing the idea and restoring its ethical appeal?

The 1857 Rebellion as Jihad

The first century of colonial rule in India witnessed a dramatic shift in Muslim political fortunes. While some Muslims profited by collaboration, colonial policies devastated many families, both the aristocratic and the salaried. Their predicament was especially grim in Bengal.[3] Local systems of patronage were left in disarray, and as a result of the colonial state's demand for revenue, the peasantry suffered greater undernourishment and oppression than ever before. Maulvis Wilayat Ali and Inayat Ali recruited men for the frontier from the Bengali Muslim peasantry in the main. Yet during the rebellion, it was the newly conquered territories in northern and central India that posed the greatest threat to the English East India Company.

Critics accused company officials of working hand in glove with Christian missionaries who published inflammatory tracts and gave public speeches attacking Indian religions. Most offensive to Muslims was the vilification of the Prophet in three treatises written by Reverend Carl Gottlieb Pfander.[4] In his article "The Mohammedan Controversy," printed in the *Calcutta Review* in 1845, Sir William Muir (1819–1905) portrayed Islam as "a subtle usurper," which, having borrowed its weapons from Christianity, had become its "mortal foe" through conquest and conversion. For twelve centuries Christian powers did nothing to combat Islam and the teachings of its "false Prophet." The same lack of resolve plagued the company's government, which was a "sad spectacle of men without a faith." Because conquest "invests the conqueror's faith and opinions with the prestige of power and authority," the British had a unique opportunity to rectify past mistakes. Outnumbered by Hindus, Indian Muslims, unlike their narrow-minded Turkish and Persian brethren, were inclined toward "enlightened liberality." By grasping the nettle and promoting Christianity, the company state could break "the bond of Mohammedan union" and "weaken the thraldom of opinion and custom" that was the source of the bigotry of "our opponents."[5]

Most ulema linked to fatwas calling for a jihad during the rebellion participated in polemical debates with their Christian counterparts in the pre-1857 period.[6] Schools, medical missions, and orphanages providing famine relief were charged with planting religious doubts in the minds of young Indians in preparation for converting them to Christianity. William Bentinck's law of 1832 protecting the civil rights of converts caused serious consternation. Population censuses showing an increase in the number of Christians in India were distributed as proof of the mala fide intentions of the British. Colonial intervention in economy and society was perceived as a conspiracy to eradicate Indian religious traditions.[7] The replacement of Persian by English as the administrative language in the upper echelons of government and the steady dismantling of the Mughal system of justice helped confirm those suspicions. For its part, the company state feared a popular uprising, backed by a stream of wily tribesmen from the northwestern frontier. The favored policy was to bribe the Pathans into submission or attempt to overawe them. But the specter of "predatory hordes" spilling into Peshawar and beyond was never far from the colonial mind.[8] The debacle of the first Afghan war of 1839 was seen as a body blow to British prestige, leading to a loosening of the bonds of respect between Indian sepoys and their English superiors.[9]

As broken promises to the rulers of successor states to the Mughals highlighted English perfidy, the widespread socioeconomic and psychological impact of the loss of sovereignty set the stage for a major conflagration. The rebellion of 1857, described as a sepoy mutiny in British accounts, has been celebrated as India's first war of independence. It is now clear that the company state in its dying moments faced a multiclass struggle that encompassed regional aristocracies, peasants, artisans, and soldiers belonging to all the major religious denominations. Although the reverberations were felt throughout the subcontinent, the rebellion itself was confined to disaffected parts of northern and central India, where the company had gradually extended its rule during the first half of the nineteenth century.

A sense of injustice, coupled with disdain for an immoral and tyrannical English government, was already widespread, even before the annexation of Awadh inflamed the soldiers of the Bengal army. Bhumihar Brahmans and Rajput Thakurs from the region resented the loss of the special perquisites formerly attendant on service abroad. Reeling under the loss of social prestige, they were further stung by the prospect of losing their caste status, because they had to bite off the ends of the greased cartridges of the new Lee Enfield rifles supplied by the British. The cartridges were rumored to be smeared with pig fat and cow fat, repugnant to Muslims and Hindus, respectively. The disaffection of soldiers from northern India soon transmuted itself into patriotic fervor in support of the deposed king of Awadh, Wajid Ali Shah. One of the king's wives, Hazrat Mahal, raised the standard of revolt. Her close circle included such leaders of the rebellion as the son of the former Maratha Peshwa Baji Rao, Nana Sahib, and his representative Azimullah Khan; the dynamic Maulvi Ahmadullah Shah Faizabadi; and the ever controversial Maulana Fazl-i-Haq Khairabadi.

Nana Sahib's decision to rebel was both personal and political. In 1853 he had sent the suave, Western-educated Azimullah to London, to plead for the reinstatement of Nana Sahib's pension. By the end of the futile mission, Azimullah had become thoroughly anti-British. On returning to India, he set up a revolutionary movement and persuaded his employer to join it. An early example of the Muslim universalist, Azimullah established contacts in Egypt and Russia. After the outbreak of the rebellion, he masterminded an effective anticolonial resistance in Kanpur with Nana Sahib's help.[10] It was, one British historian of the rebellion lamented, one of those "strange revenges," for the Maratha leader had initially agreed to use his army to protect government treasure and munitions.[11] Once the soldiers revolted in Kanpur, Nana Sahib saw a certain sense in requisitioning these items and allying himself with the rebels. The alliance—a product of political, not religious, impulse—qualifies as a patriotic war, rather than as a jihad in the way of God.

Unlike the secular partnership between Nana Sahib and Azimullah, both Ahmadullah and Fazl-i-Haq are associated with fatwas declaring a jihad against the British. Maulvi Ahmadullah Shah Faizabadi, alias Dhanka Sahib (1789–1858), was from the Qutb Shahi royal family of the Deccan. Inspired by the courage of Tipu Sultan and Sayyid Ahmad Barelvi, he visited England, where he demonstrated his skill at arms. On his way back to India, he performed hajj, and he spent the next twelve years in quest of the truth. During an extended stay in Tonk, ruled by Amir Khan's son Wazirudullah, Ahmadullah was exposed to the doctrines of Sayyid Ahmad and Shah Ismail's followers. The turning point in his life was his meeting with a saint, Mehrab Khan Qalandar, who told him to wage jihad. Ahmadullah traveled widely in India before arriving in Delhi, only to be rebuffed by the ulema, who scoffed at his ideas on jihad. He went next to Agra, where he trained Muslims for jihad. The British attempted to have him arrested, but the policemen refused to carry out the orders. The jealousy of the local ulema compelled Ahmadullah to leave the city.[12] He arrived in Lucknow dressed as a beggar and held the populace spellbound with his "miracles," which included swallowing burning coals, and preached jihad.[13]

In January 1857 Ahmadullah declared a jihad against the English, who had abandoned all semblance of justice and were "appropriating the possessions of the Mohammadans." Anyone who fell in such a war would be "venerated as a martyr," whereas "he that held back would be execrated as an infidel and a heretic."[14] Ahmadullah fought some skirmishes with the colonial army, in which he was injured, then arrested and given a death sentence. The rebels released him from jail once news of the Meerut mutiny reached Faizabad. He joined Hazrat Mahal's coterie and became the main rebel leader in Awadh. An archconspirator, in the eyes of the British, he devised the scheme of distributing chapatis among the rural population in the northwestern provinces as a prearranged signal that the sepoys had rebelled.[15] Though "not the equal of Hyder [Ali] and Shivaji," Ahmadullah has been portrayed by one British official historian as the "most determined of the men who fought against us in the Indian mutiny."[16] A political and military genius, not a religious figure, he was less interested in scoring theological points for waging jihad than in rallying popular sentiment in support of fighting the alien rulers. He succeeded in establishing his own government and would have continued defying British authority if he had not been assassinated by one of the rajas of Bundlekhand whose assistance he had solicited.[17]

If Ahmadullah had an ideological link with the martyrs of Balakot, Fazl-i-Haq Khairabadi was their bitterest opponent. Although Fazl-i-Haq was sentenced to the penal colony on the Andamans for allegedly signing a fatwa on jihad, his role as a freedom fighter has been a matter of contention. Detractors point to his family's long-standing collaboration with the British to cast doubt on his jihadi credentials.[18] As chief judge of Lucknow in

1855, he opposed, on the grounds that Muslims were in the minority, a fatwa calling for a jihad against Hindus who had demolished a mosque. Fighting established authority, even non-Muslim authority, was strictly prohibited.[19] The reasons for his conversion to the rebels' cause are unclear. There is no evidence of his signing any fatwa on jihad. In letters written after his arrest, he denies any complicity in the revolt. Munshi Jeevan Lal, the secretary to Bahadur Shah Zafar, recorded in his diary that Fazl-i-Haq had asked the emperor to dissuade the rebels because they had no chance of prevailing over the English. The rebel leaders distrusted Fazl-i-Haq sufficiently that he was debarred from attending the emperor's advisory council, of which he was a member.[20] In his account of the revolt, Fazl-i-Haq reveals his sympathy and admiration for rebel leaders like Maulvi Ahmadullah but also mentions their mistakes. He complains bitterly that "the Christians punished me with imprisonment by fabricating falsehoods and deceptive devices against me." Fazl-i-Haq had disagreed with two men over the meaning of the Quranic verse he had interpreted as stating that anyone who befriends a Christian becomes one himself. These men had retaliated by supplying false testimony against him. In attempting to downplay his own association with the British, Fazl-i-Haq held that his enemies had "turned apostate, exchanging *iman* with *kufr*" by insisting on friendship with Christians.[21]

The image of Sayyid Ahmad and Shah Ismail's adversary languishing in a British jail is all the more poignant and paradoxical when contrasted with the fate of a man who did take up arms. Maulana Muhammad Qasim Nanautawi (1833–1879), the great Deobandi scholar, fought against the British but survived a short stint in jail and lived on to promote the anticolonial cause through his educational and scholarly activities. His hagiographers portray him as an ethical man who practiced what he preached. Nanautawi maintained that there are two kinds of Quranic injunctions: those whose inner meaning and outer form are revealed, and those whose inner meaning and outer form are left to the believer's discretion. The first type of injunction can be followed readily, but the second type—of which jihad is an example—require that the inner meaning be discerned.[22]

Contemptuous of the company's government, he steered clear of the revolt until it took the form of a popular struggle. Along with Maulana Rashid Ahmad Gangohi (1828–1905), he took up arms when he was presented with clear evidence of English injustice. Nanautawi's mentor was Haji Imdadullah, who had connections with the Waliullah family and the mujahideen movement. He resided in Thana Bhawan, where the English had executed a member of a well-to-do family of *qazis* without trial, on a false charge of sedition brought by a Hindu moneylender who had an old score to settle with them. The head of the clan vowed to avenge the murder by launching a jihad.[23] A *majlis-i-shura* (assembly of advisers) was convened in which the majority of the religious divines opposed waging jihad against the English. The contention of the assembly members was that only a member of the Prophet's family could serve as imam, and he must be powerful so that success was assured. Shrugging aside these concerns, Nanautawi nominated Imdadullah as imam. After a few initial successes, the jihad fizzled out. Nanautawi went into hiding. He was later reunited with his spiritual preceptor in Mecca. On returning to India, Nanautawi served a jail sentence, though he was later acquitted of the charges against him.[24] Gangohi was also imprisoned. Upon release, Nanautawi and Gangohi helped transform the *maktab* in the Jamia Masjid of Deoband into a theological seminary. Modeled on Waliullah's Madrasa-i-Rahimiya, it emphasized hadith, without denying the authority of Hanafi law. This was the reason that not all Deobandis were unequivocally supportive of jihadi ideology, even though they celebrated the martyrs of Balakot.

Lesser-known fatwas offer further insights into the thinking of the rebels.[25] These fatwas, addressed to Muslims and Hindus, played on the religious sentiments of both communities, without being hampered by niceties of Islamic law and theology. Fatwas were often obtained by force, forged, or attributed to people without their knowledge, thereby provoking opposition from Sunni and Shia ulema, who issued rulings of their own. The contradictory fatwas on jihad illustrate how religiously informed cultural identities were articulated in the early struggles against colonialism. Recourse to jihad invariably established the outer limits of Muslim identity. But definitions of identity are always contingent. The fatwas of 1857 were different from those given by Sayyid Ahmad Barelvi in one important respect. In asking Indians to resist English injustices, the rebels made a more effective case for a just war than for *jihad fi sabil allah*. Muslim legists had laid down far too many conditions for a jihad, not all of which the Indian situation satisfied. In declaring India a *Dar-ul-Harb*, Shah Abdul Aziz had not called for either jihad or *hijrat*. The dilemma Muslims confronted during and after the 1857 rebellion was whether to take his fatwa to its logical conclusion and wage an armed jihad or to follow his example in making a conditional peace with the British.

"Consider yourselves dead even before death" was the rebel exhortation to the Royal Army of Delhi. Evoking the hadith of the Prophet "Die before you die," it bears no resemblance to the Sufi conception of annihilation *(fana)* in the Creator. The allusion here is to physical, not spiritual, death. Soldiers who did not join the rebels would be enticed by the English into their camp and "put to death." It was better to die honorably than be killed by "unclean barbarians" who ate pork, drank wine, and engaged in "lust and fornication." A common prayer was prescribed for Muslims and Hindus, who were told to rise to a man in defense of their religions, which the infidel usurpers were contaminating.

The rebels were offended by colonial laws giving women over eighteen full legal rights to take their cases to court. This "full liberty to women" was seen as "subjecting every man to petticoat government."[26] In a scurrilous attack aimed at substantiating the promiscuity of Englishwomen, Queen Victoria was accused of having an affair with her African slave! Woman's rule was declared unacceptable on the authority of a hadith in which the Prophet allegedly said that a tribe led by a woman could never prosper. Detailing oppression the English had instituted and their aim of forcibly converting Indians to Christianity, the rebels vowed to die rather than abandon their faith.[27]

The cause célèbre was Dalhousie's Caste Disabilities Act of 1850. Next on the scale of abominations was the General Service Act requiring new recruits to serve overseas—a taboo for upper caste Hindus, who called it *kala pani*—a term that in popular parlance still means a life sentence. As Sayyid Ahmad Khan commented after the rebellion, it was widely believed that the Caste Disabilities Act was "issued especially to allure people to become Christians." The Hindu community did not accept converts, and Islam prohibited converts from inheriting the property of anyone belonging to a different creed. So converts to Christianity enjoyed "great advantages," but other religious communities none whatsoever.[28] The fears of a subjugated people are never more real than in exaggeration. Hindu soldiers were afraid of losing their caste status and being left with no alternative but to convert to Christianity. Muslim concerns were primarily political. Efforts were no doubt made to instill ethical values among the rebels by suggesting that the "religious war" was not for worldly goods but for the "fruits of eternity."[29] Yet on balance, the conception of faith emerging from the proclamations owed less to the ethical principles of Islam than to the temporally expedient use the rebels made of religion.

Nothing illustrates this point better than the worldly advice to the soldiers to refuse colonial employment for more attractive service conditions in the Mughal army. "Unanimity" in "strengthen[ing] the King's cause" was vital, and soldiers would be rewarded with "lucrative appointment." Those who had "purchased loot" or received interest on pensions and stipends would be allowed to keep it after "due investigation," whereas deserters would be "deprived of this boon." Serving an infidel power was pronounced "absolutely unlawful." It was regrettable that so many of the soldiers' Hindu and Muslim brethren stood in "indescribable awe" of the English. The end of English rule exactly one hundred years after its inception had been foretold by holy men and astrologers. The prophecy of Hazrat Naimutullah Shah that "a King in the West" would be "victorious" over the infidel rulers with "the force of the sword of jihad" was widely circulated. Nothing could now save such unjust and treacherous rulers from the wrath of God. A great deal was made of the alleged fate of thirty-five thousand English soldiers, sent to assist in the conversion of India but killed by Ottoman forces.[30]

In one of the more tragic twists taken by the rebel imagination, the expectation spread that Persia and Afghanistan would declare war on the English. In May 1857, the newspaper *Sadiq-al-Akhbar* of Delhi published a facetious proclamation in the name of Shah Nasiruddin of Persia, calling on his troops to fight "a religious war of Extermination" by following the precepts of their Prophet.[31] Swearing not to "leave the English any resting place this side of London," it assured the Afghans that Persia had no interest in annexing their country. Emir Dost Muhammad Khan was reminded of his promise to aid Persia if it was attacked by "a people of different religion."[32] The unity of the *ummah* being what it was, neither the Persian nor the Afghan ruler had any interest in aiding their co-religionists in India. The Persians needed to keep fences mended with the British to hold the Russians at bay. Dost Muhammad had recently signed a subsidiary treaty with the British and was maintaining a studied neutrality. This appeared to prove that for the faithful, "love of English money was stronger than hatred of the English race."[33]

Rebel proclamations relied, in the absence of external assistance, on the power of fear. An English victory would leave Indians with the choice between conversion or death. Fighting would make them warriors of the faith *(ghazis),* while death assured the martyrs rewards in the hereafter. The English had given the order to slay "all [Indian] cavalry and infantryman" from Delhi to Allahabad; the reward on each head was said to be fifty rupees! A proclamation in Kanpur stated that Indians would be "executed indiscriminately."[34] To forestall this eventuality, the rebels recommended wholesale plunder and slaughter of the English and, in a recognition of the strategic importance of the province, told Punjabis to "cast [off] . . . the attire of the females" and join the rebels in "the garments of men." In case this slight on Punjabi honor did not light the fires of revolt, they warned that Punjabis would have their faces "blackened in both worlds" if they did not join the rebellion.[35]

In recounting stories of Indian humiliation at the hands of the English, the would-be fatwas reveal their authors' fragile sense of religious identity, which was coupled with a misogynist worldview. An insistence on the social control of women through preservation of the home, as an inner domain free of colonial intrusion, accompanied a singular concern with external aspects of identity. If these were endangered, faith itself would be jeopardized. Apart from the accusation that the new rulers were undermining Indian manhood, the most biting charge brought against the British was their alleged attempt to convert Indians by contaminating them, not just with greased cartridges but also with food. A proclamation attributed to the Mughal emperor Bahadur Shah repeatedly invoked God's name, while complaining of the company's plot to "destroy our religions" by selling rice mixed with small pieces of bones and flesh.[36] Fear of losing their religion by eating with Europeans was not uncommon among Muslims, though the taboo was borrowed from Hindus. A fatwa addressed to the royal army commented that although Muslims could seek forgiveness for an inadvertent transgression through repentance, "a Hindu's religion once forsaken can never be regained."[37] If the need to rally Hindus led the rebels to take a more lenient view of polytheists, it was more than counterbalanced by revulsion for the European "other." The rebels, in drawing the outer boundary that separated them from the treacherous infidel, called for the slaughter of the English, in order to save Indian religions and lives.

This was not just a Muslim attempt to carry out the situationally specific Quranic command to flay the infidel. As Nana Sahib realized, the need of the hour was a temporal war in which retribution was to be carried out by men, and only indirectly by God. If Indians did not act here and now, the English would "take away the[ir] faith and religion." That would put the final nail in the coffin of Indian sovereignty. God was on the side of the rebels and had destroyed the consignment of English sent by the queen to "Christianize the people and army of Hindustan." When the news reached Calcutta, the governor-general "beat his head" in sorrow. Nana Sahib responded with an allegorical poem of rejoicing at the end of the company raj:

> Early in the morning massacre began
> In the morning neither had the body a head, nor the head
>   a crown
> After one revolution of the sky
> Neither Nadir remained in his position, nor his kingdom.[38]

The mutinous soldiers often fought courageously. In many instances, though, they degenerated into a disorganized rabble of murderers and plunderers. The rebels often violated Islamic prohibitions against killing the aged, women, and children. Nana Sahib's defeat of the English division garrisoned in Kanpur led to rebel atrocities. The damage done to the rebels' cause partly explains the ambivalence many of their countrymen felt toward the rebellion.

The need to curb the rebels' excesses necessitated proclamations stating that the war against the English was a jihad. In February 1858 Mirza Firoz Shah, the Mughal emperor's grandson, gave one that was not a fatwa but a political statement amplifying on the duty of jihad. Describing himself as "a lover of justice, and a hater of oppression," the prince called on all Indians to save their religions and lives "by murdering all Englishmen." Recounting his experiences in the struggle, he admitted that in the past the "religious fervor" of the troops had become "so great that they paid no attention to discipline." Their desire for worldly goods had made a mockery of jihad. The reason the English had not been expelled was that "the army mercilessly murdered women and children" in violation of orders. The rebels had "oppressed the people" and given "themselves up so much to plunder that they turned victory into defeat." Yet there was consolation for undisciplined and selfish soldiers: killing infidels was in itself a victory![39]

Not all Muslims accepted the rebels' spin on the Sufi injunction to die before dying. Nor did most Muslims share the rebels' hatred of the British, even as they deplored the more egregious excesses of colonial rule. As Ghalib once quipped, a mere drop of water was an ocean in itself; he could not abide narrow-minded bigotry based on religious strictures.[40] Mughal sovereignty was a thing of the past. Jamshaid was the Persian emperor who could look into his chalice and see all that was happening in the world. Ghalib, likening sovereignty to a cup of wine that constantly changed hands, noted that Bahadur Shah was no Jamshaid.[41] The poet admired the British for running an effective civil administration in Calcutta and promoting rationalism and science. But he resented their policies in Awadh and bemoaned the lost glories of Mughal Delhi. In his eyewitness account of the rebellion, Ghalib strives to disguise his horror at the intensity of the British violence but stops short of endorsing the rebels, seeing no prospect for their victory, far less for a restoration of Mughal sovereignty.[42]

The historian Maulvi Zakaullah was a student at government-supported Delhi College when the rebellion broke out. He recalled visiting the Mughal court as a young boy and being shocked by the "corruption and decay." Things were appreciably better under British rule, though much remained to be done to educate Indians before the positive changes could begin to take effect. The rebels had erred in their decision to take up arms. If they had enjoyed the benefits of universal education, they would not have rebelled in the face of such heavy odds. Fed on blind superstitions and prejudices, they had misled the common people into engaging in a fruitless revolt. The rebels targeted Zakaullah, whom they held in suspicion for his presumed leanings toward Christianity, for trying to save his Christian friends at Delhi College. Ostracized by segments of his own community, he had to take refuge in his home and pray for God's mercy.[43]

Fighting a jihad for a lost cause, as men of Ghalib's and Zakaullah's erudition knew, was not sanctioned by either the Quran or the Muslim jurists. There were too many loopholes in the rebel invective against the English to justify a jihad. It was only when personal circumstances required individuals to overlook the legal niceties or, like Maulana Qasim Nanautawi, to circumvent them through interpretation that the cry for jihad was sounded. Many Muslims, including Sunni and Shia ulema, collaborated with the British. The absence of an imam to spearhead the jihad ensured Shia opposition. Several of Nanautawi's fellow seminarians in Deoband and divines of the Ahl-i-Hadith reputed for their adherence to Sayyid Ahmad Barelvi rejected the jihad. A fatwa by fifty-three ulema, including Deobandis and non-Deobandis, declared British rule to be preferable to Russian, since under the British the Indian Muslims were permitted to practice their religion.[44]

Maulana Sayyid Nazir Husain Dehalvi was the most influential of the Ahl-Hadith ulema in Delhi at the time of the revolt. The rebels coerced him into issuing a fatwa declaring a jihad. He was imprisoned during the "Wahabi trials" but released once it emerged that he had not been a supporter of the rebels. According to Dehalvi, a jihad was legitimate only if initiated by an imam from the Prophet's family with a firm base of support and sufficient arms and ammunition to fight the enemy. A proponent of *jihad-i-lafzi* (verbal struggle) for the propagation of Islam, he ruled out armed jihad in India, on the grounds that the relationship with the British government was a contract that Muslims could not legally break unless their religious rights were infringed.[45]

Although the ulema showed a certain pragmatism on the question, Muslims in the colonial service were emboldened to oppose the rebellion. None did so with greater conviction than Sayyid Ahmad Khan, who was employed with the East India Company in Bijnor when the rebellion started. Despite his family's long association with the Mughals and his own emotional identification with Muslim culture, he was motivated by the liberal ethics inculcated in him by a humanitarian and religiously oriented mother. Not only did he jeopardize his own life to save English women and children from the rebels, but he publicly opposed the call for jihad. With the help of a local landlord, he disabused people in Bijnor of the view that the rebels were fighting a jihad.[46] More than any of his contemporaries, Sayyid Ahmad Khan intuitively understood the intrinsic link between jihad and Muslim identity. Unless Muslims made some accommodation with colonial rule, they would be unable to correct the general impression of the average Muslim as "arrogant and bigoted," deserving nothing but "disdain and antipathy."[47] Whatever his later utterances about the merits of British rule, he was not initially starry-eyed about the boons of colonialism. In two of his earliest writings on the revolt, *Asbab-i-Baghawat (The Causes of the Indian Revolt)* and *An Account of the Loyal Mohomedans of India,* he spent more time outlining the shortcomings of British rule than critiquing the failings of his co-religionists.[48]

In *The Causes of the Indian Revolt,* published a year after the rebellion, Sayyid Ahmad dismissed the idea of a well-planned Muslim conspiracy against the British. Invoking Shah Ismail's authority, he noted that so long as Muslims were allowed to practice their religion, they could "not conscientiously take part in a religious war within the limits of Hindustan." Those who declared a jihad in 1857 were "vagabonds and ill-conditioned men," "wine drinkers" in the main, who "spent their time in debauchery and dissipation." Far from being a jihad, the revolt infringed the basic tenets of Islam:

> To be faithless to one's salt is to disregard the first principles of our religion. To slaughter innocents, especially women, children and old men would be accounted abominable. Can it possibly be imagined then, that this outbreak was of the nature of a religious war? The fact seems to be that some scoundrels, prompted by greed and hoping to gain their end by deceiving fools and increasing their own numbers gave the disturbances the title of a religious war. The project was worthy of the men, but there was no crusade.[49]

Most ulema in Delhi considered the Mughal emperor a "heretic." Before the revolt, they issued a fatwa prohibiting praying in mosques that he visited or patronized. How could "men holding such views . . . give a futwah in favour of a religious war and . . . plac[e] the King at the head of it?" Some associated with the fatwas on jihad "sheltered Christians, and guarded their honour and their lives." Muslims were "in every respect more dissatisfied than the Hindus," and "in many districts the greater proportion of rebels were found in their ranks." But where Hindus rebelled, "matters were carried to as great extremes." Without absolving Muslims, Sayyid Ahmad thought the government had only itself to blame. It was an "impolitic and unwise" policy to keep up the pretense of Mughal sovereignty after 1827, when the company was declared the de facto ruler in India: "The King of Delhi was a spark from the furnace which, wafted by the wind, eventually set all Hindustan in a blaze."[50]

Sayyid Ahmad used the Quran and Islamic law in the *Loyal Mohomedans of India* to prove that the 1857 rebellion was not a jihad. He resented the "passion and prejudice" that dripped from the pens of historians. Knowing "absolutely nothing whatsoever" about Islam, they were culling passages from the Quran to show that it sanctioned the "wholesale butchery of Christians" by "inciting a crusade *against them!*" As a consequence the government was imputing atrocities to one community when "the parties really guilty may have been Ramdeen and Matadeen!" Such "monstrous calumnies" were inciting "a bitter feeling of rancour and hostility" toward Muslims, thereby "sowing the seeds of animosity between the governed and their governors." Sayyid Ahmad asked, "How can religion foster cruelty, tumult, and disorder?" According to the *Fatawa-i-Alamgiri,* jihad could be fought only if no treaty arrangement or protection *(aman)* prevailed between the rulers and the ruled. It was a "sad misnomer" to call "a sanguinary rebellion" fought for purposes of "secular aggrandizement" a jihad. The self-styled men of religion leading the rebels were "heartily despised by all good Mahomedans, who had penetrated the character of these low bred-pseudo-Moulvies." Truly learned and pious Muslims did "not pollute themselves by the smallest degree of complicity in the rebellion, which they utterly denounced and condemned as infamous and criminal in the extreme."[51]

Distinguishing the temporal from the religious, Sayyid Ahmad Khan distanced the rebellion from the high ethical principles of jihad. Far from repudiating jihad, he declared it to be an article of faith for Muslims. But its purpose was "not to practice treachery and cruelty," and "no sane man" could honestly "apply that term to an insurrection characterised by violence, crime and bloodshed." Muslims were obliged to uphold treaties and not to plunder properties put in their trust. They were strictly prohibited from slaying women, children, and others under their protection. The rebels paid scant regard to these principles. Christians were forcibly converted and then slain for being insincere in their profession of faith. It was "astounding" that those "enlighten[ing] the world with their sapient views on the recent events" should claim that these "low-lived wretches" who "committed every species of revolting barbarity . . . against the children of the book" were motivated by Islam. How true were the words of the Oriental poet who had wailed that there was "no misfortune sent from heaven which ere it descended to earth, did not seek for its resting-place the dwellings of Mohammedans!"[52]

Sayyid Ahmad Khan's rationalizations of 1857 were intended to rescue the Islamic conception of jihad from the taint of a failed rebellion. But the primary motivation for his defense was the practical need to adapt to British rule. He held pragmatically that jihad was incumbent on the believers only if they were powerful enough to defeat their rivals.[53] Fighting a better-equipped enemy was suicidal and strictly illegal in Islam. In his estimation, armed struggle against a temporal ruler who protected Muslims was outright sedition, not a religious war. Muslims were obliged to fight such rebels, regardless of their creed.

Nawab Abdul Latif in Bengal echoed these ideas. He turned his Muhammadan Literary Society of Calcutta into a vehicle of opposition to a violent struggle against the British. Rejecting categorization of India as an abode of war, Latif tried dissuading his co-religionists from waging an armed struggle against the British. Instead of engaging in such futile political maneuvers, which could bring only greater ruin, Muslims would be better off solving their social and educational problems. To muster support for his strategy, he procured fatwas from leading ulema in India and Mecca declaring India a *Dar-ul-Islam*. The signatories included Maulvi Karamat Ali of Jaunpur, who considered Sayyid Ahmad Shaheed a renewer of the faith. He had broken with the Tariqah-i-Muhammadi to form his own movement, called *Taiyuni*—"to identify"—because he disagreed with the rejection of the four schools of Sunni jurisprudence by Sayyid Ahmad's "Wahabi" followers. Karamat Ali thought a jihad against the British was unjustified, and he concentrated on reforming Muslim society.[54]

Despite the best efforts of men like Nawab Abdul Latif, it was not always possible to tailor Islamic legal thought on jihad to address the technical difficulties arising from the existential fact that a non-Muslim power was acting as de facto ruler of India. In theory, Muslims living in a *Dar-ul-Islam* were obliged to fight an invasive infidel force. Realizing the contradiction resulting from the ruling by the Muhammadan Literary Society of Calcutta, a group of religious scholars in northern India issued their own fatwa declaring that jihad was illegal, even though India was a *Dar-ul-Harb.* This was a shade closer to Sayyid Ahmad Khan's thinking. Based on his study of Hanafi law as detailed in the *Fatawa-i-Alamgiri,* he argued that India was neither a *Dar-ul-Islam* nor a *Dar-ul-Harb,* but a *Dar-ul-Aman,* or a place where peace prevailed.

Long before the publication of Hunter's *Indian Musalmans,*

Sayyid Ahmad Khan had denounced categorizations of 1857 as jihad. After all, "hundreds of thousands of Mahomedans" were "innocent in heart and deed of the foul enormities, so flagrantly laid to our charge." Many in their "devoted loyalty to the State" had "sacrificed life and property, honour and reputation" and "endured hardships and trials grievous to be borne." Was it "fair and honest then," he asked, "to hurl contumely and reproach indiscriminately against Mahomedans in general as *a class,* and grieve the hearts of the well affected as well as disaffected?"[55] The question of Muslim loyalty to the raj acquired greater significance after 1870, when, as part of a review of British policy toward the community, Governor-General Mayo commissioned W. W. Hunter to investigate whether the followers of Islam were obliged to rebel against the queen.

Wahabi Conspiracies and Muslim Apologetics

Now that prominent Indian Muslims were spurning religious war, regardless whether India was a *Dar-ul-Islam* or a *Dar-ul-Harb,* armed jihad after 1857 was confined to Sayyid Ahmad Barelvi's followers. Though loosely categorized as Wahabis, the Indians so named were a far cry from their Arabian counterparts. In 1809, Wahabis had looted some English ships in the Arabian Sea. Transferring their fears of Arabian Wahabis to Indian acts of sedition was the natural response of a colonial power unsure of its bearings in a culturally alien society that had so recently erupted in revolt. In a masterstroke, the British, who wished to act on their own anxieties about Wahabis, played on the visceral hatred a vast majority of Muslims felt for the notorious demolition squad that had razed the Prophet's grave. Between 1803 and 1809 the pilgrimage to Mecca suffered a serious blow when the great human caravans from Asia and Africa ceased to arrive. The nonperformance of the hajj made the Wahabis the object of universal execration among Muslims. But some in India admired the Wahabi stance against popular superstitions and the shrine-centered rituals that masqueraded as Islam. The word *Wahabi* did not have altogether negative connotations in India before colonial policy altered its meaning. Sayyid Ahmad Khan once said he was a Wahabi if that meant the exercise of independent reasoning in matters having to do with religion.[56]

During the nineteenth century, different movements came to be labeled Wahabi, not for their religious beliefs but for acts of sedition, actual and anticipated. These movements included the Faraizis of eastern Bengal, who on the basis of their founder Haji Shariatullah's interpretation of Hanafi law, abolished Friday congregational prayers designating India as a *Dar-ul-Harb*. While calling for a return to the Quran and elimination of all forms of mediation, Shariatullah merely replaced the *pir-murid* (priest-disciple) relationship with the *ustad-shagird* (teacher-student) relationship, which implied a lesser degree of submission. The Faraizis are often linked with the reformist activities of the professional wrestler Nasir Ali (alias Titu Mir), who between 1827 and 1831 rallied Muslim cultivators and weavers in the western districts of Bengal against Hindu moneylenders and British owners of indigo plantations. Despite a common aversion to polytheism and superstition, and rejection of the four schools of Sunni jurisprudence, there was no formal connection between Titu Mir and the Faraizis. A disciple of Sayyid Ahmad Barelvi, Titu Mir concentrated on establishing the outer bounds of Bengali Muslim identity and paid special attention to food and attire. He changed the way Muslims donned the dhoti, the three-yard long loin cloth worn by Bengali peasants, and instructed his followers to grow beards. He was killed in a skirmish with the East India Company's army while protesting the local Hindu landlord's imposition of a beard tax.

After Titu Mir's death the loci of the Muslim reform movement in Bengal shifted to the eastern districts under the leadership of Haji Shariatullah. Upon returning to India after twenty years in the Hejaz, he declared shrine based-religious rituals and Hindu influenced customs to be incompatible with Islam. An admirer of Arab culture, like Waliullah, Shariatullah ordered his followers to eat grasshoppers, which resembled locusts eaten by their Arab brethren. His son Dudu Mian expanded the scale of activities, making converts and collecting taxes on behalf of the sect. Suspicions that he was working for the expulsion of the British led to the Faraizis' being lumped with Wahabis. The Faraizis found a fierce opponent in Maulana Karamat Ali, who accused them of being the new Kharajites of Islam. Although he shared the Faraizi antipathy for the excesses of shrine-based Islam and Sunni participation in Shia mourning during *muharram,* Karamat Ali accepted the principle of spiritual preceptorship.[57] What he deplored was the Faraizi insistence on treating India as a *Dar-ul-Harb,* thereby making it obligatory for Muslims to wage an armed jihad against the British.

By the time *The Indian Musalmans* revived the notion of "Wahabi conspiracies" running the length and breadth of India, neither the Patna rebels nor the Faraizis posed a real threat to the colonial state. Showing a degree of paranoia unwarranted by his own evidence, Hunter concluded that the "line between sullen discontent and active disaffection" among Muslims was "a very narrow one." He made light of Sayyid Ahmad Khan's opinion that the British had erred in perpetuating Mughal sovereignty. If they had "hastened by a single decade . . . [the] formal assumption of sovereignty," the British would have faced a Muslim uprising "infinitely more serious than the mutinies of 1857." Casting his analytical net widely but basing his findings on the case of Bengali Muslims, he noted that British "inattention to the wants of peaceable Muhammadans in Bengal has enlisted their sympathies on the side of a class whom they would otherwise shrink from as firebrands and rebels." Lack of education was one factor pushing Muslims to Wahabism. The other was the loss of state employment. If the urban educated classes were aggrieved, the indebted and emaciated rural masses of Bengal were mere cannon fodder for articulate preachers from northern India looking to sow the seeds of rebellion in the province. The real "danger" was that the "entire Muhammadan community" was being "rapidly . . . transformed into a mass of disloyal ignorant fanatics."[58]

Hunter's descriptions of the "Wahabi" preachers he encountered in eastern Bengal reflected horror mixed with admiration. While denouncing them as "dangerous firebrands," he thought they were not altogether unworthy of respect. Willing to suffer the hardships of their solitary wanderings, they were the "most spiritual and least selfish type of the sect." Though a "small fragment of a great sect," the so-called Wahabis were "absolutely conscientious" believers. By contrast, none of the younger generation of Muslims passed through government schools without "learning to disbelieve the faith of his fathers." In the same category as these skeptics, Hunter considered propertied Muslims, all of whom were "men of inert convictions" who, though they "decorously attend the mosque" to say their prayers, thought "very little about the matter."[59]

The nonchalance with which Hunter conferred the prize for religiosity on the most extreme section of Indian Muslims is the more remarkable given his own assessment of popular reactions to Wahabi missionaries. Their singeing criticisms of local customs, he observed, antagonized the predominantly Hanafi Muslims of eastern Bengal quite as often as exhortations about jihad converted them to the aim of "holy war."[60] This situation could change if nothing was done to improve the lot of Bengali Muslims. The colonial state ought to deal leniently with rebels apprehended on the frontier. Otherwise, efforts to stamp out the Wahabi conspiracy could "fan the zeal of the fanatics into a flame." Not content with "swaying the fanatical masses," "Wahabi preachers" were seeking to "bind the burden of Holy War upon the shoulders of all ranks of their countrymen." It was a troubling choice, for Muslims had either to face being denounced as apostates or to enter into a deadly conspiracy. The colonial state's enhanced powers of arrest meant that "only the more bigoted consent to take the risks." Rejecting the "Laodicaean casuistry" of the better off Muslims, the "dangerous [Wahabi] firebrands" had "drafted away to certain slaughter batch after batch of deluded youths" under the age of twenty in nearly all the districts of eastern Bengal, for the most part without the parental consent required under Islamic law. But the false propaganda of the Patna missionaries about the appearance of a "Divine Leader" to restore the glory of Islam was the best guarantee against their attraction of additional recruits. "A single returned Crescentader [that is, the obverse of a Crusader] from the Frontier" did "more to ruin the Wahabi cause in a District than a State Trial." Even the "really sincere Wahabis" were "willing to listen to any interpretation of the law which frees them from the obligation to rebel." Fatwas by Sunni and Shia ulema against jihad gave the "comfortable classes" of Muslims a pretext to "wash their hands of the business."[61]

Hunter denounced the law doctors for relying on the *Fatawa-i-Alamgiri,* rather than earlier and, in his biased opinion, more "authoritative" books on Islamic law. In his estimation, all three conditions making a country a *Dar-ul-Harb* were operative in India: 1) the laws of non-Muslims had replaced those of Muslims; 2) the country directly adjoined a *Dar-ul-Harb;* and 3) neither Muslims nor non-Muslim *zimmis* enjoyed protection. There was no question that English law reigned supreme in post-1857 India. Given that England had conquered India by sea, the latter had the status of *Dar-ul-Harb,* for no intervening Muslim power existed capable of sending help to co-religionists in the subcontinent. The third condition depended on the interpretation of protection. In Hunter's opinion, it covered the entire gamut of religious security and status enjoyed by Muslims under their own rule. The Muslims' civil law and religious law were inseparable. Such religious liberty and status as Muslims possessed were at the pleasure of the English and in any case less than Indians had enjoyed under Mughal rule. The status of non-Muslim *zimmis* had also changed, as was evident in the abolition of *sati* (burning of widows).[62] It followed that unlike the "Wahabis," Muslims who rejected jihad were distorting their own legal texts to give the British a false sense of security.

In one of his more insightful comments, Hunter found it a "misfortune" of British rule in India that the Wahabi-led "Reformation" of Muslims was so "inseparably linked with hatred against the Infidel Conquerors."[63] This was not far removed from Sayyid Ahmad Khan's view of the potentially positive effects of Wahabi strictures. Sayyid Ahmad regretted that the sect had been "little understood by the world at large." Tracing the origins of the Arabian Wahabis to the Ahl-i-Hadith movement during the Abbasid period, he noted how they were "hated by the masses" and condemned in Muslim law books. Despite their well-known excesses in curbing popular religious practices, "what the Protestant is to Roman Catholic, so is the Wahabi to the other Mahomedan creeds."[64] He found fault with Hunter's understanding of Islamic law and the equation of "Wahabism" with fanatical rebellion against the British. Nothing exposed the absurdity of the analysis more than the characterization of the staunchly Sunni frontier Pathans as Wahabis. It was vital not to confuse the Sikh tyranny in the Punjab with British rule in India. Presenting the Wahabi doctrine in its "most terrifying form," Hunter had glossed over the elementary fact that Muslims were debarred from rebelling against an infidel ruler who did not interfere with their religion.[65]

In countering Hunter's arguments, Sayyid Ahmad Khan turned

loyalty toward a benevolent infidel government into a tenet of Islam. He traced the different phases of the movement to show how Wahabis had held firm to the principle of nonrebellion against a government that allowed Muslims their religious freedom. The only jihad they had ever fought had been against the Sikhs. Even Hunter, in his fanciful account of Wahabi sedition, admitted that the Patna rebels avoided direct confrontation with the British after Sikh rule ended in the Punjab. Hunter's "sweeping assertion" that the "flames then kindled were nursed by the Mahomedan community in India" until they resulted in the conflagration of 1857 had not the "slightest foundation." Pathan tribes were notoriously irrepressible, and their attacks on villages under British control could not be blamed on the rebels. During the revolt, the rebels tried enlisting Sayyid Ahmad Barelvi's critic Mahboob Ali. The cantankerous maulvi refused on legal grounds and "reproached" the rebels for the "inhuman cruelties perpetrated by them towards the European ladies and children." Maulanas Wilayat Ali and Inayat Ali fought the Sikhs but undertook "nothing towards the furtherance of jihad" against the colonial state. They knew that fighting while their families were under English protection would deprive them of the "joys of paradise and martyrdom." Money transmitted to the rebels, according to Sayyid Ahmad, was given as alms *(zakat)* and not to bring down the British. The Akhund of Swat was "no Wahabi" jihadi, even if he did receive alms from wealthy Muslims.[66]

Sayyid Ahmad Khan conceded that after 1857 a small band had given the government trouble on the frontier. Consisting of Hindus and Muslims, it was "scarcely one which could be designated as a jihadi community." In some of the "most unjust, illiberal, and insulting sentences ever penned against" Muslims, Hunter had mischievously suggested that "the whole Mahomedan community had been openly deliberating on their obligation to rebel." Letting the power of imagination run riot, the Englishman

had "twist[ed] everything connected with Mahomadism in support of his cherished theories."[67] It was wrongheaded to conflate
"negative abstentions from the faith *(kufr)*" in the secular sphere
with "positive oppression and obstruction" in religious matters. A
jihad was justified only when Muslims were prevented from practicing the five pillars of Islam and not if it related to the civil administration of the country.[68]

In excluding political oppression from the sphere of positive
oppression, Sayyid Ahmad is seen as having heralded a break with
"classical" Islamic tradition, by restricting the scope of the duty to
wage a jihad. His separation of the religious from the political is
considered an "obvious innovation" in a religion that claims to
dominate all spheres of human activity.[69] This opinion overlooks
the great variation within the Islamic legal tradition. Classical
Hanafi law, as historically interpreted and implemented in the
subcontinent, allowed for a separation of the religious from the
political. The idea that jihad was only for defensive purposes had
roots in the early years of the Muslim community in Mecca.
Quranic verses sanctioning armed jihad were often interpreted to
be defensive in intent. The neat dichotomy between the "classical" and the "modern" conceptions of jihad assumed by contemporary Islamic scholars becomes untenable when seen through
the complex and constantly shifting prism of Muslim history.

In defending the Wahabi stance on jihad, Sayyid Ahmad was
referring to armed warfare. That he was perfectly aware of the
broader meanings of jihad is suggested by his admission that
"some bigotted and superstitious Wahabis . . . look with hatred
and contempt not only on Infidels" but also on social interac-
tion with other Muslims. But their opinions were not "infallible,"
and they "represent[ed] no principle of Wahabism." There were
"many earnest Wahabis" and other Muslims who though not formally members of the sect hoped that just as Wahabism "inculcates the unity of God . . . it may also be the means of promoting

brotherhood among the human race." If even the Wahabis were really misunderstood humanists, then no one could doubt this: "The purification of our faith and our loyalty to the Government under whom we live and serve are perfectly compatible."[70]

Although most Muslims opted for political quietism after the great tumult, for some life under a nonreligious dispensation justified culturally exclusionary attitudes aimed at making the external boundaries of the community more rigid. In the search for the correct political and ethical response to colonial subjugation, Muslims of different ideological and sectarian orientations drew on the model of the Prophet. A common source of inspiration did not guarantee unanimity of opinion. The struggle within the community was not about accepting or rejecting new ideas but about the right to interpret Islam. Muslim ulema had no qualms about incorporating new ideas if doing so furthered their own interest. Although Muslims who were the product of religious seminaries suffered from a lack of employment opportunities under British rule, the ulema as a corporate interest arguably benefited from the creation of a spurious distinction between a "secular" public space monitored by the colonial state and a private space of religious and cultural autonomy.[71]

Portraying themselves as the ethical conscience of a community besieged by alien cultural influences, the ulema used print technology and new forms of communication to assert their leadership. This course locked them in grim battle with Sayyid Ahmad Khan and his followers, who urged Muslims to take to Western learning and tried reinterpreting Islam in the light of modern ideas. Ulema affiliated with the theological seminaries at Deoband, Farangi Mahal in Lucknow, and Bareilly disapproved of Sayyid Ahmad's ideas on Islamic theology and jurisprudence. The Deobandis objected to his refusal to consider the opinions of Sunni jurists as authoritative. Sayyid Ahmad's approval of independent reasoning was closer to the Ahl-i-Hadith point of view.

But his use of religious interventions and rational criticism to arrive at a new ethical conception of Muslim identity was abhorrent to the ulema as a whole, who saw in them a threat to their preeminent status as the religious guardians of the community. They attacked Sayyid Ahmad's pro-British policy, even while disagreeing among themselves on what constituted the correct Islamic response to colonial subjugation.

Prominent among Muslims who objected to Sayyid Ahmad's efforts to accommodate colonial rule were those loosely labeled Wahabi. These included members of the Tariqah-i-Muhammadi and the internally diverse supraregional conglomeration calling itself the Ahl-i-Hadith, who claimed to be the true successors of Waliullah's reformist movement. Accusing other sects of undermining Islam through undue reliance on jurisprudence, the Ahl-i-Hadith held that the Quran and the hadith provided adequate moral and ethical guidance to Muslims. But their own literalist readings of the texts vitiated the beneficial effects of their stress on independent reasoning. In the Ahl-i-Hadith view, independent reasoning was the preserve of prominent scholars and not of individual believers. Even though disagreeing on the authority of Sunni law and the obligation of jihad, the Tariqah-i-Muhammadi and Karamat Ali's followers considered themselves part of the Ahl-i-Hadith and had no major doctrinal differences. In the course of time, however, differences within the Ahl-i-Hadith came to mirror the divisions their abrasive polemical style was creating with fellow co-religionists. Once Wahabism and fanatical disloyalty became indistinguishable in colonial discourse, the Ahl-i-Hadith openly professed loyalty to the raj. In 1887 the Ahl-i-Hadith, under the leadership of Sayyid Muhammad Husain Batalvi, editor of the Ahl-i-Hadith newspaper *Ishaat-u-Sunnat,* formally requested that the group be differentiated from the Wahabis.[72] This provided the Ahl-i-Hadith with the requisite leeway to propagate their version of Islam in colonial India.

The politics of Muslim cultural defense were not an Ahl-i-Hadith preserve. Deobandi ulema also considered themselves to be successors of the Waliullah clan.[73] Like the Ahl-i-Hadith, Deobandis were divided over colonial India's status under the sharia. Muhammad Qasim Nanautawi held that India was a *Dar-ul-Harb,* while Rashid Ahmad Gangohi thought it was a *Dar-ul-Islam.* These differences did not extend to the role of Hanafi law, which the Deobandis upheld. Deobandis shared the Ahl-i-Hadith antipathy for Christian missionaries and Hindu reformist groups like the Arya Samajists, as well as Shias and the Ahmadis. Deobandis opposed ritual excesses and innovation *(bidat)* among Muslims on the occasion of marriages, birth, and death. Where the Deobandis and Ahl-i-Hadith came to verbal blows was in the latter's taste for fatwas declaring co-religionists *kafir* and a general proclivity to get embroiled in trivial religious disputes.[74]

The Ahl-i-Hadith's aggressive posture toward local customs and shrine-based Islam generated the stiffest opposition from the Barelvis. Constituting the majority of Hanafi Muslims in India, they rivaled the Deobandi claim to be the *ahl sunnat wa jamaat* (the people of the practice of the Prophet Muhammad). Ahmad Raza Khan (1856–1921), the founder of the sect, attacked both the Deobandis and the Ahl-i-Hadith. He traced his intellectual lineage to Waliullah but did not consider him a *mujaddid* (renewer). Instead, he regarded Shah Abdul Aziz as the *mujaddid* of the thirteenth-century *hijri* (Muslim calendar).[75] Though backing popular rituals and Hanafi law, Barelvis shared Deobandi and Ahl-i-Hadith anxieties about the negative effects of alien influences on Muslim identity.[76] Barelvis were equally emphatic in opposing Shia and Hindu influences and by no means free of the taint of bigotry. In a strident assertion of Muslim difference at the cost of a universal human ethics, Raza Khan said that presented with the choice of giving water to a thirsty infidel or to a dog, a believer should make the offering to the dog.[77] His shunning of politics and his rejection of armed jihad distinguished the Barelvi response to colonial rule from that of the Ahl-i-Hadith. In Raza Khan's opinion, India was a *Dar-ul-Islam,* for Muslims had religious freedoms. Those arguing the contrary merely wanted to take advantage of the provision allowing Muslims living under non-Muslim rule to collect interest from commercial transactions and had no desire to fight jihad or perform *hijrat.*[78]

More than doctrinal differences, it was the Ahl-i-Hadith's efforts to deviate from their co-religionists in the performance of prayer, modes of dress, and cut of beard that accounted for their negative standing in the Indian Muslim community. Crafting an exclusionary identity in an ocean of difference was the Ahl-i-Hadith's way of asserting the superiority of their religious worldview.[79] But an overemphasis on the literal interpretation of selective hadith and Quranic verses led them to focus more on Islam as a marker of a different identity than Islam as a faith based on universal human values. It was not that Sayyid Ahmad Barelvi's teachings were devoid of ethical content. But the Ahl-i-Hadith construed narrowly the ethical values they prized, and made them exclusionary in effect, a permanent source of friction within the Muslim community.[80]

Under the influence of Nazir Hussain Dehalvi and Karamat Ali, the politics of the Ahl-i-Hadith were quietist by comparison with those of the mujahideen. Even Nawab Muhammad Siddiq Hasan Khan of Bhopal (1832–1890), considered by the British to be the strongest exponent of armed jihad, professed loyalty and dismissed those advocating war as mischief makers.[81] While renouncing armed struggle, the Ahl-i-Hadith called for an intellectual jihad against fellow Muslims on moral and ethical grounds. In keeping with the Waliullah tradition, Dehalvi's *ijtihad* was limited to a rejection of Sunni jurisprudence. With their literal readings of the Quran and hadith, the Ahl-i-Hadith were often more conscientious in observing Islamic rituals than were Muslims subscribing to the schools of Sunni jurisprudence.[82] Opponents labeled the Ahl-i-Hadith *zahirparast* (those who worship externals).[83]

The proliferation of hadith in the subcontinent, championed by Waliullah and popularized by the Ahl-i-Hadith, helped divide the community against itself. There were sporadic tensions in northern India between the Ahl-i-Hadith and Sufis, Shias as well as Sunnis of the Hanafi school. But they remained a minority voice, and orthodox Sunni ulema as well as modernist Muslims led by Sayyid Ahmad Khan and his Aligarh school countered them. The Prophet Muhammad is recorded as identifying over sixty kinds of faith. These included observing the five pillars of Islam, believing in angels and the day of judgment, practicing good deeds and *haya* (literally, "self-respect," but with meanings similar to "modesty," "bashfulness," "scruples").[84] It is also said that after his death the Muslim community was going to split into seventy-two sects, and he would belong to the seventy-third. With contradictory hadith at their disposal, Indian Muslims could seek to discredit the more extreme expressions of Islam.

Those discussing the obligation of jihad under colonial conditions did so from within their own tradition, arguing as Muslims have always done that in Islam there can be no separation between religion and politics. What this idea meant for ethical practice was a source of lively disputation. Many ulema did not deny that Islam was consistent with new forms of Western learning. The disagreement was temperamental, not doctrinal, a distinction highlighting that the dimensions of the deepening gulf within the community were worldly, rather than religious. The key question was how far Muslims could remain faithful to their religiously informed cultural traditions, while accepting new forms of knowledge. This was the reason Sayyid Ahmad denounced bigotry and narrow-mindedness as a product of worldly rather than religious concerns. His liberal agenda inspired some Muslims to project jihad as a defensive ethical struggle. Directly or indirectly affiliated with the Aligarh movement, they produced writings that offer interesting insights into how modernist Indian Muslims of a liberal bent conceived of Islamic ethics, while responding to colonialism and Western modernity.

Jihad and Ethics in Modernist Muslim Thought

An overly simplified conception of the relation between religion and politics in Islam obscures the myriad ways in which Muslims divorced faith from politics for tactical and pragmatic reasons. Reiterating the organic relationship between the religious and secular aspects of a Muslim's life did not mean that Islam was immune to secularization. Sayyid Ahmad Khan once commented that *din* and *duniya* had "a strange relationship." Leaving religion does not result in leaving the world, but leaving the world does result in leaving religion:

> This is worship, this is religion *[din]* and faith *[iman]*:
> When human beings help human beings in the world.[85]

Following Waliullah, he held that there is only one unchanging *din,* which is rational and just, precisely because it is consistent with human nature. He maintained that since all religions draw upon a common core of ethical values, religiously based differences are not an insurmountable obstacle to peaceful coexistence. The need of the hour was to counter the activities of Muslims who, in propagating cultural exclusivity, were erecting artificial barriers to accommodating change, thereby hastening the secularization of Islam. Muslims had grievances in plenty. But nothing in Islam propelled them to conspire against their temporal overlords. The sharia sanctioned friendship with non-Muslims.

Enmity between Christians and Muslims on religious grounds was impossible. More than any other religion except Christianity, Islam revered Christ and his teachings. Muslims had to remain loyal to a sovereign authority that granted them religious freedom, ruled with justice, maintained peace, and respected "individuality and property." The Torah offered a precedent, in recording how Joseph faithfully served Potiphar, although he did not observe the laws of Moses.[86]

Muslim discourses in the late nineteenth century reveal the intrinsic link between jihad and faith in conceptions of identity. Based on the teachings of the Waliullah family, the debates were animated by concerns about foreign rule in India. Defying simplistic categorization as traditional or modern, conservative or liberal, religious or secular, these Indian Muslim voices display a dizzying depth and range. What gives them a degree of coherence is the effort by the speakers to remain within the Islamic tradition, even while redefining the debate in the light of rational modern thinking. The themes of change and the advance of civilization invariably find their way into the writings on jihad and ethics by Sayyid Ahmad Khan, Maulvi Chiragh Ali, Syed Ameer Ali, Maulana Shibli Numani (1857–1914), and Mirza Ghulam Ahmad, to mention a select few.

The immediate context was the uproar in Muslim circles over the publication of William Muir's *Life of Mahomet* in four volumes between 1856 and 1861. Writing at the suggestion of the Muslim bugbear Reverend Pfander, Muir attacked the moral principles of Islam for being incompatible with modern ethics. By permitting polygamy, divorce, and slavery, the Prophet of Islam was seen to have struck at the core of public morals, poisoning domestic life and creating perpetual imbalance in society. Freedom of religion had been "crushed and annihilated." The "sword is the inevitable penalty for the denial of Islam." It was "a miserable delusion" to believe that Islam was a religion for all mankind. Islamic teachings were a barrier to "the reception of Christianity," and "no system could have been devised with more consummate skill for shutting out the nations over which it has sway, from the light of truth." Parts of Africa and Asia which "once rejoiced in the light and liberty of Christianity" were "now overspread by gross darkness and a stubborn barbarism." Muir rejected the authenticity of Quranic revelation but acknowledged the historical validity of hadith as a source for the life and times of the Prophet. He derided Muhammad's "licentious self-indulgence" and "flagrant breaches of morality" for "political and personal ends," on the pretext that he was the "favourite of Heaven." Not only were "wholesale executions inflicted, and territories annexed," but the Prophet was accused of "gloat[ing] over the massacre of an entire tribe" and "savagely consign[ing] the innocent babe to the fires of hell." There was no question that "the sword of Mahomet and the [Qu]ran are the most fatal enemies of Civilization, Liberty, and Truth, which the world has yet known."[87]

There was enough ammunition here for a million Muslim mutinies. Muir's work was seen as a threat to the faith of the younger generation of Western-educated Muslims.[88] The first to retaliate with a verbal jihad was Sayyid Ahmad Khan, taking heart in the Prophet's saying that the ink of the scholar is weightier than the blood of the martyr. Locating himself within the Islamic tradition, he borrowed the polemical methods of Christian apologists. To counter the allegation that Islam was the cause of Muslim decline, he wrote twelve essays in Urdu, which were translated into English and published in 1870 as *Essays on the Life of Mohammed*.[89] He used Quranic verses to argue that "Islam inculcates and demands a hearty and sincere belief in all that it teaches" and that "genuine faith which proceeds from a person's heart cannot be obtained by force or violence." Unlike Moses, who was "allowed to use the sword . . . to extirpate all idolaters and infidels," he pointed out, "Mohammedanism grasped the sword . . . not to force men to become Moslems . . . but only to proclaim . . . the unity of the Godhead, throughout the . . . globe." Some of the later Muslim "conquerors were guilty of cruelty and intolerance." But Islam could not be judged by their actions. Muslim rulers who respected the doctrines of their religion "granted amnesty, security, and protection to all their subjects, irrespective of caste or creed."[90]

Categorizing Sayyid Ahmad's writings as an apologia undermines their intellectual value and denies Muslims a right of response to ill-informed denunciation. At the time he was writing, however, Christian apologists were held in a positive light. In both his essays on Muhammad and other works on theology, history, and ethics written over two decades, Sayyid Ahmad oscillated between a defensive and an offensive approach.[91] He defended the ethical principles of Islam and attacked Muir for inconsistency, ignorance, and prejudice. Christianity was hardly free of dogmatism and bigotry. As Godfrey Higgins had confessed, nothing could be found in Muslim history "half as infamous as the Inquisition, nor a single instance of an individual burnt for his religious opinion, nor . . . put to death in a time of peace . . . for . . . not embracing . . . Islam." Sayyid Ahmad also cited John Davenport, who in his *Apology for Mohammed and the Koran* spoke of "the massacres and devastations of nine mad crusades of Christians against unoffending Turks" over a period of almost two hundred years, in which millions perished. Internal schisms within Christianity had left a long, dark trail of blood. It was Islam's "emancipation of the human mind" from "slavish servility" that inspired Martin Luther's Protestant reform. Instead of casting aspersions, Davenport thought, "Christianity should for ever remain thankful to Islam."[92]

In his commentary on the Bible, Sayyid Ahmad had applauded Christ's exhortations to love one's neighbor and to turn the other cheek. By the time Sayyid Ahmad was working on his translation of the Quran, he had developed a full blown critique of this "beautiful" ethical principle. Ethical values were meaningless if they were inconsistent with human nature. None of the ethical principles of Christianity had been observed by its followers, who throughout history had engaged in bloodletting, injustices, and cruelty. Islamic ethics were consistent with the laws of nature. Revenge and fighting were permitted within prescribed bounds. Muslims were allowed to wield the sword when non-Muslims through sheer prejudice attempted to eradicate Islam. But war was the last resort, and Muslims were expected to be merciful and forgiving to the extent that was humanly possible. When faced with oppression in non-Muslim countries, Muslims were told to put up with it or migrate. They could take up arms to save co-religionists in another country if they were being oppressed because of their religion: "Who can say that such a war is unjust or unfair? Who can say that such a war is against ethics? Who can say that such a war is against the laws of nature and human nature? . . . Who can say that in such circumstances offering the other cheek is according to God's wishes?"[93]

Syed Ameer Ali and Maulvi Chiragh Ali continued the strategy of taking the offensive against non-Muslim detractors in defending the religion, yet not shying away from an internal critique of Islam. Ameer Ali, a member of a Shia family from Orissa that had served the Nawab of Awadh, was educated in Calcutta before being called to the bar in London. Western in orientation and elitist in approach, Ameer Ali avoided difficult theological issues and had recourse to history to explain the rise of Islam. In keeping with the trend among Muslims to write works focusing on the Prophet, he initially entitled his book *A Critical Examination of the Life and Teachings of Muhammad,* before expanding it into his best-known book, *The Spirit of Islam.*[94] While disagreeing with Sunnis on the apostolic succession, Ameer Ali concurred with them on most other issues. He presented the Prophet's life

The voice of Muslim modernism, Sayyid Ahmad Khan, with members of the Educational Society in 1883 at the Bashir Bagh Palace, Hyderabad Deccan. Seated, left to right: Sayyid Husain Bilgrami, Nawab Muhsin al-Mulk; Sayyid Ahmad Khan, Nawab Musahib Jang, Justice Maulvi Khuda Bakhsh, and Maulvi Chiragh Ali. Photo: Raja Deen Dayal, Copyright Omar Khalidi.

as a story of exemplary humanism in the face of untold persecution. Even if the "modern professors of Islam" had "dimmed the glory of their Prophet," and he could write an entire volume "on the defects of modern Mohammedanism," a "religion which enshrines righteousness . . . deserves the recognition of the lovers of humanity." A "true Muslim" is "a true Christian," because he or she accepts the morality preached by Christ. But the humility taught by the Prophet of Nazareth was "forgotten in the pride of power."[95]

Turning the tables on Christian critics of Islam, Ameer Ali charged the Church with shedding more innocent blood than any other institution in human history. "Islam seized the sword in self-defence" and for that reason would forever hold it in its grasp. But Christianity had "grasped it in order to stifle freedom of thought and liberty of belief." Through "a strange perversion of the human intellect," Christians assumed that moral norms regulating individual conduct did not apply to relations with non-Christians. The Prophet not only preached humanism, but he embodied it into law at a time when international obligations were unknown. Islam condemned proselytism by the sword and honored treaties with non-Muslims in letter and spirit. "Designing chieftains," whether Muslim or Christian, used religion as "a pretext for the gratification of ambition." Yet the principles on which Muslim jurists divided the world between *Dar-ul-Islam* and *Dar-ul-Harb* showed "a far greater degree of liberality than . . . evinced by Christian writers on international law." Isolationist and exclusivist, Christianity valorized aggression against non-Christian nations, in complete "infringement of international duties and the claims of humanity." Christians regarded differences in matters of faith as a "crime"; in Islam they were a mere "accident." An "uninterrupted chain of intolerance, bigotry and fanaticism" had accompanied Christianity's historical ascent in the world. Far from being dead, the "spirit of persecution" was "lying dormant, ready to burst into flame at the touch of the first bigot." Islam, a liberal and humanizing religion, was "opposed to isolation and exclusiveness" and demanded nothing from nonbelievers except "a simple guarantee of peace and amity."[96]

Maulvi Chiragh Ali belonged to Hyderabad Deccan. Less abrasive in his defense of Islam, he was also far more critical of Muslim jurists than Ameer Ali was. Like many of his contemporaries, Chiragh Ali also wrote a book on the Prophet. But his reputation as a Muslim apologist is based on his book on jihad, which he dedicated to Sayyid Ahmad Khan. Written in a self-consciously modern idiom, it attempted to dispel the "erroneous impression from the minds of European and Christian writers" that the Prophet "held the Koran in one hand and the scimitar in the other." Fighting against religious oppression was the "natural right of every individual and nation" and was justified by international law, both ancient and modern. Not only were the early wars that the Prophet fought defensive, but he never resorted to compulsion in matters of faith. "Every sanction" of natural and international law entitled the Muslim community in Medina—humiliated, persecuted, and expelled by the Quraish—to fight for the "civil rights of freedom and religious liberty." Even when forced to wage war to protect his community, the Prophet was merciful and forgiving. He promoted the ethical ideals of truth, sincerity, and honesty in a society afflicted by superstition and vice. "Lay[ing] stress on the propensities of the mind," he made "the actions of the heart answerable to God, and preferred holiness to outward form." The charges of moral licentiousness, hypocrisy, and cruelty leveled against Muhammad by European writers applied better to the teachings of Islamic *fiqh,* which was not "a divine or unchangeable law."[97]

Echoing Waliullah at a distance and his mentor more closely, Chiragh Ali took pains to show that the ethical values of the Quranic revelation had little to do with the secularly based precepts of the sharia. "Social reform was a secondary question" for the Prophet. Since it was impossible to carry out sweeping reforms, the "gradual amelioration of social evils had necessarily to pass several trials." Owing to gross "oversight" on the part of legal scholars, the intermediate and transitory civil precepts "adapted for the dwellers of the Arabian desert were pressed upon the neck of all ages and countries."[98] The Quranic injunction to "abandon the outside iniquity and its inside"[99] proved that inner purity was vital to true faith. Specific precepts to regulate social life, moral conduct, and religious ceremonials were intended for the Arabs, who were living in a state of "barbarism." Commands enjoining balance and justice in social dealings, abstention from wine and gambling, and kindness toward one's fellow human beings were meant for a people who had not reached a higher level of civilization. But the Quran also mentioned higher principles for those "possessing . . . higher forms of civilization." Its teachings about the virtues of truth, honesty, temperance, and mercy and its emphasis on inner thought were for those who had "outgrown" the need for precepts regulating conduct in minute detail. "A social system for barbarism," Chiragh Ali maintained, "ought not to be imposed on a people already possessing higher forms of civilization." The Quran never elucidates "a precise system of precepts regulating in minute details the social relations of life and the ceremonial of worship." Its aim was to "counteract the tendency to narrowness, formality, and severity" that is the consequence of "living under a rigid system of positive precepts."[100]

This was a spirited reminder of the distinction between Islamic ethics and ritual practice geared toward delineating the external boundaries of Muslim identity. Chiragh Ali denied that the Quran prescribed any fixed times or specific forms of prayer, other than the act of prostration. The absence of precision aimed to counteract the tendency toward formalism, which "stunted and retarded" moral development by leading people to see intrinsic virtue in the mere performance of duties and religious ceremonies. It was a crying shame that morality had become concretized for Muslims in external rituals, instead of being "a certain disposition of heart towards God and man." Far from confining "practical morality and piety" to the ritual exertions of believers, the Quran "lays the foundation of that far-reaching charity which regards all men as equal in the sight of God, and recognizes no distinction of races and classes." These teachings were capable of keeping "pace with the most fully and rapidly-developing civilization" if "rationally interpreted" and "enforced by the sentiment of a nation." It was the sharia, based on inauthentic sayings of the Prophet, that with the "chimerical concurrence" of Muslim law doctors had "blended the spiritual and

the secular" and "become a barrier" in the way of "social and political innovations for the higher civilization and progress of the
nation."[101]

The essence of Chiragh Ali's argument was that Islam was being judged by the standards of the sharia, created by men, rather
than the ethical principles of the Quran. The division of the
world between *Dar-ul-Islam* and *Dar-ul-Harb* was a construct of
legists that had no basis in the Quran. Even the detractors of
Islam conceded that the real meaning of jihad was exertion and
striving in a noble cause. Only in the post-Quranic period had
Muslim legal scholars developed the theory of unprovoked war,
tribute taking, and conversion to Islam at sword point. The
Quran sanctioned only defensive wars under the most adverse
circumstances, and it strictly prohibited aggression. References
in the Quran to fighting were "transitory" and could not be interpreted as "positive injunctions" specifying a duty incumbent
on future generations.[102] By "justifying" Muslim conquests, legal
scholars "committed the unpardonable blunder of citing isolated
parts of solitary verses of the Koran" and ignoring others that explicitly prohibited aggressive war. The author of the *Kifaya,* a
commentary on the *Hedaya,* had turned unprovoked aggression
into a binding obligation for all Muslims. Another legist made
perpetual warfare mandatory. Far from being of divine or super-
human origin, the sharia was a hodgepodge of "uncertain traditions, Arabian usages and customs . . ., frivolous analogical de-
ductions from the Koran, and a multitudinous array of casuistical
sophistry of the canonical legists." Striking out at the religious
guardians, Chiragh Ali asserted that the sharia had "not been held
sacred or unchangeable by enlightened Mohammadans of any
Moslem country and in any age since its compilation in the
fourth century of the Hejira."[103]

One contemporary scholar, calling Chiragh Ali an apologist
whose analysis has "not much to commend itself," has disparaged
his attempt to "prove that Islam and pacifism are synonymous."[104]

Such a judgment accords precious little attention to the historical context in which Muslim "apologists" were writing. Their partiality to Islam was intended to offset brazen attacks by Christian authors and cannot be judged by the standards of latter-day critical scholarship. At no stage in their impassioned defense of the Islamic concept of jihad as warfare did they overlook the excesses of Muslim rulers or fail to rail against the jurists who legitimated their wars. If Ameer Ali made attack the better part of defense, Sayyid Ahmad and Chiragh Ali went to considerable lengths to disentangle the Quranic meaning of jihad from the historical evolution of the concept. Sayyid Ahmad in the *Tafsir* recounted instances when Muslims flouted established rules on warfare by committing acts of murder and oppression. Those who murdered Umar, Usman, Ali, and Husain and burned the Kaaba were also Muslims. They had ignored the laws of Islam. Was it really fair to hold the religion responsible?[105]

The answer to this deceptively simple question depended on one's perspective on Islam as a personal religion and a precise code for civic behavior. In his treatise on jihad, the Ahl-i-Hadith scholar Muhammad Husain Batalvi substantiated Sayyid Ahmad's argument by distinguishing between political and religious jihad. States fought a political jihad to subjugate others. Religion played no part in it whatsoever. A religious jihad was undertaken solely to preserve Islam, not to oppress members of another religion through plunder and murder. From "a scientific point of view," religious jihad was "a matter of history . . . since the lawful caliph ceased to exist." Some Muslims had gone to the frontier in the hope of becoming *ghazi* or *shaheed* in contravention of the doctrines of Islam. It was the "height of ignorance to die an unnatural death" and consider "such disturbances as Jihad." Indian Muslims would be foolhardy to follow that example, for they were living comfortably in a *Dar-ul-Islam* and observing their religious obligations.[106]

Critics who take Muslims to task over delivering apologias for their religion note that classical Islamic thought recognizes no distinction between religion and politics or between the private and the public. On the basis of this view, Sayyid Ahmad, Chiragh Ali, and Muhammad Husain Batalvi could be seen as invoking a false dichotomy between *din* and *duniya* by juxtaposing the Quranic message and the sharia. A succession of Orientalist scholars have suggested that Muslims cannot reconcile faith and reason. Sayyid Ahmad Khan and his school, however, linked revelation with human progress in reason and knowledge. This scheme was closer to the European idea of a linear development in intellectual, moral, and religious thought than it was to Waliullah's notion of the four stages of socioeconomic development.[107] Whereas Waliullah restricted *ijtihad,* or independent reasoning, to a select group of ulema, Sayyid Ahmad, by linking *ijtihad* to the very idea of faith in Islam, proclaimed that the right of rational interpretation belonged to every believer. This was arguably not the first time such an assertion had been made from inside the bounds of Islam. Only exclusive focus on the legal scholars and the more rigid ulema, to the neglect of mystics and philosophers, can support the conclusion that in Islam reason is incompatible with faith. Neither Sayyid Ahmad nor Chiragh Ali separated reason from faith. Underscoring the intrinsic relationship between *din* and *duniya,* they accused the legal scholars of devaluing the religious dimensions of jihad to legitimate secular wars.

Even if Hunter, Pfander, and Muir attributed to Islam the Muslim proclivity toward sedition and fanaticism, some Orientalist scholars agreed with Sayyid Ahmad Khan and Chiragh Ali without being consigned to the category of apologists. Representative of these writers on jihad was the erudite Hungarian educationist and linguist G. W. Leitner, who served as director of public instruction and principal of Government College in Lahore. Using the methods of philology and his own considerable knowledge of

Arabic, he showed in an article how meanings of jihad were situationally specific. *Jihad,* which connotes exertion against adversity, could have any number of meanings. It could apply to the suffering of a patient, the endeavors of a student to read a book, a merchant's attempt to increase his wealth, or a farmer's efforts to plough the land. When used for religious matters, *jihad* meant, strictly, "exertion under religious difficulties on behalf of the true religion." In certain circumstances, Muslims could legitimately fight a jihad against non-Muslims. But this was not very different from a Christian soldier's duty to join a crusade against the oppressors of his community. Sacred war in Islam was so encumbered by conditions that it was "impossible for any modern Christian Government to commit . . . acts which would alone give a colour of justification to a jihad by its Muhammadan subjects." Those who reduced jihad to the Muslim duty to wage war against a non-Muslim government were "really talk[ing] nonsense" and "pass[ing] an undeserved libel on a religion with which they are not acquainted."[108]

The concrete meaning of *jihad* as exertion in the face of difficulty never changed, unlike its applied connotations. The "purest Arabic word in all its concrete, allegorical, and abstract applications," it was the "noblest duty of a pious Muhammadan," which Islam had "rendered identical with prayer." None of its many applied meanings implied fighting people simply on account of their belonging to a different religion. Despite certain commonalities, *jihad* did not go so far as the word *Crusade* in "animating a community . . . to oust the unbeliever from [a] foreign land in order to obtain the guardianship of the Holy Sepulchre, or to simply wrest land from the Muhammadans for the glory of a most Christian King." The "ground is cut off from under the feet of those people who maintain that Jihad is intended to propagate the Muhammadan religion by means of the sword." The Quran states that the purpose of jihad was to protect places of religious worship. Leitner did not know of a single "Christian crusader whose object it was to protect mosques or synagogues." After Muslims were driven out of Spain, the "modern meaning of Jihad as hostility to Christianity was naturally accentuated." Yet jihad's intrinsic role as a means of protecting Islam was highlighted by the explicit prohibition against destroying any place of religious worship in which the call to prayer could be given or where a single Muslim could "live unmolested as a witness to the faith."[109]

The impartial views of a Christian scholar in the service of the colonial state militate against hasty assumptions about any inherent hostility toward Islam in Orientalist scholarship. At the same time, such perspectives serve as a warning against the blanket rejection of Muslim "apologists." Ameer Ali avoided direct reference to jihad and adopted the methods of Western rational historicism for his counterattack, and Sayyid Ahmad and Chiragh Ali felt constrained to restrict their rebuttals to criticizing armed warfare in Islam and correcting the errors of Muslim legists. The obviously subjective nature of their critique may dismay readers still convinced of late nineteenth-century scientific "objectivity." But to make these writers' subjectivity the pretext for dismissing the scholarship in its entirety would in itself represent a subjective judgment! Because his religious identity was not under attack, Leitner had more room for maneuver. Even though he threw much the same light on the ethical conception of jihad in the Quran as Sayyid Ahmad and Chiragh Ali had, his defense of Islam, rather than being challenged for its scholarly merits, was simply ignored. This double standard offers a telling insight into the inequality of discursive authority in late nineteenth-century colonial India.

One way to compete on an uneven playing field was to make better use of polemics. Mirza Ghulam Ahmad was a master of the art. Despite Muslim aversion to his claim to be the "promised messiah" of the age, his vitriolic attacks against Christian missionaries and Hindu revivalists initially earned him support within the community. Matters came to a head in 1892, when the Arya Samaj propagandist Pandit Lekh Ram, in an impertinent book, endorsed the Christian depiction of Islam as a warmongering faith. Directed at Sayyid Ahmad Khan and Muhammad Husain Batalvi, it caused widespread disquiet among Muslims.[110] After infuriating Hindus in northern India by accurately predicting Lekh Ram's death, Ghulam Ahmad wrote an Urdu treatise on jihad. As his follower Muhammad Ali explained in the preface to the English translation of the work, the harshness of the tone "afforded an exit to the excited passions of the community" aroused by the "scurrilous and abusive language" used against Islam. Unless the government put a stop to such attacks, its policy of religious freedom would be "taken in another light" and would begin to sow the seeds of serious discontent.[111]

Striking deep into enemy territory, the "promised messiah" admitted to a "sense of shame" at the way Muslims had distorted the original meaning of jihad. This distortion had provided Islam's enemies with an opportunity to attack a great religion that was in perfect accord with the laws of human nature. *Jihad,* meaning simply "endeavor," had been applied metaphorically to religious wars. The Sanskrit word *yuddh,* meaning "war," was, according to Ghulam Ahmad, a corruption of the Arabic *juhd* (which has the same root as *jihad*). He attacked the clergy and monks of all religious systems for looking upon any pious reformer as "an intruder," out of fear of losing their social position. Though endorsing the modernist Muslim argument about the Prophet's defensive jihads, he maintained that the permission had been valid only so long as there had been a threat to the nascent Muslim community. It was a grievous mistake to assume that such an interpretation of jihad was intended to "extend over the whole future of Islam."[112]

The wars fought by Muslims after the death of the Prophet and first four caliphs went against the grain of the Quranic concept of jihad. If the Christians violated the rights of Allah by making a man their god, "Muslims did violence to humanity by unjustly drawing the sword upon their fellow-beings under the guise of *Jehad*." Both had turned their respective violations into symbols of their salvation and the road to paradise. Although violating the rights of God is the worst possible form of crime, Ghulam Ahmad was more concerned about the violation of human rights by Muslims. The doctrine of jihad spread by maulvis was "altogether unknown in Islam" and "serves only to generate savage qualities in the ignorant masses and blot out all noble qualities of humanity." The Quran and the hadith stated that the coming of the messiah would mark the end of warfare—prayer would be his only implement and resolution his sword. "The days of *Jehad* are gone," Mirza Ghulam Ahmad announced. Its continued propagation was a "death-blow to all moral and social laws and lays the axe to the root of all kind-heartedness and fellow-feeling." By a strange quirk of fate, religious charlatans among Muslims, known as mullahs, had joined Christian mullahs to hide the "real excellence of Islam" by "drawing a veil on the true significance of *Jehad*." As the promised messiah, he commanded Muslims to "refrain from . . . shedding blood for the sake of religion." In his imperious words:

> If still you do not abstain from such blood-thirsty deeds and hold your tongues from such preachings, you shall be deemed to have turned your backs upon Islam . . . Had I not come, the error would, to some extent, have been pardonable. But now that I have come . . . those who take up the sword under the pretence of the support of religion . . . shall be called to account before their Lord . . . [for their] false hankering after Paradise.[113]

Ghulam Ahmad's status as a messiah and the blanket prohibition on armed jihad set the Ahmadis at loggerheads with the
rest of the Muslim community. Their founder's claim was rooted
in Islamic mystical tradition. He understood the concept of
khatm al nabuwwat as implying the superiority and not the
finality of Muhammad's spiritual prophethood, which would
always remain with the Muslim community. This was a throw-
back to Ibn al-'Arabi's distinction between the legislative and
nonlegislative functions of prophecy. It was the legislative and
not the spiritual function of prophecy that had ended with Muhammad's death, the thirteenth-century theosophist had argued.
In India, Sheikh Ahmad Sirhandi and Sayyid Ahmad Barelvi,
among others, claimed to be the recipients of spiritual communications from God. The Ahmadi leader never denied the
special status of the Prophet or present laws overruling the Muslim sharia. As the repository of the divine light with which the
Prophet had been blessed *(nur-i-Muhammadi)*, Ghulam Ahmad
believed he had been sent to correct the fallacies into which Muslims had fallen.

He told his followers that although "*Jehad* with the sword is
now at an end," the "real *Jehad* . . . remains and much must still
be done for the purification of the soul." In the modern age, a
common sense of humanity was the best way of ensuring the
spread of Islam. He had appeared "in the spirit of Jesus Christ"
to establish peace by rejuvenating the ethical dimensions of Islam. Instead of being "a model of . . . unsurpassed moral excellence," Islam had been so thoroughly corrupted by selfish and
semiliterate maulvis that Muslims thought killing non-Muslims
was a passport to paradise. Not a single verse in the Quran or the
hadith condoned the shedding of innocent blood. It was just that
"fanatics," having heard about jihad, sought to "gratify sensual
desires or led by delusion perpetrate bloody deeds." This was especially true of the Pathans, who, having absorbed incorrect ideas

about their faith from local mullahs, considered killing members of another religious community an act of virtue. It might help if Emir Abdur Rahman of Afghanistan, an Islamic universalist who had written on the merits of fighting the infidels, issued a fatwa declaring that jihad under the present circumstances would be a rebellion and not a religious war.[114]

Moving from the eschatological to the mundane, Mirza Ghulam Ahmad demonstrated his true loyalist colors. He marveled at the peace and tranquility prevailing in colonial India, in sharp contrast to the Punjab under the Sikhs. The British had given Islam a fresh lease on life in the Punjab. But maulvis in India were as misled as those on the Afghan frontier. So long as they awaited the coming of "a bloody Mahdi," they would not stop preaching their false doctrine of jihad. If the British recognized him as the promised messiah and stopped followers of different faiths from inveighing against one another, Muslim and Christian maulvis would not be able to spread their nefarious message.[115] Ghulam Ahmad's egotistical pronouncements about being the promised messiah made him suspect in the eyes of Muslims incensed by his rejection of the finality of Muhammad's spiritual prophethood. They overlooked the subtle distinction he drew between a *rasul*—a prophet who came with a set of laws—and a *nabi*, who, like Christ, came to correct the deviations from Moses' law. Moreover, the ulema could not stomach the Mirza's claim to be the recipient of heavenly guidance. That pretence undermined the Prophet's authority and their own role as the keepers of his tradition. On the political front, his rejection of jihad and laudatory remarks about British rule were seen as a cover for Ahmadi proselytizing.

Despite occasional hints of intellectual liberalism, displays of fellow feeling among Ahmadis were reserved for their own number. Their social conservatism on issues of gender and the exclusionary tendencies in social and religious matters bred hostility toward Ahmadis. If even their most explicit statement of jihad as a struggle to be human did not avoid the stigma of sectarian narrow-mindedness, to what extent were Muslims in late nineteenth-century India successful in translating into practice their assertions about jihad as an ethical concept? An answer to this key question requires some examination of the movement for ethical reforms that Sayyid Ahmad Khan initiated while still embroiled in debates with Hunter and Muir.

When not wielding the pen against Christian critics of Islam or fighting turf battles with ulema of varying stripes, Sayyid Ahmad thought his primary concern was the reform of Muslim social ethics through modern education. His critique of Muslim society and efforts to steer his co-religionists away from narrow-minded bigotry are one reason he cannot be dismissed as a mere apologist. Nor can he legitimately be portrayed as an abject loyalist whose sense of Muslim identity clouded his vision of Indian unity. Criticisms of Sayyid Ahmad Khan as either a loyalist or an apologist fray at the seams when we locate them within the historical context of nineteenth-century colonial India.

After 1857 Sayyid Ahmad, who despaired of remedying the predicament of his countrymen, had contemplated migrating to Egypt. He found solace in national service based on promoting education and friendship with the British. He told the Muhammadan Literary Society of Calcutta in 1863 that "nothing but patriotism" motivated him. Religious differences veiled the real unity among all created beings. One way to end the "seeming disunion" was "to exert ourselves for the good of our fellow-creatures just as we would do for our own." He remarked on how "many of our fellow countrymen though not co-religionists" were "excelling" only because of their knowledge of English. He said this without "any envious feelings" and only "to encourage and incite . . . fellow countrymen to strive to equal them." Calling for an educational jihad, he urged Indians to "diligently strive to master English," so that as in the past they might "surpass the rest of the races of the East."[116] In Ghazipur, thanks to subscriptions from wealthy Indians, he helped set up a school that taught Urdu, English, Arabic, Persian, and Sanskrit. His friend Raj Har Dev Narayan Singh was one of its first patrons.[117] Sayyid Ahmad's high hopes for national unity were dashed once Hindus in Benares began agitating to replace Urdu in the Persian script with Hindi written in Devanagari in government institutions. Convinced that cooperation between the two communities would become increasingly more difficult, he opted to focus on the education of his own co-religionists.[118]

Sayyid Ahmad Khan's trip to England in 1869 was an invigorating and transformative experience. Without absolving the English for looking down on Indians as animals beneath contempt, he attributed British prejudice to lack of understanding. Compared with the English, who had superior education and were well mannered and upright, Indians might seem like "imbecile brutes." The English also observed their religion with unsurpassed beauty and excellence because they educated both their men and their women. If Indians became civilized through education, they could equal if not surpass the English.[119]

After returning from London in 1870 Sayyid Ahmad launched a journal called *Tehzib-ul-Akhlaq,* after Miskawayh's famous work on ethics. It was patterned on the *Tatler* and the *Spectator,* started by Richard Steele and Joseph Addison in the early eighteenth century to improve English ethical life. Sayyid Ahmad hoped to emulate their achievement by encouraging rational, critical discussion among Muslims. Islam was flexible enough to allow Muslims to take up any challenge. Nothing rational and in accord with human nature was prohibited for them. The publication's English subtitle, "The Muhammadan Social Reformer," indicates his intention to use ethical debate as an instrument of social change.[120] An ethical revolution could make Indians, and Muslims in particular, "desirous of the best kind of civilization." This would "remove the contempt" in which they were held by "civilized people in the world." Knowledge in which Indians had once taken great pride was no longer useful in worldly or religious matters. Debates focused on trivial or artificial topics, and Indians rejected alternate points of view in petty and disputatious fashion. Poets wrote endlessly and without elegance about love but were silent on the subject of human goodness.

The message of the "innocent, straight forward and kind hearted Prophet" who had explained God's laws in "a clear and simple way to the ignorant and illiterate Arab nation" was "distorted with petty criticisms and philosophical proofs and argumentation to such an extent that there was nothing clear or simple left in it." Muslims had abandoned the Quran and hadith to follow the worldly principles of Zayd and Umro, and deception and pretense had supplanted ethics. Cleverness had come to entail "dishonesty and betrayal." Abusive language characterized verbal exchanges even among the respectable classes. Steele and Addison had improved English culture without dwelling on religion. "We too would like to avoid religious issues," Sayyid Ahmad asserted. But in India, one no sooner advocated giving something up than it was proclaimed a religious virtue; one no longer advocated learning something than it was declared forbidden on religious grounds. Consequently, one had no choice but to engage in religious debate when discussing the advancement of culture and the betterment of society.[121]

Because his agenda for reforming Islam proclaimed complete freedom of opinion in religious matters, it outraged the ulema, who attributed it to Sayyid Ahmad's overexposure to Western values. He was charged with infidelity and labeled a *nechari* (someone who reduces religion to worldly matters). The sayyid attacked his detractors' apparent monopoly on Islam. They had deviated from the teachings of the Prophet and imputed the wrong ideas to him. Sayyid Ahmad ridiculed the bearded, pajama-clad maulvis who questioned his faith. They penned pages filled with useless accusations of unbelief, apostasy, and the like. Why should Muslims obey clerics whose teachings ran counter to the Quran? Certain maulvis believed something to be bad only because it was declared to be bad. Reason played no part in their thinking. They could deceive a poor innocent woman or steal a person's goods and legitimate their actions by using legal stratagems *(hiyal)*. Having bathed at the mosque, combed their beards, and put on fresh clothes, they delivered eloquent sermons from the pulpit that demonstrated no sense of shame before God or the world.[122]

The absence of moral rectitude among the guardians of the faith had deprived the community of any sense of fellow feeling. The hearts of the Muslim populace, "darkened by the sermons of the maulvis," had become "harder than stone and" retained "not an element of *iman.*" Fed on the teachings of maulvis and pirs, who were enemies of reason as well as of God and the Prophet, Muslims had become fatalistic, slothful, and allergic to any attempt to better their lives. While the vast majority were destroying themselves thinking of the hereafter rather than the present, the so-called sacred personages of Islam were busy working for their own worldly advancement by spreading religious bigotry. Nothing could be more contemptible than, under the guise of piety, to fill one's pockets with worldly goods and then tell others to leave the world![123]

Sayyid Ahmad blamed the ruination of the individual and the community on bigotry. Bigots, being self-absorbed and limited in their worldview, were too arrogant to enter into reasoned debates with others, take the slightest criticism, or accept that they might be in the wrong. They avoided important and beneficial actions for reasons of prejudice. Given the depths of bigotry among the Indian ulema, the community was riven with extreme forms of cultural prejudice, which were wrongly ascribed to religion. The Quran condemns false pride and lack of consideration toward others, traits that are characteristic of bigots.[124] Moreover, the Quran warns against stubborn refusal to acknowledge the signs of the times as signs of God.

If only a series of articles written with lucidity and rare courage could have arrested the decline in the ethical standards of the Muslim community! In 1876, the sayyid suspended publication of the *Tehzib al-Akhlaq* to focus on establishing Aligarh College. Although Sayyid Ahmad restarted the paper twice in the 1890s, the sense of urgency that had motivated him in the beginning had dissipated. While retaining a keen interest in ethical issues, he focused toward the end of his life on building an institution for educating young Muslim men, and some Hindus too, in the spirit of fellow feeling and liberality that he believed would be the building blocks for national unity. Unfortunately for the sayyid, institution building requires more than goodwill and commitment. In his dependence on continued financial patronage for Aligarh College from the colonial state, Sayyid Ahmad made loyalty his politics. In his desire to rend the veil that obscured from his co-religionists the power of reason that Islam conferred on them, he instituted a policy of aloofness from the Indian National Congress. That policy helped breed new kinds of bigotry between the very two communities he hoped in due course to unite. And finally, for a man who placed reason above emotion and disliked slavish imitation, Sayyid Ahmad Khan remained committed to Islamic cultural values that were the source of the mental and spiritual subjugation of Muslim women. He supported women's education and approved of giving them the property rights conferred on them by Islam. But the education he advocated for women, which had to take place within the confines of the Muslim home, was restricted to study of the Quran and the traditions set down by the Prophet. Even though his ideas on the role of women thwarted his modernist agenda for the ethical reform of the Muslim community, Sayyid Ahmad inspired a range of projects whose effects continue to be felt more than a century after his death.

His educational jihad, enshrined in the Aligarh Muslim University, is only the best-remembered of his achievements. Equally significant was his influence in getting Shibli Numani to write a monumental biography of the Prophet Muhammad. Ameer Ali's and Chiragh Ali's books on the Prophet's life in English were aimed at a Western audience. Shibli, by contrast, wrote his magnum opus, *Sirat-ul-Nabi,* in Urdu, to offset the negative effects of Christian writings about Islam. Although he broke with the Aligarh school in 1894 to form the Nadwat-ul-Ulema at Lucknow, Shibli shared Sayyid Ahmad's concerns about the need for an ethical reformulation of Islam. Nawab Sultan Jahan Begum of Bhopal was the patron for the book, whose first volume was published in 1914, after Shibli's death. Printed in seven volumes with the help of Shibli's associate Maulana Sayyid Sulaiman Nadwi, the *Sirat ul-Nabi* aimed to correct the centuries-old neglect of an ethics based on the Quran.

The fourth volume discusses faith, and the fifth and the sixth are devoted to ethical behavior. In the opening chapter of the sixth volume, whose subject is righteous deeds *(amal-i-salah),* Shibli gave scholarly depth to Sayyid Ahmad and Chiragh Ali's contention that although *iman* as an idea has deep Islamic roots, Muslims are not committed to performing good deeds. Yet *iman* is the basis for *amal-i-salah.* Forty-five verses of the Quran begin with the words "Those who attained to faith and did good works"—making it clear that *iman* and *amal-i-salah* are inseparable. Some mention only *islam,* implying obedience, and substitute virtuous actions for *amal-i-salah*. *Amal-i-salah* encapsulates worship *(ibadat)*, ethics *(akhlaq)* and social relations *(muamalat)*. Worship in Islam has multiple meanings and includes works done to win God's pleasure. *Akhlaq* and *muamalat* carried out with the intention of winning Allah's favor are forms of *ibadat*. The Muslim jurists, however, kept the three distinct. *Amal-i-salah* was of two kinds—*ibadat* relating to God and *akhlaq* and *muamalat* dealing with human relations. *Akhlaq* had to do with human obligations while *muamalat* established legal responsibility. Consequently, the absence of good deeds in the presence of *iman* is regarded as merely performing a duty *(farz)* when in actuality neglect of good deeds indicates weakness of faith. Only when both are operative is it possible to lead a balanced life in this world, the key to salvation and a place in paradise.[125]

Turning to jihad, Shibli commented that although Islamic law did not consider it as an aspect of worship, the Quran and the hadith accord higher status to jihad than to acts the jurists considered as worship. The opposite of *jihad* in the Quran is *qaood,* which literally means "to remain sitting," with the implication of laziness and dereliction of duty. Shibli regretted that the meaning of such an important concept had been reduced to the idea of war against the enemies of Islam. There is a world of difference between jihad in the way of God and fighting *(qital)*. Not all forms of jihad entail fighting. Though he avoided saying the converse—namely, that not all forms of *qital* are jihad—Shibli defined permanent jihad as the struggle every Muslim is expected to wage at every moment in life. It entails supporting the *din,* propagating knowledge about the faith, struggling to secure victory for the truth, assisting the poor and handicapped, and preaching what is good and prohibiting what is wrong.[126]

If Shibli's magnum opus was a posthumous tribute to Sayyid Ahmad's reconceptualization of Islamic ethics, the internal critique of Muslim society he initiated bore fruit in his lifetime with the publication in 1879 of the *Musadas-i-Hali,* by Altaf Husain Hali. A student of Ghalib and a devoted follower and biographer of Sayyid Ahmad Khan, Hali wrote the long poem in accessible Urdu, charting the ebb and flow of Islam, to rouse his co-religionists from their intellectual, moral, and spiritual torpor. The *Musadas-i-Hali* contrasted the history of Muslim achievements in the realm of science and culture with the educational backwardness, religious bigotry, and cultural decadence of Indian Muslims. The *Musadas* was a sensational success. It went through several editions within months of its first publication. Describing it as a veritable lament *(marsiya)* about the Muslim condition in India, Sayyid Ahmad, who wept while reading it, considered it a milestone in the history of Urdu literature. He wanted to lift the legal constraints on its distribution that were attendant on the copyright Hali had given Aligarh College. Nothing would delight him more than to hear boys chanting it, dancing girls singing it to the accompaniment of music, Sufis intoxicating their audiences by reciting it at shrines, and the imams reading its verses in prayers and sermons at the mosques. He felt like inviting the elite of Delhi to listen to a musical rendition of the poem. If God asked him about his good deeds, he would point to Hali's *Musadas* as his crowning achievement.[127]

There was a flip side to these self-congratulatory words. Sayyid Ahmad's sensitive and discerning mind could not have failed to note the discrepancy between his stated aims and his actual achievements, masterfully captured in Hali's stab at the coreligionists for whose ethical reform the sayyid had struggled so long in vain:

> If the stranger worships idols, he's an infidel;
> If he believes in the son of God, he's an infidel;
> If he calls fire his god, he's an infidel;
> If he attributes miracles to the sun, he's an infidel.

But for believers the ways are expansive.
They may happily worship whom they like,
Turn the Prophet into God if they wish,
Give imams a status higher than the Prophet,
Visit shrines to offer gifts day and night,
Or pray to martyrs if they so desire.
The unity of creation is not impaired
Nor Islam distorted, nor does faith take its leave.[128]

❦ 5 ❧

Jihad as Anticolonial Nationalism

THE INTELLECTUAL discourse on jihad after 1857 was dominated by Indian Muslims advocating accommodation with colonial rule. Their pragmatic response to British temporal sovereignty in India was aimed at securing better safeguards for the
defeated and demoralized Muslim community. They found the
persuasiveness of their argument seriously undermined by Western imperialist forces' growing encirclement of Muslim countries
over the course of the late nineteenth century. Since the end of
the Mughal Empire, Indian Muslims had taken solace in the idea
of God's sovereignty over the universe, consistent with a sense of
belonging to the worldwide community of Islam. For a cross-section of politically conscious Indian Muslims who looked upon
that empire as the last bastion of Islam, the European pincer
movement against the Ottomans helped revitalize the bonds of
affinity with the *ummah*.

Anxious about their own minority status and sympathetic to
the plight of co-religionists in Asia and Africa, a vocal segment of
the Indian Muslim intelligentsia acknowledged Sultans Abdul
Aziz (1861–1876) and Abdul Hamid II (1876–1909) as the tempo-

ral and spiritual leaders of the *ummah*. In a break with the Mughal past, imams at Indian mosques read sermons in the name of the Ottoman sultan. This practice elicited a sharp reproof from Sayyid Ahmad Khan and his followers, who, apart from questioning the religious basis of the sermon, argued that Indian Muslims fell under the jurisdiction of the British and had no religious obligation to accept the Ottoman claim to the caliphate. Taking their cue from Waliullah, they maintained that a caliph had to belong to the Prophet's family. With three different conceptions of sovereignty—the divine, the spiritual, and the temporal—shaping their sense of religious identity, Indian Muslims could come to no agreement on jihad in either its reductive or its more expansive meaning.

Muslims who were indifferent or opposed to the policy of accommodation to alien rule often tended to be cultural exclusivists and with a few significant exceptions supported the principle of armed jihad for political, religious, and psychological reasons. But there was a world of difference between principles and actions, and Muslims found even less room for agreement on what constituted legitimate armed struggle. While a handful did take up arms, many considered resistance to established government seditious and suicidal. The frontier rebels became icons of anticolonial nationalism by cultivating their jihadi credentials and consciously associating themselves with the martyrs of Balakot.[1] More political than religious in intent, the notion of jihad articulated by Indian Muslim rebels in the second half of the nineteenth century came closer to the idea of a just war than to the theistic Quranic conception of war in the way of Allah.

It was not that Muslims ever lost sight of the finer points at the level of intellectual discourse; but as one Muslim country after another was crushed by the juggernaut of Western military and economic power, the idea of jihad as legitimate armed struggle could not fail to attract anticolonial nationalists. If modernist

Muslims considered freedom of speech, as granted by Western liberal thought, an opportunity to reform Islam, anticolonial intellectuals were willing and able to redefine jihad in their search for an authoritative ideology to help them resist alien rule. During the closing decades of the nineteenth century European rivalries played out in bitter battles for the choicest colonies in Asia and Africa. In 1881, France occupied Tunisia; the British, aided by Indian troops, took Egypt in 1882, and by the late 1890s they had moved up the Nile into Sudan to defeat the Mahdist state. Spain controlled the Western Sahara, but the French had the ultimate say in Morocco. Germany netted the Cameroons and Tanganyika, Belgium seized the Congo, and Italy, unwilling to be left out of the European power grab in Africa, swallowed up Eritrea and Libya. Muslims, finding themselves on the defensive against the rising tide of Christendom, tended to revolt quite as often as they did to reflect and reorient themselves toward a dramatically changed world.

An emotional affinity toward the *ummah* had never kept Muslims from identifying with patriotic sentiments in their own homelands. Rather, the aggressive expansion of European power and the ensuing erosion of Muslim sovereignty formed the backdrop for refashioning the classical doctrine of jihad to legitimate modern anticolonial struggles. An overview of international politics in the late nineteenth and early twentieth centuries provides the general context for an examination of the globalist vision of Sayyid Jamaluddin al-Afghani, the peripatetic Persian propagandist and political activist who is credited with shaping the modern form of Islamic universalism. It is useful to trace his ambiguous intellectual legacy in India by examining the thought and politics of such pro-Congress Muslims as Maulana Abul Kalam Azad (1888–1958) and Obaidullah Sindhi. Both were anticolonial nationalists who shared Afghani's universalist vision of Islam. A major theoretician of Islamic law and ethics, Azad was the most prominent Muslim leader of the Congress in preindependence India. A Sikh convert to Islam, Sindhi tried translating Waliullah's ideas into practice and started a transnational jihad by cultivating ties with Germans, Russians, and Turks during World War I. Adopting the language of an Islamic humanist ethics, they tried to maintain amicable relations with non-Muslims, even while calling for an armed jihad against the Western aggressors. Muhammad Iqbal was an anticolonial nationalist of a different ilk. More of a poetic visionary than a political radical, he wrote stirring verse invoking the power of the sword to cut through the cobwebs of a defeatist mentality. Muslims could become true Muslims only if they broke the chains of servitude by waging an armed jihad against Western colonialism. The difficulty, as Iqbal sensed intuitively and Azad and Sindhi learned from bitter political experience, was that Muslims had little inclination, and far less capacity, to rise to the occasion and launch an effective challenge to Western imperialism.

Islamic Universalism and Afghani's Anticolonial Vision

A theme of enduring interest in modern history has been Muslim anticolonial resistance based on selective appropriations from the ideology of jihad. As early as the eighteenth century, Tipu Sultan (1750–1799) invoked the idea of universal Islamic sovereignty when he endorsed the idea of a caliphate centered in the Ottoman Empire to counter European expansionism. His defiant struggle against the East India Company's armies and Sayyid Ahmad Barelvi's valiant jihad against the Sikhs have represented the most potent symbols of resistance in Indian Muslim consciousness. Their power to inspire anticolonial sentiments was buttressed by other stories of heroic armed struggle against Western imperialism emanating from different parts of the Muslim world. Resistance to the Russian presence in Dagestan and Chechnya, led by

Imam Shamil, for instance, held romantic appeal for politically conscious Indian Muslims, even if few dared follow in his footsteps. Identification with the struggle of co-religionists in the colonized Muslim world was reinforced by the questions that commonly arose with the onset of Western colonialism. From India to West and Central Asia, as well as in Africa, Muslims in the late nineteenth century pondered over the obligation to fight a jihad or perform *hijrat* and reacted in diverse ways to the appearance of every new Mahdi claiming to lead the faithful out of infidel rule.

Beginning with Abdul Qadir (1808–1883), who fought against the French between 1832 and 1834, several Mahdist revolts were staged in Algeria during the second half of the nineteenth century. As in the case of Sayyid Ahmad Shaheed, Abdul Qadir's efforts to raise taxes by establishing centralized control over the tribes and religious brotherhoods led to his downfall. During the Mahdist revolt in the Sudan, the guardians of orthodoxy rejected the claims of Muhammad Ahmad (1844–1885) to be the Mahdi (divinely guided vice-regent), on the grounds that established authority had to be obeyed. Although he failed to preserve Sudanese independence, Muhammad Ahmad's courageous stand against the joint British and Egyptian forces aroused widespread respect and admiration in the Muslim world.

Jamaluddin al-Afghani was among those who looked on the Mahdist revolt as a model worthy of emulation in struggles against British imperialism. Unlike Sayyid Ahmad Khan, whose vision was limited to India, Afghani took a global view of the Muslim predicament. A "strategist of defeat and survival" for the dejected Indian Muslim community, Sayyid Ahmad has been contrasted with Afghani—the "strategist of defence" for the *ummah* against an encroaching and predatory West.[2] Although Afghani lived briefly in India, his ideas had limited appeal there until after the outbreak of World War I. Not only were his ideas impracticable in the conditions prevailing in late nineteenth-century India, but an effective strategy of defense required a rearguard attempt

Sayyid Jamaluddin al-Afghani, paragon of Islamic universalism. Courtesy *Dawn.*

to ensure the survival of the community. Sayyid Ahmad Khan's emphasis on correcting British misconceptions about the inherent disloyalty of Britain's Muslim subjects has to be seen in context: all religious communities in late nineteenth-century India vied with one another in professing loyalty to the raj.

Like all matters of temporal expediency, Sayyid Ahmad's policy of collaboration was overshadowed by the changing tenor of global politics. Between 1875 and 1882 a series of political events dramatically altered Europe's relations with West Asia. For Indian Muslims, the outbreak of the Russo-Turkish war of 1877–78, coinciding with the proclamation of Queen Victoria as empress of India, marked the start of an inexorable process of disillusionment with the policy of unconditional collaboration. A vibrant popular press widely disseminated news of the proclamation of jihad issued by the Sheikh-ul-Islam of Constantinople. In the sanguine opinion of Sayyid Ahmad Khan's *Aligarh Institute Gazette,* the Indian Muslim response to the call for jihad was unlikely to extend beyond pious prayers to heaven. Even the "most bigotted Musalman [*sic*] cannot but confess that peace and security, such as exists under the British rule, though it is not altogether free from faults is not to be found in any Muhammadan kingdom on the earth."[3] One Urdu newspaper promptly countered this assertion by publishing emotional verses showering blessings on the Ottoman sultan and invoking the curse of God on his enemies: "May the whole Russian army perish under the Turkish arms; may the earth split under the infidel army of the czar and the sky fall down upon their heads; may the heart of the czar burn with the fire of repentance, and his life be in the claws of death; may the angel Israel snatch his soul from his body and hell dress its fires to receive him."[4] Muslims donated enthusiastically to the Turkish relief fund and some even contemplated taking up arms in response to calls for jihad issued at local mosques. At the end of the war, the Indian Muslim press blamed Britain for its ineffectual assistance to the Turks in their hour of need and for engaging, even more unforgivably, in intrigues at the Congress of Berlin that resulted in the loss of four-fifths of the Ottomans territory in Europe.

India, where pro-Ottoman sentiment was running high, offered fertile ground for Afghani's hopes of reviving the idea of a universal Muslim caliphate as the first step toward a coordinated Muslim jihad against European imperialism. If jihad was his preferred antidote to the rapid shrinkage in the territories of *Dar-ul-Islam,* he favored a universal caliphate to correct the fragmentation of religious authority that he identified as the cause for the decline of Islam. A savvy political operator rather than a profound or original thinker, Jamaluddin left a limited corpus of writings, which does not include a treatise on jihad. Being less interested in the form than in the substance of the struggle against the British imperial presence in the East, Afghani adapted his spoken and written words to suit his audience. With the threat of colonialism hovering over Egypt and India, he promoted territorial nationalism rather than the Islamic universalism for which he is renowned. Instead of making appeals in the name of religion, he tried to instruct Egyptians and Indians on the power of a common language and shared history to unify diverse communities. Without unity and patriotism, neither the Egyptians nor the Indians had any hope of fighting colonialism.

Afghani was a remarkable but cryptic man. He concealed his Persian national origins and, despite his heterodox beliefs, went to great lengths to appear as Sunni as the next Muslim. Duplicitous in his thought and inscrutable in his actions, he was a shadowy presence that appeared to be everywhere and nowhere at the same time. Who was Jamaluddin al-Afghani? In some rare and insightful rhymed prose that anticipates later questions about his identity, he wrote:

> The English people believe me a Russian [*Rus*]
> The Muslims think me a Zoroastrian [*Majus*]
> The Sunnis think me a Shi'i [*Rafidi*]
> And the Shi'i think me an enemy of Ali [*Nasibi*]
> Some of the friends of the four companions have believed
> me a Wahhabi
> Some of the virtuous Imamites have imagined me a Babi

The theists have imagined me a materialist
And the pious a sinner bereft of piety
The learned have considered me an unknowing ignoramus
And the believers have thought me an unbelieving sinner
Neither does the unbeliever call me to him
Nor [does] the Muslim recognize me as his own
Banished from the mosque and rejected by the temple
I am perplexed as to whom I should depend on and whom
   I should fight
The rejection of one requires affirmation of the other
The affirmation of one makes the friends firm against its
   opposite
There is no way of escape for me to flee the grasp of one
   group
There is no fixed abode for me to fight the other party.[5]

Single-minded in his opposition to British imperialism but un-sure of what fate had in store of him, Afghani made a virtue out of the Shia strategy of dissimulation he had learned in his youth. Though he posed as an Afghan, it is now known that Sayyid Jamaluddin was born in Asadabad near Hamdan, into a family that traced its lineage to the family of the Prophet. He received training in the traditional Islamic sciences in Iran, Iraq, and Afghanistan before visiting India for the first time 1854. During a stay lasting over a year, he gained his initial exposure to the methods of Western science. His next visit was in 1869, when he made a timely escape from Afghanistan after ending up on the wrong side of the succession dispute among Emir Dost Muhammad's sons. Although the British Indian government received him with honor, Afghani was prevented from meeting Indian Muslim opinion makers. After a month, the colonial state put him aboard a ship to Suez. He arrived in Cairo for the first time and came into contact with the faculty and students of Al-Azhar.

Afghani next headed for the Ottoman capital abuzz with Sultan Abdul Aziz's attempts to promote himself as the universal caliph of Islam. Here Afghani rubbed shoulders with the Ottoman ruling elite and spoke freely about religion. Jealous of his growing prestige, the Sheikh-ul-Islam of Constantinople castigated him for giving a lecture exalting philosophy and reducing prophecy to a mere craft, thereby implying that the Prophet was an artificer or a craftsman. Jamaluddin had not dared deny the superiority of prophecy over philosophy. Prophecy was a divine gift whose infallibility was unquestionable, whereas a philosopher, whose knowledge was acquired through thought and study, could fall into error. But like prophecy, a correct philosophical point of view was the means to spiritual perfection through ethical refinement and moral purification.[6] Charged with blasphemy, Afghani was forced to leave Constantinople. After this close shave, he scrupulously avoided entering into theological controversies with the ulema and instead concentrated on promoting the study of philosophy in the light of modern knowledge. He returned to Egypt, where he attracted droves of students. He taught them philosophy and Western science, to the outrage of traditional theologians. Suspicious of the political activities he undertook in concert with the "Young Egyptians" led by Arabi Pasha, the British engineered Afghani's expulsion from Egypt.

This turn of events brought Afghani to India, where he lived in Hyderabad and Calcutta between 1879 and 1882. The colonial state, alarmed by Arabi Pasha's revolt in Egypt, feared an uprising in India and kept him under close surveillance. It was during this period that Afghani emerged as a virulent opponent of Sayyid Ahmad Khan's loyalist policy. There is no evidence that he had contacts with the so-called Wahabi followers of Sayyid Ahmad Barelvi or, if he did meet them, that he became close to any of the leading Indian Muslim modernists or ulema.[7] There are surprisingly few references to him in colonial archives. The most often cited is a letter written in June 1883 by Sayyid Husain Bilgrami of Hyderabad to the British resident, describing Afghani as "a free thinker of the French type, and a socialist" who was "shallow in his acquirements."[8] This description stands in complete contrast to the standard portrayal of him as a defender of Islam who exhibited a revulsion toward the Aligarh variety of intellectual modernism.

Though Afghani couched his antipathy in religious terms, the difference between him and Sayyid Ahmad Khan was political and did not, as is often mistakenly held, result from their conflicting conceptions of Islam.[9] Sayyid Ahmad maintained that he supported the colonial government not out of love or loyalty for the British, but because the best course for Indian Muslims was to win safeguards from the established government of the time. This position was unacceptable to Afghani, who described British imperialism as "a dragon which had swallowed twenty million people" and, having drunk up the waters of the Ganges and the Indus, was "still unsatiated and ready to devour the rest of the world and to consume the waters of the Nile and the Oxus."[10]

Fancying himself as the Martin Luther of Islam, Afghani was an improbable opponent of Sayyid Ahmad Khan's modernist rationalism and reformist ideas. But Afghani despised the Aligarh movement's religious and educational agenda, which smacked to him of political servitude to the British. Education that served the interests of foreign rulers was worse than no education. Instead of their hollow imitation of the conqueror's values, Indian Muslims needed an education that inculcated pride in their own "civilization" and helped them develop an indigenous ideology for reform and self-strengthening. Any policy of collaboration with the oppressors could only tighten the bonds of subjugation and had to be countered with all means, fair and foul. Sayyid Ahmad Khan's excessive admiration of British rule amounted to an "abandonment" of Islam, which by "disparag[ing] . . . the interests of the fatherland" was fanning "discord among the Muslims."[11]

Like those he mocked as *necharis* and referred to as *Aghuris,* the lowest and most despised of sects in India, Afghani took an evolutionary view of history. He shared Sayyid Ahmad's belief that scientific knowledge not only was consistent with Islamic teachings but represented an outgrowth of the past achievements of Islamic civilization. But unlike his Indian counterpart, Afghani did not engage in hair-splitting disputes with the ulema by trying to promote a new theology. This restraint did not prevent him from lambasting the guardians of Muslim orthodoxy for their prejudice against philosophy and their stubborn refusal to accept modern science, simply because it had originated in the West. Nothing could be stranger than the ulema's arbitrary division between "Muslim science" and "European science." They had "not understood that science is that noble thing that has no connection with any nation."[12]

Without having actually delved into the Indian Muslim reformer's writings, the eminent Middle Eastern historian Albert Hourani thought that Afghani's claim that Islam was consistent with human reason was a far cry from Sayyid Ahmad's attempt to interpret Islam on the basis of a rational understanding of natural law. While Afghani is depicted as "a convinced Muslim" who "accepted the fundamental teachings of Islam with all his mind," Sayyid Ahmad is presented as a secular modernist, who held human reason to be above divine revelation. His Muslimness is deemed suspect because he wanted a rational interpretation of the Quran in order to formulate a moral and legal code governing the laws of nature.[13] Such a sweeping claim can be easily twisted to justify the fatwas given by ulema in Mecca and Medina against Sayyid Ahmad Khan. These condemned him as an apostate and a dangerously misled man who was better dead than alive. Muslims were instructed not to support the Aligarh Muslim College, which was imparting an irreligious education contrary to the sharia.[14]

Even if Sayyid Ahmad in his interpretation of the Quran overdid the attempt to justify Islam in terms of modern rationalism, he cannot be judged on the basis of facile generalization about distinctions between the religious and the secular. Far from denying the importance of religion or revelation, he contended that historical processes of secularization in Islam had transformed the sharia from a divine law into a man-made law. To allude without analytical rigor to the categories of religious and secular does a disservice to modernist Muslim thought as pioneered by men like Sayyid Ahmad Khan and Chiragh Ali. Erecting false dichotomies between faith and reason deflects attention from the strands that linked the intellectual thought of men as far apart politically as Sayyid Ahmad and Jamaluddin al-Afghani. It also distracts the historian from considering the extent to which Afghani, instead of merely putting his imprimatur on anticolonial thought in India, may have used some of Sayyid Ahmad's insights to refine his own ideas.

Afghani, who is credited with inculcating Islamic universalism into Indian Muslim minds, diligently avoided that subject for the duration of his visit, in the broader interests of promoting Hindu-Muslim unity against a common enemy. He made few disciples in India but won the esteem of two relatively unknown journalists, who had their own reasons for reporting his barbs against the Aligarh movement.[15] None of his Indian writings mention the Ottoman sultan's claim to be the universal caliph or the need for Muslims to unite behind a single leader. The decisive phase of his career as a champion of Islamic universalism began only after his departure from India, around the time of Britain's occupation of Egypt. After a brief stint in London, Afghani arrived early in 1883 in Paris, where he joined with his Egyptian protégé Muhammad Abduh (1849–1905) to launch an

Arabic newspaper, *Al-Urwa al Wuthqa* (Indissoluble Link). The paper fulminated against British policy in Egypt and evinced only a marginal interest in Indian affairs. It was through this paper that Afghani's ideas on Islamic universalism were disseminated throughout the Muslim world. But the impact remained limited in India, because of the British ban on the paper and the difficulty Indian Muslims had in gaining access to its Arabic content. By 1885 Afghani's few contacts in India had begun to dry up.[16]

The remaining years of Jamaluddin's life are an intricate tale of his involvement in the politics of Iran and Ottoman Turkey and futile efforts to get Russia to declare war on the British. He was expelled from Iran for inciting the ulema to resist the tobacco concession and, though Sultan Abdul Hamid II used him to underwrite his claim to the caliphate, kept in virtual confinement in Constantinople, where he died in 1897. A victim of the syndrome that had led Waliullah to decry monarchy and yet work to strengthen it, Afghani, in an elusive quest to promote a jihad against Western imperialism, cultivated the very rulers of the Muslim world whom he charged with opening the gates to foreign aggression. Despite his intense distrust of the Ottoman sovereign, he endorsed Abdul Hamid as the universal caliph in the vain hope of initiating jihad against the West and forcing internal reforms in the Muslim world. An immensely ambitious man who was fatally attracted to power, Afghani could lay claim to only one political achievement of note: having influenced his former servant to assassinate the Iranian sovereign Nasiruddin Shah in 1896. A fortnight before the event, he had been found reciting in a state of frenzy: "There is no deliverance except in killing, there is no safety except in killing."[17] With a little bit of prescience he might just as well have exclaimed, there can be no deliverance but in death, in death will be my deliverance.

And indeed Jamaluddin al-Afghani in death posed a bigger

threat to the colonial masters than he had managed to in his life-time. His legendary impact on the subcontinent is a construct of a later period and, like most belated recognition, tends to over-state his role in shaping the politics of Islamic universalism in India. Even before Muhammad Abduh and Rashid Rida hailed Afghani in articles in *Al-Manar* as the apotheosis of Muslim anticolonial resistance, Indian Muslims unfamiliar with his ideas had reasons of their own to break ranks with Sayyid Ahmad Khan on the question of loyalty to the raj. Their romantic affinity with Ottoman Turkey was heartfelt. By the 1890s most Urdu newspapers considered Sultan Abdul Hamid as the spiritual leader of the Muslims and the custodian of the holy shrines of Mecca and Medina. Even those who doubted his claims to the caliphate supported his stand against the European powers out of religious solidarity. This, more than Afghani's invective against Sayyid Ahmad Khan's lack of piety and policy of collaboration, was the reason Indian Muslims were inclined to take a universal-ist view of politics.

A new generation of educated middle-class Muslims, per-turbed by the spread of Western imperialism and uncertain about their own future as a minority in India, gave vent to their suspi-cion of Britain's ultimate intentions toward the Ottomans. In 1897 the Indian Muslim press celebrated Ottoman victories, only to find itself under attack by Anglo-Indian– and Hindu-owned newspapers agitated by a treatise on jihad written by Emir Abdur Rahman of Afghanistan and a recent uprising of Pathan tribes-men in Tochi and Malakand. These different occurrences were seen as part of a common thread which provided proof positive of the visceral disloyalty of Muslims to British rule. Wondering how Indian Muslims could be held "responsible for the doings of their co-religionists in such remote places," the pro-Congress *Paisa Akhbar* inquired "why the Anglo-Indian papers were so put off by Muslim rejoicing at Turkey's victories." Only the "lynx-eyed Editors of the Anglo-Indian papers" could read "signs of a Muhammadan revival" in pro-Ottoman sentiments, the emir's treatise, and the tribal uprisings.[18]

The Turkish victories had "not instilled any new life into Islam," but they had "gladdened the hearts of the Muhammadans." Why should Muslims be "afraid of expressing their sympathy with the Sultan"? Given that the British were not party to the war, it ought to be "a matter of indifference to the Government whether the Muhammadans rejoice over the Turkish victories or not." At the same time the *Paisa Akhbar* attacked Sayyid Ahmad Khan for suggesting that there was no history of animosity between Islam and Christianity.[19] More insightful onlookers could see that the policy of keeping the "sick man of Europe" alive had less to do with altruism than with the strategic need to check Russian ambitions. Coupled with the disenchantment with colonial policies in India, the thread of intrigue running through imperial policies in Asia and Africa was sufficient grounds, without Afghani's intervention, for Indian Muslims to spurn the policy of collaboration. A significant exception was Shibli Numani who, being influenced by Muhammad Abduh, began opposing his former patron's policy of keeping Muslims out of the Congress. But it was not until Maulana Abul Kalam Azad's meteoric rise that the mystique of Afghani affected Indian Muslim ideas about Islamic universalism and, more specifically, jihad as the answer to Western aggression.

Jihad in Anticolonial Indian Muslim Thought and Politics

Islamic universalism in India was a by-product of European imperialist policies and predated Jamaluddin al-Afghani's efforts to rally Muslims behind the Ottoman bid for the caliphate. Afghani's posthumous reputation as the intellectual progenitor of Islamic universalist politics in India was not unearned. After all, he had preached Hindu-Muslim unity and waxed eloquent on the virtues of territorial nationalism. For Muslims in the colonies, the attractiveness of Afghani's anti-imperialist ideas lay in his astute analysis of contemporary politics. Whatever his own beliefs on any particular subject, he went to great lengths not to transgress the consensual limits of Islam, and his efforts paid handsome dividends. His appeals for forming a united Muslim front to fight a jihad against European imperialism and for reconciling a spiritual caliphate with the establishment of independent states based on human reason and divine law, not to mention his emphasis on the right to revolt against unjust rulers, were the building blocks for Muslim anticolonial politics in Asia and Africa. Given Afghani's global focus, coming to grips with his intellectual legacy for anticolonial Muslim thought and politics in India is an intellectually rewarding enterprise. It underscores the continuing cross-fertilization of ideas between India and West Asia at a time when the Western liberal paradigm had purportedly established its dominance, if not hegemony, over the thought and politics of the colonized. Moreover, it reveals how Muslim intellectuals in the age of European colonialism invoked the wider world of Islam to strengthen, not undermine, their attachment to territorial nationalism.

Maulana Abul Kalam Azad was the foremost Indian Muslim intellectual to blend the politics of Islamic universalism with a comprehensive anticolonial vision derived from close study of the Quranic concept of jihad. If Afghani can be described as "the most complete Muslim of his time," Azad was the exemplar of the erudite Muslim scholar.[20] His independence of mind was hemmed in only by a conviction that the Quran and the practice of the Prophet were the perfect guides for all aspects of life. Azad grasped the wider ethical meanings of jihad to make a forceful case for fighting colonial injustices. Thus his ideas on jihad owed less to Afghani than to the Islamic tradition in which he was reared. His father was a spiritual preceptor with a succession of disciples. Although he refused to assume the hereditary mantle, Azad had an understanding of Islamic mysticism that gave his thought much greater poignancy than Afghani's political writings could ever achieve. Where Azad's ideas converged with those of Afghani, Abduh, and Rida was in stringent opposition to the contemporary ulema, who had compromised religion for worldly gain. Although he remained in constant dialogue with like-minded co-religionists in other parts of the Muslim world, Azad's universalistic vision was shaped by the experience of subjugation under British rule.

A child prodigy and a precocious adolescent, Azad blazed onto the public scene at the age of fifteen, brimming with ideas of social justice and religious reform and filled with abhorrence at British rule. Though he had been impressed by Sayyid Ahmad Khan's translation of the Quran, it was his exposure to the Bengali militant groups Jugantar and Anushilan and his contacts with the frontier rebels that did most to shape his political worldview. In 1908 he traveled through West Asia and met anticolonial nationalists in Iraq, Turkey, and Egypt. In Egypt Azad kept company with the followers of Mustapha Kamil, the leader of the National Party (Al Hizb al-Watani), who proposed confronting the British and who rejected the relatively more accommodating line taken by Abduh's Al Manar group. Kamil's preference for territorial rather than Islamic nationalism and his policy of zero tolerance for British imperialism helped Azad formulate his own anti-imperialist political agenda.[21] Azad not only retained these contacts but named his first paper, an illustrated Urdu weekly called *Al-Hilal* (The Crescent), after a publication of the same name and format, which appeared in Egypt.

Published in Calcutta in July 1912, *Al-Hilal* provided Azad with a perfect medium for expounding his views on jihad as legitimate anticolonial struggle. Peppered with quotations from the

Quran, the paper was designed to stir Muslim sympathy for co-religionists fighting imperialist powers in Asia and Africa. Article after article extolled the gallant Muslims resisting European aggression on the charred and bloody battlefields of Tripoli and the Balkans. The message was stirring and unequivocal. Part of a seamless worldwide *ummah,* Muslims were bound by their religion to reject arbitrary lines on the map drawn by European imperialists with the aim of further dividing and weakening the Muslim world. Muslims, being answerable only to Allah, could not suffer subjugation but must fight to regain their sovereignty. They could do so with greater efficacy by forming a united Muslim front under the Ottoman caliph.

Azad had as his aim not merely to report but to educate and guide Indian Muslims. He was at one with Sayyid Ahmad Khan in considering ethical reform a requisite for Muslim social and political revival. But this is where their agreement ended. In one of his earliest pieces in *Al-Hilal,* he declared that the correct ethical path was thin and sharp like the edge of a sword below which burned the fires of hell. An ethical conception of life entailed love, service, and respect for humanity, irrespective of religious or racial differences. It was best to avoid conflict and refrain from criticism. But to take this precept to an extreme by falsifying the truth to please the oppressors was the obverse of decency. The Quranic injunction *amar bil maruf wa nahi anal munkur,* to command what is good and prohibit what is wrong was, in Azad's opinion, the effective meaning of jihad. Commanding what is good without prohibiting what is wrong was impossible.[22]

Muslims were described as the best community in the Quran because they were expected to eradicate instability and injustice. They would be replaced by another, more deserving community if they failed to act against the forces of disequilibrium. Muslims were exhorted to follow the middle path to establish a just and virtuous society—"give full measure when ye measure and weigh with a balance that is straight: that is the most fitting and the most advantageous in the final determination" (17:35). This duty had been compromised by the confusion caused by two apparently contradictory verses of the Quran. "Let there arise out of you a band of people inviting to all that is good, commanding what is right and prohibiting what is wrong; they are the ones to attain felicity" (3:104) suggests that the duty is limited to a select group. But verse 3:110, addressed to the *ummah,* applies to all: "Ye are the best of peoples evolved for mankind commanding what is good, prohibiting what is wrong, and believing in Allah. If only the People of the Book had faith, it were best for them; among them are some who have faith but most of them are perverted transgressors."[23]

Seeing no contradiction between the two verses, Azad rejected the consensus among Quranic scholars that only the ulema can preach what is good and prohibit what is wrong. This was a "dangerous error," which had cost Muslims dearly. The obligation to preach the good and prohibit wrong was the duty of the entire community and required exertion (jihad) to understand the Quranic message. By restricting it to a small group, Muslims had lost the universal vision of Islam. He attributed the decline of all religions to the assumption of godly authority. Islam had attempted to avoid the pitfall by ruling out any sort of clergy and making the preaching of good and prohibiting of wrong incumbent on all believing Muslims. Islam had been established to prevent religion from becoming the private preserve of priests, but the very problem it was intended to eradicate was undermining the faith. The ulema had turned the general duty to God into one of their private rights, and no one else had a right to interfere. The result was that they preached the wrong and prohibited the good! Unaware of their primary responsibility, Muslims were ignorant and beholden to the ulema. They could not feel the presence of God's government over them; their eyes were closed to virtuous action, and wrongdoing was overlooked, as if no one had eyes to see.[24]

A religiously inspired ethics could not rest on belief alone but must manifest itself in virtuous action. As a core Islamic principle, spreading good and removing wrong was the essence of jihad, and sometimes it was necessary to undertake nonpeaceful actions for the sake of maintaining peace. Just as the law on homicide allows the taking of life in the interests of deterring further murders, the Quran sanctions the use of the sword to eliminate sedition. God approves of mercy, but mercy cannot be established unless those who use force are put in their place. In addition to being merciful, God is just. When disequilibrium becomes too great, the sword must be wielded. Azad held that to humiliate those who humiliate was in accordance with God's mercy and love. Since Muslims are urged to cultivate an ethics derived from God, those with true faith must express disapproval of wrongdoing openly and forcefully.[25]

Azad identified himself with the great Sindhi mystic and martyr Sarmad Shaheed, who preferred death to compromising his conscience.[26] The life of a believer is a constant struggle to emulate the Prophet. Like the mystics, he held that a believer's love of God is the essence of true faith. Without love of Allah, it is impossible to fulfill the responsibility to enjoin good and prohibit wrong. Persons prompted by selfish interest rather than love of God cannot create the inner space to fight evil. They are polytheists, though they might profess to have faith. It behooves the true believer to give everything to others except himself, which can rightfully belong only to God. Muslims wage true jihad when they see and hear nothing but God and perform the duty of commanding the good and prohibiting wrong solely to win the approval of their beloved (the One who is loved). Without going into the all-important question of how God's approval is to be gauged, Azad sanctions rebellion and, better still, "arrogant jihad" against all satanic temporal authorities.[27]

A discussion of the deeper ethical purposes of jihad served as the springboard for Azad's political treatment of the idea in both theory and practice. The concept of jihad meant that when "deviations from the prescribed path assumed the form of weapons of war, the devotees of truth and keepers of the unity of creation [*tawhid*] should also have the sword in their hands." This was jihad against an external enemy. But when transgressions were a result of spiritual depravity and ignorance, the principle of commanding the good and prohibiting wrong provided the rationale for waging jihad through the spoken and written word. Following earlier scholars of Islam, Azad identified three kinds of jihad: 1) verbal proclamations commanding good and prohibiting wrong, 2) contributions of property and goods for the cause, and 3) fighting *(qital)* and the actual waging of war.[28] He refused to restrict jihad to spiritual struggle but disagreed with those who advocated the indiscriminate killing of infidels. The idea that Muslims are allowed to murder all non-Muslims, which so terrified Europeans, formed no part of Islamic teaching. Islam sanctioned only the right to fight those who opposed and oppressed Muslims as Muslims.[29]

Affirming that armed conflict was one possible means of countering Christian hostility toward Islam, Azad endorsed a jihad against the British. Any struggle to break the chains of oppression and reestablish truth and justice constituted jihad. Indian Muslims must awaken from their slumber and see how their co-religionists elsewhere had risen up in the cause of freedom as granted to them by Islam. He valorized the Sanusiya struggle against the Italian invasion of Libya in 1911 and told moving stories about European atrocities. During the First Balkan War, *Al-Hilal* printed photographs of Turkish freedom fighters, along

with scenes of gory battlefields, and described instances of religious oppression by the European powers.[30] These were provoca-
tive images for Indian Muslims, who were licking their wounds
after the display of British arrogance and brute power that had
led to the Kanpur massacre in August 1913. Muslims protesting
the demolition of a lavatory attached to a mosque in Kanpur
were fired on indiscriminately, and several were left dead. Seeing
the opportunity to strike the Islamic universalist chord in Indian
Muslim hearts, Azad wrote a moving piece blasting the colonial
government for trampling on religious freedoms: "The earth is
thirsty, it demands blood, but of whom? Of the Muslims." Tripoli was drenched in Muslim blood, as were the plains of Persia
and the Balkan Peninsula. Hindustan too was athirst for Muslim
blood. At long last it had rained blood in Kanpur; the dust of
Hindustan was saturated with it. "Oh, you Muslims," Azad asked
tauntingly, "where will you now reside?"[31]

By desecrating the Kanpur mosque for a mundane reason like
straightening the road, the British had forfeited the right to
Muslim loyalty. Likening the Kanpur killings to the massacre in
Karbala, Azad noted that the real casualty of the bullets fired at
an unarmed crowd was British justice. The Christians accused
Muslims of believing that women had no soul. But did they believe Muslims had no soul? Muslims had a soul, but the British
had killed it, forgetting the primary law of all religions: "You shall
not kill." By committing an unpardonable blunder, the British
had turned the Kanpur incident into a matter of grave concern
throughout the Islamic world. "Muslims from every corner of the
globe" had already made many "sacrifices in blood." At last, Indian Muslims had offered their co-religionists "the gift of our
spilt blood."[32]

Backed by a potent ensemble of local, national, and transnational symbols, Azad's *Al-Hilal* venture was a sensational success.
Although closely monitored by the colonial state, it was not until

after the start of World War I that the paper was forcibly closed down in November 1914. A year later, it reappeared as *Al-Balagh*. But with Azad labeled the "most mischievous of agitators" in India, its run lasted a mere five months.[33] Journalism was not the only medium Azad chose to use in disseminating his anti-imperialist ideas. The spoken word was an equally important component of his efforts to educate Muslims on the importance of Islamic unity and the obligation of resisting Western aggression. In speeches given over a long and productive public career, Azad developed the ideas on jihad to which he had first given expression in the pages *Al-Hilal* and *Al-Balagh*.

In a rousing speech in Calcutta on 27 October 1914, he compared the Muslim community to a human body. A pinprick sustained by Muslims in a distant corner of the world was felt by the entire *ummah*. How could Indian Muslims not feel wounded and agitated by the sufferings of co-religionists? Muslims who had sold their souls to foreign masters might consider an affinity with the extraterritorial *ummah* a dangerous manifestation of religious bigotry that had to be suppressed, or better still eliminated.[34] They were entirely mistaken in their reading of international politics. Picking up Jamaluddin al-Afghani's point about Islam as a "civilization" and the West as a correlative and antagonistic historical phenomenon, Azad raised the specter of the civilizational divide between a menacing and conniving Europe and the unsuspecting and ill-prepared Muslims of Asia and Africa.[35] The threat was not to countries, but to Islam as a living religion.[36]

Europe's solution to the "Eastern problem," Azad contended, was a nefarious plot to hammer the last nail into the Ottoman coffin. Christians took as their model the natural justice enunciated by Jesus, the "Prince of Peace," in the Book of Luke (19:27): "But as for these enemies of mine, who did not want me to reign over them, bring them here and slay them before me." It was no surprise that Europe did not consider the eradication of Islam as oppression. The natural laws of nations were meaningless in this game of domination. Azad compared the European powers to a pack of wolves whose sole concern was to curb their rivals' appetite for the Islamic body politic, so that all could claim a piece of the prey. Europe considered the subjugation of Muslims its greatest cultural service to the world in the twentieth century. The sacred sword of the Ottoman caliphate was the only security left for God's religion and the Islamic way of life. Unless the entire Muslim world threw its weight behind the Turks, nothing could stop the armies of European Christendom.[37]

Azad belittled Europe's arrogant claims about the superiority of European culture and civilization and pointed to evidence of its inhumanity in the blood-stained desert of Tripoli and the mutilated corpses of Marrakech. The Turks were the quintessential barbarians. But in contrast to the European armies, which had perpetrated heinous crimes against Muslims, the Turks had treated Italian prisoners of war graciously. If Muslims had a shred of the pan-Islamism they were accused of favoring, they would not be humiliated and ruthlessly killed. The hands that held the white flag of peace were undoubtedly blessed. But only those would survive whose hands controlled the sword. Force alone guaranteed a people's existence. It was the means of establishing justice to save human life and protect the oppressed. Faced with Western political and cultural aggression, all believers had a duty to engage in jihad in the way of Allah and must remember that while others were masters of their own lives, the lives of Muslims were the property of God.[38]

This was as categorical a call for jihad as any given by an Indian Muslim under British colonial rule. Azad did not delve into the delicate issue of how Muslims, who in his estimation had made a charade of Islam, could serve the cause of God by fighting Western aggression. The omission was more than just a matter of expediency. In his articles in *Al-Hilal,* he referred to the wars in Tripoli and the Balkans as jihad, well aware that the word sent shivers up the spine of some people. He justified this wording on the grounds that it was Europe that was waging another religious crusade against Islam. European armies were Christian armies when the Ottomans were the enemy. To consider the wars in Tripoli and the Balkans as Christianity's temporal wars was to release Muslims from the strictures of their religious laws governing warfare. The potential effects of doing so might be explosive: Muslims in other parts of the world might retaliate by opposing and killing Europeans at random. Fighting and warfare were not the same as jihad. The Quran prohibited Muslims from taking up arms to oppose people who were not waging a religious war against them. This prohibition acted as a floodgate, holding Muslims back from breaking off relations with Christians in India and fighting the British government. Those who abhorred jihad had to decide whether they wanted Muslims to abandon this Quranic restraint on warfare and instead learn the European military methods.[39]

In a treatise on the Islamic conception of war, Azad elaborated on the difference between temporal warfare and jihad. The Quran referred to the cruelty and carnage in the killing fields of Europe as war *(harb),* sedition *(fitna),* killing *(qital),* and controversy *(jidal).* Unlike wars in which human beings were mercilessly slaughtered and subjugated, jihad had as its purpose the establishment of peace, tranquillity, and freedom. As a means of putting an end to bloodshed and restoring the dignity of man, jihad was the exact opposite of war as *qital, harb,* or *fitna.* This was why the Quran used the word *harb* to refer to the political wars the Prophet fought against those who broke treaties or who acted like highway robbers, by exacting interest. Temporal wars had nothing to do with jihad. A warrior enamored of his own success ceases to be a jihadi, for there is no room for self-praise or arrogance in jihad fought in Allah's cause. The worldly conqueror wreaks havoc in the places he conquers, whereas the true jihadi is moderate in his treatment of the vanquished and thinks only of winning favor with God.[40]

Unfortunately, Muslims did not understand the meaning of jihad, Azad asserted. Instead of developing political methods based on the noble tenets of their religion, they had either entangled themselves in the slavish and suicidal politics of the Muslim League or looked to the Congress for their salvation. There was "no greater blot on the sacred message of Islam than for Muslims to borrow the lessons of human freedom and the welfare of their country from other nations." In their educational, ethical, social, and political affairs, the leaders of Muslim opinion could think of nothing better to do than to follow the Europeans. If Muslims had been true to their faith, they would have known that whatever was good and beautiful in the world existed because of Islam.[41]

God had created human beings to live ethical lives. Human ethics were subjected to the most extreme test during periods of strife between nations. This was why Islam had selected jihad as the training ground for its ethical teachings.[42] A strong belief in the ethical superiority of Islam propelled Azad to wage a jihad of tongue and pen. He also engaged in the second form of jihad, by spending his resources on the cause. Before the outbreak of war, he was planning to initiate an Islamic movement by setting up an outfit called Hezbollah (or Party of Allah). The British suspected it of being a secret society, a view confirmed when a Dar-ul-Irshad (House of Learning) was opened to train teachers for Hezbollah.[43]

Once Turkey sided with Germany in the war, Azad pulled out all the stops in his effort to warn Indian Muslims of the grave error they were committing by supporting the British war effort. The Ottoman fatwa of November 1914 declaring jihad against Britain, France, and Russia lent weight to his efforts. Its most salient feature from Azad's point of view was the stipulation that Muslims living under Allied rule in India, Central Asia, North Africa, and the Balkans were obliged to come to the rescue of the Turks by attacking the non-Muslim rulers in those countries.[44] At a juncture when India's would-be preeminent anticolonial leader, Mohandas K. Gandhi, was backing the government's recruitment drive, Azad favored allying with Germany and Turkey, in order to acquire the military means to fight a jihad against the British. He was interned in April 1916 and kept in Ranchi for the next four years.[45]

Before his arrest he became embroiled in a chain of activities originating in the Dar-ul-Ulum at Deoband under Maulana Mahmudul Hasan (d. 1920). Popularly known as Sheikhul Hind, Mahmudul Hasan had given an oath of allegiance to Muhammad Qasim Nanautawi's spiritual preceptor, Haji Imdadullah, and Azad considered Mahmudul Hasan the heir of the "Waliullah Caravan."[46] Together with his enterprising student Obaidullah Sindhi, Mahmudul Hasan sketched out a secret plan to hasten the demise of the British in India. The "silk letter conspiracy" gave the colonial state concrete evidence of the disloyalty of a politically vocal faction of its Muslim subjects. This was seen as justification for the Rowlatt Act, which turned wartime ordinances into harsh peacetime legislation. Such measures as the British took to root out the sedition in India did not prevent Sindhi from giving practical shape to global anticolonial activities, of which Azad approved heartily.

Few turn-of-the-century anticolonial nationalists in India matched Obaidullah Sindhi in his penchant for high political adventure. A devotee of Shah Waliullah educated in the finest traditions of Deoband, Sindhi espoused a revolutionary nationalist ideology that bordered on romantic idealism. He was eclectic in his thinking and more ingenious than Mahmudul Hasan, whom he more often led than followed. Instead of being ill-disposed to European thought and culture, like his mentor, he was broadminded about borrowing ideas that served his purposes. Without compromising on the essentials of his adopted religion, Sindhi, like Afghani before him, drew from a variety of influences, and it mattered little whether they were Eastern or Western, so long as they furthered the cause of Indian independence. He traced the genealogy of jihad movements in India to Waliullah and divided the process, which he dubbed *Hizb-i-Waliullah,* into three phases. The first, starting with Waliullah and Shah Abdul Aziz, ended with the defeat at Balakot in 1831. In the second phase, Shah Muhammad Ishaq carried on his father's movement, to which Haji Imdadullah gave practical shape. Sindhi, considering himself the successor to his esteemed teacher, believed he was playing a pivotal role in the third phase of the movement, which he dated to Mahmudul Hasan's death in 1920.[47]

As early as 1909, Mahmudul Hasan had deputed Sindhi to organize the Jamiat-ul-Ansar from among former students of Deoband. Its two-fold objective was to engineer a revolt against the British by enlisting the support of Muslim countries. To facilitate a unified Muslim response cutting across class and ideological lines, Mahmudul Hasan for the first time initiated a dialogue between Deoband and Aligarh. An academy of Quranic learning was set up in Delhi whose main patrons included Nawab Waqar-ul-Mulk of Aligarh College. Sindhi headed the institution and met anticolonial Islamic universalists and Western-educated Muslims like Azad, Mohamed Ali (1878–1931), and Dr. Mukhtar Ahmad Ansari (1880–1936).[48] These exchanges lent momentum to Mahmudul Hasan's objective of awakening Indian Muslims to the plight of the *ummah* in the face of Western aggression and stirring the autonomous tribal areas of the northwest frontier to attack the British with the help of Afghanistan. It was an audacious plan, which ran into the same wall of apathy, however, that had prompted Azad to print rousing articles on the need for Muslim unity under the Ottoman banner. Commenting on the problem after his return from incarceration in Malta, Mahmudul Hasan noted that the hearts of pious people sank when they were told to rise and save the Muslim community from the infidel onslaught. What they feared was not the wrath of God but the power of "a few individuals and their weapons."[49]

The accusation was only partly true. Muslims opposed to the Ottoman caliphate were no less God-fearing than those who rallied behind the Sheikh-ul-Hind. But the opponents saw no merit in supporting a distant sovereign whose main enemy was their principal benefactor. As far as they were concerned, transnational religious affiliations could never replace the political requirement of loyalty to the rulers of their own country. They were accused of dividing the Muslim community by serving Western interests. Anticolonialists like the Sheikh-ul-Hind considered loyalty to the British conditional on the preservation of Muslim religious freedoms. Ever since the crisis in the Balkans, the theme of Islamic universalism had been highlighted in the anticolonial polemics of *Al-Hilal* and *Al-Balagh,* the *Comrade* (Calcutta) and the *Hamdard* (Delhi) started by Mohamed Ali, and in the *Zamindar* in the Punjab, edited by Maulana Zafar Ali Khan (1873–1956). They elicited a mixed response from Muslims, many of whom were wary of coming under colonial surveillance on account of their community's notorious disloyalty. Despite the spread of pro-Turkish sentiments, not all Muslims were ready to heed the Ottoman call for a jihad. "What can we do with neither guns nor swords!" was one line of response. Some Indian Muslims, anticipating an Ottoman victory, wanted Greece to join the Allied powers, so that Turkey could regain its lost territories. They were encouraged by rumors that a Turkish army of eighty thousand, led by German officers, was advancing on Egypt and would soon "proceed to India" with the help of the Muslim powers.[50]

Mahmudul Hasan and Sindhi wanted to cash in on pro-Turkish feelings by organizing an invasion of India. Before leaving for Kabul in August 1915, Sindhi met with representatives of the mujahideen party based on the northwest frontier. With a free hand to do anything that was necessary to put the colonial masters to flight, he spent the next seven years in the Afghan capital plotting armed action against the British. In keeping with the plan to coordinate trouble on the northwest frontier with an uprising in India, Maulana Muhammad Mian Mansoor Ansari was sent to the autonomous tribal areas to promote jihad.[51] Azad visited Peshawar at Mahmudul Hasan's behest in 1915 and arranged for Maulana Saifur Rahman to cross the border to raise the Mohmands with the help of Haji Sahib Turangzai, who had fought the British in Malakand in 1897.[52] In a parallel development, a group of young students at Government College in Lahore crossed the border into Afghanistan. Inspired by Azad's writings and the Ottoman fatwa, they decided, upon being approached by the mujahideen, to wage jihad against the British. The autobiography of one of the students, Zafar Hasan Aybek, recounts Sindhi's activities in Afghanistan, the Soviet Union, and Turkey. The nephew of Maulvi Muhammad Jafar Thanesari and the son of a Deobandi father, Aybek had impeccable credentials as an Islamic revolutionary.[53] Azad had a hand in the decision of the students to leave India to abet Sindhi's activities.[54] With his loyal foot soldiers working closer to home, Mahmudul Hasan left India in September 1915 on the pretext of performing hajj. He got in contact with Ghalib Pasha, the Turkish commander-in-chief in the Hejaz, from whom he secured a proclamation of jihad. The document, known as the *Ghalibnama,* was distributed in India as well as among autonomous Pathan tribesmen.

As Afghani had learned to his cost and Sindhi was about to discover, it was easier to procure fatwas on jihad than to mobilize Muslim rulers against Western imperialism. Once in Kabul,

Sindhi began a long and futile attempt to win Emir Habibullah Khan over to the cause of Indian independence. But the emir was beholden to the British, from whom he received a grant for his "neutrality" in matters to do with India. Without consulting Mahmudul Hasan or the Congress leadership in whose name he claimed to operate, Sindhi made an outlandish offer to the emir, whereby his son Amanullah Khan would be placed on the throne in Delhi in return for Afghanistan's military help in invading India and defeating the British.[55] This won him the emir's bemused support for the idea in principle but not in practice. As Sindhi tried to negotiate the byzantine web of Afghan politics to secure India's freedom, Emir Habibullah's complicity with the British emerged as the most formidable obstacle.

Mindful of the precarious financial condition of Muslim countries, Sindhi came up with an innovative way to create a steady flow of funds for the jihad. He set up an organization called Junud Allah, patterned on the Salvation Army, to collect the skins of animals slaughtered in the Hejaz on Eid. The hides would be processed in a leather factory and exported to Muslim countries. The profits were to be managed by a transnational Islamic company based in the Hejaz, and an Islamic bank was to be established to finance the project. Before Sindhi's ideas could materialize, the Afghan authorities intervened to nip his plans in the bud.[56] This was just the start of a bumpy relationship between Emir Habibullah and the Indian revolutionaries. Tensions soared with the arrival in Kabul of an Indo-German mission led by Raja Mahendra Pratap of the American-based Ghadr [Revolution] Party. Sindhi used his contacts with anti-British Afghan nationalists to assist the mission in securing Afghanistan's support in the war against the Allied powers. When the Ghadr Party established a "provisional government of India" with Raja Mahendra Pratap as president and Barkatullah as prime minister, they made Sindhi home minister in recognition of his usefulness in keeping lines of communication open with Afghans opposed to Habibullah. Alarmed at the prospect of being pushed into a war with the British, the emir sent the mission packing and placed Sindhi and his young associates in state detention.[57]

In a measure of Maulana Obaidullah Sindhi's resourcefulness quite as much as of loopholes in Afghan security, he sent letters on behalf of the provisional government to the governor of Russian Turkistan as well as to the czar, urging them to declare war on Britain and establish contacts with Turkey. On 9 July 1916 Sindhi wrote to Mahmudul Hasan asking him to prepare the ground for a Russian-Turkish entente. In another letter Maulana Mansoor Ansari referred to the *Ghalibnama* and proposed establishing an army called Hezbollah, which would be recruited from India. Sindhi's letter contained details of the organizational structure of Hezbollah, which was to have its command center in Medina and regional centers in Constantinople, Tehran, and Kabul. Mahmudul Hasan was named supreme commander, and Sindhi became the commander in Kabul.[58] The letters were carefully woven into yellow silk handkerchiefs, to escape detection by Afghan and British intelligence. A breach in the secret arrangements resulted in the silk letters' ending up in British hands in August 1916.[59] When the "silk letter conspiracy" scotched, Mahmudul Hasan and four of his associates were arrested in December with the help of the pro-British Sharif of Mecca and transferred to a high-security jail on the island of Malta for prisoners of war.

Sindhi described the setback as "worse than death."[60] But it did not deflect him from his ultimate goal. His opening came when Emir Habibullah was assassinated in February 1919. Amanullah's accession to the throne brought to power nationalist Afghans with whom Sindhi had been in communication since his arrival in Kabul. Amanullah, who was eager to secure Afghanistan's independence from Britain at all costs, accepted Sindhi's scheme for invading India. The Afghan declaration of jihad was timed to take strategic advantage of Britain's continuing woes in the immediate aftermath of World War I. The better part of the colonial army was still deployed on the fronts where the war continued to smolder. The troops that remained in India had their hands full trying to control widespread public unrest over the Rowlatt Act. The colonial state used the silk letter conspiracy to justify arrogating to itself draconian powers to detain Indians without trial. But the social and economic dislocations of the war, taken in conjunction with Muslim concerns about the future of the Ottoman caliphate and the holy places in Mecca and Medina, posed the more immediate danger for the British. A brigade of voluble maulvis in India was giving impassioned sermons about how Islam had been disgraced by the Ottoman defeat and would, with the occupation of the holy places, be altogether effaced. Some Muslims likened the fall of the Ottoman capital to the day of judgment.[61] The situation became especially sensitive in the strategically vital province of the Punjab after soldiers fired mercilessly on a peaceful crowd in Jallianwallah Bagh in Amritsar protesting the colonial state's black laws that allowed detention without trial. There were rumors that money was being collected surreptitiously in the Punjab for the mujahideen.[62]

Seeing the turmoil in India as Afghanistan's best opportunity, Amanullah ordered his fledgling army to take up positions along the border. Sindhi was instructed to prepare the ground in India, so that the approaching army would meet with welcome, not resistance. The best-case scenario would be for Indians to revolt, thereby forcing the British to make concessions to the Afghans. Unaware of Amanullah's ultimate aims, Sindhi circulated a memorandum addressed to "Brave Indians! Courageous Countrymen," congratulating them for their "gallant deeds done for the noble cause of liberty." Their government in exile had taken all the necessary steps in seeking outside help to "liberate them from the iron clutches of the English and to establish indigenous government." It was the duty of Indians to "murder the English wherever [they found] them, cut the telegraph lines, destroy the railway lines and the railway bridges, and assist the liberating armies in all respects." If they complied with these orders, they would not be "molested" and their homes and properties would be safe.[63]

Apart from an accidental skirmish on 2 May 1919 in Jalalabad, the third Afghan war did not cause any agitation in the British military high command. In spite of Sindhi's meticulously worked-out plans, which included diplomatic missions to Russia and other European countries, the Afghans did not even cross the Indian border. Army discipline had completely disintegrated, and soldiers refused to obey orders. The situation of the mujahideen was no better. Some tribesmen looted the property of their co-religionists, "as if the purpose of jihad was to obtain a few yards of cloth."[64] Before the maneuver backfired on him, Amanullah started negotiations with the British that led to his securing Afghanistan's independence, after which he left the Indians in the lurch. The Khilafat movement led by Gandhi and the Ali brothers, Mohamed and Shaukat, was in full swing in India at this time. Having set the stage for the migration *(hijrat)* pandemonium, the emir retracted his offer to welcome Indian Muslim migrants *(muhajirin)* to his domains. Thousands of homeless and destitute Indian Muslims had sold everything to seek the protection of a Muslim sovereign, only to be robbed of their worldly belongings by his subjects. The spectacle was a grim reminder of the limits of Islamic universalism. It was also a fitting end to Sindhi's pipe dreams of winning Indian independence by installing an Afghan in power in Delhi.

He had not been alone in believing that an Afghan invasion backed by autonomous Pathan tribesmen could topple the British in India. While Azad was cooling his heels in Ranchi in the immediate postwar period, educated anticolonial Muslims had plotted with the usual suspects among the ulema to whip up pro-Ottoman hysteria. Indian Muslims, although they still acknowledged the Ottoman sultan as the caliph and regretted the fall of Constantinople to Allied forces, were more agitated about the future of the holy places in Mecca and Medina. If these came under the control of the Allied forces, they feared, jihad would become incumbent upon them, because their loyalty to infidel rule was contingent on the preservation of their religious freedoms. In a letter to the viceroy dated 14 May 1919, Mohamed Ali and Shaukat Ali rebuked the British for showing disrespect, in violation of their promises, to Muslim religious sentiments. Unless steps were taken to redress Muslim grievances, there could be disruptions in the empire. In a postscript the Ali brothers noted that the British were on the verge of "involving Indians in a war with a neighbouring Moslem kingdom, which in view of its small size and resources, could never have dreamt of attacking the Indian Empire." Truth, justice, and religious tolerance demanded that before thrusting Muslims into this conflict, the British consider whether "the outbreak of hostilities was not due to this very attitude which has caused Indian Muhammadans to contemplate migration because they are too weak to resort to *Jehad*."[65]

If this was a barely veiled threat, Shaukat Ali felt no compunction in stating at the All-India Muslim League session in December 1919 that a jihad proclaimed by the caliph would be obligatory on all Muslims. "Muslims had degraded themselves by becoming the disciples of expediency," which in his opinion, was tantamount to "renouncing their religion." He "yearned to go to Turkey and die in that country" but could hardly show his face to the Turks now that Indian Muslims had helped defeat them. Holding the "lowest Turk" to be "superior to the best Indian Muslim," he declared that "true Muslims obeyed the orders of God and of no other ruler."[66] Such clarity of exposition was noticeably missing in the statements of Indian ulema on whether

Theorist of jihad Maulana Abul Kalam Azad with secular Congress leaders. Standing left to right: Harekrishna Mahtab, Sarat Chandra Bose, J. Daulatram, Pattabhi Sitaramayya, Subhas Chandra Bose, Jawaharlal Nehru, Vallabhbhai Patel, Abul Kalam Azad, J. B. Kripalani. Courtesy Netaji Research Bureau.

Muslims were obliged to wage jihad against the British if control over the holy places was not restored to the Turks. Indian Muslims of all denominations condemned the transfer of Palestine to the Jews. This was seen as a brazen attempt to place the holy places under Jewish control. Pro-Congress ulema quoted Quranic verses prohibiting friendship of Muslims with Christians and Jews. Since Muslims were under Christian rule, there was no objection to their uniting with Hindus in the cause of Islam and Indian independence.[67] Other ulema, not all of whom were on the British payroll, vehemently opposed the idea. Many Muslims reproached the Khilafatists for allowing Hindus inside mosques, and even Farangi Mahal maulvis expressed their "disapproval."[68]

Maulana Abdul Bari of Farangi Mahal was one of the leading lights of the Khilafat movement. He instructed his followers to declare jihad and mobilize Muslims if Mecca and Medina were invaded by infidel forces. On 24 November 1919, Bari gave a fiery oration at the All-India Khilafat Conference in Delhi. In deference to Gandhi, who was opposed to both *hijrat* and jihad, he avoided direct mention of jihad. But the idea was implicit in the statement he gave, and subtly linked with his sense of identity. Bari noted that although Gandhi had converted him to oppose the sacrifice of cows, he, Bari, had not taken the vow of non-violent struggle, because killing was sometimes unavoidable. A choice had to be made between "becoming a Kafir by killing Muslims and being [a] true Muslim." In violation of religious freedom, the government had compelled Muslims to become infidels by forcing them to fight the Turks. Personally, Bari preferred death, but he wanted to know "how many of the seven[ty million] . . . Indian Muslims were true Muslims."[69] Not all ulema of Farangi Mahal agreed with Bari. Many of them countered his opinions in a fatwa stating that if non-Muslims attacked a Muslim country, waging jihad would be incumbent on Muslims in neighboring territories only if they had the power to do so successfully. Suicidal efforts and mere slaughter were strictly forbidden in Islam.[70]

Azad's release from jail in January 1920 gave a boost to the pro-jihad lobby in India. During the Khilafat and noncooperation movement, Azad called upon Muslims to stop serving the British Indian army. Islam prohibited Muslims from killing co-religionists. Muslims were also forbidden to forge friendship with those who were killing and oppressing Muslims. The Quran distinguished between two kinds of Muslims, those who fight or oppress other Muslims and those who do not. Muslims were bound by their faith to fight the aggressor with all the means at their disposal; and Muslims were supposed to befriend people who did not fight them. It followed that Muslims should fight to remove the illegitimate British government in India by uniting with their Hindu countrymen.[71] To dispel Muslim fears about letting Hindus inside mosques, Azad wrote an essay to prove that the gesture was consistent with the sunna and the sharia.[72] Freedom of opinion and national independence were the lifeblood of ethics. Nothing was more dangerous and disgraceful for a nation than the fear of death and of the punitive force of temporal power.[73] Azad capitalized on the hadith identifying opposition to an unjust ruler as the greatest jihad. Equating the anticolonial struggle with jihad, he accepted the charges of sedition brought against him by the colonial state. But he was not bound by laws contrary to the fundamental precepts of Islam. He could not as a matter of conscience remain loyal to a government that violated his religious freedoms.[74]

Azad followed his courageous defense at the Karachi trial with a fatwa declaring *hijrat* mandatory for Muslims.[75] Since Indian Muslims could not wage a successful jihad against the British, they were religiously obliged to take refuge in a neighboring Muslim country. If it had been genuine, which it was not, Amanullah's offer to welcome fellow co-religionists to his domain could have presented the British with a problem. Shifting the debate from jihad to *hijrat* was a calculated political gamble on Azad's part. But dressing temporal calculations in a religious idiom had catastrophic results for thousands of Muslims, who sold their belongings for a pittance in the vain expectation of a better quality of life in Afghanistan. Given that the ulema celebrated the *hijrat* movement as an achievement, no one has dared point an accusing finger at those who helped in the making of this human debacle.

Left to his own devices in Afghanistan, Sindhi had only the most erratic communication with like-minded anticolonial nationalists in India. The emir's betrayal, together with mixed signals from India on the question of jihad, prompted Sindhi to make tactical readjustments. After the Anglo-Afghan truce, he spent two more years in Kabul in an unavailing attempt to set up a Hindustani university. Described as "an institution for the whole world," whose aims were "synonymous with humanity," the university was to work toward "elevating mankind" by providing education in the arts and sciences to "all nationalities" without discrimination on the basis of gender, race, color, or creed. The estimated starting cost of two hundred thousand pounds was not nearly as formidable a stumbling block as the insistence by Sindhi on Urdu as the medium of instruction. He was accused of destroying Afghan nationality and making the country subordinate to India. There was an element of truth in the charge. Sindhi envisaged amalgamating Afghanistan and India. Though he did not abandon that objective, the controversy over language taught him something about national pride. In later years he abandoned the vision of Muslims living under a universal caliphate, instead preferring the model of the nation-state as the vehicle for Islamic unity.

Hampered and humiliated by his hosts in Afghanistan, Sindhi left for the Soviet Union in October 1922 in the hope of striking a deal with the Bolsheviks to oust the British from India. He was able to persuade the Soviets to give ten million rupees in financial aid for the cause of Indian independence. In an interesting come-down for an advocate of armed jihad, he turned down the offer of military assistance, on the grounds that Congress was fighting a nonviolent movement against the British. He advised the Soviets to pay an equivalent amount to the Afghans, so that they would not be tempted to repeat the treachery of 1919. On 23 July 1923 he left for Turkey to make arrangements for the Congress to conclude an alliance with the Soviets.[76] Sindhi's idea of sending Soviet aid to India through Afghanistan failed to elicit interest in Congress. Lala Lajpat Rai, on hearing about the plan during his visit to the Turkish capital, was visibly disturbed. Sindhi thought

Rai had conveyed the news to his mentor, Madan Mohan Malaviya—the leader of the right-wing Hindu Mahasabha. As a result, Hindu-Muslim relations soured to an appreciable degree.[77] With a little empathy and a better grasp of history, he might have realized that it was difficult for Rai and Malaviya to envisage Afghan involvement in Indian independence in a form other than an invasion!

Hindu-Muslim relations in India had been strained ever since the emir's abortive jihad. By openly supporting an Afghan invasion of India, Congress Muslims like Shaukat Ali touched a raw nerve among their Hindu counterparts, some of whom saw this as a barefaced attempt to reimpose Muslim rule. In the words of the Hindu nationalist leader Swami Shradhanand, the real danger to Hindu-Muslim unity came from Muslim leaders who considered jihad a religious duty. Equally rebarbative was the claim of Muslim intellectuals like Khwaja Hasan Nizami that conversion of Hindus to Islam was not inimical to Hindu-Muslim unity.[78] Commenting on Nizami's invitation to Gandhi to embrace Islam, one Hindu-owned paper recalled how Aurangzeb had offered his daughter to Shivaji's son Sambhaji. No ploy could be more abject: a "religion which seeks to induce a person to embrace it by throwing to him the bait of wealth, women or *jagirs* loses in the estimation of all good men."[79]

Anticolonial Muslims considered it legitimate to use any means to undermine the British in India. Their call for jihad and attempts to secure outside military assistance for Indian independence were in line with this view. The people who dismissed them as Muslim supremacists in nationalist clothing were not always right-wing Hindu bigots. The passion with which Azad, the Ali brothers, or Sindhi gave expression to their Islamic identity was a source of consternation even for relatively broad-minded Congress Hindus. It is important, therefore, to consider how far the commitment of anticolonial Muslims to the cause of Indian independence was compromised by their attachment to the idea of jihad.

For someone who stayed outside the Congress and worked for Indian independence in Kabul, Moscow, Ankara, and the Hejaz, Sindhi held a conception of jihad as anticolonial politics that makes for instructive study. A commitment to Islam in general and to Waliullah's revolutionary ideology in particular did not deter him from selectively incorporating socialist ideas that aimed to achieve socioeconomic justice. While under surveillance in Kabul, he examined the British parliamentary system of government and tentatively concluded that India should be a constitutional monarchy on the British model. He changed his mind after studying European labor history and the principles of socialism and communism in Moscow. Taking Islam and India as his points of reference, Sindhi sought an antidote to the atheistic and antireligious ideals of communism and their doctrinal rigidities. The elimination of private property was not incompatible with Islam, he reasoned, provided Muslims recognized that the private ownership of property endangered their faith. Nevertheless, keeping Indian conditions in mind, he deplored the Soviet emphasis on the dictatorship of the proletariat at the expense of merchants, farmers, and industrialists.[80]

During his stay in Turkey, Sindhi sought Zafar Hasan Aybek's help in writing and publishing *The Constitution of the Federated Republic of India,* in which he outlined his vision for the future government of independent India. Even though he was a Deobandi and an admirer of Waliullah, Sindhi did not seek a religious solution to Hindu-Muslim differences. His answer to India's religious dissensions was to recognize that national and class differences were based on existing economic and political conditions. The main objectives of the draft constitution were 1) to establish a federal form of government for independent India, 2) to protect Muslims and other minorities, 3) to set up a government of the working-class majority, by eliminating feudalism and capitalism, and 4) to create an Asiatic federation to counter the forces of imperialism. Geographically, he saw India as comprising three distinct regions—northwestern, eastern, and southern. These regions were to be divided into provinces on the basis of language and cultural traditions, and each province would have a homogeneous socioeconomic system. Later these provinces were to become democratic countries that would hold elections on the basis of universal adult franchise.[81] They would exercise all the functions of an independent state except foreign affairs, defense, and external trade, authority for which was to be vested in a federal government of India. Its constituent units would be represented according to their economic, cultural, and military significance as well as their population. Independent countries with a common culture might also decide to form subfederal unions. For instance, Western Punjab, the NWFP, Kashmir, Sind, and Baluchistan could create a federal system before joining the all-India federation.[82] Sindhi's ideas about the grouping of Muslim provinces in the northwest, which he expressed as early as 1926, foreshadowed the efforts of a succession of Muslims seeking to grapple with ways to handle the issues of identity and sovereignty in an independent India.

Sindhi's draft constitution differed from later schemes in important ways. He believed that the Hindu-Muslim "problem" was "not being considered in its true perspective." Instead of assuming some nonexistent unity of religion, one had only "to look a little below the surface" to see that "differences exist not only between these two communities, but that each community is itself cleft into various sections on account of national and social divergences." A central government of federal India had to guarantee the constituent units autonomy in religious and cultural affairs. Grouping members of a single religious community so that it enjoyed a clear majority could alleviate dissension, as in the case of

Muslims in the northwest. To safeguard minority rights, representation in the independent democratic countries of the federation was to be determined on "the basis of class differentiations and not religion."[83]

Whereas the Muslim schemes of the late 1930s were mainly political in nature, it was India's socioeconomic problems Sindhi was interested in solving. The success of the liberation movement depended on winning the sympathy of the masses. It was possible to gain their backing only if the stated aim was to replace the capitalist system with a system promoting the welfare of the laboring majority. Sindhi was careful to point out that uprooting capitalism in India would not entail restraints on religion or on smallholding.[84] But restrictions would be placed on unbridled accumulation of private property. A proper system of taxation was to be introduced, and interest taking banned. All means of production for the common good would be state owned. Landlordism was to be eliminated, and the land distributed according to the needs and abilities of the peasantry. State-owned industries were to be run by organized labor, which would receive a share of the profits. Primary and middle school education was to be free, and health facilities would be provided to the laboring classes at state expense. Internal trade was to be conducted by cooperative societies whose membership would be open to merchants.

Finally, securing the sovereignty of independent countries required the formation of an Asiatic federation that could combat Western imperialism. Sindhi did not claim originality for the idea, which Japan and Turkey had put forward in the past. He conceded that it was unlikely to inspire colonized Indians, who had developed "a sort of repugnance to establishing foreign relations." This attitude would change once political power was in their hands. He justified including the Soviet Union in the federation on the basis that its support would be useful in repelling the

British. Glossing over Moscow's colonialism in Central Asia, Sindhi held that the Soviets had "discarded imperialism." They could assist India in creating a system in which political and economic power was in the hands of the toiling masses. He acknowledged the need to guard against unnecessary Soviet interference but warned against excessive caution. India had "lost her greatness," by refusing to learn from the French Revolution. The new federation would be signing its own "death sentence" by ignoring the achievements of the Russian Revolution in replacing private property with a system geared to industrial and agricultural production for the public benefit instead of for private profit.[85]

To execute his revolutionary plans, Sindhi proposed the creation of the Mahabharat Swarajya Party, which would strive for an independent government of all Indians, irrespective of color, creed, or wealth. Its members were to live like ordinary peasants, and India was to be a federation of different nations, each with its own language and distinctive traditions.[86] The motto of the party was to "mitigate the evils of racial hatred and religious bigotry." Every member would protect and defend the "honour of an Indian woman or the sacred place of an Indian religion in danger." Hindu members of the party were to treat outcastes on equal terms and extend the same treatment to "all those persons . . . who ha[d] made India their home." In return, Indian Muslims, in the interest of national unity, would abandon the slaughter of cows. To make his socioeconomic ideas accessible, Sindhi quoted extensively from Hali's *Musadas,* to throw light on the greed of capitalists and the dignity of labor. Well aware of the power of poetry, he had concluded the introduction to the constitution with a Persian couplet subtly extolling his life as a jihadi:

> Even though our cause appears without resources, yet think
> it not insignificant

For in this field, poverty carries with it the dignity of
Regality.[87]

Eager to give his ideas the widest possible dissemination,
Sindhi decided in the spring of 1926 to attend the Mutamar-i-Is-
lam Conference taking place during the annual pilgrimage in
Mecca, where he anticipated meeting with Indian Muslim leaders. While waiting for a ship in Italy which could take him to the
Hejaz, he met Jawaharlal Nehru and informed him of his plans.
Nehru's silence on the subject of the meeting suggests that the
Congress leader thought little of them. By the time Sindhi arrived in the Hejaz, the hajj was over. Seeing no real prospect of
advancing his program in Turkey and unable as yet to head back
home, he chose to remain in the holy cities. He abstained from
politics and instead concentrated on his own research and teaching the Quran and the hadith according to Waliullah's precepts.
During the hajj in 1927, he did meet with influential Indian Muslims, only to be thoroughly disappointed by their lack of enthusiasm.[88] Sindhi stayed in the Hejaz for thirteen years, the longest
stretch of his quarter of a century in exile, until his supporters
prevailed upon the colonial government to allow him safe passage
back home.

By the time Sindhi returned to India in 1939, he had recast
the revolutionary ideas absorbed in the Soviet Union in the light
of Waliullah's philosophy and the exigencies of life as a British
colonial subject. He still described the unity of creation, jihad,
and revolution as the three pillars of his ideology, but he renounced violence and offered unconditional support to the British during World War II. He justified this stance by arguing that
European scientific knowledge and military equipment and tech-
niques would help Indians bring about the revolution.[89] Equally
significant was his confession that he had forsaken Islamic universalism to become a dedicated supporter of nationalism. But he

Obaidullah Sindhi, practitioner of transnational jihad, in his later years.

had no love lost for Gandhi, who had "kept the nation back-
ward" through his stubborn insistence on winning Indian independence with a spinning wheel and hand loom. The Congress
had to be overhauled and made into a truly revolutionary party.
Whether Sindhi had, after years of efforts to mobilize outside
help, come to a pragmatic realization of the limits of the possible
or a painful acceptance of the colonial stranglehold on India, he
valued the power of the vote and believed that democracy would
devise a solution for the elusive Hindu-Muslim problem and allow for an understanding with the British.[90]

When it came to the socioeconomic and religious aspects of

his program, Sindhi asked his compatriots to adopt a simple life-style, offer service to the country, and work for Hindu-Muslim unity. He blamed the colonial education system for giving Indians a superficial understanding of politics. Muslim youth were told to read Hindu philosophy and acquire knowledge of modern science and technology. At the same time, Sindhi invited them to join him in bringing about a revolution based on Quranic teachings. Islam would be restored to its full vigor, but it would be different in its "outward appearance." In calling for a modern understanding of the Quran and the hadith, Sindhi noted, "The sooner Muslims adopt this new form of Islam the better will it be for them." In the true Waliullah tradition, he applauded Sufism as containing the "real genius of humanity," whereas Islamic jurisprudence concerned itself with the external form of religion. Both were inseparable parts of Islamic practice that had to be in the spirit of religion rather than purely ceremonial. Only by maintaining a fine balance between form and spirit could Muslims usher in a revolution in the political, social, and economic spheres of life.[91]

In December 1939 Sindhi established the Jamna, Narbada, Sind Sagar Party, whose membership was open to all religious communities. While other parts of India were free to join, the party was to concentrate on Sind, the valley of the Indus, its tributaries controlled from Lahore, and the Gangetic Jamna Plain, including Ajmer and Benares, with Delhi as the center. The party was to peacefully strive for Indian independence within the British Commonwealth, until such time as the Indian federation had become operational. In addition to improving the social and economic conditions of the masses, the party would work for the advancement of the different nationalities residing in India, by promoting democracy, to the "exclusion of racial and religious superiority." Members would be open-minded about the "adoption of [the] European mode of living," in order to introduce advanced industries and teach men and women to serve courageously and defend their motherland. Without "joining the political brotherhood of European nations," India was in danger of succumbing to the forces of reaction.[92]

Yet when it came to giving the party's program ethical and political uniformity, Sindhi had no doubt about the intellectual superiority of Waliullah's philosophy. In his opinion, Waliullah's thought was the culmination of efforts made by Indian Muslim thinkers since the sixteenth century to perfect the philosophy of Ibn al-'Arabi, which Sindhi equated with Vedantism and saw as capable of laying the political foundation for a united India. The inclusion of "Europeanism" in the party's program was aimed at winning over Western-educated Muslims, who Sindhi believed held out more promise for the future than did the products of madrassas. He admitted that in the past he had opposed Indians' becoming Europeanized. But now he wanted to "Europeanize" the peasantry, not in a cultural but in a technical sense, so that it could benefit from modern knowledge and improve agricultural productivity. Toward that end Sindhi recommended writing Urdu in the Roman alphabet, which was easier to read and learn than the Arabic script. This was not an unthinking endorsement of Europe's cultural hegemony or its godless revolutions. Religion was to remain the basis of the party: "We want to instill in our educated youth the Quranic principle of self-sacrifice for the betterment of humanity."[93]

If Sindhi was reviving the substance of Waliullah's philosophy, he was also revolutionizing its form. His hopes of making the Jamna, Narbada, Sind Sagar Party an instrument to serve humanity showed none of the bigotry that had tended to creep into the injunctions of his intellectual preceptor.[94] That Sindhi failed to rally support for his program should not detract from its intellectual contribution to anticolonial Muslim thought at a time when religious tensions were at their height. Although he remained a voice on the margins and conceded that few people had understood him, Sindhi tried to solve India's manifold problems without abandoning jihad in its more expansive meaning of nonviolent ethical struggle. He did not succumb to the inverted prejudice that was the shortcoming of many so-called religious-minded Muslims. His greater objectivity may have had something to do with his remaining outside the rough-and-tumble of the political mainstream, as represented by the Congress and the All-India Muslim League.

By contrast, Azad gave some of his most eloquent depositions on jihad as Islamic ethics in the service of Congress's anticolonial politics. The Indian national struggle was a jihad because the British were waging a war to exterminate Muslims. If Muslims had any spark of faith left in them, they would befriend snakes and scorpions rather than make peace with the British government, he asserted. Referring to the Prophet's constitution at Medina, in which Muslims and non-Muslims were described as one nation, Azad asked Muslims to perform their religious duty by uniting with Hindus.[95] Sindhi did not seek religious justifications for Hindu-Muslim unity. Taking as his premise Indian diversity within a broad framework of unity, he pushed for a revolution in line with Waliullah's philosophy. Although jihad was vital to Azad's and Sindhi's conception of Muslim identity, their variants of anticolonial nationalism left open the possibility of collaboration with a predominantly Hindu Congress. It was not only supporters of inclusionary nationalism who advocated jihad as ethical struggle. Like Sayyid Ahmad Khan and his Aligarh associates, the poet and philosopher Muhammad Iqbal kept his distance from the Gandhi-led Congress, while urging his co-religionists to resist imperialism as a religious duty. It remains to be seen how far Iqbal's mainly poetic invocations of jihad were tainted by religious bigotry owing to his endorsement of the Muslim League's communitarian politics.

The Living Stream: Jihad in Muhammad Iqbal's Thought

In his inimitable way, Muhammad Iqbal conveyed the meaning of jihad as ethical struggle in these two Persian couplets from the *Javidnama* (Pilgrimage to Eternity), which forms part of nine dictums attributed to Hindu rishis.

> O enlightened conscience, infidelity is death
> Jihad with the dead does not befit a warrior of the faith
> One who has faith is alive and at war with himself
> He leaps on himself like a cheetah on a deer[96]

Although he distinguishes the Islamic conception of faith from Hindu idol worship, Iqbal was not denigrating Hinduism. The pungent comment on what jihad entailed for the believer was followed by the damning lines:

> An infidel sitting before an idol alive at heart
> is better than a Muslim asleep in the holy shrine.[97]

An overture to Muslim awakening in the face of colonial subjugation, his poetry is a calculated attempt to rouse believers to conscious action. A lawyer from a middle class Kashmiri family based in the Punjab, Iqbal was trained in the Islamic tradition before being exposed to Western education. He lived in Europe between 1905 and 1908 and had a better grasp of Western philosophy than most of his contemporaries. When it came to global politics, Iqbal shared the anxieties of Muslim anticolonialists about the Western imperialist thrust, and he advocated jihad as a legitimate struggle against foreign aggression. He denied that his ideas on Islamic universalism were influenced by Azad's writings in *Al-Hilal* and insisted rather that they were the result of his own independent reasoning since 1907.[98]

Even if one accepts Iqbal's claim, there can be no question about the broad parallels between the thought of the two men. These were not surprising, given that both wrote some of their most famous works on Islamic universalism in the context of international politics around World War I. Both turned to the Quran for answers and acclaimed jihad in both its expansive and more reductionist forms. But there were subtle differences. Iqbal disagreed with pro-Congress anticolonial nationalists when it came to politics in India. The pettiness fueling Hindu-Muslim tensions in India in general and the Punjab in particular made him skeptical of Congress's inclusionary nationalism. Iqbal's attempts to fashion a Muslim identity and his call for a Muslim state in the northwest of India has earned him a reputation as the poetic visionary of Pakistan.[99] It may be more appropriate to call him by his own chosen designation, *zinda rawad* (the living stream) traversing the Muslim tradition, someone who cast a critical glance at the present, while optimistically harkening to the call for a brighter and more meaningful future.

The thread running through Iqbal's poetic and philosophic corpus is the idea of *khudi* (self or personality), which he uses to refer to the self-conscious and dynamic individual—the man of faith or the perfect human being *(insan-ul-kamal)*. Jihad as inner struggle is intrinsic to the process by which the individual, a mere speck of dust, attains self-awareness and knowledge of reality. The image of the sword of self-consciousness *(khudi)* is a recurrent motif in Iqbal's poetry, as is the use of *la ilaha ilallah*—there is no God but God. Iqbal likens self-awareness to the sharp rim of the sword that cuts through the veils of untruth and self-deception. The self-aware individual can take command of life and throw down a real challenge to the world. Instead of being firm,

Living Stream: Muhammad Iqbal. Courtesy Oxford University Press Pakistan Archives.

like a sword, Muslims were limp in faith, fragile in purpose, and unstable in action. In imitating the West and its godless, soul-destroying materialist culture, Muslim youth had lost their spirituality and vitality.

Without the sword of negation represented by *la,* the life-affirming faith in Allah is rendered meaningless. India's Muslim youth, so intoxicated by the West, were like an empty sheath covered with decorative gilt:

> To your mind God's existence seems unproved
> Your own existence seems not proved to mine.
> He whose Self shines like a gem, alone exists;
> Take heed to it! I do not see yours shine.[100]

Not to question was to capitulate. In an age of political servitude, that translated into complacency. If Muslims had remained self-aware, they would not have been subjugated. A nation with a steely sense of identity could dispense with the sword, but light borrowed from others could neither enlighten nor embolden a nation. The spirit of modern culture permeating Muslim minds was Western to the core. In his lectures on the reconstruction of religious thought in Islam, Iqbal accused Europe of being "the greatest hindrance in the way of man's ethical advancement."[101] Europe's cold-blooded rationalism was devoid of moral values and fostered doubt instead of certitude. The results were hostility, self-serving actions, impatience, and greed. Muslim youth were jealous of one another and had no scruples about selling their souls for a pittance. Iqbal blamed this on their education, which was like a knife shedding blood and spreading sedition. For all the trivial problems it purportedly solved, modern education blinded its recipients to the reality of human life. Western philosophers dismissed religion as an unstable passion. Yet every great act in the world required passionate conviction and a touch of madness. "Even if you are the wisest of men," Iqbal quipped, "do not remain without some madness!"[102] This sentiment he praised is *ishq*, which literally is "love" but whose true meaning is closer to "intuition," the creative power that energizes and transforms.

Though distinct from pure reason, *ishq*, God-given intuition, should not be confused with antirationalism. Iqbal, who has been credited with giving the word a new meaning, considered the idea of love as creative energy to be firmly rooted in the Islamic mystical tradition.[103] From Al-Ghazali to Azad, Muslims of a mystical bent identified love as the key to knowledge of God. Iqbal's originality lay in giving poetic expression to love of God as the driving force in a believer's quest for self-knowledge. But knowledge of the self was meaningless unless it sought to transform the world. Iqbal, who deplored the life-denying teachings of the Sufis, noted that Muslims did not know the difference between self-abnegation *(faqr)* and otherworldliness. Withdrawal from the turmoil of life is not spirituality. True spirituality is an affirmation of life and a means of correcting the world. Abnegation is a feat born of inner struggle. Like the sword of negation, it paves the way for affirmation.

If Westerners were wary of the word *Islam,* they could call it *faqr,* which was its other name. *Faqr* was impossible without love, which Iqbal defined as freedom and revolution. While confessing love for God, Muslims were worshipping idols. Since they loved idols, why did Muslims disapprove of the Brahmans? Muslims were letting the West place its new gods in the house of Allah! Even the temple deities were sympathetic to the Kaaba's complaint.[104] He regretted being born in an age deprived of the fire of love. And while it made him restless as a flame, this state of dissatisfaction was immeasurably better than the self-contentment of the youth fed on spells and fiction in schools. Iqbal placed a high premium on education. But the education he favored was to be found in neither Western institutions nor Muslim madrassas:

> Love is dead in the West, owing to its irreligious thought;
> Reason is enslaved in the East, owing to incoherency of
> ideas.[105]

Iqbal saw his poetry as an elucidation of the Quran, which he believed held all the answers to meet the challenges of the present. Scholars and poets had to help Muslims internalize the message of the Quran. Revelation could inspire passionate conviction, whereas a purely intellectual outlook generated only fear and doubt—the characteristics of a defeated and subjugated people:

> In slavery, neither swords nor designs are of use,
> But if there is certainty of faith, chains are broken.
> Can anyone assess the strength of his arm?
> One look from the true Muslim can change fate. . .
> Certitude, action, and love of triumph in the world,
> These are the swords of men in the life of jihad.[106]

Iqbal identified Shah Waliullah as "the first Muslim who felt the urge of a new spirit" and inspired Indian Muslims to the essential jihad.[107] In keeping with his view that the Quranic emphasis was on deeds, rather than on the ideal, he singled out Shah Ismail Shaheed as the one truly great scholar India had produced who had combined a life of scholarship with action, ultimately sacrificing his life in a jihad against the infidels. He hailed Jamaluddin al-Afghani as a "living link between the past and the future," who "fully realized the immensity of the task" with his "deep insight into the inner meaning of the history of Muslim thought and life." The Islamic world would have been on "a much more solid ground today," if only the "indefatigable" Afghani had not dissipated his energy but had instead "devoted" himself "entirely to Islam as a system of human belief and conduct."[108] What troubled Iqbal was that he could not find one self-aware Muslim in India who could approximate Afghani's zeal, far less emulate Shah Ismail's commitment to a life of jihad. The Sufis were absorbed in contemplation of the unknown, the worldly mullah had turned the sharia into a stream of disconnected words, and contemporary poets were more dead than alive:

I cannot see the man of jihad anywhere
In whose veins runs force of character.[109]

A male chauvinist who had little use for women except as
mothers, Iqbal was surprised to find the spirit of struggle in a
young Muslim girl, Fatima bin Abdullah, who was killed during
the Balkan War of 1912 while serving water to the soldiers. He
marveled at her courage—what a jihad she had fought, without
a sword! Iqbal envisaged the birth of a new nation near her
grave.[110] To stress the importance of effectively countering Western imperialism, Iqbal in several other poems extolled the valor of
Muslims fighting the Europeans. In the *Javidnama,* his opening
question to Jalaluddin Rumi during an imagined spiritual quest
through space was whether the world was "some prey and we the
huntsmen, or are we prisoners, utterly forgotten?"[111]

Patterned on the Prophet's ascension to the heavens, the poet's
journey through the different levels of heavenly space represents
his mature thought about the nature of life as an ethical struggle
to be human. Even before his views crystallized in the *Javidnama,*
Iqbal had provided important glimpses into what he considered
the most acceptable Muslim response to the age of Western empire. In one of his longer poems, *Khizr-i-Rah,* he converses with
Khizr—the eternal prophet associated with the green of everlast-
ing freshness who guides seafarers and searchers after truth with
pearls of divine wisdom. In response to Iqbal's question, Khizr
comments that subjugation to any other than God is worse than
unbelief. Democracy and freedom, the two pillars of capitalism,
are designed to hoodwink the subjugated peoples of Asia. Muslims' deliverance lies in abandonment of politics and protection
of Islam. These would require Muslim unity from the shores of
the Nile to Kashgar (in other words, from Africa to Turkey).[112] In
a later encounter, Khizr proposes a remedy for European imperialism that cuts like a sword:

An infidel is lost in the skies;
The skies are lost in a true Muslim.[113]

In brazenly drawing this distinction between the believer and the nonbeliever, Iqbal sets a standard for Muslim identity that, as he was the first to concede, was impossible to realize in an age of political servitude. Through his emotional outpourings on the inherent potential of a free Muslim, he turns the spotlight on the more important fault lines between the Islamic and the Judeo-Christian worlds. In criticizing Europe's arrogant imperialists for riding roughshod over the Muslim world, Iqbal was redefining, not closing, the debate with the West. The deliberately exclusionary overtones of his message to Muslims are counterbalanced by a willed engagement with the wider world. Nothing demonstrates this better than his imaginary escapade through seven levels of space in the *Javidnama,* where he meets up with some of the greatest figures in human history. In evidence of his open-mindedness to other religious traditions, Iqbal first stops on the moon, where he meets a Hindu sage, the Buddha, and Zoroaster. The exchanges reassure him that regardless of differences in religious tradition, human beings are locked in a common quest for an ethical existence in conformity with God's commands. But this realization serves only to affirm his faith in the Quran as the ultimate answer to humanity's ills.

The next stage of the heavenly journey takes him to the planet Mercury, where he rubs shoulders with Jamaluddin al-Afghani and the Turkish reformer Halim Pasha. Afghani asks him about the state of the Muslim world. Assuming the form of the *zinda rawad,* the living stream, Iqbal replies that although the purpose of the *ummah* is to eliminate untruth, Muslims are agitated over religion and nationhood. Weakness of faith has killed their spirit and they have lost all hope in Islam. Whether Turk, Iranian, or Arab, all are subjugated to foreign ideas, and their necks are in foreign nooses. If imperialism has imprisoned the Muslim self, socialism has killed both religion and nation. Afghani blames Muslim abasement on the West's territorial nationalism and expounds on the ideal Islamic state. Halim Pasha predicts that the West is on the verge of killing itself with its own sword. But Muslims are in no position to seize the opportunity. The modernizing reforms of Mustafa Kemal Pasha (Atatürk) in Turkey are old and lifeless ideas with no future, and the mullah is unfamiliar with God and treats the Quran as an epic.[114]

In the remaining stages of the spiritual journey, Iqbal converses with several historical luminaries, including Tolstoy, Ghalib, and the great Persian Sufi martyr Mansur al-Hallaj. From Tolstoy Iqbal learns the extent of Christianity's failures in Europe and vows to combat atheistic materialism. Ghalib teaches him how to bear witness to new worlds in the making:

> To create is to give existence its due
> And to imbue it with the passion to move forward—
> This is the beginning and God's mercy the end.[115]

Elaborating on the point, Hallaj notes that wherever a world is astir with a desire to come alive, we sense either a manifestation of the Prophet or something in search of his spirit. True love of the Prophet and of God requires following their teachings and not distorting them like the Sufi who after witnessing the divine presence seals his lips and suspends his breath:

> He did not establish the commands of God in the world;
> He ate the barley bread but did not adopt the courage of
> the Prophet;
> He found the *khanqa* but stayed away from the Battle of
> Khyber
> If you have any sign of truth in you, go search the world—

Your fate will follow the methods you adopt.
The present is challenging you: Prove God to this *kafir*.[116]

Iqbal asks how he can prove God's existence. With love or conquest, proclaims Hallaj. But since love of God manifests itself in mercy, it has a higher status than conquest and is more easily attained by the passionate lover than the pious worshipper. True knowledge of God is not attained through annihilation, as the mystics wrongly believe, but through self-awareness in the presence of the divine. These encounters confirm Iqbal's belief in the individual's potential to re-create the world through internal and external jihad. But the conclusion only heightens his anxiety, aware as he is of his own limited capacities, as well as those of his enslaved and benighted co-religionists. The confessions of Satan underline the difficulties Iqbal anticipates in arousing Muslims and, through them, humanity as a whole to create a just and orderly world. Man is only too eager to be hunted, the devil complains. He prefers a real challenge: "Oh God, give me one live man of truth, so that I may enjoy the taste of defeat."[117]

The tension between Iqbal's romantic faith in a revitalized Islam capable of confronting Western modernity and his despair at the abysmal state of Muslims gives an explosive unity to his poetic corpus. He does not attribute Islam's malaise to intellectual stagnation but to the loss of the Muslim will to struggle against adversity. In his poem "Hindi Islam," Iqbal dismissed the idea that religious freedom was restricted to saying prayers and performing rituals. Muslims needed sovereignty and power to spread Islam's teachings in the world but had accepted the conditions of servitude instead. The Muslim defeat was complete: Sufis had lost their warlike spirit, and meanwhile the ulema, reluctant out of deference to foreign rulers to assert Islamic truths, were busy instigating sectarian battles.[118]

Islam could become a force again if a Mahdi led a revolution to spread humaneness and decency in all walks of life. But there was no saying when a true Mahdi might appear. So Iqbal settled for an imam who could turn Muslims away from the immorality of Western culture and make them thirst for martyrdom. He applauded the war between Islam and unbelief as one between truth and untruth. A slave could not understand the joy a warrior found in the war for truth.[119] It would be facile to interpret that enthusiasm as jingoism. Although armed struggle was part of his repertoire on jihad, he was more focused on the internal jihad—the struggle with the self. He realized that armed jihad without the self-strengthening achieved through leading an ethical life had no religious meaning. In one of his most popular poems, Iqbal defines a believing Muslim *(momin)* as possessing four characteristics—strength, mercy, purity, and heavenly guidance. Such a Muslim shuns temporal gods such as territorial nationalism and attacks the enemy like a fearsome storm, while showing kindness and mercy to friends.[120]

An attachment to Muslim identity did not blind Iqbal to the wider matrix of human relationships:

> A man of God is neither of the East nor the West,
> My home is not a city, nor a clime.
> I always tell what seems to me the truth
> I am neither a mosque's fool nor culture's slave.[121]

Though he defies easy categorization, Iqbal can be described as an Islamic global humanist who was uncomfortable with the limitations of territorial nationalism:

> Thou art yet region-bound
> Transcend the limits of space

Transcend the narrow climes
Of the East and the West
. . . . .
With a mountain-cleaving assault
Bridging the East and West
Despise all defences,
And become a sheathless sword
Thy imam is unabsorbed
Thy prayer is uninspired,
Forsake an imam like him,
Forsake a prayer like this.[122]

Although he glorified Islam, Iqbal remained an unrelenting critic of ranting mullahs who distorted religion and spread hatred. He once scoffed at the suggestion of some Muslim divines that the community should suspend trade relations with Hindus who dealt in impure things, by sarcastically noting that the faithful had nothing to worry about, for they could always find Muslim wine sellers.[123] Instead of heeding the mullahs, Muslims must listen to their own hearts. *Ijtihad,* the jihad of the mind, was the moving principle of Islam.[124] It demanded concentrated endeavor and the courage of a lover of truth, who was the true warrior of the faith. Subjugation to Western imperialism had stripped Muslims of courage and love. Without an inner struggle Muslims could not recover the ethical virtues embodied in the Quranic revelation. Until then, jihad as armed struggle would be a distant dream for believers but, ironically enough, provide a convenient pretext for continued Western aggression against Muslims. In a poem titled "Jihad," Iqbal poignantly sums up the Muslim anticolonial plaint:

To protect the aura and power of untruth,
Europe is drowned in armaments from shoulder to waist.

We ask the sheikh overawed by the church,
If for the East war is unhallowed, is not war unhallowed for
   the West?
And if your goal is truth, is this the right road:
The West's faults glossed over and Islam held to so strict an
   account?[125]

6

Islam Subverted?
Jihad as Terrorism

In trying to retrieve the notion of jihad from the grip of defeatism, anticolonial Muslims sparked a religious and political debate whose effects were felt well beyond the subcontinent. Iqbal, pointing an accusing finger at Muslims who had "lost the taste for death," made a wry comment on the hypocrisy of Western imperialism, "drowned in armaments," that inspired the Islamic revivalist agenda of Abul Ala Mawdudi and found echoes in the writings of the Egyptian political activist Sayyid Qutb (1906–1966). Along with Ibn Taymiyya, Mawdudi and Qutb are considered the intellectual forebears of "Muslim fundamentalism."[1] Authors tracing the roots of "Islamic terrorism" have seized on Mawdudi's and Qutb's definitions of *jihad* as authoritative, glossing over the contested interpretations of the word throughout Muslim history.

Temporally specific in its uses, the idea of jihad has been variously interpreted in Muslim thought and practice. The prevalence of its derivative in the Urdu phrase *jihd-o-jihad* in everyday parlance in the subcontinent testifies to the meanings of *jihad* as both an inner and an outer struggle. *Jihad*'s myriad significations in the Muslim world are borne out by examples like the Ministry of Jihad for Agriculture in Iran and the use of the word in development terminology, especially relating to eradicating poverty and illiteracy. Dismissing these as aberrations from the concept's primary meaning in the heartlands of Islam is a feeble excuse for not addressing this complexity. The emphasis on the spread of Islam through the sword makes it all the more important to assess the meaning and practice of jihad in the conquered territories. Modern technology and economic globalization have made the old idea of centers of authority with dependent peripheries untenable. Al Qaeda is fighting a jihad in the Middle East from Afghanistan and the autonomous northwestern regions of Pakistan. Whether "holy war achieves its purest Islamic form" in the Central and South Asian periphery is a debatable proposition. But there can be no denying the emphasis that Al Qaeda places on the ethical nature of its struggle against the enemies of Islam.[2]

Instead of debating whether jihad is primarily warfare or a spiritual struggle, it is intellectually more challenging to contend with its multiple meanings in Muslim thought and practice.[3] Al Qaeda's ethical claims are based on selective appropriations of the Islamic tradition that are disputed by other Muslims. In that sense, Osama bin Laden has thrown down the gauntlet not to the West but to his co-religionists. The crucial issue facing Muslims is not that Islam has been "hijacked" by modern-day Kharajites, but the more difficult one of Muslims' clarifying their understanding of this key concept in Islam. The rush to explain jihad after the attacks on the United States has generated a veritable industry in both print and cyberspace, whose main victim has been the idea itself. Contrasting claims about the purely spiritual or the primarily aggressive connotations of jihad have prevented a nuanced understanding of its multiple meanings in Muslim thought and practice. Often narrowly policy-oriented in approach, arguments based on a reductive view of jihad make only superficial references to the Quran. The current focus of these works on Al Qaeda's brand of "holy war" obscures the historical links between the ideologues of radical Islam and anticolonial nationalists in South Asia and the Middle East.

The silences and ambivalences in Muslim reactions to the September 11 attacks on the United States may seem unfathomable unless we take into account the nexus between nationalism, informed by anticolonial sentiment, and Islamic political radicalism. Although no neat equivalence exists between these two dynamics, it is important to clarify their commonalities and differences.[4] While sharing a distaste for Western imperialism, they avoid making a rigid separation between worldly and religious points of view. Unlinking the anticolonial from the religious impulse, in the interest of sustaining the dichotomy between Islam and secularism, has prevented an understanding of the psychological and political fault lines running through Muslim societies. What Samuel Huntington has infamously described as the "clash of civilizations" is more aptly characterized as a problem of mutual incomprehension.[5] As if the misperceptions based on a long and contentious history between the Judeo-Christian world and Islam were not enough, the American-led "war on terror" targeting Afghanistan and Iraq has inflamed a significant segment of Muslim opinion. Only by going beyond the limited and sterile dichotomy between the religious and the secular is it possible to discern the contours of the Muslim disenchantment.

Mawdudi's radical reformulation of jihad was based on selective appropriations of the thought of some of his worthier intellectual forerunners in the subcontinent. But he differed from them as well as from Islamic traditionalists in important ways. In rejecting the authority of traditional interpretations of the Quran, Mawdudi, like Qutb, was following in the footsteps of modernist Muslims like Sayyid Ahmad Khan and Muhammad Abduh. The centrality for Mawdudi of the nation-state underscores the extent to which his engagement with the "secular" rivals that of any of his secular opponents. It was this aspect of his thought and politics which influenced militant Islamic concepts of jihad in the postcolonial period. By deftly conflating the religious and the secular, Mawdudi transformed the ethical and political dimensions of the contemporary discourse and practice of jihad in South Asia. That is why reasserting the distinction between the greater and the lesser jihad cannot adequately address the ethical challenges posed by the politics of Islamic militancy. Instead of dwelling on its ethics or lack thereof, it is more important to ask what kind of ethics the militants are promoting and to what degree it has the sanction of other Muslims.

Beyond Disbelief: Mawdudi on Jihad

Sayyid Abul Ala Mawdudi was born in Aurangabad, Hyderabad Deccan, into a family associated with the Chishti Sufi order. After completing his early education at home and at a local seminary under the tutelage of Deobandi ulema, he graduated from the Fatihpuri madrassa in Delhi. His literary skills drew him to journalism at the age of twelve. He participated in the Khilafat and noncooperation movement and joined a secret society working to dislodge the colonial government. During the *hijrat* movement, Mawdudi considered emigrating to Afghanistan but thought better of it. Instead, he remained in India, where he gave expression to his anticolonial and Islamic universalist sentiments in the newspapers.[6]

The concept of jihad engaged Mawdudi's attention very early on, but the demands of a journalistic career prevented him from setting down his thoughts on the subject. All this changed with the assassination on 23 December 1926 of Swami Shradhanand in Delhi at the hands of a Muslim named Abdur Rashid. Hindu propagandists claimed that Islam enjoined Muslims to murder unbelievers as a pious duty. Some Hindus baldly asserted that there could be no peace on earth unless the Quran was banned. Such "erroneous and ill-founded charges," Mawdudi complained, had led even Gandhi to say that "Islam was born in an atmosphere of violence" where the sword was paramount and that it was still a little too much in evidence among Indian Muslims.[7] Gandhi later issued a retraction in *Young India:* "The more I study the more I discover that the strength of Islam does not lie in the sword."[8] But the Mahatma's initial statement rankled with Mawdudi. It seemed to corroborate the depiction by the Hindu reformist Arya Samaj of Islam as an aggressive religion whose followers were intent on looting, arson, and rape. In 1924 a bookseller in Lahore called Rajpal had published an anonymous tract provocatively entitled *Rangila Rasul* (The Playboy Prophet). It noted that whereas the founder of the Arya Samaj, Swami Dayanand, preached celibacy, the life and faith of the Prophet of Islam were marked by relationships with women.[9] Aided by the bigotry of the provincial press, communitarian hostility in the Punjab reached new heights.[10]

This was the historical context that shaped Mawdudi's exclusionary discourse on Indian Muslim identity. Eager to draw the external boundaries of Muslim identity, he had no qualms about stretching the logic of the Islamic message to meet the needs of the situation at hand. He attributed Hindu attacks on Islam to Western attempts to subjugate Muslims. In February 1927 he began writing an essay on jihad, which was published in the Jamiat-ul-Ulema-i-Hind's paper, *Al-Jamiat,* in several installments, before being abruptly discontinued. The complete essay was printed in September 1927 as *Al-Jihad fi-ul Islam.*[11] Directed more at the West than at the Hindus who had precipitated its writing, it is the earliest source on Mawdudi's concept of jihad. Mawdudi found it remarkable that the image of Islam as a religion of the sword started gaining prominence from the moment the dragon of Western expansionism began devouring the weak and infirm nations of the world. The West, being in self-denial about its tyrannical acts and anxious to escape the antipathy and hatred that they had created, had succeeded in shifting the blame to Islam because Western dominance extended to controlling the production of knowledge. Consequently, the concept of Islamic jihad had been thoroughly distorted, he thought, and the distortion accepted wholesale, without investigation. During the nineteenth and the twentieth centuries, Muslims had repeatedly tried to refute the false interpretation of jihad. But they had either adopted the position of apologist or, Mawdudi said, passed over certain aspects of Islam to curry favor with the West. It was unacceptable to tinker with Islamic teachings merely to satisfy others.[12]

That critique of Muslim "apologists" has earned Mawdudi the criticism of scholars who doubt that jihad was ever interpreted as anything nobler than warfare against infidels.[13] Like anticolonial Muslims, he did not reject jihad as armed conflict, but he denied the allegation that Islam taught its followers to kill. He quoted the Quranic verse (5:32): "If anyone slay a person unless it be for murder or for spreading mischief in the land, it would be as if he slew the whole people: and if anyone saved a life, it would be as if he saved the life of the whole people." The right to life is the first law of human society, and no religion preached the killing of one person by another, Mawdudi asserted. Unlike secular laws, which employ coercive measures to prevent people from killing, Islam creates revulsion for killing in the hearts of men.[14] If "apologetics" is taken to mean glorifying one's own religion, Mawdudi can be reproached for saying that Islamic teachings are more humane than the Sermon on the Mount and the message of *ahimsa*. Like Azad, he maintained that *haq* (truth or justice), was more sacrosanct in Islam than human life. To kill a human being who murders or causes social disruption *(fitna)* is just. Islam, as a practical code for living based on freedom of conscience, justifies the shedding of blood to establish peace and root out evil. Even Christianity modified the ban against killing once Christians gained political power. However peaceful the message of Hinduism, Manu's laws prescribe death to those who offend against custom. The Quranic law of *qisas* not only protects the individual from violence but corrects the greed and arrogance of the collective. Individual sedition affects a few, but that of the collective creates havoc among nations through economic, political, and spiritual exploitation.[15]

War against oppression becomes an ethical imperative when verbal persuasion fails to stop the community from engaging in evil and malicious practices. True faith demands that the friend of humanity should take up the sword and should not rest until the rights of God's creation have been restored. To oppose shedding an oppressor's blood on idealistic grounds is sheer cowardice—a policy of inaction incapable of securing the world against tyranny and oppression. By turning a war against injustice into a war for God, Mawdudi conflates a just war with *jihad fi sabil allah,* making no distinction between the greater and the lesser jihad or, for that matter, between jihad and *qital.* The two are indistinguishable in his mind when the battle is against disbelief, the source of moral insensitivity and inhumanity. In one example of the literalism that characterizes quantitative notions of virtue and goodness in his view of Islam, Mawdudi spoke of "this war for the truth in which staying awake one night is equivalent to staying awake for a thousand nights to pray and for which fighting resolutely on the battlefield is greater than staying at home and praying for sixty years." Tyranny was rife because Muslims had abandoned jihad. Revealing his anticolonial agenda, Mawdudi asserted that a nation incapable of resisting external domination was devoid of self-respect and guilty of inflicting oppression *(zulm)* on itself. In order to prosper, not perish, nations must cultivate the spirit of self-sacrifice; otherwise they will be ruled by outsiders, and that is the lowest form of existence. Spiritual and mental subjugation in a sense precede physical and material conquest, because a people strong in spirit and mind could never allow themselves to be ruled by others.[16] He attacked the nineteenth-century modernist Indian Muslim view of a defensive jihad. The success of Islam as a world religion lay in its use of the sword—not to compel people to convert, but to tear away the veil from their understanding, so that they voluntarily accepted its teachings. Just as it was wrong to say that Islam had by the sword forced people to become Muslims, it was incorrect to say that the sword had no role in its propagation. The truth lay somewhere in between. No civilization in history had established itself in which both the power of the sword and the power of preaching had not played a vital part.[17]

In his widely quoted lecture "Jihad in Islam" Mawdudi chided the West for "conjur[ing] up the vision of a marching band of religious fanatics with savage beards and fiery eyes brandishing drawn swords and attacking the infidels wherever they meet them and pressing them under the edge of the sword for the recital of the *Kalima*." It was paradoxical that those now "pillaging" the world for markets and raw materials, "armed to the teeth with all kinds of deadly weapons," were berating Muslims for their blood-stained past. Whatever the Muslims may have done was "now part of history," but "their deeds are a present matter witnessed by the world day and night." Asia, Africa, Europe, and America—"which portion of this planet has been spared from blood-bath resulting from their unholy war?" He derided Muslim "apologists" for taking the Western depiction of jihad as religious mania to heart: "Sir, what do we know of war and slaughter? We are pacifist preachers like the mendicants and religious divines. To refute certain religious beliefs and convert the people to

some other faith instead, that is the be-all and end-all of our enthusiasm."[18]

Firing cannons and shooting guns was now the sole privilege
of the British, while jihad for Muslims meant "wagging tongues
and scratching . . . pens." But this was mere political expediency.
The real obstacle to understanding jihad as "Holy War for the
Cause of God" was the mistaken idea that Islam is a religion and
Muslims a nation in the conventional sense. Islam is "a revolutionary ideology" which seeks to "alter the social order of the
whole world and rebuild it in conformity with its own tenets
and ideals." Concerned with "the welfare of mankind," Muslims
aimed to "destroy all States and Governments" opposed to the
ideology of Islam. Jihad is the composite term for establishing an
ideological state that can revolutionize the mental and practical
outlook of humankind. All work done for the well-being of humanity with "perfect sincerity" is "an act in the way of God."
Making no distinction of class, race, nation, or country, the International Revolutionary Party of Islam (Hezbollah) captures
state power because "no party which believes in the validity and
righteousness of its own ideology can live . . . under a system different from its own."[19]

Support for God's party was the true measure of a Muslim's
faith. Obeying laws inimical to Islam, even if they have been
made by a Muslim government, was evidence of lack of faith and
made one complicitous in "upholding . . . un-Islamic doctrines."
With this scarcely veiled threat against Muslims disagreeing with
his Islamic ideology, Mawdudi asserted that jihad has both offensive and defensive dimensions. It can be seen as offensive in that
"the Muslim Party assaults the rule of an opposing ideology," and
"defensive" in that it is "constrained to capture State power" to
establish the principles of Islam. Instead of coercing people to
abandon their un-Islamic ways, the party of God "abolishes the

government which sustains these principles." The Islamic idea of war was unlike the temporal wars of Western imperialism. Although both conquer other countries, "an elemental difference" existed, akin to the space between heaven and earth. As Iqbal had put it: "Both fly in space, yet the world of the Eagle is far removed from that of the Crow."[20]

A political practitioner and a journalist by training, Mawdudi may have lacked the uplifting quality of Iqbal's poetic and philosophic vision or the depths of Azad's scholarship. But he made up for it by offering a piercing critique of Muslim societies and their hapless servitude to Western imperialism.[21] He attributed the demise of the Ottoman caliphate to the narrow calculations of Turkish and Arab nationalists. Calling for God's government to replace the tyrannical government of man over man, Mawdudi's writings and speeches aimed to help Muslims deal with the dichotomy between the precepts of Islam and their political and cultural subjugation. That so few rallied to the banner of the Jamaat-i-Islami, which Mawdudi founded in 1941, lent greater force to his condemnation of their *jahaliya,* a term for pre-Islamic Arabia, but which he used to refer to anything not conforming to his idea of Islam.

His belief that Islam could not borrow from lesser civilizations shows up Mawdudi as a cultural exclusivist.[22] The most antidemocratic characteristic of this uncompromising attitude lies in the refusal to coexist with difference. As the antithesis of Islam, *jahaliya* justified a jihad to bring about a revolution in the mental and emotional outlook of humankind. Mawdudi saw a relationship between pagan and Western civilizations in their practice of polytheism. A civilization is as good as its ethics. The Islamic worldview based on God's sovereignty over the universe was ethically superior to those of other civilizations. Unfortunately, Muslims had reverted to *jahaliya* after the establishment of the Umayyad dynasty. This amounted to a counterrevolution. But because the opportunistic state paid lip service to the tenets of Islam, Muslims refused to disturb the status quo. The result of this disingenuousness was that instead of the teachings of Islam, the art, literature, and philosophy of *jahaliya* had taken hold of Muslim consciousness. Dance, music, and painting, in Mawdudi's estimation, were *jahaliya* art and the source of social discord. Muslims were treading the path of moral degeneration because some ulema permitted polytheism to parade as Islam. In spite of such worldly corruption, elements of Islam's ethical teachings survived, and for that reason Muslim nations always maintained a higher moral status than non-Muslim ones. Individual Muslims continued to practice true Islam, but individual piety was not enough. An organized collective approach was needed to restore Islam to a state of purity.[23]

This is where the role of a *mujaddid*—a renewer of faith—acquires significance for Mawdudi. He dismissed the popular view that *mujaddids* appeared only at the beginning or end of the century. They had existed in all periods of Muslim history and often coexisted in time. An aspirant to the position, Mawdudi differentiated between a partial *mujaddid* and the promised Mahdi. A partial *mujaddid* was capable of assessing the contemporary political situation and determining what was Islamic and un-Islamic. He had to be prepared to seize political power and establish an Islamic system, not just in one country but the world over. Mawdudi conceded that the idea of the Mahdi had contributed to laxity of morals among ordinary people—or at least no good had come from the vision of the Mahdi as a mystic with beads in hand who would wage jihad against the enemy's planes and tanks with the help of a mysterious spiritual force. In actuality, the Mahdi would be the "most modern of the modernists" and would be attacked by the religious leaders of the day. Like other revolutionary leaders, he would initiate a powerful movement for cultural and political reform. This would enable him to seize power and establish a state based on Islam and the latest scientific knowledge.[24]

Among the *mujaddids* whom Mawdudi singled out for praise were Taymiyya, Ahmad Sirhandi, and Waliullah. Living in an age of Mongol ascendancy and the devastation of Muslim lands, Taymiyya presented Islam in commonsensical terms to ordinary people. Sirhandi was the savior of Islam in India at a time when it was being maligned and was contaminated by Akbar's pro-Hindu policies. Waliullah was a *mujaddid* worthy of emulation, for he had carried out the most thorough critique of Indian Muslim religious practices. Even though he had not wielded the sword, his successors had made up for the omission. Shah Ismail and Sayyid Ahmad Barelvi, though not *mujaddids,* had propagated Waliullah's thought. Lacking interest in material and worldly matters, they pursued *jihad fi sabil allah.* Their army was exemplary in discipline and in its regard for the Islamic laws of war. The soldiers did not mistreat women or endanger any life unnecessarily. These men sat on horseback during the day and on the prayer mat at night. When a government was formed, a life of simplicity and poverty was the norm. There was complete equality for all. A consultative assembly dispensed advice, and enforced justice in accordance with the sharia.[25]

Mawdudi noted how Muslims in the subcontinent revered the mujahideen and praised their sacrifices. But not delving into the reasons for the failure of this quintessential example of *jihad fi sabil allah* would encourage the line of thinking of the Aligarh school—namely, that there was no place for religious reform and piety, much less jihad, under British rule. This assumption was patently false. Tracing the historical reasons for the debacle, Mawdudi noted that all the work by reformists from Sirhandi to Waliullah to correct Sufi practices had been in vain: deviations had been unwittingly reintroduced. Even these two giants of Muslim religious thought could not resist proclaiming themselves *qutb,* the towering spiritual masters of their time. In doing so, they revived the very master-disciple system that their reforms had discredited. They used careless language to describe their mystical experiences. Mawdudi did not allude to the possibility that Sirhandi and Waliullah, and Sayyid Ahmad after them, chose not to undercut the popular beliefs that gave them mystical stature.

Mawdudi thought that Sayyid Ahmad and Shah Ismail had erred on a more practical level, in not preparing the tribesmen for the Islamic revolution. They had naively assumed that since the Pathans were suffering under non-Muslim rule, they would welcome an Islamic government. What ultimately doomed the cause was the gross military imbalance between Sayyid Ahmad's followers and European power. Libraries in Europe were overflowing with books by philosophers, scientists, and thinkers whose critiques of ancient society had brought a revolution in mental attitudes. Waliullah and his sons had written books for a small circle of people. In India the debate on philosophy, ethics, collective life, politics, and economics remained in the early stages. In Europe entire systems were constructed on the basis of such debates. Scientific discoveries transformed the balance decisively. New discoveries in engineering and modes of waging war had made the French Revolution and the industrial revolution possible. It had not occurred to Sayyid Ahmad and Shah Ismail to send a delegation of ulema to Europe to find out the reasons for its rapid strides in scientific knowledge. Nor had they realized that the English and not the Sikhs posed the real threat to Islam in India.

The failure of the jihad proved that religious reform cannot be carried out simply by reviving the sharia. A comprehensive Islamic movement is needed based on the exercise of *ijtihad.* Modern *jahaliya* had created new problems for which the Quran and the sunna provided answers. Muslims should avoid restricting themselves to the doctrines of any one scholar from the past. A

modern *mujaddid* could not be a replica of the prophets of yes-
teryear. He might even be devoid of elementary signs of piety.
Those who made outward displays of piety or made uncorroborated claims to mystical experience were like counterfeiters. The
Indian Sufi tradition abounded in examples of localized cults pitting their own sovereignty against that of God. Mawdudi warned
Muslims not to be hoodwinked by such men. Adopting the
Sunni attitude of postponing moral judgment, he held that anyone capable of engaging in religious reform should leave it to
God to decide whether that work was meritorious or not. He
considered Sirhandi and Waliullah *mujaddids* because of their
work but did not believe in their claims to be God's anointed.
Mawdudi strongly denied Maulana Sulaiman Nadwi's allegation
that he was posing as a *mujaddid* and intended to declare himself
a Mahdi.[26]

The doubt has remained in the minds of those who have taken
exception to his claim to be an authoritative interpreter of Islam.
Conservative ulema object to his rejection of traditional authority. The liberal intelligentsia is repelled by the cultural exclusivity
and authoritarianism inherent in his thought. But there was some
overlap in the ideas of Mawdudi and his Muslim opponents. His
extended essay on jihad impressed Iqbal, who thought he had
discovered a young scholar capable of revising the sharia to meet
the demands of the modern age. Apart from helping Mawdudi
get a job in Gurdaspur, Iqbal is said to have recommended him as
imam of the Badshahi Mosque in Lahore. The two met toward
the end of 1937 and considered collaborating on a systematic reform of Islamic law.[27]

The project was aborted with Iqbal's death in 1938, fueling
misconceptions about his affinity with Mawdudi. Some Western
scholars find no difference between the poet of the East and the
ideologue of radical Islam. Conflating the two is to misinform
and mislead. Where the entire thrust of Iqbal's thought was on

the dynamic individual using the right of independent judgment, Mawdudi reposed that authority in a *mujaddid*. Iqbal posed the paradox of being a Muslim in a witty couplet:

The religious bigot considers me an infidel
And the infidel deems me to be a Muslim![28]

Mawdudi had a sterner conception of Muslim identity. Being a Muslim was not an inborn characteristic but a state attained by striving for Islamic knowledge.[29] Like Iqbal, Mawdudi considered faith to be more important than life itself. But unlike this ideo-logue who could not countenance a believer's doubt, Iqbal, the poet-philosopher, had emphasized the importance of the initial negation in the Muslim profession *la ilaha ilallah*. An affirmation of faith after sincere doubt is qualitatively different from ideolog-ical indoctrination drawing on a particular view of Islam.

After a cursory study of Marxism, Mawdudi concluded that there was no room for disagreement in a revolutionary program. An astute reader of his times, he saw the modern state as the key to the realization of his ultimate aims. He interpreted *din* as gov-ernment, the sharia as its law, and worship as submission through obedience to the law. Acceptance of a ruler entailed submitting to the sovereign's religion and obeying his laws. A human being can-not follow two religions. To believe in divinity and also obey temporal law constituted polytheism, because the dual allegiance caused confusion between the ruler's law and God's sharia. The prayers of a Muslim who does not conform to the sharia are arti-ficial, because it is actions that count, and not belief. No scope is left for God's religion where democracy or territorial nationalism is worshipped as *din*.

Until God's laws were enforced in the courts and his sover-eignty recognized, the practice of Islam in India was pure self-de-ception. Mawdudi marshaled Quranic verses in support of his arguments, but he conveniently overlooked the fact that most of them proclaim the supremacy of God rather than reject the legitimacy of diversity in religious practices. He was closer to the mark in his assertion that like any other religion, Islam is not satisfied with the mere declaration of faith or the demonstration of ritual piety. Islam left Muslims with no alternative but to wage jihad to establish God's government on earth:

> This is the litmus test for the truth or certitude of your faith. If your certitude is genuine, then you will not be able to sleep peacefully being part of another *din*. To follow Islam and abide by the norms of another religion would mean that every moment in life would be like sleeping on a bed of thorns, food would be like poison, and the desire to establish God's religion would be an all-consuming desire. But if one was at peace co-existing with another *din*, then one would not be a *momin*, no matter how many genuine prayers and other forms of worship one might perform or [how much] Islamic philosophy one might expound.

Such a stark distinction between Muslims and nonbelievers excludes the majority of the faithful from Mawdudi's brand of Islam. He was contemptuous of Muslim hypocrites who fought jihads for democracy: "If such people consider themselves to be Muslims, they are grossly mistaken . . . One cannot subscribe to one religion and work to establish another one."[30]

There is no denying the originality of Mawdudi's contribution to the contemporary discourse on jihad. His understanding of Islam's mission to save humanity from moral and cultural depravity through jihad and the acquisition of state power sets him apart from other anticolonial Muslim thinkers. Iqbal had considered it "a mistake" to suppose that the idea of the state is dominant in Islam. Muslims needed independent reasoning *(ijtihad)* to adapt to social change. The state in Islam was "theocratic" only insofar as its aim was to establish a "spiritual democracy." There was no place for "a representative of God on earth who can always screen his despotic will behind his supposed infallibility." Iqbal was confident that the "inner catholicity of the spirit of Islam is bound to work itself out in spite of the rigorous conservatism of our doctors." With the end of the Ottoman caliphate, the right of *ijtihad* had to be vested in an elected Muslim assembly, which "in view of the growth of opposing sects" in Islam was the "only possible form Ijma [consensus] can take in modern times." He applauded the Turks for vesting responsibility for collective *ijtihad* in an elected assembly. The "republican form of government is not only thoroughly consistent with the spirit of Islam, but has also become a necessity in view of the new forces that are set free in the world of Islam."[31]

Mawdudi's notion of God's government forecloses the possibility of vesting sovereignty in the people. He accepted the consensus of the community as opposed to one restricted to the ulema. But this concession to democracy was qualified by an insistence on leaving interpretations of the sharia to the state, which would receive advice from ulema knowledgeable in Arabic and the juristic literature. Although he differentiated between the immutable and the mutable aspects of Islamic law, he restricted human legislation by equating the sharia with state law. There was no chance for citizens to influence state policy or question the infallibility of the party of God. This exclusion he justified on the grounds that since justice and equity would prevail in an ideal Islamic state, dissent would amount to apostasy. Submission to Allah meant obeying whoever could claim to be the authoritative interpreter of divine will.[32]

Mawdudi considered himself a contender for that job. He ends all debate by privileging ideology over individual choice and prohibiting critical dialogue about the merits and demerits of his Islamic state. Iqbal's most exuberantly Muslim expressions exhibited none of the narrow cultural and religious outlook, if not outright bigotry, that marked Mawdudi's utterances. A good example of this is the assertion that a Brahman can be a Brahman without knowledge, but to be a Muslim requires knowledge of Islam.[33] Iqbal had put it more delicately: he preferred the idol worshipper alive at heart to the Muslim asleep in the holy sanctuary of Mecca. An act belonged to the temporal world, Iqbal noted, if it was carried out in a "spirit of detachment from the infinite complexity of life," and it could be considered "spiritual if it [was] inspired by that complexity."[34] Sayyid Ahmad Khan, for his part, held that narrow-mindedness is a product of worldly and not religious concerns. In Iqbal's and Sayyid Ahmad's view, bigotry is based on an arrogant refusal to enter into reasoned debates with others.

Nowhere is this tendency more in evidence than in Mawdudi's literal-minded interpretation of the Quran and hadith to promote his bigoted view of women's role in Islam. Although he was a critic of the ulema's obsessive attachment to custom, he exceeded even their social conservatism and perverted sense of justice when it came to women. Social control of women was the ultimate line of defense for a Muslim whose stated aversion to Western culture often bordered on the pathological. He decried the "white jaundice" that had assumed epidemic proportions among Westernized Muslims, the "fifth columnists," in his political terminology. He shared Iqbal's opinion that a woman's role was to be a nurturing mother, doting sister, devoted wife, and dutiful daughter. But he went further, arguing that women should be excluded from the public sphere altogether because their menstrual cycles left them so physically and mentally infirm that they were unsuited for jobs outside the home. The West denied women their feminine identity in the name of progress and development. What was being called women's emancipation in the

West was in fact exploitation of women by the forces of capitalism.[35]

Mawdudi's critique of Western imperialism seems flawed by comparison with Iqbal's, on account of its cultural and religious arrogance. Mawdudi cannot countenance any disagreement with his belief in the ethical superiority of Islam. Morality was impossible without religion. A godless social ethics cannot judge between good and evil, right and wrong. The absence of any authority behind moral law had resulted in chaos and confusion. One nation's ethical standards conflicted with those of another. Powerful nations infringed the rules of morality they expected others to observe. The "conscience of humanity had been deadened" by man's "escape from the Lord." Islam provided an authentic, reliable, and comprehensive code of life that could rescue humanity from the pit of moral depravity. It was "a perfect ethical system" with "no [possibility] of escape from moral responsibility" such as that found in "the ethics of idolatrous religions and of secular creeds." Nor did it "divide humanity into warring sections" along lines of class, clan, or country. The Islamic moral outlook was "dynamic and progressive." While allowing for the "development of civilization and the advancement of society," Islam does not permit its adherents to behave like "moral weathercock[s]" with "no set of uniform ethical norms."[36]

Asserting God's absolute sovereignty in all matters of morality evades the issue of who ultimately interprets his law and will. Non-Muslims had no possibility of debating with Muslims on the ethical validity of Islamic ideas. Though assured of "perfect freedom of religious belief," non-Muslims were barred from the administration of the Islamic state, for their lack of faith in its ideology might compromise the public interest. As soon as "the Ummah of Islam capture[d] State power," it would ban usury and all forms of business and financial dealings prohibited by Islamic law, close down dens of prostitution, and put a stop to all other vices. It would be "obligatory for non-Muslim women to observe the minimum standards of modesty as required by Islamic Law." The Muslim party would "clamp censorship on the Cinema" and put a stop to non-Muslim cultural activities "corrosive of moral fibres." Anticipating criticism, Mawdudi declared that "no creed in the world" had "shown more tolerance to the votaries of other faiths" than Islam. It offered "full opportunity for self advancement to the people of other faiths under conditions of peace and tranquility and displays such magnanimity towards them that the world has yet to show a parallel example."[37]

That Muslims fare even worse in Mawdudi's scheme of sociopolitical transformation is cold comfort for non-Muslims. The faithful have no choice but to fulfill the demands of an all-encompassing *din* and are denied the satisfaction of spiritual and mental salvation in personal faith. In attempting to pull humanity out of the maelstrom of moral relativism, Mawdudi broke with Islamic tradition, by shifting the purpose of religious practice away from individual piety and toward a worldly ideology capable of mobilizing Muslims to submit themselves actively to God. Only an Islamic society and polity could guarantee the believer's piety and salvation. Instead of saving human souls in the hereafter, Mawdudi's Islamic revolution seeks success in this world. To add to the secular character of his ideology, he considered the ulema and not the spiritual community as the architects of a God-based ethics. Like the legists who focused on monitoring the outward behavior of the believer, he considered as law only that part of the sharia which required backing from the coercive power of the state. This expectation left the domain of conscience, the core of individual ethics in Islam, outside the purview of the state. Since Mawdudi subsumed human free will under state power, the ethical society he envisioned relied on draconian enforcement of the principle of preaching what is good and prohibiting what is wrong.

In transferring faith into the realm of politics, Mawdudi rationalized and secularized religion. His neat division of the world into Islam (as interpreted by him) and *jahaliya*—which now included the overwhelming majority of Muslims—negated the possibility of establishing an ethical polity, let alone a humane ethics. In principle, the immediate jihad had to be fought against "bad" Muslims who were in collusion with the Western infidels. Yet it was one thing to proclaim an ideology of world revolution and quite another to translate it into practice. Mawdudi the political practitioner proved to be more moderate and conservative than Mawdudi the theoretician of radical Islam. After rejecting the demand to establish a separate state of Pakistan, he pragmatically accepted its legitimacy and tried to influence the constitutional debate by demanding the establishment of an Islamic state. Instead of being revolutionary, his political approach to state power turned out to be evolutionary. He rejected violent overthrow of the established government and distanced himself politically from the Muslim Brotherhood in Egypt. In keeping with his belief in constitutional change, the Jamaat-i-Islami has participated in electoral politics ever since the creation of Pakistan, even if its student wing has resorted to sporadic violence in pursuit of its aims.

Looking to establish his Islamic credentials in a country whose creation he had opposed, Mawdudi showed political guile in exploiting two issues that have remained central to the self-definition of the Pakistani state: the dispute with India over Kashmir and the controversy over the status of the Ahmadi community in Islam. In 1948 he challenged Pakistan's endorsement of a jihad declared by local religious leaders in Kashmir during a ceasefire with India.[38] So long as Pakistan maintained diplomatic relations with India, its covert assistance to the Kashmiri mujahideen was contrary to the sharia. Mawdudi considered the Kashmiri *jihd-o-jihad* a just war that qualified as jihad according to the standards of

Islamic *fiqh*. Thus, believing that Kashmir's rightful place was in Pakistan, he advocated breaking off relations with India. Doing so would have eliminated the ethical and sharia-based constraints on Pakistan's throwing its full weight behind the Kashmiri cause.[39]

Mawdudi's role in the 1953 agitation to exclude Ahmadis from the Muslim community was linked to his conception of jihad in Kashmir.[40] The Pakistani state, having been created in the name of Islam, had an obligation to define what it meant to be Muslim. Ahmadis were apostates, and Islamic law demanded waging a jihad against them. Pakistan also had to fight the Kashmir jihad in accordance with the sharia. Snapping diplomatic ties with India and stirring up a hornet's nest with such definitions was too radical for the Pakistani establishment. Mawdudi found no takers for his extreme views in 1950s Pakistan. Instead of praising him for his hard-line positions, a military court charged him with sedition in 1953 and sentenced him to death. The offence, interestingly enough, was not his intervention in the Kashmir jihad but his stance on the Ahmadi question.

His opposition to the Ahmadis was a bid to establish himself and the Jamaat-i-Islami as the intellectual and moral bulwark of Islam. Charging the followers of Mirza Ghulam Ahmad with offending faith, Mawdudi argued that declaring them a non-Muslim minority was "a natural and reasonable result" of the course they had chosen. In considering their leader a prophet and renouncing jihad, the Ahmadis violated fundamental tenets of Islam. Most unacceptable were the political irritants that Ahmadis had imposed on Muslims. By avoiding social and religious relations with Muslims, they had separated themselves from the community. It was wrong to say that setting such a dangerous and misguided group outside the bounds of Islam would open the floodgates to the exclusion of other sects. No sect posed a bigger threat than the Ahmadis, who "hide behind Islam" and sow disunity among Muslims. "By their cunning method of pretending Islam [*sic*]," they had grabbed "more administrative positions and employments." This subterfuge was harmful to the community, which could not tolerate a minority that was persecuting the majority.[41]

The 1953 agitation brought the sectarian pot in Pakistan to a dangerous boil. Some Barelvis demanded that Deobandis be declared a separate minority—and included Mawdudi among the prominent representatives of the sect![42] Undeterred, the anti-Ahmadi protesters billed their struggle as a jihad against infidels and called on police and military personnel not to fire on their Muslim brethren. Branding the Ahmadis agents of the British, the agitators demanded to have them removed from top government posts. Chaudhry Muhammad Zafrullah Khan, Pakistan's Ahmadi foreign minister, was the main target of the attack. Yet all the ulema, with the exception of one Shia divine, insisted that the demands were based on religious convictions.

The commission of inquiry investigating the movement considered this a tactical ploy "to avoid . . . being held responsible for the disturbances for a worldly reason." The principal agitators, particularly the Majlis-Ahrar, had been supporters of the Congress ideal of secular nationalism. Together with the Jamaat-i-Islami, they had opposed the Muslim League's demand for a separate state of Pakistan. Consequently, they "found themselves distinctly embarrassed and in a position of inconsistency and self-contradiction in view of their previous utterances." After all, "if the demands were religious . . . [and by implication] both immutable and inflexible, then it becomes somewhat difficult to comprehend how ideology which is based on religion changes from time to time and from place to place." After this jibe at the sincerity of the agitators, the commission dealt the decisive blow, by pointing out that "the most important . . . parties . . . clamouring for the enforcement of the three demands on religious grounds were all against the idea of an Islamic State." Even Mawdudi had

conceded that the "form of Government in the new Muslim State
. . . could only be secular."[43]

Mawdudi, who had long been adept at changing tack and rein-
venting himself, easily got around the commission's charges. His
international fame and his national stature combined to bring
about his pardon and release in 1955. The experience left him
chastened. In his later years, he toned down the more authoritarian features of his scheme. He argued that curbs on individual
rights that would have been permissible if imposed by a genuinely Islamic state were not justified in a non-Islamic state, which
he likened to a tyranny. Until the establishment of an Islamic
state, the sharia was an ideal, not a practical set of religious injunctions and laws that could be enforced piecemeal.[44] Before independence, he had proclaimed armed jihad a legitimate weapon
to replace human government with divine sovereignty. In 1954, he
was more circumspect. A jihad could be declared, he told the
commission of inquiry, only if the state was at war with a non-
Muslim country. It was not necessary for an Islamic state to give
the call to jihad; a Muslim national government could do so in its
legitimate interest. This alternative had the merit of being more
acceptable to the Pakistani state. As the governmental commission put it, if jihad meant the "spread of Islam by arms and conquest," then "Pakistan [could not] be a party to it," for that was
tantamount to sanctioning "aggression" and "genocide," which
were "offences against humanity."[45]

If Mawdudi had watered down his "revolutionary" agenda to
respond to political exigencies, his enthusiasm for an armed jihad
remained unabated—provided a Muslim victory was assured. After his initial jab at the Pakistani state's misuse of jihad, he was
cautious about taking the extraconstitutional route. A willingness
to swim with the tide, even to the extent of modifying a cherished ideal like jihad, helped the Jamaat-i-Islami survive the political storms of military-dominated Pakistan. Using the state's

Abul Ala Mawdudi, theorist of contemporary jihad. Courtesy *Dawn*.

self-professed Islamic identity as his point of entry, Mawdudi launched an ethical and cultural critique of Pakistani society and politics. He identified immorality and forbidden acts rather than issues of socioeconomic injustice as the primary barrier to an Islamic state. Given that revolution had become more of a slogan than a cherished concept, Mawdudi had settled for a long secular trek toward the attainment of an Islamic state.[46]

Using the educational system to carry out a potent kind of sociocultural engineering was the first step toward seizing state power. At the ideological level, the Jamaat-i-Islami has remained committed to Mawdudi's ideal of precipitating an intellectual revolution through education and the systematic infiltration of key state institutions like the army. Instead of opening its membership to all, the Jamaat prides itself on being a party of ethically upright and religious individuals. With its limited social base, it has fared poorly at the hustings. It has made up for this by playing the role of a hypervigilant and well-organized cultural police, ready and able to embarrass the Pakistani state and its personnel for their lack of Islamic rectitude. Armed with Mawdudi's dictums in simple Urdu and the zeal of its student wing, the Jamiat-i-Tulaba, the Jamaat has made a mark on the moral economy of Pakistani society in the Punjab and the North West Frontier Province. But political engagement has also entailed deviation from the precepts of the party's founding father. This has created internal schisms and allowed sectarian and other Islamic revivalist organizations to try to steal the Mawdudian thunder in the field of educational and cultural reform. Although the Jamaat has scrupulously refrained from exploiting Muslim sectarian divisions for political purposes, its electoral alliances and public stances have been based on the same calculations as those of secularly aligned parties in Pakistan.

Mawdudi's ideas, thanks to their skillful dissemination by the Jamaat-i-Islami's publicity wing, have continued to enliven political and cultural debates in Pakistan and other parts of the Muslim world. Yet the cutting edge of those ideas in initiating revolutionary change and ethical reform has been blunted by the weight of temporal compromises. Followers of Mawdudi have lost sight of his principles in the rush to achieve practical implementation. The Jamaat-i-Islami's influence in Pakistani politics remained limited until Mawdudi's death in 1979, which coincided with the Iranian revolution and the Soviet invasion of Afghanistan. Mawdudi's impact on contemporary Islamic radicalism is best understood in the light of the criticisms his ideas elicited not only within the Jamaat-i-Islami but also from rival organizations in Pakistan.

A Bitter Harvest? Mawdudism and Its Critics

An inauspicious beginning on the wrong side of Pakistan's military authoritarian state left Mawdudi whistling ultra-nationalist tunes and posing as the moral conscience of the Muslim nation. If a belated endorsement of Pakistani nationalism spared him the wrath of the state's intelligence agencies, his sniping at the ethical lapses of his countrymen won him more enemies than friends. Pakistan's first constituent assembly produced a document that alluded in only the most perfunctory way to Mawdudi's notion of God's government. While acknowledging God's sovereignty over the entire universe, the constitution vested sovereignty in the people. Far from being a religious theocracy, Pakistan was to be based on Islamic principles of democracy: freedom, equality, tolerance, and social justice were guaranteed for all, including minorities. The only concession to the religious lobby was that the state undertook to ensure that its Muslim citizens lived according to the tenets of Islam.[47]

The constitution afforded the Jamaat-i-Islami opportunities to carp about the misguided secular path the nation was taking, but the party's vacillation over state authoritarianism left it open to criticism. Disagreements within the party led to defections and the setting up of alternative organizations directly or indirectly inspired by Mawdudi's Islamic revivalist philosophy. In 1957, Maulvi Israr Ahmad broke away from the Jamaat-i-Islami, on the grounds that electoral participation was incompatible with revolution. Although Ahmad is a vocal advocate of jihad, his organizational network has focused on education rather than politics.[48] During the era of General Zia-ul-Haq, Ahmad erupted onto the public scene with his socially conservative and misogynist opinions. A man of considerable financial means, Israr Ahmad has wielded political influence without contesting elections. His admirers included Mian Nawaz Sharif, who was twice prime minister in the 1990s. Sharif asked him to frame the 15th Amendment (the Shariat Bill of 1998) making the Quran and the sunna the supreme law of the land.

Across the great divide of 1947, the Indian wing of the Jamaat-i-Islami had to adapt to the realities of a formally democratic state in which Muslims are in a minority. Maulana Wahiduddin Khan, decrying Mawdudi's emphasis on politics over the spiritual reform of the individual believer, left the party after more than fifteen years of dedicated organizational work. The author of several hundred books on Islam and modernity, Wahiduddin has been one of the principal voices accusing Mawdudi of distorting Islam to serve his political agenda of resisting colonial subjugation and Western cultural dominance. Wahiduddin, being committed to a democratic and pluralist India, condemns Mawdudi's cultural exclusivism and hostile perceptions of the "other." Islam promotes dialogue, not confrontation with non-Muslims. In foregrounding politics to achieve narrowly construed temporal objectives, Mawdudi undermined the principle of the unity of creation *(tawhid),* which is the heart of Islam. As the central concern of all Islamic activity, *tawhid* can be realized only through propagation of the faith, which is one form of jihad as peaceful struggle. A prolific writer, Wahiduddin has recently published *True Jihad,* which dispels misconceptions about the term as limited to armed warfare against non-Muslims. In his opinion, jihad is "a continuous action" to live a virtuous life through strict observance of God's commands.[49]

The stress on spiritual perfection through propagation of the faith connects Wahiduddin with a series of traditional scholars who have accused Mawdudi of damaging Islam. Sayyid Abul Hasan Ali Nadwi denounced the shift in emphasis from the spiritual salvation of the believer to the achievement of worldly power. These views found their most energetic expression in the Tablighi Jamaat, a Deobandi organization focusing on individual character building through acts of piety and spiritual devotion, which would then lead to a religious revival and the establishment of an Islamic state.[50] The organization rivals Mawdudi in missionary zeal, something that initially elicited his admiration for the movement, but the Tablighi Jamaat considers criticism of traditional authority to be a deviation from Islam.[51]

Established in the late 1920s by Maulana Mohammad Ilyas (1885–1944), the organization avoids politics and debates on Islamic jurisprudence, out of preference for a life of spirituality modeled on the sunna. The Tablighi Jamaat aimed to move Islam out of the religious seminary, so that Muslims of all walks of life, from the lowest laborer to the wealthiest businessman, could share the obligation of exhorting their co-religionists to faithful religious practice. Educated in the Deobandi tradition, Maulana Ilyas came from a family devoted to the Waliullah clan. Some of his ancestors had given the oath of allegiance to Sayyid Ahmad Barelvi.[52] Ilyas received his early education from his spiritual mentor, Rashid Ahmad Gangohi. Later he studied hadith with Maulana Mahmudul Hasan and joined the circle of mujahideen organized to fight against British imperialism.[53] According to

Abul Hasan Ali Nadwi, he was gripped by the spirit of jihad: "Throughout his life, he was never without it, and had, in fact, taken the pledge of Jehad at the hand of Maulana Mahmood Hasan for that very reason."[54]

Yet Maulana Ilyas did not participate in an armed jihad. Dedicated to a life of piety and worship, he concentrated on spreading Islamic religious practices among the Meos of Mewat, an area south of Delhi. Mewat was the focal point of Arya Samajist and Muslim proselytizing activities after the collapse of the Khilafat movement. Even though the Tablighi Jamaat maintained a studied aloofness from politics, the organization was as much an exponent of Muslim identity as any other. Unlike the Jamaat-i-Islami, which sought an exclusive following, the Tablighi Jamaat cast its net widely among all classes of Muslim South Asian society. At the organizational level, it has avoided the hierarchical strains that, as Mawdudism demonstrated, are implicit in the favoring of a select group of ulema who derive religious authority by following a *mujaddid*.[55] But political and organizational fluidity has made the Tablighi Jamaat prone to manipulation by the state as well as by mainstream political parties, secular and religious. The military regime of General Ayub Khan (1958–1968) tried to pit the Tablighis against the Jamaat-i-Islami. Maulana Zakariya Khandhlawi, a leading ideologue of the movement and a nephew of Maulana Ilyas, was deputed to condemn Mawdudi's ideology as un-Islamic, a task he duly fulfilled with the publication of the *Fitna-i-Mawdudiyat* (the sedition of Mawdudi) in the early 1950s.[56]

A revival based on the reaffirmation of individual faith is closer to the traditional Islamic view than the one that Mawdudi's born-again Muslim followers attempted. But in entrusting the faith to individual Muslims, the Tablighi Jamaat effectively relegated the attainment of an Islamic state to an indefinite future. While Mawdudi served one jail sentence after the other, the Tablighi

Jamaat made it through the postcolonial transition relatively unscathed. Political neutrality has helped its followers come to terms with their minority status in a democratic and secular India.[57] State bureaucrats and army personnel in Pakistan have been able to join the Tablighi Jamaat in large numbers because of its apolitical image. This has played an important role in its rapid growth within Pakistan as well as worldwide. Since many state officials are also sympathizers of the Jamaat-i-Islami, the overlapping membership has acted as a brake on their otherwise withering critiques of each other. Jamaat-i-Islami's spokesmen chide the Tabligh for its disengagement from politics. They claim that it has killed the spirit of armed jihad, a point that accords with the opinion of several other so-called jihadist outfits in contemporary Pakistan. Tablighi activists, for their part, exalt the virtue of personal piety over the Jamaat-i-Islami's worldly politics.

One of the most virulent modernist critics of Mawdudi in postindependence Pakistan was Ghulam Ahmad Parvez (1903–1995), a follower of the anti-hadith Ahl-i-Quran movement. A graduate of the Punjab University, Parvez was among the Muslim government servants who elected to move to Pakistan where he retired in 1955 to concentrate on studying Islam. In 1938 he had started a journal called *Tulu-i-Islam,* apparently on the advice of Iqbal and Mohammed Ali Jinnah, the founder of Pakistan. An avid admirer of Iqbal, Parvez is said to have been among those responsible for arranging the poet's meeting with Mawdudi. But whatever camaraderie may have existed between Parvez and Mawdudi was short-lived. Before partition, the *Tulu-i-Islam* attacked the Congress and its affiliate, the Jamiat-ul-Ulema-i-Hind, and voiced support for the Muslim League. After the creation of Pakistan, Parvez, backed by a state bureaucracy looking for ways to deflect the Jamaat-i-Islami's calls for an Islamic state, turned his venom against Mawdudi.[58]

A brilliant propagandist, Parvez likened Mawdudi's commentary on the Quran to "a mouse-trap: the mouse can get in, but cannot escape."[59] In weekly lectures in Lahore during the late 1950s, he castigated Mawdudi on the basis of his own interpretations of the Quran. While agreeing that Islam was a *din* and not a religion *(mazhab)*, Parvez went a step further, in claiming that the two were mutually contradictory. Echoing Waliullah, he held that there was only one *din*, which he defined as a social ethic or a code of law. Different prophets taught the true *din*, but their followers made a *mazhab* out of it. Human history was "a perpetual conflict between *din* and *ma[z]hab* terminating in the success of one over the other." The idea of "religion" was "a deliberate creation of the minds of men devoted to the pursuit of self-interest." Lacking spirit and soul, "*ma[z]hab* is in fact the embalmed corpse of *din*." Religion was a rope trick mesmerizing people through "a sustained process of indoctrination" in such a way that "the masses learnt to hail and bless those who cheated them." In all their attempts, "the standard-bearers of 'religion' had always relied . . . on one technique: they attributed their own aims and ambitions . . . [to] the 'Will of God.'"[60]

In this blistering attack on impostors claiming the authority of God, Parvez reiterated many of Iqbal's ideas. But Parvez's interpretation of Islam was influenced by the standoff between the religious lobby and supporters of the postcolonial state in Pakistan during the 1950s and 1960s. The 1954 commission of inquiry had offered the best exposition of the Pakistani state position on religion. Its published findings, known as the *Munir Report*, noted that "no two learned divines . . . agreed" on the definition of a Muslim: "If we attempt our own definition as each learned divine has done and that definition differs from that given by all others, we unanimously go out of the fold of Islam. And if we adopt the definition given by any one of the *ulama*, we remain Muslims according to the view of that *alim* but *kafirs* according to the definition of every one else."[61] In the absence of agreement on the definition of a Muslim, it was hardly possible to talk about an Islamic state. Parvez made this the bedrock of his attack on self-serving ulema who peddled religion for cheap publicity.

Mawdudi claimed that in 1951 thirty-one ulema representing different sects had endorsed a common minimum program. According to the agreement, the constitution would be based on the sharia accepted by a majority of Muslims, but each sect could follow its own individual laws. Parvez dismissed this as a pack of lies. Not only were the ulema bitterly divided on the definition of a Muslim, but each member had his own peculiar interpretation of the sunna. The Ahl-i-Hadith was ready to declare a jihad against Mawdudism. Whereas Hanafis considered several hadith in the authoritative collections of Bukhari and of Muslim to be suspect, the Ahl-i-Hadith dubbed them infidels. Sunnis thought all hadith from Shia sources were spurious. Shias had the same opinion of Sunni hadith. Mawdudi opposed the Hanafi conception of the sharia, which the majority of Pakistani Muslims upheld. If no agreement could be reached on the sharia, the only course available was to base the constitution on laws that were not repugnant to Islam, as had already been done. In harping on the topic of the Islamic state, Parvez claimed, Mawdudi had been laying the groundwork to seize political power and impose his own ideas on the people. This was a sure recipe for chaos, rebellion, and bloodshed.[62]

Even if state power remained beyond the reach of the Jamaat-i-Islami, the concordat it had concluded with the traditional ulema and some mainstream political parties could create mayhem and confusion. The Ahmadi controversy showed how pressure politics clothed in Islamic rhetoric could be applied in Pakistan. The demand to expel Ahmadis from the community, although it had met with categorical rejection in the early fifties, remained the focal point of the movement for Islamization of the state. By buckling under pressure and declaring Ahmadis a non-Muslim minority in 1974, the elected government of Zulfikar Ali Bhutto undermined the basis of the nation-state in affirming an exclusionary conception of citizenship. The counternarrative of an Ahmadi critic of Mawdudi is eye-opening. It both conveys the apprehensions of non-Muslim minorities in Pakistan and encapsulates the opinion of Pakistan's liberal intelligentsia, who were appalled by the cynical use of religion for political ends.

In the early fifties Mirza Tahir Ahmad, the fourth caliph of the Ahmadi community, wrote *Murder in the Name of Allah,* a searing critique of Mawdudi's understanding of jihad. To assert that Islam had been spread by the sword was to parrot the accusation of "biased orientalists." Mawdudi's mania for political power "so dominated his thinking that . . . he converted . . . the Holy Prophet . . . into . . . a warrior putting the world to rights with the blade of a sword." Mawdudi's plan to overthrow existing government by force amounted to letting "the fires of civil war . . . consume the very fabric of society." It was false to say that members of God's party were "pious" and "free of lust and greed," whereas their opponents were "cruel, unjust or evil." Mawdudi and his followers could preach what they wished in Pakistan or Saudi Arabia, "but let them take their creed of 'Islam by force' elsewhere and just see what reception it gets." The Jamaat-i-Islami made Islam "a target of ridicule." The movement was "devoid of spiritual values" and "hungry for power," and it was furthermore "inspired by Moscow, not Mecca." Since Mawdudi could not institute reform through "persuasion, patience and humility," he had adopted the Marxist-Leninist "policy of violence and disorder." Tahir Ahmad excoriated Mawdudi for saying that killing an apostate was an act of mercy because it was better to die than to live like a hypocrite. His assertion that all Muslims who disagreed with him were committing apostasy punishable by death showed "the Maulana's dictatorial, manipulative and intolerant personality." There was no possibility of non-

Islamic minorities' carrying out missionary work in a state wedded to a foreign policy of perpetual war against neighboring non-Muslim states.[63]

The objects of Mawdudi's aggression were not non-Muslims living in other countries but homegrown Muslim sects. Although the maulana's followers claimed to promote nonsectarian views, the insistence on capital punishment for apostasy was an implicit declaration of jihad against Muslims who refused to embrace the Jamaat-i-Islami's ideology. Once the Pakistani state took the novel step of winnowing out Muslims from non-Muslims, no sect was safe from the charge of apostasy, not even the Jamaat-i-Islami. Deobandis and the Ahl-i-Hadith issued fatwas declaring Mawdudi an infidel, thereby highlighting the dangers of a state policy based on a set definition of what it meant to be Muslim. Far from resolving the ethical dilemmas posed by the concept of jihad, Pakistan after 1974 was up for grabs for anyone who could muster the street power to pronounce any Pakistani a non-Muslim. The nation had started unraveling; any external shock would suffice for religious bigotry to tear apart the fragile social weave of a country where an all-powerful military exercised authority in the name of Allah.

Allah's War? Jihad and the Embarrassment of Ethics

Pakistan's descent into sectarian hatred, violence, political instability, and economic chaos is attributable to the policies pursued by a military-dominated state anxious to exploit opportunities at the international level to strengthen its domestic and regional profile. It is possible to discern three interlocking phases in the military establishment's flirtation with the idea of jihad. They help elucidate the shift in Pakistan's role from "frontline" state in the war against communism to hub of Islamic "terrorism," before the country became a key ally in the war against terror. The first phase lasted from 1979 until 1996, when the Taliban seized control in Kabul; the second, ending in 2000, was the golden age of Deobandi power; the third, following attacks on the United States in September 2001, forced the military regime of General Pervez Musharraf to crack down on the militias without jeopardizing the army's much-vaunted Kashmir policy. Charting the chronological trajectory of Pakistan's jihadist policies in each of the three phases makes it possible to assess whether the uses the state and the different militant organizations have made of jihad have been in line with its ethical basis in the Quran or have rather been ignored for strategic, economic, and political advantage.

Following the Soviet invasion of Afghanistan in 1979 the Jamaat-i-Islami found the opportunity to make a decisive breakthrough in Pakistani politics. By throwing its weight behind the Afghan resistance movement, the organization catapulted itself onto center stage in the American-backed jihad orchestrated with the help of the Pakistani army and its intelligence services. The July 1977 military coup by General Zia-ul-Haq gave the Jamaat-i-Islami unprecedented political influence. In July 1979, a few months before Mawdudi's death in Rochester, New York, U.S. President Jimmy Carter allegedly gave his secret sanction to fostering the spread of Islamic "fundamentalism" in Central Asia, to "destabilize" the Soviet Union.[64] The aim was to overthrow the Soviet-backed Marxist regime in Afghanistan. Communist haters in Washington had found an opening to deal a blow to America's archenemy. Charlie Wilson, a Texas Congressman, is said to have single-handedly transformed a routine CIA assignment into the largest covert operation in American history.[65]

Once America began pouring billions of dollars into financing the Afghan jihad, Pakistan became a hotbed of religious extremism. The state's intelligence agencies were acting as patrons to madrassas projecting a bigoted and violent form of Islam to boys between the ages of five and eighteen. The main recruits were youth from deprived socioeconomic backgrounds with no prospect of finding jobs in a stagnant economy. General Zia-ul-Haq, who craved the cachet of legitimacy, was quick to cash in on the windfall. In a decisive break with the past, he changed the motto of the Pakistani army to "Islam, Piety, and Jihad." Mohammed Ali Jinnah, the architect of Pakistan who had pronounced religion to be of no concern to the state, had reiterated the theme of "unity, faith, and discipline" in a nation where all citizens would be on an equal footing, free to practice their different creeds. The melding of American strategic interests with the institutional concerns of the Pakistani military, however, tarnished the founder's ideals. Domestically, the die had been cast in 1974 with Bhutto's cynical policy to appease the religious lobby to achieve narrow political gains. But Pakistan in the late seventies was still a relatively moderate Muslim state. The American- and Saudi Arabian–funded Afghan jihad gave extremist forces a crucial opening to alter the tenor of politics in Pakistan.

Future members of Al Qaeda were trained by American and British intelligence with the enthusiastic help of Pakistan's own Inter-Services Intelligence (ISI). With plenty of money to back the cause, jihad was lucrative business for the merchants of death. Over three million Afghan refugees fled to Pakistan in the early 1980s. Gulbadin Hekmatyar, the Afghan leader, was an ardent admirer of Mawdudi. Until the mid-1990s, Pakistani sponsorship of Hizb-i-Islami, the party Hekmatyar led, gave the Jamaat-i-Islami a preeminent position in the Afghan jihad. The Jamaat-i-Islami also called the shots in the Kashmir jihad through its militant wing, Hezbul Mujahideen. But the Jamaat-i-Islami was soon overshadowed by Deobandi parties. A considerable portion of the monies had been funneled into Deobandi madrassas in the NWFP, which shared a Pathan culture with the Afghan refugees. The main beneficiaries of state largesse were the Deobandi party, Jamiat-i-Ulema-i-Islam (JUI), headed by Maulana Fazlur Rahman, and its breakaway faction led by Maulana Samiul Haq. It was at Haq's Dar-ul-Ulum Haqqania that future leaders of the Taliban, including Mullah Omar, learned the Quran by rote, with a smattering of traditional jurisprudence for good measure.

State support for Deobandis upset the sectarian balance in the country, where Barelvis represented by the Jamiat-i-Ulema-i-Pakistan were in the majority. Before it became an assembly line supplying jihadists for America's covert war in Afghanistan, Pakistan was a Barelvi-Deobandi state that subscribed to the Hanafi school of jurisprudence. Mawdudism served as a sort of buffer between the Ahl-i-Hadith and the Hanafites. Deobandis have their strongest following among Pathans in the NWFP and Baluchistan. Pakistan's largest province, the Punjab, is over-whelmingly Barelvi. State patronage of Deobandi imams in gov-ernment-run mosques and the rise of the sect's militias spurred both the Barelvis and the Ahl-i-Hadith into action. As the poli-tics of local influence tilted in favor of the Deobandis, the Barelvis and the Ahl-i-Hadith entered the business of exploiting religion for profit by building mosques and madrassas with money contributed by the Pakistani expatriate community.

The burgeoning of rival madrassas altered Pakistan's sociopolitical landscape in decisive ways. Most madrassas have a sectarian base. Their curricula are adaptations of the eighteenth-century Waliullah and Nizami models of Muslim education. Students are forced to memorize the Quran, so that they can serve as religious functionaries. The teacher is not merely a vessel of knowledge but a sage divinely endowed with unquestionable authority. Stiff discipline is paired with an isolationist worldview. The beliefs of the sect are held sacred. Muslims who do not ad-here to them are instantly declared infidels. Students are taught to refute the beliefs of other sects and hate all manifestations of Western modernity.[66] The contempt for secular and rational forms of knowledge transformed madrassas into factories for turning out a lethal kind of religious bigotry. Pitched battles between militant bands of Sunnis and Shias, as well as Deobandis, Barelvis, and the Ahl-i-Hadith, are fought out against the backdrop of a flourishing black market in arms and drugs encouraged by the state's intelligence agencies. The Jamaat-i-Islami has its own madrassas but has kept its sights on capturing state power by steering clear of sectarian politics.

There are no reliable figures for the total number of madrassas in Pakistan. Most are unregistered. Estimates have varied from several thousand to tens of thousands. What is undeniable is the astronomical increase in madrassas since independence, and especially since the Afghan jihad. In 1947 there were only 137. The number rose from 210 in 1950 to 563 in 1971. During the early 1980s 893 larger and smaller Pakistani madrassas were in existence, with a total of 3,186 teachers and 32,384 regular students. More tended to spring up in smaller towns and in the countryside than in the major cities.[67] Once Pakistan was awash in greenbacks, enterprising maulvis rushed to fill the demand for recruits by offering their students for jihad. Since they are a means of establishing political dominance, self-proclaimed religious parties of all sectarian denominations, as well as the Jamaat-i-Islami, set up madrassas in places where they saw an opportunity to extend their influence.[68] In 1980 there were 700 such institutions in the country. By 1986 there were approximately 7,000. Most were set up in the NWFP, the southern Punjab, and Karachi and served as nurseries for jihad. As the ISI became used to the influx of American money, the maulvis became addicted to the business of jihad.[69] The existence of a well-run jihad industry made Pakistan a haven for foreign students excited by the prospect of attaining martyrdom by fighting the godless and satanical governments of Afghanistan and the Soviet Union.

Deobandi seminaries run by the two factions of the JUI in the

NWFP had the greatest stake in the new dispensation. In an off-shoot of the Iran-Iraq war and General Zia-ul-Haq's social and political engineering, the Anjuman-i-Sipah-i-Sahaba emerged as the main Sunni sectarian organization in the country. Formed in Jhang, Punjab, in 1984 by Maulana Haq Nawaz Jhangvi, the Sipah-i-Sahaba spouted hatred against Shias, who were the land-lords and spiritual leaders in the district. After 1986 the organiza-tion started a campaign of targeted assassinations of Shias. In December 1990 its operatives killed the Iranian Consul General in Lahore, an act that brought relations between Pakistan and its Shia neighbor to an all-time low. The Sipah-i-Sahaba disowned responsibility, but Jhangvi was sentenced and executed for his hand in the conspiracy. This made him a martyr in the eyes of Shia haters and strengthened the organization's base of support in the Punjab. With a string of madrassas in the province, the Sipah-i-Sahaba actively provided recruits for the Afghan jihad. It curried favor with other Deobandi parties to become an influen-tial political force in Pakistan. It got easier once Azam Tariq rose to the helm of the organization. He had given an oath of alle-giance to the prominent Deobandi figure, Maulana Yusuf Ludhianvi, a virulent opponent of Mawdudi and the spiritual mentor of the JUI's Maulana Fazlur Rahman. The Sipah-i-Sahaba shares the Deobandi idea of an Islamic society. Long before his assassination, Azam Tariq vowed to convert several of Pakistan's large cities into "model Islamic cities," by enforcing five rules: 1) the closure of all shops at the time of the Muslim call to prayer, 2) designation of Friday as a holiday; 3) boycott of busi-nesses based on bribery or illegal money; 4) the elimination of ca-ble television; and 5) calling on the ulema to vet all decisions from an Islamic point of view.[70]

The Wahabi-Deobandi alliance was cemented in 1989 after Osama bin Laden's meeting with the Taliban leader Mullah Omar at the Deobandi Banuri Mosque in Karachi. The Banuri

Mosque, headed by Mufti Nizamuddin Shamzai, became the hub of Deobandism in Pakistan. Azam Tariq and Fazlur Rahman had close links with Shamzai and through him with Mullah Omar and the Al Qaeda network. The emergence of "the grand Deobandi consensus" eclipsed the Jamaat-i-Islami in Afghanistan and Kashmir and heightened sectarian tensions in Pakistan. Once the Taliban gained power in Afghanistan, the JUI acquired greater prominence. Meanwhile, the Deobandi Harkat-ul-Ansar overshadowed the Jamaat's Hezbul Mujahideen in Kashmir. An estimated 80,000 Taliban students from Deobandi seminaries in the NWFP and the Federally Administered Tribal Areas (FATA) were dispatched to help the Taliban fight against the Iranian-supported Northern Alliance directed by the Tajik leader, Ahmad Shah Masud. Pakistan and Saudi Arabia's recognition of the Taliban government strengthened the anti-Shia Deobandi–Wahabi coalition.[71]

Another important support arm for the ISI-managed Afghan and Kashmir jihads has been provided by Lashkar-i-Tayyiba, a branch of the Ahl-i-Hadith's Markaz Dawat-al-Irshad with contacts in the Arab world. The Lashkar enjoys a flow of funds from expatriate Muslims living in the West. General Zia-ul-Haq granted the Markaz several acres of land in Muridke for the construction of its headquarters. The pro-Wahabi leanings of its founder, Hafiz Mohammed Saeed, a former teacher of Islamic studies at the government-owned Engineering University of Lahore, made the Lashkar a natural ally of Al Qaeda. Its influential contacts with the ISI and its training camps in Afghanistan and Central Asia have made the Lashkar one of the most enterprising militant organizations operating in Indian-occupied Kashmir.[72]

When the Kashmir jihad started in 1989, it was the secular-oriented Jammu and Kashmir Liberation Front (JKLF) and the Jamaat-i-Islami that enjoyed the most militant support on both sides of the Line of Control separating the Indian- and Pakistani-occupied parts of the state. Once the Afghan jihad began to peter out, the ISI redirected the returning warriors to Kashmir. The entry of war-hardened militants from Afghanistan injected sectarian and Wahabi tendencies into what had started as a freedom struggle with no specific religious agenda. Both the Pakistani and Indian intelligence agencies set about smashing the JKLF, which splintered into as many as twenty different organizations. The Hezbul Mujahideen in Indian-held Kashmir shared intelligence with the Indian army to help it locate JKLF militants; as a result five hundred of them died.[73] The ISI wanted to weaken the JKLF and gain control of the freedom struggle by converting it into a jihad. As in Afghanistan, which local warlords plunged into civil war after the Soviet withdrawal, the fragmentation of the jihad in Kashmir has caused its Pakistani paymasters to lose control to smaller outfits operating under the direction of local commanders.

In the second phase, starting in 1996, the Jamaat-i-Islami's Hezbul Mujahideen paid for its sins (helping undermine the JKLF) by losing out to Deobandi groups. The eventual beneficiary proved to be the Lashkar-i-Tayyiba, which introduced the Ahl-i-Hadith's pro-Wahabi doctrines into the Kashmiri struggle. The Deobandi-Wahabi combine was at its height once Mullah Omar, with Osama bin Laden's financial backing and advice, turned Afghanistan into a clone of the emirate. Arab funding and state support helped the membership of the Tablighi Jamaat grow by leaps and bounds in Pakistan, even though the organization formally opposes jihad in both Afghanistan and Kashmir. An estimated two million people typically converge at the Tablighi Jamaat's annual meeting in Lahore, of which 90 percent are said to be Pathans from Peshawar and the tribal areas bordering Afghanistan.[74] Not all members of the Tablighi Jamaat are "the stealthy legions of jihad," though some belong to sectarian and militant groups like the Sipah-i-Sahaba and the Harkatul Ansar, which was renamed Harkatul Mujahideen after being declared a terrorist organization by America in 1997.[75]

More than two decades of state support for militant organizations flush with money from Saudi Arabia, Iran, and expatriate communities in the West, not to mention the state's own welfare funds, had left Pakistan languishing on the fringes of the international polity. During the nineties, the Pakistani army had sought to gain "strategic depth" for its policy of jihad, by extending its influence in Afghanistan and undertaking a punishing low-intensity war with India in Kashmir with the assistance of its underlings. Between 1979 and 1990 there was a 100 percent increase in the number of militant parties, and sectarian parties grew by 90 percent. Taking advantage of the religious sentiments of socially marginal groups, these organizations converted the lesser jihad of the sword to the greater jihad, in an inversion of the Islamic tradition. An estimated thirty thousand young Pakistanis were martyred in Afghanistan and Kashmir. Two thousand more were killed in sectarian clashes in Pakistan; some two hundred thousand young men belonged to militant and sectarian organizations.[76] The impact on the social landscape of Pakistan has been devastating. Deobandi dominance was resented by Shias and Barelvis alike. Both reacted by creating their own militant organizations, initially to carry out revenge killings against the Sipah-i-Sahaba and later to wield political influence in their own right.

The Tehrik-i-Nifaz-i-Fiqha-i-Jafaria had rallied Shias against Zia-ul-Haq's Islamization policies. In the 1990s it founded the Sipah-i-Mohammadi to combat the menace posed by the Sipah-i-Sahaba. While staying away from the Afghan and Kashmir jihads, some members of the Fiqha-i-Jafaria's student wing participated in the Hezbollah's war against Israel in Lebanon. The Barelvis have for the most part avoided jihad and have tried to make common cause with the Shias. The Sunni Tehrik was established to counter Deobandi influence and restore some semblance of Shia-Sunni amity after a rash of horrific killings by the Sipah-i-Sahaba. Sunnis fed up with sectarian tensions and Deobandi extremism flocked to Allama Ilyas Qadri of the Dawat-i-Islami and Allama Tahirul Qadri of the Pakistani Awami Tehrik. Both claim spiritual status and attract handsome sums of money from expatriate Pakistanis with no direct involvement in the state-sponsored militant network.[77] Barelvi reassertion in Pakistan has not been entirely salutary in effect. Incensed by creeping Deobandism in what had been their stronghold, the Barelvis condemn their rivals as infidels and apostates who, if they cannot be killed at random, at least ought not to be befriended. The Barelvis have protested the appointment of Deobandis in mosques and have tried to reassert control over the anti-Ahmadi Khatm-i-Nabuwwat movement, which was started by Maulana Abul Sattar Niazi of the Barelvi Jamiat-ul-Ulema-i-Pakistan.

The sectarian component of the Deobandi alliance became several shades more dangerous with the release of Maulana Masood Azhar from an Indian jail after the hijacking in December 1999 of an Indian Airlines plane from Kathmandu to Kandahar in Afghanistan. Azhar, a follower of the Sipah-i-Sahaba leader, Haq Nawaz Jhangvi, split the Harkatul Mujahideen in January 2000 to form the dreaded Jaish-i-Muhammad, which has a militant sectarian orientation. The ISI's complicity in this development was revealed when Azhar traveled to Lahore, escorted by scores of armed guards sporting Kalashnikovs. This was extreme provocation for New Delhi, which was still reeling under the decision to exchange Azhar and other extremists for the passengers on the hijacked Indian Airlines plane marooned in the wilds of Kandahar. Its revenge was not long in coming. Since the May 1998 nuclear tests by India and Pakistan, Washington had been pressing Islamabad to suspend its Kashmir jihad in the interests of dialogue with New Delhi. Facing international isolation for its support of the Taliban and a rising graph of sectarian violence domestically, the military regime of Pervez Musharraf was taking preliminary steps to begin dislodging the militant infrastructure when the September 11 attacks on American soil dramatically altered old alignments and compelled the choice of new and more difficult ones.[78]

Musharraf's volte-face on Pakistan's Taliban policy met with ferocious resistance from organizers of madrassas as well as leaders of religious parties as far apart as the Jamaat-i-Islami and the JUI. But when it came to demonstrating their strength on the streets, the pro-jihadi Pak-Afghan Defence Council failed to muster popular backing. It did have the support of the independent tribes in Pakistan's wild northwest, but most agitators in the urban areas were madrassa-educated youth whose average age was nineteen.[79] By comparison with the half-million protestors who had thronged the streets of Karachi during the first Gulf War against Iraq in 1991, no more than fifty thousand assembled this time to raise clenched fists, while shouting slogans against America and its stooges in the Pakistani establishment. The reason for this poor showing was quite simple: the state was urging moderation, instead of encouraging the extremism that had fueled the militant culture. Several supporters of the Taliban were imprisoned or placed under preventive detention. The tide had turned. But there was a qualitative difference between stated intentions and actual achievements. The deweaponization campaign had ended in failure because the military was unwilling to disarm the militias by force.[80]

It had long been characteristic of the Pakistani state for the left hand not to know what the right hand was doing. For the cornered regime of Musharraf such a lack of coordination could produce deadly results. His resolve to clamp down on militias was counterbalanced by a firm determination not to compromise the army's Kashmir policy. Walking a tightrope in his attempt to reverse the culture of militancy previously nurtured by the state, Musharraf made duplicity the better part of valor. The crackdown on militias and religious seminaries offering military training was highly selective. Since sectarian militias posed the greatest threat to the regime's agenda for economic revival, they were the first to come under fire. But cleansing Pakistan of its sectarian malaise was no mean enterprise.

The militant infrastructure cultivated by the ISI over a period of twenty-two years was too closely enmeshed with the sectarian militias to be dismantled without damaging the army's strategic doctrine. This situation gave Musharraf some scope to bargain with Washington. If Americans could help resolve the Kashmir dispute, the Pakistani army was ready to abandon support for the militants. But neither America nor India was convinced that Musharraf could deliver the peace dividend. Such success as the regime has had in eliminating the most objectionable sectarian militias has come at a great risk to Musharraf's personal security. He has survived six assassination attempts linked to individuals and militias that the state's intelligence agencies had once propped up.

Many analysts fear that disarming the militias will lead to internal conflict and the collapse of Pakistan.[81] A member of the Jaish-i-Muhammad conceded that Pakistan was next in line for jihad, given that injustices were quite as prevalent there as in Kashmir. The leader of the Kashmiri Jamaat-i-Islami confirmed that after the jihad had been won against India, the system in Pakistan would be set aright.[82] If sectarian tendencies in the jihad threaten Shias, Ahmadis, and religious minorities, the class composition of the fighters makes it the ideal instrument for an onslaught against the pro-Western ruling elites. The products of religious seminaries come mainly from the lower and middle classes and have the support of middle-class officers in the army and the state bureaucracy. Agencies of the state often let those involved in sectarian killings off the hook and permitted other lawbreakers to go underground. Popular support for the militias has been another obstacle, and one that a military dictator is least well placed to overcome. Pakistan's robust Urdu press has championed jihad to score points against English newspapers catering to the upper middle classes. One prominent journalist complained that when the English press "agonises over the extremism and defiance of the jehadi groups," influential Urdu columnists "deliver warnings of bodily harm" to them for "adopting an anti-Islamic posture at the behest of Pakistan's enemies."[83]

The predicament of Musharraf, who has no real base of political support outside the army, is as unenviable as his resolve to hold on to power has been remarkable. Before and after the 2002 general elections, the regime won the grudging support of a six-party religious-political alliance called the Mutahida Majlis-i-Amal (MMA). The MMA, which includes the Barelvi Jamiat-ul-Ulema-i-Pakistan, the Jamaat-i-Islami, the two factions of the Deobandi JUI, the Jamiat Ahl-i-Hadith and the Shia Tehrik-i-Jafaria, is an inherently volatile grouping. Although Samiul Haq's faction of the JUI has parted company with the MMA, political ambitions have kept the alliance together in form more than in substance. Apart from lambasting Musharraf for refusing to give up his position as chief of army staff and for serving as the civilian president of a democratic country, the MMA accuses him of compromising state sovereignty and secularizing Pakistani culture and politics, actions it equates with *la-diniyat* (irreligiousness). The clerics, while falling short of declaring a jihad against Musharraf's godless regime, have shown no signs of diminished opposition to his alliance with America. The MMA, already incensed by the state's betrayal of the Afghan and Kashmiri jihads, sees his appeals for enlightened moderation as adding insult to injury.

Whether Pakistan implodes under the weight of the tensions

between the state's jihadi and anti-jihadi policies will depend on Musharraf's ability to practice what he preaches. If Pakistan is to adopt a moderate and enlightened view of Islam, it cannot avoid an open debate on the ethical basis of the Quranic concept of jihad. The military-dominated state has used jihad, which is intrinsic to faith and ethics in Islam, to advance its strategic, economic, and political ends. Such a skewed strategic vision, backed by political denial and policies of economic exclusion, violates elementary Islamic principles of equity and justice. The army has capitalized on the jihadi industry to further ensconce itself in the power structure. If Pakistan is to turn over a new leaf, the army will have to drastically modify its strategic vision. The monumentality of the task can be gauged from the discourse on jihad that state policies have helped promote. The vast literature on the subject, which focuses narrowly on jihad as war against infidels, variously defined, reaches a wide market in Pakistan. During the heyday of state sponsorship for jihad, militant outfits published newspapers, journals, books, and pamphlets on jihad, in addition to hosting Web sites as propaganda and marketing tools. Apart from being hugely profitable for its promoters, jihad is a powerful means for militant organizations to extend their political influence by making sensational claims about their members' courage and spirit of sacrifice. Some continue to do so with gusto, most notably the Lashkar-i-Tayyiba, which has flourished as the Jamaat-ud-Dawah since the crackdown on sectarian and pro–Al Qaeda outfits. The Lashkar-i-Tayyiba, created by the ISI, played a critical role in the Kashmir jihad after 1990. The Lashkar has escaped the tightening noose on militant groups because the state's intelligence agencies needed an alternative to the troublesome Jaish-i-Muhammad, which was directly involved in the murder of the *Wall Street Journal* reporter Daniel Pearl and has well-advertised links with Al Qaeda.[84]

Picking up on themes promoted by several of the now defunct

militant organizations, the Lashkar-i-Tayyiba has pieced together a coherent ideology of jihad that merits careful analysis. The appeal of its message is best understood against the backdrop of popular ideas about fighting in the way of Allah to gain the ultimate honor of martyrdom. By lauding death on the field of battle as the highest service to Islam, the militias have created a compelling incentive, the promise that jihadis can attain worldly status and religious virtue simultaneously. This perception has dramatically altered Pakistan's cultural ethos. Young men, and some women too, long to die for their religion.[85] Martyrs' families are promised material comforts, respect, and the greatest reward of all—a guaranteed place in paradise. Parents, who are encouraged to send their sons to battle Hindu infidels, celebrate news of their death by distributing sweets and offering prayers of thanksgiving to Allah. Jihad has done roaring business in Pakistan because it appeals to the imagination of people whose prospects are severely limited. Death offers worldly glory and security in the hereafter, whereas their lives would otherwise promise nothing but oppression and humiliation. The political culture that supports the ideology of jihad is rooted in both material culture and religion, albeit religion reduced to a series of formulaic rituals and customs based on a superficial understanding of Islamic ethics.

Contrary to the perception that extremism incubates in religious seminaries, most recruits to militant organizations in major cities of the Punjab have come from government schools and colleges. The province provided nearly half the manpower to all militant organizations in the country. Most Pakistanis killed in Afghanistan and Kashmir have been Punjabis. A sampling of statements by the recruits reveals the mindset of contemporary militants. Many recruits to the Jaish-i-Muhammad were trained in a madrassa in Balakot named after Sayyid Ahmad Shaheed. One of its members quipped that there was "more honor in jihad" than in any other profession, and "the money too was good." Another said jihad was the only honorable thing left for Muslims. Asked if the focus had not shifted from the greater to the lesser jihad, he remarked that several religious parties in Pakistan had taken up the struggle against the existing system. This was the greater jihad, and Jaish's purpose was to "bring more people around to this objective." A Harkatul Mujahideen militant with seven years of schooling decided to join the jihad after hearing about the treatment of Kashmiri women. A twenty-year-old high school graduate said that since he had joined the Harkatul Mujahideen, jihad had become a complete way of life for him and he could not conceive of doing anything else. He denied that the organization was sectarian in orientation. Deobandis believed only in what was correct unlike the sectarian Lashkar-i-Tayyiba, which forced new recruits to position their hands in a strictly prescribed manner while praying.[86]

Since the personal ambition of the leaders outweighs ethical considerations, a distinguishing feature of militant groups has been the intense rivalries that erupt into verbal abuse and physical violence. Before Musharraf pulled the plug in response to the Indian outcry against the militant infrastructure in Azad Kashmir, the mujahideen were a law unto themselves, and the local administration abetted their behavior rather than curbing it. They flaunted their weapons and extorted money and other services from local shopkeepers. Members of one militant Kashmiri outfit took to visiting a billiard hall and, to the owner's distress, using grenades with the pins pulled out as billiard balls. Others acted in a lewd fashion, teasing schoolgirls and displaying weapons to advertise their heroism—a tendency that assumed epidemic proportions. One local commander named himself Commander Shah Rukh Khan, after the popular Indian Hindi film star![87]

All militant outfits attribute miracles to their men and describe them as models of Islamic ethics, purity, and heroism. Such portrayals, intended to generate enthusiasm for the jihad, paint a dazzling canvas in which fantasy and passion, blood and glory blend in improbable ways to erase distinctions between the imaginary and the rational, the spiritual and the temporal. Harkatul Mujahideen's monthly, *Sada-i-Mujahid,* in its April 2000 issue recounts the story of three mujahideen traveling in pitch darkness who suddenly find their hands and feet lit up in miraculous fashion. A *mujahid* injured in an encounter with Indian troops is carried off by an angel and wakes up in a jungle with no sign of the injury. In the *Majallah Al-Dawah* Lashkar-i-Tayyiba delights in publicizing the amazing deeds of its men. Some read like spoofs in a humor magazine, especially stories about bears, cats, and monkeys helping the mujahideen. The more glamorous yarns could put some Bollywood scriptwriters out of business. In one the clothing of a *mujahid* is riddled with bullet holes, but his body remains unscarred. Stories of knives directing tanks and armored vehicles outdo the best science fiction![88]

Amid the bravado and glitzy romanticism of the would-be warriors of Allah, the idea of jihad popularized by militant groups displays a deeply troubling side. By far the most disturbing aspect is the slogans deployed to attract impressionable youth to the cause. The Lashkar-i-Tayyiba's call for recruits in September 2002 reads like an advertisement for a trendy health spa. Under the caption "Let Us Become Mujahids" appear four rhetorical questions:

1. Do you want the dominance of Allah's D[i]n, the destruction of forces of evil and disbelief, the death of systems of injustice and oppression?
2. Do you want Muslim Ummah to rise again as a dignified nation and do you want that a befitting reply is given to all activities and machinations against Muslims?
3. Do you want that peace and tranquility prevail in Muslim

society, humanity is adored with the virtues of piety, morality and other attributes of good character?

4. Do you want an end to all evils and western culture? Do you want that the rights of Allah and the rights of people are taken care of?

Those answering in the affirmative were asked to join the Dawat-al-Irshad's training camps, which "prepare such pious individuals and Mujahideen" who "do not like any evil prevailing anywhere in the world." Thousands of such brave and virtuous souls, the organization stated, were fighting unbelievers and propagating faith and jihad among Muslims. Training for jihad was ordained by both Allah and the necessity of the moment. Muslims had to learn the use of swords, spears, and daggers to attack the forces of unbelief and master the art of planning an ambush and laying siege to the camps and cantonments of the enemy. They also had to know how to protect themselves and "other oppressed Muslims during crackdowns and blackouts." When Muslims were being trampled under the feet of infidel armies, it was inappropriate to "waste . . . precious time in playfields, or in enjoying useless things like music, films, vulgar novels and magazines." The time had come to "spread Allah's D[i]n and destroy disbelief."[89]

Elaborating on the theme of militarization, the Lashkar's main spokesman, Hafiz Mohammed Saeed, rebuked the West for asking Muslims to renounce jihad in the interest of economic progress at a time when India was brutalizing Kashmiris and Israel had "unleashed a horrible reign of terror" in Palestine. Muslims had to "stand united and raise the banner of Jihad." Breaking with Islamic tradition, Saeed asked Muslims to join the jihad on an individual basis if their governments were unwilling to take action. In deference to his patrons, he added that those who chose jihad must not create conflict with their governments or expect help from them. Their "earnestness," courage, and sacrifices would, by the grace of Allah, suffice to "open up new avenues." Muslim youth should not to be daunted by the power of the unbelievers. Non-Muslim hegemony would prevail only so long as the mujahideen kept "sitting on the fence." Once jihad was launched, "the storms of evil and disbelief [would] soon subside," as had happened in Afghanistan and was now happening in Kashmir.[90]

The success of the mujahideen in Kashmir had forced India to seek help from Israel, the United States, and Russia. Given that "all decisions were made in the heavens," it was owing to the grace of God that the enemies of Islam were coalescing. In keeping with the heavenly plan to "foil the machinations of the enemies," their attention had been diverted to Palestine. Hafiz Saeed was proud of the Kashmir jihad's power of demonstration. The Lashkar-i-Tayyiba's activities were "creating an understanding of Jihad in the Muslim world." Palestinians were resisting their oppressors, and that resistance in turn was "benefiting Jihad in Kashmir." Saeed warned Muslims of the "conspiracies of the disbelievers" and the futility of engaging in negotiations with the enemy. If Muslim leaders could not take up jihad, they ought to at least ban American and Indian products and withdraw investments from non-Muslim countries. They should expel all non-Muslim workers and give the jobs to their own people. Muslims had to cooperate with one another. They had to realize that "Muslims are distinct from non-believers and our friendship with them can be anything but fruitful."[91]

Hafiz Saeed's exclusionary vision would have done Mawdudi proud. But the two are radically at odds on the legality of the Kashmir jihad. Saeed's notion about individual Muslims fighting a jihad without state sanction or the consensus of the religious scholars is without parallel in the Islamic tradition. In opposing Pakistan's policy toward the Kashmir jihad in 1948, Mawdudi had placed the burden of responsibility on the state, not the individual. He believed in the legitimacy of a jihad fought by Kashmiris and denied saying that Pakistanis killed in Kashmir would not die a martyr's death. Pakistanis could send food and medical aid and even sell arms to their co-religionists. But so long as Pakistan maintained diplomatic relations with India, its citizens were not permitted under the sharia to fight in Kashmir. Anyone who maintained the opposite was treading on thin ice.[92]

The Lashkar-i-Tayyiba, which is acutely vulnerable to the charge, has expended considerable energy countering the impression that jihad is not an individual duty. It has issued a spate of pamphlets and books in both English and Urdu to put an end to the controversy.[93] These publications, which have prefaces by Hafiz Saeed, invoke the authority of the Quran and the hadith, even as they refuse to be hemmed in by traditional Muslim scholarship. The reprint of a book by Maulana Fazal Illahi Vazirabadi from the late 1940s defending the Kashmir jihad has lent support to the Lashkar's ideology.[94] In 1915 he was instrumental in assisting the group of Punjab University students to reach the mujahideen center on the frontier and cross the border into Afghanistan to join Obaidullah Sindhi.[95] The Lashkar's own publication *Jehad in the Present Times* draws on Vazirabadi's arguments and targets an English-speaking audience. Apart from providing a rationale for waging an armed struggle in Kashmir, both works offer vivid glimpses into the Lashkar-i-Tayyiba's conception of Islamic ethics.

An active participant in the 1948 Kashmir jihad, Vazirabadi was a devotee of Sayyid Ahmad Shaheed and a staunch Pakistani nationalist. He wrote the book in response to a questionnaire inquiring whether the war being waged in Kashmir since August 1947 was a *jihad fi sabil allah*. The bulk of Vazirabadi's work is devoted to answering this question, with references to the history of the jihad in Kashmir and suitable quotations throughout from the Quran, the hadith, and Sayyid Ahmad's and Shah Ismail's writings. A dogged insistence on the Kashmir jihad as the panacea for all evils explains Vazirabadi's appeal for the Lashkar-i-Tayyiba. In his preface, Hafiz Saeed decries America's designation of jihad as terrorism. While admitting that the international situation is not conducive to jihad, he endorses Vazirabadi's thesis, and incidentally also the ISI's, that Pakistan can become the strongest force in the subcontinent by helping the Kashmiris. He categorically asserts that freeing Kashmir from India will result in the success of other Muslim dissidence movements in the world.[96]

Like Mawdudi, Vazirabadi did not distinguish between jihad and *qital* (fighting) or forcible and voluntary conversion. Despite assurances from the Indian government, Muslims had been forced out of areas with Hindu majorities. Vazirabadi called for a decisive war against India, so that in future it would not dare break agreements with Muslims. This would not be a national war but a *jihad fi sabil allah.* What Hindus had done to Muslims in India was akin to what the Meccan Quraish did to the fledgling Islamic community. The loss of Muslim sovereignty in India had weakened Islam. Instead of worrying about the causes of ethical degeneration, Muslims needed to concentrate energy and resources on fighting a continuous jihad until victory was won. Making use of Quranic stories about Moses and the Pharaoh as embellishment, Vazirabadi argued that a war to wrest political control from non-Muslims was the primary religious duty for Muslims. Restoring Kashmir as *Dar-ul-Islam* and merging it with Pakistan would secure both of them, as well as Afghanistan, from the threat posed by Hinduism. Muslims who opposed the jihad on grounds that it was a nationalistic war were doomed; seventy intercessions by the Prophet would not spare them the fires of hell! India was in flagrant violation of its agreements and it was legitimate for individual Pakistanis to plot its demise. The woeful condition of Indian Muslims hinted at what awaited Pakistanis. Any who opposed the Kashmir jihad were helping the enemy achieve what it otherwise could not with all the military power at it disposal.[97]

The questionnaire had asked whether the imam and the mujahideen had to be men of high ethical character. Drawing on Islamic law, Vazirabadi retorted that the imam could be the most unethical of men. Even if he was a model of immorality, Muslims would be obliged to wage jihad under his command. There was no need for the mujahideen to be upright men. If saying prayers was mandatory for sinful Muslims, why not jihad? This was not to suggest that Islam was devoid of ethical concerns. Jihad had to stand alongside the other pillars of Islam. The lovers of God put a premium on spiritual virtues and abstinence from material pleasures. But their preoccupation with ascetic practices ran counter to the Quran and the Prophetic sunna. The only way to achieve nearness to God was to wage *jihad fi sabil allah*. Jihad was a magic wand that washed away the sins of the warrior and could turn the unethical into the ethical.[98]

If Vazirabadi provided a dubious ethical gloss to the Kashmir jihad, *Jehad in the Present Times,* by Abdus Salam Bin Muhammad, exposes the inherent bigotry of the Lashkar-i-Tayyiba's worldview. Infidels had not damaged the cause of jihad as much as the "so-called virtuous preachers and scholars of Islam" had. They had set impossible conditions for jihad, condemning Muslims to remain in their "present position of disgrace and slavery." There was no need for an Islamic state or caliphate to wage a legitimate jihad. A "believer is quite free to start a war against the disbelievers, particularly when it is with a view to saving his life." While jihad is not obligatory for all Muslims, those who did not fight had a lesser religious status. "Muslims had to continue fighting against the disbelievers" anywhere in the world, if they had the power to persecute Muslims or prevent anyone from accepting and practicing Islam. As a corollary, Muslims had to defend their co-religionists if they were oppressed or attacked and retrieve any conquered territories. Muslims were also obliged to fight against a nation that broke its pledge to them. Revenge had to be taken against unbelievers who killed Muslims. Whereas a Muslim murdering a Muslim can pay blood money or secure forgiveness from the victim's relatives, conversion to Islam is the only escape available to an unbeliever accused of killing a Muslim. It was "binding and incumbent upon the Muslims" to fight the infidels until they agreed to pay the *jizya* and Islam became the dominant way of life in the world.[99]

The pamphlet also tackles the delicate issue of why a jihad is not being fought in Pakistan, where persecution and oppression are as rampant as in Kashmir. The reasoning has all the hallmarks of the Pakistani statist mentality. Unlike India's Hindu rulers, the rulers in Pakistan did not disown Islam, even if their policies were hypocritical. Muslims are prohibited to kill people because they are hypocrites. The "restlessness and violence" in Pakistan were akin to a civil war among Muslims, "not a struggle between Islam and disbelief." Indian Muslims were being slaughtered for professing Islam. Their possessions were plundered, their women disgraced, and their mosques razed to the ground. The Shiv Sena leader Bal Thackeray had given Muslims three choices: they could convert to Hinduism, leave India, or face death. Pakistani Muslims were under no such threat. It was the Lashkar-i-Tayyiba's "utmost desire to have in Pakistan a just Islamic society where no one was wronged" or made to suffer violent oppression as in Kashmir. But the most effective way of waging jihad in Pakistan was to fight the unbelievers. This battle would unite Muslims, who were "bound to go on fighting among [them]selves" if they renounced jihad. Muslims had to avenge "the oppression, wholesale massacre, wrongs and persecution" they had suffered in 1947 at the hands of the Hindus.[100]

In a classic statement of the exclusionary doctrine, Abdus Salam warned Muslims of the perils of not maintaining boundaries with the other. "It really pains me very much," he professed, "to find any of my Muslim brothers equalizing India and Pakistan, as he, then, is following and advocating the Hindu point of view." He accepted that strengthening the outer aspects meant neglecting the inner facets of Islam, which continued to be a sham in his opinion. But it is through jihad that "we strengthen the outer as well as the inner parts of the building of Islam." Only those with a sense of honor can fight the unbelievers. Pakistan's rulers were "devoid of any sense of honour." He who "fights the disbelievers for a cause no other than their disbelief is surely a true believer, a Man of Faith." God would "bless us with inner (as well as outer) establishment, strength and integrity" because of such men.[101]

Those objecting to the Kashmir jihad were in "a strange dilemma" and behaving in "a ridiculous manner." While evading their duty, they claimed to believe in jihad. Not one of these "esteemed scholars" of Islam could load a gun. This showed that "they were not true in their claims and . . . just gossip." They may have good reasons for not going to the front, "but what hindres [sic] them from attending a military camp to prepare themselves for Jehad if they sincerely intend to take part in it?" It was puerile to say that since no one qualified as caliph, jihad was impossible. There was "no such condition" in Islam. The caliphate had ended in 1924. If Muslims had no need of guns, they would have to "polish the shoes" of the unbelievers to "enjoy . . . the sweet sleep of peace and rest."[102]

A living death in humiliation and oppression is far less attractive than the rewards of martyrdom promised by the propagandists of jihad. Although Pakistan has formally disavowed a two-decade-long jihadist policy, the legacy has been difficult to dispel. The Lashkar-i-Tayyiba, banned in January 2002 as part of Musharraf's purported dismantling of the jihad infrastructure, has continued to thrive, by exploiting the Pakistani state's anti-Indian stance. After the carnage at Gujarat, Hafiz Mohammed

Saeed used the ideology of Pakistan to his advantage to ask the state to allow Indian Muslims to emigrate. It was wrong to say that they were Indian citizens; they had every right to come to Pakistan and were suffering only because they had supported the creation of a Muslim homeland. Pakistan had to protect the Muslims of the subcontinent. If the rulers of Pakistan, who claimed to be admirers of Allama Iqbal, could not understand their faith according to the Quran and the hadith, they should at least try to understand the ideology of Pakistan according to the statements of that poetic visionary. The borders were for Hindus, not Muslims. If the borders were unlocked for Afghan Muslims, they ought to be thrown open for Indian Muslims. In India, Hindus called Muslims Pakistanis and referred to parts of Gujarat as little Pakistan. It was unconscionable for Pakistani Muslims not to aid Indian Muslims.[103]

The American-led war against terror in which the principal victims have been Muslims has lent force to the militants' claims. In highlighting Western duplicity in Palestine, Chechnya, Kashmir, and other parts of the world, groups like the Lashkar-i-Tayyiba have recast anticolonial ideas in a new mold. The militants' focus is on fighting not just imperialism but the forces of unbelief in every nook and cranny of the world. Freely drawing on Mawdudi's thought, modern-day militants of Hafiz Saeed's breed are hard-nosed political practitioners who are not daunted by legal niceties, least of all the charge of terrorism. Even before the Lashkar-i-Tayyiba was declared a terrorist organization by the United States and forced to change its name, it insisted that its operations in Kashmir were directed at the Indian army, with the "sole purpose of protecting the local population from its repression." It harbored no ill will toward Hindus or any other community in Kashmir, it claimed, and had scrupulously avoided targeting civilians. Those killed during encounters with the Indian security forces were, like other collateral damage, "a regrettable exception." The Lashkar-i-Tayyiba had engaged in "no direct confrontation with any nation, Muslim or non-Muslim," and there was no question of its being "involved in any activity that may endanger US property or citizens either in US or anywhere else in the world."[104]

When pleading failed to do the trick, the Lashkar renamed itself the Jamaat-ud-Dawah, making only nominal changes to its logistical operations in Kashmir. Saeed publicly fulminated against Musharraf's "cowardly" policy of "bow[ing] down before the US pressure." He proclaimed: "For us jihad is sacred like praying and fasting." India had raised the specter of "cross-border terrorism" to "befool the world." There was no border between the two parts of Kashmir, "just a control line and no world forum or institution acknowledges it as border [sic]." Kashmiris were fighting for their freedom, and "no law could stop them crossing the LoC [line of control], because it was their territory that is under Indian occupation." He sneered at the suggestion that Pakistan wanted only to extend moral support to the Kashmiris. "It is sheer immorality," he declared, to offer consolation, after the Indian army killed, maimed, and tortured Kashmiris, besides burning their property. His courageous legions would never call off their jihad until they had rid the world of injustice.[105]

The Lashkar-i-Tayyiba and its offshoots have been involved in a series of suicide bombings in Kashmir and India. Though he denies the charge, Hafiz Saeed has been quoted as saying that suicide bombing is the best kind of jihad in the contemporary world.[106] The attack on the Indian parliament in December 2001 and the targeting of civilians in New Delhi and Benares punctures his claim that the Lashkar-i-Tayyiba attacks only Indian military personnel and installations. A little tactful prodding brings out the secular nature of his agenda. Asked how he could justify sending young men to their certain death in Kashmir when the jurists of Islam maintain that jihad is legitimate only if it has a chance of military success, Saeed's disingenuous reply is that his organization is fighting a guerilla war against India and the question of superior and inferior strength does not come into the equation.[107] Calling a guerilla war a jihad is a novel claim, as is his confident assertion that because Kashmiris are fighting a struggle against tyranny, the only ethical course for individual Muslims to adopt is to join them in defeating the oppressors.

Hafiz Saeed's ethical challenge is difficult to counter in a country where civil society has been pulverized by decades of military rule. In the post–September 11 global scenario, the theme of Western hypocrisy has dominated popular Muslim discourse the world over. After an initial surge of sympathy for Americans, Pakistanis were revolted by the cluster bombing of Afghanistan. The daily death toll in postwar Iraq has only deepened resentments: Muslim lives are cheap; American lives sacred. The "silence" of the moderate Muslims is laden with significance, because at one level it strikes an anticolonial chord in common with the militants' message. Like those whom they oppose as "religious" obscurantists, "secular" and liberal Muslims do not question the legitimacy of fighting injustice in Kashmir. Rather they point to those in their own society who have allowed extremist views to gain prominence. That the Lashkar-i-Tayyiba has been operating in full view of the state's security apparatus underscores its continuing utility to Pakistan's Kashmir policy.

In such an ambiguous situation, marred by the denial of democratic freedoms and the absence of critical debate, bouts of moderation and enlightenment are unlikely to dissipate the fog hovering over notions of jihad in Pakistan. Voices from a broad cross-section of society continue to speak out against the militaristic connotations assigned to this key ethical idea in Islam. Leading the resistance is the Human Rights Commission of Pakistan, which has chosen to name its journal *Jahd-i-Haq* (The Struggle for Rights). A liberal Urdu literary publication is called

Jid-o-Jehad. Attacks on unarmed civilians—one definition of terrorism—are regularly condemned.[108] But daily doses of disquieting news from Iraq, Afghanistan, and Pakistan's own independent tribal areas ensure guarded sympathy for the would-be warriors of Allah. And so the business of jihad continues, albeit less overtly, for the state is as yet uncertain whether peace with India will be worth the price it may have to pay for a solution of the Kashmir dispute. Until then, Pakistan's democratically enfeebled society is unlikely to succeed in restoring the broader meanings of jihad as an ethical struggle to be human. Not only are noncivil actions the bane of civil society in Pakistan, but ideologues like Hafiz Saeed justify them as ethical. With belief *(aqida)* in sectarian teachings replacing faith as the central feature in a believer's life, jihad is a weapon to be unleashed in a particular time and place against unbelievers, whether Muslim or non-Muslim. Jihad has gone from being the core ethical principle of Islam to becoming a justification for unethical actions, in the pursuit of worldly aims. Muslims opposed to armed jihad for humanistic reasons are routinely dismissed as heretics and apostates.

The contextually specific nature of the debate on jihad is evident in the opinions of an anonymous Ahl-i-Hadith scholar in India who condemns the terror networks of the Lashkar-i-Tayyiba in unequivocal terms: "Islam enjoins upon Muslims to cultivate good relations with others," not to fight a perpetual war to dominate and decimate them. The Lashkar was giving the Ahl-i-Hadith "a very bad name" by spreading hatred against non-Muslims. Most of its members were "ignorant, crazy and stupid youth." Hardly any scholar of note was associated with the Lashkar, which abused many respectable ulema of the Ahl-i-Hadith in Pakistan. In talking of an "Islamic state," they did not "observe the rules of Islamic morality." The Lashkar was "defaming Islam by empty slogans of flying the Islamic flag atop the Red Fort in Delhi!" By dragging Islam through the streets like a commodity, the Lashkar-i-Tayyiba was "spreading oppression." The "Lashkar," he said, "has nothing to do with Islam"—its operatives were "simply puppets in the hands of the Americans and the Pakistan government."[109]

Moderate Pakistanis share many of these opinions. But mindful of the Lashkar's close relations with the ISI, most have desisted from pressing the point aggressively. Transgressing the limits of public discourse on jihad can have fateful consequences. The military authoritarian state is of two minds about the value of jihad for strategic and political ends, and with homegrown militias using jihad to fight the "other," an informed critical debate on its meaning as an ethical struggle to be human runs the risk of being labeled both antinational and un-Islamic! In the absence of democratic norms in Pakistan, and given the frequent recourse to the untenable dichotomy between the religious and the secular, discussion of what kind of ethics Pakistani Muslims need to uphold will remain stifled, as always. The paradox of an American-led war on terror serving to promote a military dictator in Pakistan while seeking to spread democracy in the Middle East may be lost on Washington. In failing to practice what it preaches, the United States through its policy is helping delay the debate that Pakistanis must inevitably conduct if they are to recover the ethical basis of jihad and clear away the cobwebs of a militaristic and exclusionary mindset.

Conclusion

THESE TWO sets of utterances celebrating death for the love of Islam are different not merely in poetic quality, but in what they convey about the religious and ethical sentiments of the two composers:

> Die now, die now, in this Love die: when you have died in
> this Love, you will receive new life. . .
> Be silent, be silent; silence is the sign of death; it is because
> of life that you are fleeing from the silent one.[1]

> We drink the wine of martyrdom, swaying in ecstasy;
> This living is not living, we live by getting our heads cut
> off.
> We love to receive the gifts of our religion;
> When we bequeath gifts, it is of our lives.
> We became homeless for your religion—
> Oh, Allah, accept our sacrifices.[2]

The first, by Jalaluddin Rumi, is a variant of the Sufi injunction to die before dying in the struggle to be human, the greater jihad. The second, by Abdullah Shaban Ali of the Lashkar-i-Tayyiba, speaks of physical death in armed struggle against the enemies of Islam, the lesser jihad, as leading to promised rewards in the hereafter. Both kinds of jihad have animated Muslims in varying measure, depending on the historical context. To say that Rumi's conception of death is life-affirming, whereas the other is life-denying does at first sight seem a trifle unfair to the unknown young militant who cheerfully embraced martyrdom after killing thirteen Indian soldiers in his quest for eternal life in paradise. Suspension of moral judgment in the true Sunni tradition might be a tempting alternative, given the human incapacity to second-guess the will of Allah.

The ethical dilemma confronting Muslims in the contemporary world does not permit the luxury of postponement. The demonstrated urge among some Muslims to die fighting injustice needs to be understood before it can be expected to abate. The hope that practical accommodation will miraculously ensue if peaceful methods are given preference is a vain one. It does not even begin to address the discourse on the ethics of resistance, which has complex links with religion as faith and identity. Yet uncritically seeking recourse in the Islamic tradition can be a double-edged sword: far too many ambivalences suffuse the debate on whether or not Muslims are justified in taking up arms against oppression in any given situation. Paradoxically enough, this lack of clarity is the one glimmer of hope on an otherwise dark horizon. The contested and fluid meanings of jihad in Muslim history suggest that the issue is not settled, certainly not for all time to come. The vigorous debates of the past merely underscore the imperative of continuing debates in the present and the future.

If Muslims today show signs of reluctance to conduct an open-ended debate on the meanings of jihad in light of both Islamic faith and ethics, the reasons are political and have nothing to do with the presumed rigidity of the religion. If we ignore its multiple and shifting meanings throughout history, jihad in the aftermath of the attacks on American soil has come to signify the opposition between the Islamic world and the West. Perceptions of the threat posed by Muslims to the established global order has provided an instant market for journalistic pieces and hastily devised works on jihad. The popular notion that although not all Muslims are terrorists, all terrorists are Muslims has vitiated the debate and become the single biggest obstacle to restoring some semblance of perspective on the much-maligned concept of jihad. A columnist for the *Washington Post* conceded that any attempt to "penetrate the mysteries of Islam" invariably begins with a discussion of the idea of jihad as propagated by groups like Islamic Jihad and Al Qaeda. But just as code breakers using the wrong combination misinterpret the message before them, people who hold such a narrow view of jihad attack an idea that is central to "the daily life of ordinary Muslims worldwide, while the terrorists get away with wrapping their crimes in religious phraseology."[3]

Politically motivated interpretations of Islam serve only to reinforce the lines of division between Muslims and non-Muslims and provide grist for the overactive terrorist mill. Some Muslim and Western analysts have been belaboring the point that the war against terror is strengthening the very groups it purportedly is trying to eliminate. This observation has been misconstrued as sympathy for the terrorists rather than a genuine attempt to clear the air for a meaningful exchange across the great divisions both within and between the two monoliths of Islam and the West. Equating jihad with violence and terror makes a sheer travesty of a concept that, for all the distortions and misinterpretations, remains the core principle of Islamic ethics. In inviting Muslims to abandon jihad, the Western spokespersons for several political and academic establishments are erecting walls of religious opposition in an ineffectual attempt to disguise their political bias against Islam. There are those within the Muslim community who have their own reasons for encouraging the misconceptions of their rivals. Both parties are guilty of deliberately confusing temporal concerns with supposed religious divisions for opportunistic reasons.

While challenging the arbitrary distinction made between the religious and the secular, in this study I have retained the analytical separation between the two in discussing the evolution of Muslim political thought. In this way it has been possible both to recover the Quranic roots of the dichotomy and to shed light on the later temporal uses made of the key ethical concept of jihad. The idea of jihad as warfare against infidels has drawn on Muslim legists' arbitrary division of the world between the abode of Islam *(Dar-ul-Islam)* and the abode of war *(Dar-ul-Harb)*, which finds no sanction in the Quran. Yet ever since the inception of Islam, Muslims have contested an exclusive association of jihad with "holy war" against infidels. In fact, once the early wars of the expansion were over, by the tenth century, the interpretation of jihad as armed warfare became far less salient than it had been in the early defense of the incipient Muslim community. An overreliance on legal and theological texts at the expense of mystical, philosophical, and ethical writings gives a one-dimensional view of a concept that historically has been deployed to justify peace with nonbelievers quite as often as it has been to justify war. This assertion is borne out by the uses made of jihad and its obverse, *aman* (protection), in South Asia's precolonial history. Even as Muslim rulers evoked the idea to justify wars against their non-Muslim and Muslim rivals, it was the discourse on *aman* that tended to govern relations between the rulers and the ruled. India was described as a *Dar-ul-Islam,* even though non-

Muslims outnumbered the faithful. The Mughal emperor Akbar's policy of *sul-i-kul,* peace for all, was only the most dramatic and prominent manifestation of the desire of Muslim sovereigns to reach a creative accommodation with other faiths and to mediate the religious and cultural differences among their subjects. Muslims like Ahmad Sirhandi who frowned on such accommodation saw more sense in focusing on Islam as a marker of identity between Muslims and non-Muslims than on Islam as an ethical and humanistic religion for all humankind.

The false dichotomy between text and context in many writings on intellectual history is untenable. Important elements of continuity and change have marked the thought of key figures in the history of South Asian Islam. Even the most original thinkers borrowed from the intellectual legacy of the past, while striking out on a new path determined in part by a changed historical environment and in part by the predilections of the individual thinkers. Almost everyone relied on the Quran and the sunna, which were variously interpreted at different times. Shah Waliullah, the towering Muslim intellectual figure of the early eighteenth century, drew on facets of Sirhandi's thought but introduced important variations of his own. If Sirhandi had been the dissenter in the high Mughal era, during the reigns of Akbar and Jahangir, Waliullah lived through a period of decentralization, if not decline, during the age of the lesser Mughals. Waliullah's location in Delhi, as the Mughal influence was becoming attenuated, undoubtedly colored his perspective on the relationship between politics and ethics. Yet he was a master of textual sources. His interpretations are characterized by great creativity and independent reasoning. This has made him the point of reference for all subsequent Muslim thinkers on the subject of jihad and earned him the title of father of Muslim modernism.

Despite the depth of Waliullah's thought, his pivotal role in giving precedence to the outer husk rather than the inner kernel

of Islam strengthened Sunni orthodoxy and had important consequences for Indian Muslim views of identity and faith from the
late eighteenth century on. A tendency toward rationality and
modernity provided no guarantee against prejudice, once identity
achieved pride of place over faith and ethics. The worldview
Waliullah espoused, therefore, took on the rather stern and aus-
tere quality of a rational bigotry. Having had the potential to be
the founder of a generous conception of modern Muslim ethics
based on independent reasoning, he became in the end the foun-
tainhead of Sunni sectarian orthodoxy in the subcontinent.
Waliullah's invitation to the Afghan warlord Ahmad Shah Abdali
to invade Delhi signaled the drowning of Islamic ethics in the
torrent of eighteenth-century Indian politics. With the erosion of
Muslim political power in India, jihad came to be seen by many
as a means to assert identity against the encroachment of the
infidels, rather than as a spiritual and ethical struggle to be fully
human.

There were continuities and discontinuities between Waliullah
and Sayyid Ahmad of Rai Bareilly, who translated Waliullah's idea
of jihad into practice. Although influenced to some degree by intellectual currents in the Arabian peninsula, the Waliullah clan's
frame of reference was shaped to an even greater extent by the Indian environment in which its members lived. The attachment of
the label "Wahabi" to Sayyid Ahmad Barelvi and his followers
was more a function of British insecurity than an accurate characterization of their doctrines and methods. Indian thinkers and
practitioners of jihad never abandoned their Sufi inspiration and
camaraderie. Sayyid Ahmad Barelvi was less a thinker than a man
of action. If his reform movement initially fostered an attitude of
religious and moral positivism that was more this-worldly than
concerned with the hereafter, his jihad against the Sikhs between
1826 and 1831 could hardly avoid being influenced by temporal
factors.[4] A narrative of this jihad shows up the slippage between

the theory and the practice. Sayyid Ahmad Barelvi was constrained not just to seek help from Hindu rulers, financiers, and warriors, but more painfully to fight against fellow Muslims on the northwest frontier.

The history of the subcontinent's only undisputed jihad, which thrust Muslims against Muslims, ought to have supplied a cautionary tale for the future. Yet it was not the inadequacies of jihad as armed struggle that served as a lesson from history. Instead, Muslims remembered the martyrdom of Sayyid Ahmad Barelvi, Shah Ismail, and their gallant band of mujahideen, who sacrificed their lives in the battle of Balakot. To offer a critical history of jihad is not to diminish the sacredness of the martyrdom of Sayyid Ahmad Barelvi and his followers. In death they had upheld the high ethical principles of Islam, which often had to be set aside in the course of the armed struggle. A later historical conjuncture would make possible another appropriation of the legacy of this jihad. Sayyid Ahmad Barelvi's teachings compiled in the *Sirat-i-Mustaqim* had rejected jihad for this-worldly purposes. But the moral positivism inherent in his teachings allowed for considerable flexibility, inviting some writers to claim his jihad against the Sikhs as a nationalist struggle, although such a notion is at odds with the idea of sacred war. Fazlur Rahman had argued that the moral positivism of the movement helped the more enlightened segments of society adapt to modernity.[5] But for all the emphasis Sayyid Ahmad placed on ethics, the political nature of the movement required compromises of convenience. These served to widen still further the gulf between jihad and Islam as faith and virtuous actions.

Between the jihad of 1826–1831 and the aspiration to wage jihad in the period leading up to World War I lay another fascinating phase in the history of Muslim thought and politics in India. The reverberations of Sayyid Ahmad Barelvi's jihad could be heard along the frontier as late as the 1860s. Yet when superior

British military forces crushed the great rebellion of 1857 and inaugurated the crown raj in 1858, the Muslim intelligentsia had to adapt to a qualitatively different temporal context. Colonial officials charged Muslims with disloyalty, and English authors and Christian missionaries portrayed Islam as an aggressive religion lacking in ethics. In reacting to these unwarranted attacks on their religion, modernist Muslims like Sayyid Ahmad Khan, Chiragh Ali and Mirza Ghulam Ahmad were not prisoners of their context or mere apologists. Through his spirited critique of W. W. Hunter's misperceptions and scathing commentary on William Muir's egregious opinions about the Prophet Muhammad, Sayyid Ahmad Khan pioneered the Indian Muslim effort to recover the expansive dimensions of jihad as an ethical ideal rather than as perpetual warfare against infidels. Far from repudiating jihad as armed struggle, he underlined its intrinsic importance to faith on the basis of creative interpretations of canonical literature and Muslim history. Together with his protégé, Chiragh Ali, he deflected the Orientalist critique away from Islamic doctrines toward the temporal uses made of them by Muslim legists. In framing the sharia, they had separated religion and the world. It was the secularization of Islamic law, and not Islam's religious teachings, the two argued, which was the main obstacle to Muslims accommodating modernity. Taking his cues from Sayyid Ahmad Khan, the Ahmadi leader Mirza Ghulam Ahmad declared the very idea of an armed jihad obsolete. Although more anxious to press his own claims to be the promised *messiah,* the Ahmadi leader shared the modernist Muslim view that what Indian Muslims needed most in an age of political and mental subjugation was a revitalized conception of jihad as an ethical struggle. Their intellectual contributions to redirecting the debate on jihad have continued to influence Muslim liberal circles, even though their loyalism came in for sharp questioning as early as the last decade of the nineteenth century.

The politics of collaboration with the colonial authorities advocated by late nineteenth-century Muslim intellectuals certainly ran out of steam by the turn of the twentieth century in the face of Western imperial aggression. What survived was their use of reason to challenge critically some of the cherished precepts of their own community, while exposing the limitations of Western liberal rationality in accommodating alternative points of view. One of the first to launch a blistering critique of European expansionism was Jamaluddin al-Afghani, the mercurial Iranian propagandist who shifted intellectual gears quite as often as he did habitations. Although reputed to be the forerunner of Islamic universalism in the age of empire, al-Afghani propagated territorial nationalism to his Indian audiences, in the interest of Hindu-Muslim unity against the British. His anticolonial thought and politics made no inroads on the Indian scene until the emergence of Abul Kalam Azad, an intellectual giant with a populist touch, who energized Indian Muslims with his Islamic universalist vision during World War I. Azad is best remembered as a "secularist" in retrospectively constructed Indian nationalist pasts; his credentials as a theorist of jihad have been curiously ignored by historians of modern South Asia. Azad and his compatriots fashioned a discourse on jihad that made it compatible with anticolonial struggle. Although they were seeking an ethical basis for that struggle in Islam, this line of thought also avoided the pitfalls of drawing a sharp demarcation between Muslims and Hindus. This moment of creative accommodation between extraterritorial Islamic universalism and territorial Indian nationalism coincided with the advent of Mahatma Gandhi as the preeminent leader of a mass-based anticolonial movement. Figures like Obaidullah Sindhi tried to translate the theory of the extraterritorial dimension of anti-imperialism into practice by seeking the help of Britain's enemies during an international war crisis. Just as the uncertain allegiance of the Pathan tribesmen had wrecked

Sayyid Ahmad Barelvi's jihad, the fickleness of the Afghan ruling elite hampered Sindhi's efforts at mounting a transnational anticolonial jihad—a sobering reminder of the ever-elusive nature of Muslim unity.

Muhammad Iqbal was not unaware of the formidable obstacles in India and beyond that stood in the way of invigorating the Muslim *ummah.* Yet in his poetry and philosophical treatises he supplied the most subtle evocations of jihad both as an ethical endeavor to be human and as an armed struggle against Western imperialist injustice. His work displaying the most exquisite literary touches along with the broadest imaginative reach is perhaps the *Javidnama,* patterned on the Prophet's ascension to the heavens with no less a personage than Jalaluddin Rumi as the guide. The conversations with a range of Muslim universalist thinkers that he narrates in this extended poem are indicative of the vitality of an Islamic philosophical tradition that had survived the onslaught of European colonialism. The persistence of Islamic philosophy did not mean, however, that there was no need for the poet to awaken Muslims from their slumber. As he put it sarcastically in his poem "Satan's Parliament":

> Sufi and mullah are now wedded to foreign rule;
> This was just the opium the East needed:
> Their theological artistry is no less stupefying than
>   *qawwali.*
> So what if there is commotion over the circumambulations
>   of hajj?
> Blunt is the *momin's* sheathless sword—
> Under whose hopeless command is this newfangled canon?
> "Jihad in this age is forbidden for the Musalman!"[6]

The poet-philosopher who gave lyrical expression to the dream of Islamic universalism in time achieved recognition as the spiritual founding father of the nation-state of Pakistan. A journalist and ideologue who had opposed the creation of this state until the very last moment came forward to enunciate a theory of jihad for the postcolonial predicament of Muslims. Abul Ala Mawdudi's thought shows certain connections with Iqbal's philosophy and the general orientation of anticolonial discourse and politics. Yet the transformations turned out to be more compelling than the continuities, for Mawdudi aspired to temporal power at the head of an Islamic state. The beacon of individual freedom celebrated by Iqbal was now extinguished in favor of a darker theological absolutism. This shift cleared the way for an eschatological justification of jihad against fellow Muslims who did not conform to Mawdudi's version of Islamic ideology. Mawdudi suffered setbacks, and his success in Pakistani politics was at best limited. Yet his idea of jihad, which set the temporal quest for power above personal ethics, would have powerful echoes in the Middle East, especially Egypt and Saudi Arabia, as well as among militant groups in South Asia that sprang up after his death.

The Soviet invasion of Afghanistan in 1979 and the resistance that built up against it triggered a decisive transformation in both the theory and practice of jihad in South Asia and beyond. With American and Saudi financial and ideological backing, Pakistan enjoyed frontline status in the jihad against communism that would have broad implications. The current confrontation between Islam and the West is being played out on a global stage. Yet its center of gravity lies in Pakistan, especially in its northwest frontier region. Contemporary ideologues of jihad whose storm troopers have fought in Afghanistan and Kashmir find some inspiration in the legacy of Maulana Mawdudi. They depart, however, from his certitude that jihad must be sanctioned and directed by the state on the advice of its religious guardians. In a dramatic break from Islamic tradition, today's partisans of Allah have no qualms about declaring and waging jihad without the blessing of the state. This is not to say that they do not revere the heroes of the past. Sayyid Ahmad Barelvi remains an iconic figure in South Asian jihad, and the sacredness of his martyrdom obscures the many shortcomings of his temporal struggle. The eagerness to become a martyr *(shaheed)* is seen by contemporary militant organizations as sanctifying armed warfare against perceived injustices perpetrated by enemies of Islam. Abdullah Shaban Ali's last will and testament urging his mother not to weep for him, along with his poem on death before dying, must undoubtedly have a powerful emotional impact. But in exemplifying a widespread desire among militants to become martyrs, and not just warriors of the faith, that testament raises a troubling question about the erosion of an ethics of humanity amid the brutalizing effects of war.

South Asian Muslim voices have always upheld jihad as a spiritual and ethical struggle to be human. Notable among them was that of Mirza Asadullah Khan Ghalib. His assertion that giving up one's life in a jihad is insufficient repayment for the debt owed to God, the ultimate life giver, has never ceased to inspire Muslims. It was this ethical view that prevented Ghalib from plunging into Sayyid Ahmad Barelvi's jihad. He was probably aware of a spurious tradition, aimed at discrediting the Kharajite threat to early Islam, according to which the Prophet is said to have declared:

> During the last days there will appear some young foolish people who will say the best words but their faith will not go beyond their throats [that is, they will have no faith] and will go out from their religion as an arrow goes out of the game. So, wherever you find them, kill them, for whoever kills them shall have reward on the Day of Resurrection.[7]

Instead of being an intrinsic part of faith, jihad, claims to the contrary notwithstanding, has become the belief of certain segments of the Muslim community—most notably the Ahl-i-Hadith and its contemporary manifestation in the militant Lashkar-i-Tayyiba—whose religion is based on a series of closures, internal as well as external. It is this constricting of the heart and narrowing of the mind among the would-be partisans of Allah which has reduced the concept of jihad to violent struggle against infidels, whether armed or unarmed—innocent men, women, and children. Like an arrow that has left the bow and flown wide of the mark, jihad in the modern world has become a political weapon with which to threaten believers and unbelievers alike. Only by retrieving the arrow and straightening its jagged edges and twisted feathers can Muslims aspire to attain those high ethical values which are the embodiment of faith *(iman)* based on submission to God *(islam)*. Until then the doyen of Urdu poetry in the subcontinent is unlikely to stir from the grave to assert that things in life can be easier for Muslims if they try to repay their debt to the Creator by respecting the rights and dignity of fellow human beings, irrespective of their ideological or religious denominations.

GLOSSARY

NOTES

INDEX

Glossary

adab	culture; correct social behavior
adl	justice
ahimsa	nonviolence
akhlaq	ethics
alim	religious scholar
amal-i-salah	correct deeds
aman	peace; protection
amir-ul-momineen	leader of the faithful
aqida	religious belief
aql	reason
baqa	salvation
bhakti	devotion
bidat	innovation
Dar-ul-Aman	abode of peace
Dar-ul-Harb	abode of war
Dar-ul-Islam	abode of peace
dawah	propagation of faith
dawla	government
din	Islamic notion of religion as an all-encompassing way of life

duniya	world
fana	annihilation
farz	duty
fiqh	Islamic jurisprudence
fitna	social discord; sedition
fitrat	original nature
fuqaha	legists
futawa	chivalry
ghair muqallid	one who does not adhere to any school of jurisprudence
ghazi	warrior of the faith
hadith	tradition
haq (pl. *haqiqah*)	truth
harb	warfare
hijrat	migration
hijri	Islamic calendar dating from the migration of the community to Medina
holi	spring festival of colors in Hinduism
hud (pl. *hudood*)	limits
huquq al-abad	private rights of individuals
huquq al-allah	rights of God
ibadat	worship
ihsan	virtuous action
ihtisab	accountability
ijma	consensus of the community
ijtihad	independent reasoning
ilm	knowledge
iman	faith
insaniyat	humanity
irtifaqat	different stages of civilization
irtiqadat	religious consciousness
ishq	love; intuition
islam	peace; submission
itisihan	equity
jahaliya	[literally] ignorance; term used for pre-Islamic Arabia

jihad	struggle
jihad al-akbar	the greater jihad
jihad al-asghar	the lesser jihad
jihad fi sabil allah	jihad in the way of Allah
jihd-o-jihad	exertion in a positive endeavor
jizya	poll tax
kafir	infidel
kalima	Muslim confessional
khairaj	tax on newly converted Muslims
khalifa	temporal and spiritual leader of Muslims, caliph
khanqa	Sufi shrine
khilafat	institutionalized spiritual and temporal authority over the Muslim community; caliphate
khudi	self
kufr	infidelity
khutba	religious sermon
maktab	religious school
maulana	learned man
maulvi	title given to Muslim religious preacher
mazhab	religion
millat	religious community
miraj	Prophet Muhammad's ascension to the heavens
momin	a true believer
muamalat	social relations
muharram	Shia festival of mourning to commemorate the martyrdom of Husain at Karbala
mujaddid	renewer of the faith
mujtahid	one who has legal training to exercise independent reasoning
mustamin	non-Muslims protected under Muslim rule
nechari	naturalist; one who reduces religion to worldly matters
pir	spiritual guide
qanun-i-shahi	secular law
qawwali	a genre of Sufi devotional music

qazi	judge
qisas	just retaliation
qital	fighting
qutb	pole, axis; spiritual medium through whom God and the Prophet Muhammad communicate
shaheed	martyr
shirk	polytheism
shuhudi	adherent of the principle of *wahdut al-shuhud*
tanzih	God's transcendence
taqlid	blind imitation
tariqah	correct path
tashbih	God's likeness in created beings
tawazun	balance
tawba	repentance
tawhid	Islamic principle of the unity of creation
tazir	civil punishment(s) not specified in the Quran
taziya	consolation; Shia passion play(s) during muharram
tehzib	culture
ummah/ummat	worldwide community of Muslims
urf	customary law
ushr	tithe, tax on one-tenth of the proceeds from the land
wahdut al-shuhud	unity of appearances
wahdut al-wujud	unity of creation
wujudis	adherents of the principle of *wahdut al-wujud*
zakat	Muslim alms tax
zawabit	secular law
zimmi	protected non-Muslims living under Muslim rule
zina	adultery

Notes

1. Jihad as Ethics, Jihad as War

1. Interview with author, November 2005, Lahore.

2. In Ghulam Rasul Mehr (comp.), *Nawa-i-Saroosh* (Lahore: Sheikh Ghulam Ali and Sons, n.d.), p. 69 (henceforth, Ghalib, *Nawa-i-Saroosh*). All translations from Urdu are mine unless otherwise indicated.

3. Ibid., p. 560.

4. Reuven Firestone, *Jihad: the Origin of Holy War in Islam* (New York: Oxford University Press, 1999), pp. 121–122.

5. Ibid., p. 81n22. See Abdullah Yusuf Ali, *The Holy Quran* (Brentwood, Calif.: Amana Corporation, 1989), Surahs 9:73, 22:78, 25:52, 29:69, 47:31, 49:15, 60:1, 61:11, 66:9.

6. An exception is verse 29:8, where *jahada* refers to nonbelieving parents who strive to prevent their children from practicing God's religion.

7. Yusuf Ali, *The Holy Quran,* Surah 60:8–9.

8. For instance, ibid., Surah 61:4.

9. Fazlur Rahman, *Islam* (New York: Anchor, 1966), p. 37.

10. Toshihiko Izutsu, *The Concept of Belief in Islamic Theology: A Semantic Analysis of Iman and Islam* (Tokyo: Keio University, 1965).

11. For an insightful study of the rather guarded and pragmatic Muslim scholastic response to this Islamic principle, and its implications for ev-

eryday life in the Islamic world, see Michael Cook, *Forbidding Wrong in Islam* (Cambridge: Cambridge University Press, 2003).

12. See Fazlur Rahman, *Revival and Reform in Islam: A Study of Islamic Fundamentalism* (Oxford: Oneworld, 2000); and *Islam and Modernity: Transformation of an Intellectual Tradition* (Chicago: Chicago University Press, 1982).

13. Rahman, *Islam and Modernity,* p. 155.

14. Cited in Abu Hamid al-Ghazali, *Ihya Ulum-id-Din,* trans. Fazlul Karim (Karachi: Darul Ishat, 1993), 3:58.

15. Fazlur Rahman, *Major Themes of the Quran,* 2nd ed. (Minneapolis: Bibliotheca Islamica, 1980 and 1989), p. 63.

16. See Dwight Donaldson, *Studies in Muslim Ethics* (London: Society for Promoting Christian Knowledge, 1953), pp. 109–110.

17. Ira Lapidus, "Knowledge, Virtue and Action," in Barbara Metcalf (ed.), *Moral Conduct and Authority: The Place of Adab in South Asian Islam* (Berkeley: University of California Press, 1984), pp. 56–61.

18. Ibid., pp. 43–45; Donaldson, *Studies in Muslim Ethics,* chap. 5, and Majid Fakhry, *Ethical Theories in Islam* (Leiden: Brill, 1994), chap. 6.

19. Ghazali, *Ihya Ulum-id-Din,* 3:9–10, 47–49, 69.

20. R. A. Nicolson (trans. and ed.), *The Mathnawi of Jalaluddin Rumi* (Lahore: Islamic Book Service, 1989), bk. 5, nos. 3780–3830, pp. 227–230.

21. Reverend W. R. W. Gardener, "Jihad" in *Moslem World* 2, no. 4 (1919) is a particularly biased analysis. See also Rudolph Peters, *Jihad in Mediaeval and Modern Islam* (Leiden: Brill, 1977). There has been a profusion of works on militant Islam in recent years that thoroughly distort the meaning of jihad in the Islamic tradition.

22. Aziz Al-Azmeh, *Muslim Kingship: Power and the Sacred in Muslim, Christian and Pagan Polities* (London: Taurus, 1997), chaps. 1 and 2.

23. The correspondences and differences between Islamic and Christian conceptions of a religious war are examined in James Turner Johnson, *The Holy War Idea in Western and Islamic Traditions* (University Park: Pennsylvania State University Press, 1997).

24. For an encyclopedic study of the concept through the ages, see Richard Bonney, *Jihad: From Quran to bin Laden* (New York: Palgrave Macmillan, 2004).

25. See Talal Asad, *Formations of the Secular: Christianity, Islam and Mo-*

dernity (Stanford, Calif.: Stanford University Press, 2003) for a historically nuanced analysis of the constitution of the term *secular* in the Western and Islamic traditions.

26. William Cantwell Smith, *The Meaning and End of Religion: A New Approach to the Religious Traditions of Mankind* (New York: Macmillan, 1962), pp. 19–20; Syed Muhammad Naquib Al-Attas, *Islam and Secularism* (Lahore: Suhail Academy, 1998), pp. 15–49.

27. See, for instance, Sachiko Murata and William C. Chittick, *The Vision of Islam* (Lahore: Suhail Academy, 1994), p. xxxii, Seyyed Hossein Nasr, "The Interior Life of Islam," in *Islamic Life and Thought* (Lahore: Suhail Academy, 1981), p. 193, and Frithjof Schuon, *Understanding Islam* trans. D. M. Matheson, reprint (Lahore: Suhail Academy, 1999), p. 118.

28. Schuon, *Understanding Islam,* pp. 118–119.

2. Jihad in Precolonial South Asia

1. See Barbara Metcalf (ed.), *Moral Conduct and Authority: The Place of Adab in South Asian Islam* (Berkeley: University of California Press, 1984).

2. *The Hedaya or Guide: A Commentary on the Mussulman Laws,* Charles Hamilton (trans. and comp.), reprint (Delhi: Islamic Book Trust), 1982. See also Barbara Daly Metcalf, *Islamic Revival in British India: Deoband, 1860–1900* (Princeton, N.J.: Princeton University Press, 1982); and M. R. Anderson, "Islamic Law and the Colonial Encounter in British India," in David Arnold and Peter Robb (eds.), *Institutions and Ideologies* (London: Curzon, 1993), p. 171.

3. Ali ibn Hamid Kufi, *The Chachnama: An Ancient History of Sind,* trans. Mirza Kalichbeg Fredunbeg (Karachi: Commissioner's Press, 1900), pp. 164–169.

4. See Baber Johansen, *Contingency in a Sacred Law: Legal and Ethical Norms in the Muslim Fiqh* (Leiden: Brill, 1999), p. 191.

5. See Thomas Patrick Hughes, *Dictionary of Islam,* reprint (Calcutta: Rupa, 1992), p. 710.

6. Johansen, *Contingency in a Sacred Law,* pp. 192–194.

7. See, for instance, Muhammad Qasim Fareeshta, *Tarikh-e-Fareeshta,* Abdul Hayee Khwaja and Abdur Rahman (trans. and comp.) (Lahore: Doost, 1998), 1:68.

8. See Saiyid Athar Abbas Rizvi, *Muslim Revivalist Movements in Northern India in the Sixteenth and Seventeenth Centuries* (Agra: Agra University, 1965), p. 9.

9. Johansen, *Contingency in a Sacred Law,* pp. 119–120, 127.

10. Muhammad Habib and Asfar Umar Salim Khan, *The Political Theory of the Delhi Sultanate* (Allahabad: Kitab Mahal, 1961), pp. 136–137; Muhammad Basheer Ahmed, *The Administration of Justice in Medieval India* (Aligarh: Historical Research Institute, 1941).

11. See Dwight Donaldson, *Studies in Muslim Ethics* (London: Society for Promoting Christian Knowledge, 1953), for the role of *akhlaq* literature in the Sultanate period. For a discussion of the impact on the Mughals, see Muzaffar Alam, *"Akhlaqi* Norms and Mughal Governance," in Muzaffar Alam, Franchise "Nalini" Delvoye, and Marc Gaborieau (eds.), *The Making of Indo-Persian Culture: Indian and French Studies* (New Delhi: Manohar, 2000); and Saiyid Athar Abbas Rizvi, *Shah Wali-Allah and His Times* (Canberra: Marifat, 1976), p. 59.

12. Alam, *"Akhlaqi* Norms and Mughal Governance," pp. 71–73.

13. Muhib-ul-Rahman wa Ayn-ul-Hedaya (comp.), *Fatawa-i-Alamgiri,* trans. Maulana Sayyid Emir Ali (Lahore: Maktaba Rahmaniya, n.d.), vol. 5, *Kitab Adab-i-Qazi,* pp. 112–114.

14. See Johansen, *Contingency in a Sacred Law,* pp. 452–454.

15. Johansen, *Contingency in a Sacred Law,* p. 200; *Islami Qanun Faujdari,* a translation of Maulvi Salamat Ali, *Kitab-al-Ikhtiyar* (Lahore: Sang-e-Meel, n.d.), henceforth *Kitab-al-Ikhtiyar,* pp. 1–2; Ahmad Hasan, *Principles of Islamic Jurisprudence* (Islamabad: Islamic Research Institute, 1993), 1:279–285.

16. Johansen, *Contingency in a Sacred Law,* p. 200; *Kitab-al-Ikhtiyar,* pp. 2–3.

17. Zafrul Islam, *Socio-Economic Dimensions of Fiqh Literature in Medieval India* (Lahore: Research Cell, Dyal Singh Trust Library, 1990), p. 2.

18. Ibid., p. 6.

19. Ross E. Dunn, *The Adventures of Ibn Battuta: A Muslim Traveller of the 14th Century* (Berkeley: University of California Press, 1989), pp. 1, 3, 200, 205.

20. *Kitab-al-Ikhtiyar,* chap. 3.

21. Ibid., pp. 29, 26.

22. Islam, *Socio-Economic Dimensions of Fiqh Literature in Medieval India,* pp. 4–5.

23. Mansura Haider (comp. and trans.), *Mukatab-i-Allami (Inshai Abul Fazl): Letters of the Emperor Akbar* (New Delhi: Indian Council of Historical Research, 1998), pp. 8–10, 42–47.

24. Popularly known as the *Mujaddid-i-alf-thani,* or the renovator of the second millennium, a title he bestowed upon himself, Sirhandi was a virulent critic of Akbar's policies of religious reconciliation, known as the *sul-i-kul,* or peace for all. He sought to reform Sufi doctrine and practices in the light of the sharia. The crux of his critique of Indian Sufism addressed its negative, world-denying spiritualism, one that he juxtaposed against the positive, world-affirming teachings of the sharia.

25. Sirhandi's letter to Khan-i-Azam Mirza Aziz Koka, cited in Rizvi, *Muslim Revivalist Movements,* p. 234.

26. Rizvi, *Muslim Revivalist Movements,* p. 247.

27. The *Fatawa-i-Firuz Shahi* was based on Firoz Shah's exchanges with Muslim jurists on such issues as the imposition of *jizya,* or taxes not sanctioned by the sharia, and the treatment of apostates and leaders of heretical sects. Islam, *Socio-Economic Dimensions of Fiqh Literature in Medieval India,* chap. 2.

28. See *Fatawa-i-Alamgiri,* vol. 5, *Kitab Adab-i-Qazi.*

29. Ibid., 3:339.

30. Ibid., pp. 340–342.

31. Ibid., pp. 346–347.

32. Ibid., pp. 353–356.

33. "Suhrawardi saints rolled in wealth, accepted government service but they could not be dubbed as immoral or impious." Rizvi, *Muslim Revivalist Movements,* p. 12.

34. The most famous warrior saint is Sayyid Salar Masud Ghazi, who lived during the Ghaznavid period; he is said to have conquered areas east and west of Awadh and was killed in a battle in Bahraich. Others include Sheikh Jalal of Sylhet and Sayyid Qutubuddin, an ancestor of Sayyid Ahmad Shaheed, who defeated Raja Jaichand of Kanauj. Saiyid Athar Abbas Rizvi, *Shah Abdul Aziz: Puritanism, Sectarian Polemics and Jihad* (Canberra: Marifat, 1982), pp. 472–473.

35. Schoun, *Understanding Islam,* p. 139, and Saiyid Athar Abbas Rizvi, *A*

History of Sufism in India, vol. 2, *From 16th Century to Modern Century,* reprint (New Delhi: Manohar, 1992).

36. See Rizvi, *Muslim Revivalist Movements.*

37. For a nuanced view of Simnani's attitude toward Ibn al-'Arabi and later interpretations of his thought by the Indian Naqshbandiya, see Jamal J. Elias, *The Throne Carrier of God: The Life and Thought of Ala ad-Dawla as-Simnani* (Albany: State University of New York Press, 1995), pp. 57–58.

38. Annemarie Schimmel, *Pain and Grace: A Study of Two Mystical Writers of Eighteenth Century Muslim India,* reprint (Lahore: Sang-e-Meel, 2003), p. 5.

39. William C. Chittick, *Imaginal World: Ibn al-'Arabi and the Problem of Religious Diversity* (Albany: State University of New York Press, 1994), pp. 23–29; *The Self-Disclosure of God: Principles of Ibn al-'Arabi's Cosmology* (Albany: State University of New York Press, 1998), pp. 95–96.

40. See Alexander D. Knysh, *Ibn 'Arabi in the Later Islamic Tradition: The Making of a Polemical Image in Medieval Islam* (Albany: State University of New York Press, 1999).

41. Rizvi, *Muslim Revivalist Movements,* p. 249.

42. For a preliminary study of Ibn al-'Arabi's impact on Indian Muslim thought, see William C. Chittick, "Notes on Ibn al-Arabi's Influence in the Subcontinent," *Muslim World* 82, nos. 3–4 (July–October 1992), pp. 218–241.

43. Schimmel, *Pain and Grace,* pp. 245, 248–249.

44. Sheikh Yahya Manyari, from the village of Manyar near Patna, was a member of the Firdausi Sufi order and a contemporary of Sultan Firoz Shah Tughluq. A pragmatist, he believed that the sharia had to be interpreted according to the emergent needs of Muslims. His ideas had a stronger influence on Aurangzeb than did the bigoted views of Sheikh Ahmad Sirhandi. See Rizvi, *Muslim Revivalist Movements,* pp. 49–50.

45. Ibid.

46. As Titus Burckhardt has pointed out: "Pantheism arose from the same mental tendency which produced, first nihilism and then materialism. Pantheism only conceives of the relationship between the Divine Principle and things from the point of view of substantial or existential continuity, and this is an error explicitly rejected by every traditional doctrine." Titus Burckhardt, *An Introduction to Sufism,* trans. D. M. Matheson (Wellingborough, Eng.: Aquarian, 1990), p. 28.

47. Frithjof Schuon, *Understanding Islam,* trans. D. M. Matheson, reprint (Lahore: Suhail Academy, 1999), pp. 147–150; Martin Lings (Abu Bakr Siraj ed-Din), *The Book of Certainty* (Lahore: Suhail Academy, 1988), p. 10.

48. Fazlur Rahman (comp.), *Selected Letters of Shaikh Ahmad Sirhandi* (Karachi: Iqbal Academy, 1968), p. 27.

49. See Annemarie Schimmel, *Mystical Dimensions of Islam* (Lahore: Sang-e-Meel, 2003); Aziz Ahmad, *Studies in Islamic Culture in the Indian Environment,* reprint (Delhi: Oxford, 1999).

50. Rizvi, *Muslim Revivalist Movements,* p. 255.

51. Ibid., pp. 59–60. Also see Rizvi, *A History of Sufism in India,* 2:413–424.

52. Waliullah to Shah Nurullah, in *Nadar-i-Maktubat,* Maulana Naseem Ahmad Faridi (comp. and trans.) (Lahore: Adara-i-Siqafat-i-Islamia, 1999), pp. 101–102.

53. Cited in J. M. S. Baljon, *Religion and Thought of Shah Wali Allah Dihlawi: 1703–1762* (Leiden: Brill, 1986), pp. 1–2.

54. Marcia K. Hermansen, *The Conclusive Argument from God: Shah Wali Allah of Delhi's Hujjat Allah al-Baligha* (Islamabad: Islamic Research Institute, 2003), p. 330—henceforth Waliullah, *Hujjut.*

55. Rizvi, *Shah Waliullah and His Times,* pp. 87, 90; and Rafat M. Bilgrami, *Religious and Quasi-Religious Departments of the Mughal Period, 1556–1707* (New Delhi: Munshiram Manoharlal, 1984), chap. 8.

56. Rizvi, *Shah Waliullah and His Times,* p. 306.

57. Rizvi, *A History of Sufism in India,* 2:431.

58. Waliullah to Shah Nurullah, in *Nadar-i-Maktubat,* p. 115.

59. See Aziz Ahmad, *Studies in Islamic Culture in the Indian Environment,* p. 201; and Fazlur Rahman, "The Thinker of Crisis Shah Waliy-Ullah," *Pakistan Quarterly,* Summer 1956, p. 44.

60. A. J. Halepota, "Shah Waliyullah and Iqbal, the Philosophers of Modern Age," *Islamic Studies,* December 13, 1974, pp. 227–228.

61. Waliullah, *Hujjat,* p. 7.

62. Various scholars have pointed this out. See, for instance, G. N. Jalbani, *Teachings of Shah Waliyullah of Delhi* (Lahore: Sheikh Muhammad Ashraf, 1967), pp. 107–108; and Muhammad al-Ghazali, *The Socio-Political Thought of Shah Wali Allah* (Islamabad: International Institute of Islamic Thought and Islamic Research Institute, 2001), pp. 87, 104–105.

63. Waliullah to Shah Nurullah, in *Nadar-i-Maktubat,* pp. 108, 112.

64. Ibid., p. 141.

65. Shah Waliullah, *Hujjut Allah al-Baligha,* Urdu trans. Maulana Mohammed Manzur al-Wajaidi (Lahore: Sheikh Ghulam Ali and Sons, n.d.), pp. 895–896—henceforth Waliullah, *Hujjat* [Urdu].

66. Ibid., pp. 899–901.

67. A host of scholars have made this suggestion, notably Ghazali, *The Socio-Political Thought of Shah Wali Allah,* and Bashir Ahmad Dar, *Studies in Muslims Philosophy and Literature,* collected by Shima Majeed (ed.), Iqbal Academy Pakistan (Lahore: Iqbal Academy, 1996).

68. Shah Waliullah, *Al-Budur-Al-Bazigah,* trans., G. N. Jalbani (Islamabad: National Hijra Council, 1985), p. 167.

69. Waliullah, *Hujjat,* pp. 115–117.

70. Ibid., p. 53.

71. Waliullah, *Hujjat,* pp. xviii, 115–118.

72. Shah Waliullah, *Al-Budur-Al-Bazigah,* Urdu trans. Qazi Mujibur Rahman (Lahore: Mohammed Nadeem, 2000), p. 105—henceforth Waliullah, *Al-Budur* [Urdu].

73. Ibid., p. 109.

74. Waliullah, *Hujjat,* p. 159.

75. Waliullah, *Al-Budur* [Urdu], p. 97.

76. Ibid., p. 896; Ghazali, *The Socio-Political Thought of Shah Wali Allah,* p. 260.

77. Waliullah, *Hujjut,* p. 211.

78. Ibid., p. 344.

79. Ibid., p. 341.

80. Ibid., pp. 124–125.

81. Ibid., p. 103.

82. Ibid., p. 131.

83. Waliullah, *Al-Budur,* [Urdu], pp. 109–111.

84. Ghazali, *The Socio-Political Thought of Shah Wali Allah,* p. 96.

85. Waliullah, *Hujjut,* p. 230.

86. Waliullah, *Hujjut,* [Urdu], pp. 915, 917.

87. See K. A. Nizami, *Shah Wali-Allah Dihlawi ke Siyasi Maktubat* (Aligarh, India: Muslim University Press, 1950).

88. Shah Waliullah to Shah Nurullah, *Nadar-i-Maktubat,* p. 111.

89. Rizvi, *Shah Wali-Allah and His Times,* pp. 295, 299.

90. Nizami, *Shah Walli-Allah Dihlawi ke Siyasi Maktubat,* pp. 90–91.

91. Ibid., pp. 102–103, 105.

92. Baljon, *Religion and Thought of Shah Wali Allah Dihlawi,* p. vii.

93. Cited in Rizvi, *Shah Wali-Allah and His Times,* pp. 304–305.

94. Waliullah, *Hujjut* [Urdu], p. 901; Ghazali, *The Socio-Political Thought of Shah Wali Allah,* pp. 263, 265.

95. Waliullah, *Hujjut* [Urdu], pp. 898–899; Ghazali, *The Socio-Political Thought of Shah Wali Allah,* pp. 262–263.

96. Waliullah, *Hujjut,* p. 345.

97. In a letter to Mullah Imanullah and Mullah Sher Muhammad, Waliullah asked them to inform their contacts in Abdali's army about him, so that when they invaded Delhi, he and his family would be spared. Nizami, *Shah Walli-Allah Dihlawi ke Siyasi Maktubat,* p. 161.

98. Rizvi, *Shah Wali-Allah and His Times,* p. 305.

99. Mir Muhammad Taqi Mir, *Zikir-i-Mir: the Autobiography of the Eighteenth Century Mughal Poet: Mir Muhammad Taqi Mir (1723–1810),* trans. and annot. C. M. Naim, 2nd paperback ed. (New Delhi: Oxford University Press, 2005), p. 85.

100. Cited in Khurshidul Islam and Ralph Russell, *Three Mughal Poets: Mir, Sauda, Mir Hasan,* 2nd paperback ed. (Delhi: Oxford University Press, 1998), p. 67.

101. Khushwant Singh, *A History of the Sikhs,* reprint (Delhi: Oxford University Press, 1991), p. 1167.

102. Obaidullah Sindhi, *Shah Waliullah aur unki Siyasi Tehrik, Yani Haji Waliullah Dehalwi ki Ijmaii Tehrik ka Muqaddimah,* 2nd ed. (Lahore: Sind Sagar Academy, 1952); Husain Ahmad Madni, *Naqsh-i-Hayat* (Deoband: n.p., 1954), 2:11; Ghulam Rasul Mehr, *Jamat-i-Mujahideen* (Lahore: Sheikh Ghulam Ahmad and Sons, n.d.).

3. The Martyrs of Balakot

1. Cited in Khawaja Manzoor Hosain, *Tehrik-i jihd-o-jihad bataur-i mauzu'-i sukhan* (Lahore: National Book Foundation, 1978), p. 143.

2. Ibid., p. 144.

3. Mohammad Sadiq, *A History of Urdu Literature,* 2nd ed. (Delhi: Oxford University Press, 1995), p. 238.

4. Hosain, *Tehrik-i jihd-o-jihad,* p. 148.

5. As he once declared: "There is no restriction regarding Muslim or infidel / Whether a man is a sheikh or a Brahman, he should be human." Cited in Sadiq, *A History of Urdu Literature,* p. 193, my translation.

6. Hosain, *Tehrik-i jihd-o-jihad,* pp. 180–181.

7. Asloob Ahmad Ansari, "Tehrik-i jihd-o-jihad bataur-i mauzu'-i sukhan: Ghazal ki Nai Tabir o Tafsir," in Asloob Ahmad Ansari (ed.), *Naqd-o-Nazr* 7, no. 2 (1975): 179–197.

8. Obaidullah Sindhi, *Shah Waliullah aur unki Siyasi Tehrik, Yani Haji Waliullah Dehalwi ki Ijmaii Tehrik ka Muqaddimah,* 2nd ed. (Lahore: Sind Sagar Academy, 1952); K. A. Nizami, "Socio-Religious Movements in Indian Islam," in S. T. Lokhandwalla (ed.), *India and Contemporary Islam: Proceedings of a Seminar* (Simla: Indian Institute of Advanced Studies, 1971); Maulana Syed Muhammad Mian, *Ulema-i-Hind ka Shandar Maazi,* vol. 2 (Karachi: Maktab-i-Rashidiya, n.d.); Ghulam Rasul Mehr, *Sayyid Ahmad Shaheed,* reprint (Lahore: Sheikh Ghulam Ali and Sons, n.d.).

9. Alim Nasiri, *Shahnamah-yi Balakot: Tehrik-i jihad ki dastan* (Lahore: Idarah Matbu'at Sulaimani, 1995), p. 15.

10. Ibid., pp. 29–30.

11. Khwaja Abdul Wahid, *Shah Shaheed ke Akhari Aram Gah, Shah Ismail Shaheed Mujmua-e-Muqalat* (Lahore: Makki Dar-ul-Kutub, 1999), p. 98.

12. For a discussion of these hagiographical accounts, see Qeyamuddin Ahmad, *The Wahabi Movement in India* (Calcutta: Firma K. L. Mukhopadhyay, 1966), pp. xi–xx.

13. Muhammad Jafar Thanesari, *Tawarikh-i-Ajibah Mawsum bih Sawanih Ahmadi* (Delhi: Matba Faruqi, 1891). See also Muhammad Hedayetullah, *Sayyid Ahmad: A Study of the Religious Reform Movement of Sayyid Ahmad of Ra'e Bareli* (Lahore: Sheikh Muhammad Ashraf, 1970), pp. 14–15.

14. *Gazetteer of the Peshawar District, 1897–98,* reprint (Lahore: Sang-e-Meel, 2004), p. 68.

15. Memorandum by T. E. Ravenshaw, magistrate of Patna, *Selections from the Records of the Bengal Government, no. 42—Papers Connected with the Trial of Moulvie Ahmedoolah of Patna and Others for Conspiracy and Treason* (Calcutta: Alipore Jail Press, 1866), p. 127 (henceforth *Trial of Moulvie Ahmedoolah*).

16. Sheikh Muhammad Ikram is one of the few historians who alludes to Waliullah's possible links with Muhammad bin Abdul Wahab, even though Ikram has no definite evidence that the two met in Medina. See Sheikh Muhammad Ikram, *Rawad-i-Kausar* (Lahore: Islamic Cultural Centre, 1997), p. 543.

17. Memoirs of Sir Harford Jones, "The Whabee," 1799, Home Miscellaneous Series, H/737, part 2, India Office Library (henceforth IOL).

18. Edward E. Oliver, *Across the Border; or Pathan and Biloch* (London: Chapman and Hall, 1890; reprint, Lahore: Sang-e-Meel, 2000), pp. 289–291.

19. This view was favored by anticolonial nationalists who mainly wrote in Urdu, and it is endorsed by several historians of modern South Asia. See, for instance, Mujeeb Ashraf, *Muslim Attitudes towards British Rule and Western Culture in India* (Delhi: Idarah-i-Adabiyat-i-Delli, 1982), chap. 4.

20. Cited in Saiyid Athar Abbas Rizvi, *Shah Abdul Aziz: Puritanism, Sectarian Polemics and Jihad* (Canberra: Marifat, 1982), p. 80.

21. Cited in Mushirul Haq, *Shah Abdul Aziz: His Life and Times* (Lahore: Institute of Islamic Culture, 1995), pp. 38–39.

22. Sindhi, *Shah Waliullah aur unki Siyasi Tehrik*, pp. 8–9; Hafeez Malik, *Moslem Nationalism in India and Pakistan* (Washington: Public Affairs Press, 1963).

23. Ashraf, *Muslim Attitudes towards British Rule*, p. 123.

24. Extract of Political Letter from Bengal, 10 June 1807, Board Collections, F/4/217/4758, IOL.

25. Ibid.; Rizvi, *Shah Abdul Aziz*, pp. 84–86.

26. This pronouncement stands in contrast to the attitude expressed by the Faraizi movement, which abolished Friday prayers because Bengal was no longer under Muslim rule. Ibid., p. 539.

27. Haq, *Shah Abdul Aziz*, pp. 44–50.

28. Ibid., p. 49; quotation in Rizvi, *Shah Abdul Aziz*, p. 148.

29. Haq, *Shah Abdul Aziz*, pp. 50–51; Hedayetullah, *Sayyid Ahmad*, pp. 88–89.

30. Sindhi, *Shah Waliullah aur unki Siyasi Tehrik*; Mian, *Ulema-i-Hind ka Shandar Maazi*, 2:164.

31. Mehr, *Sayyid Ahmad Shaheed*, pp. 131–132.

32. On Muslim denials, see, notably, Sayyid Ahmad Khan, "Review on Dr. Hunter's Indian Musalmans: Are They Bound in Conscience to Rebel against the Queen?" in Hafeez Malik, ed., *Political Profile of Sir Sayyid Ahmad Khan* (Islamabad: Institute of Islamic History, Culture and Civilization, 1982), pp. 272–304; and Nawab Muhammad Siddiq Hasan Khan, *Tarjuman-i-Wahabiya* (Agra: n.p., 1884). For a historian's point of view, see Ahmad, *The Wahabi Movement in India,* pp. 18–22.

33. Hedayetullah, *Sayyid Ahmad,* p. 7.

34. W. W. Hunter, *The Indian Musalmans,* reprint (Lahore: Sang-e-Meel, 1999 [181]), pp. 14, 50–51.

35. *Trial of Moulvie Ahmedoolah,* pp. 131, 136.

36. Ashraf, *Muslim Attitudes towards British Rule,* pp. 136–140; *Trial of Moulvie Ahmedoolah,* p. 129.

37. *Trial of Moulvie Ahmedoolah,* pp. 68, 79, 112.

38. Ibid., p. 115.

39. Ibid., pp. 138–40.

40. Marc Gaborieau, "Criticizing the Sufis: The Debate in Early Nineteenth-Century India," in Frederick De Jong and Bernd Radtke (eds.), *Islamic Mysticism Contested: Thirteen Centuries of Controversies and Polemics* (Leiden: Brill, 1999), pp. 465–466.

41. Cited in Hedayetullah, *Sayyid Ahmad,* pp. 69, 144.

42. Sayyid Ahmad Shaheed, *Sirat-i-Mustaqim,* trans. Mohammad Akram (Lahore: Islamic Academy, n.d.), pp. 17, 22, 83–85.

43. Ibid., pp. 29–30, 50, 54–55, 84, 87.

44. Hedayetullah, *Sayyid Ahmad,* p. 121.

45. Ibid., p. 15.

46. For a discussion of the evolution of the concept, see Yohanan Friedmann, *Prophecy Continuous: Aspects of Ahmadi Religious Thought and Its Medieval Background* (Berkeley: University of California Press, 1989), pp. 49–82.

47. Ibn al-'Arabi interpreted it as openness to different religious traditions and claimed that he was initiated by Moses, Jesus, and Muhammad on the road to sainthood. A judicious stance in the context of thirteenth-century Andalusia, Ibn al-'Arabi's accommodative attitude was inimical to the worldview of the Waliullah clan and its adherents.

48. Ghulam Rasul Mehr, *Jamat-i-Mujahideen* (Lahore: Sheikh Ghulam

Ahmad and Sons, n.d.). Mian, *Ulema-i-Hind ka Shandar Maazi.*

49. Maulvi Ismail, *Support of the Faith* [*Taqwiyat-ul-Iman of Maulvi Ismail Hajji*], Hashmat Ali (trans.) (Lahore: Orientalia, n.d.), pp. xvi, 18–19.

50. For an insight into the key distinction between faith *(iman)* and belief *(aqida),* see Wilfred Cantwell Smith, *Faith and Belief* (Princeton, N.J.: Princeton University Press, 1979).

51. Ismail, *Support of the Faith,* pp. 36–37.

52. Rizvi, *Shah Abdul Aziz,* p. 504.

53. Ashraf, *Muslim Attitudes towards British Rule,* p. 140; Mohammad Ayub Qadri, "Maulana Fazl-i-Haq Khairabadi: Dur-i-Mulazamat," in Muhammad Saeed-ur-Rahman Alvi (ed.), *Allamah Fazl-i Haq Khairabadi aur Jihad-i Azadi* (Lahore: Sunni Publications, 1987), pp. 88–91.

54. Altaf Husain Hali, *Yadgar-i-Ghalib,* reprint (Lahore: Maktaba Alia, n.d.), pp. 79–81.

55. Ibid., p. 519. Fazl-i-Haq's detractors maintain that while serving a sentence in the Andamans for his supposed role in the 1857 rebellion, he regretted opposing Shah Ismail. See Afzal Haq Qureshi, "Jihad-i-Azadi aur Shah Ismail Shahid" in *Allamah Fazl-i Haq Khairabadi aur Jihad-i Azadi,* pp. 51–52.

56. Hunter, *The Indian Musalmans,* pp. 65, 108–109.

57. W. Connor (Honorary Magistrate, Aligarh) to Syed Ahmad Khan, 8 July 1872, *Letters to and from Sir Syed Ahmad Khan,* Muhammad Ismail Panipati (ed.) (Lahore: Board for Advancement of Literature, 1993), pp. 300–301.

58. Hunter, *The Indian Musalmans,* p. 52.

59. Rizvi, *Shah Abdul Aziz,* p. 506.

60. Hedayetullah, *Sayyid Ahmad,* p. 25.

61. Shah Ismail Shahid, *Mansab-i-Imamate,* trans. Muhammad Husain Alvi (Lahore: Haji Hanif and Sons, 1994).

62. This section is based on my reading against the grain of the comprehensive but hagiographical account in Mehr, *Sayyid Ahmad Shaheed,* of the *hijrat* cum jihad.

63. Ibid., pp. 273–276.

64. Ibid, pp. 284–310.

65. Ibid., pp. 332–344.

66. Ibid., pp. 347–350.

67. Ibid., pp. 353–354.

68. Ibid., pp. 360–365.

69. Charles Masson, *Narratives of Various Journeys in Balochistan, Afghanistan and the Panjab* (London: Bentley, 1842), 1:132.

70. Mehr, *Sayyid Ahmad Shaheed,* pp. 368–370, 377; Masson, *Narratives of Various Journeys,* 1:132.

71. In 1857 he refused to sign the declaration of jihad against the British. After the revolt was crushed, the British offered him eleven villages. But Mahboob Ali tore up the award, saying that whatever he did was not for the British but because he thought it was the right thing to do. Mehr, *Sayyid Ahmad Shaheed,* pp. 431–435.

72. Ibid., pp. 436–437, 457n.

73. Ibid., pp. 449–451.

74. Ibid., pp. 455–456.

75. Ahmad, *Wahabi Movement in India,* pp. 51–52.

76. Mehr, *Sayyid Ahmad Shaheed,* pp. 461–465.

77. Ibid., pp. 491–492.

78. Ibid., pp. 510–517.

79. Ahmad, *Wahabi Movement in India,* p. 53.

80. *Gazetteer of the Peshawar District,* p. 67.

81. Mehr, *Sayyid Ahmad Shaheed,* pp. 575–576.

82. Ibid., pp. 570–581.

83. Ibid., pp. 589–595.

84. Ibid., pp. 596–602.

85. Ibid., p. 618.

86. Ibid., p. 621.

87. Ibid., p. 640–659.

88. *Gazetteer of the Peshawar District,* p. 67.

89. Sayyid Ahmad to the ulema of Peshawar, in *Makatab Sayyid Ahmad Shaheed* (Lahore: Maktaba-i-Rashidiya, 1975), p. 116.

90. Rizvi, *Shah Abdul Aziz,* p. 494.

91. *Gazetteer of the Peshawar District,* p. 68.

92. Hunter, *The Indian Musalmans,* p. 17. Rizvi, however, maintains that according to the new rule, any girl who had not been sent to her husband

because of nonpayment of bride money had to be dispatched immediately, and all mature girls married within a month. Rizvi, *Shah Abdul Aziz,* p. 495.

93. *Gazetteer of the Peshawar District,* p. 68.

94. Oliver, *Across the Border,* p. 290.

95. *Gazetteer of the Peshawar District,* p. 68.

96. Mahtab Singh corroborates this in his *Tawarikh-i-Hazara,* on which Mehr bases his account of the battle of Balakot. See Mehr, *Sayyid Ahmad Shaheed,* pp. 859–860.

97. Ibid., p. 860.

98. *Gazetteer of the Peshawar District,* p. 68.

99. Mehr, *Sayyid Ahmad Shaheed,* pp. 806–807.

100. Hedayetullah, *Sayyid Ahmad,* p. 106. See also Ishtiaq Husain Qureshi, *Ulema in Politics: A Study Relating to the Political Activities of the Ulema in the South-Asian Subcontinent from 1556 to 1947,* 2nd ed. (Karachi: Ma'aref, 1974), p. 171.

101. Hunter, *The Indian Musalmans,* p. 66.

102. *Sunan of Abu Dawood,* #3105, *Alim* (compact disk).

103. Rizvi, *Shah Abdul Aziz,* pp. 504–506.

104. Ashraf, *Muslim Attitudes towards British Rule,* p. 188.

105. Cited in Hosain, *Tehrik-i jihd-o-jihad,* pp. 151–152.

106. Ibid., pp. 160–162.

107. Ibid., pp. 6–10.

108. Ibid., p. 296; Ghalib, *Nawa-i-Saroosh,* Ghulam Rasul Mehr (comp.) (Lahore: Sheikh Ghulam Ali and Sons, n.d.), pp. 1040–1041.

109. Ghalib, *Nawa-i-Saroosh,* p. 70.

110. Hosain, *Tehrik-i jihd-o-jihad,* p. 306.

111. Ibid., p. 311n.

112. Ibid., pp. 315–326.

113. This is an oblique reference to the hadith of the Prophet stating that the ink of the scholar's pen is weightier than the martyr's blood.

114. For a discussion of this imagery, see Ayesha Jalal, *Self and Sovereignty: Individual and Community in South Asian Islam since 1850* (London: Routledge, 2000), chap. 1.

115. Ghalib, *Nawa-i-Saroosh,* p. 34.

116. Annemarie Schimmel, *Mystical Dimensions of Islam* (Lahore: Sang-e-Meel, 2003), p. 136.

117. Ghalib, *Nawa-i-Saroosh,* p. 34.

118. Ibid., pp. 34–35; Hosain, *Tehrik-i jihd-o-jihad,* p. 309.

119. Ghalib, *Nawa-i-Saroosh,* p. 20.

120. Ibid., p. 107.

121. Ibid.

122. Ibid.

123. Ibid. Significantly, Hosain omits this key verse in his discussion.

4. Jihad in Colonial India

1. W. W. Hunter, *The Indian Musalmans,* reprint (Lahore: Sang-e-Meel, 1999 [1871]),p. 113.

2. See Ghulam Mohammad Jaffar, "The Repudiation of Jihad by the Indian Scholars in the Nineteenth Century," in *Hamdard Islamicus* (Autumn 1992), pp. 93–100.

3. Hunter, *The Indian Musalmans,* chap. 4, passim.

4. These were the *Mizân-ul-Haqq,* or a resolution of the controversy between Christians and Mohammedans. Written in Persian in 1835, it was translated into Urdu and published in Mirzapore in 1843. The second was *Miftâh-ul-Asrâr*—a treatise written in Persian proving the divinity of Christ and the doctrine of the holy Trinity, which was translated into Urdu and published in Agra in 1843. The third work was called *Tarîq-ul-Hyât,* a treatise on sin and redemption, also in Persian. Sir William Muir, *The Mohammedan Controversy: Biographies of Mohammed, Sprenger on Tradition, the Indian Liturgy and the Psalter* (Edinburgh: Clark, 1897), p. 1.

5. Sir William Muir, "The Mohammedan Controversy," *Calcutta Review* (1845), reprinted ibid., pp. 2–6.

6. See Avril Ann Powell, *Muslims and Missionaries in Pre-Mutiny India* (London: Routledge, 2003), pp. 272–282.

7. See Sayyid Ahmad Khan, *The Causes of the Indian Revolt,* in Hafeez Malik (ed.), *Political Profile of Sir Sayyid Ahmad Khan: A Documentary Record* (Islamabad: Institute of Islamic History, Culture and Civilization, 1982). His views are echoed by historians like Mujeeb Ashraf, *Muslim Atti-*

tudes towards British Rule and Western Culture in India (Delhi: Idarah-i-Adabiyat-i-Delli, 1982), pp. 23–24; and Bashir Ahmad Dar, *Religious Thought of Sayyid Ahmad Khan,* 2nd ed. (Lahore: Institute of Islamic Culture, 1971), chap. 1.

8. John Kaye, *The History of Indian Mutiny: A Detailed Account of the Synchronous Incidents at Mirath, Delhi, Calcutta, Banaras, Allahabad, Kanpur, Punjab, N. W. F. P. and Kashmir During 1856–57,* reprint (Lahore: Sang-e-Meel, 2005), 2:348.

9. Colonel G. B. Malleson, *The Indian Mutiny of 1857,* reprint (Lahore: Sang-e-Meel, 2001), p. 9.

10. Ashraf, *Muslim Attitudes towards British Rule,* pp. 173–174.

11. Kaye, *The History of Indian Mutiny,* p. 252.

12. Ashraf, *Muslim Attitudes towards British Rule,* pp. 170–171.

13. Nadar Ali Khan, *A History of Urdu Journalism, 1822–1857* (Delhi, Idarah-i-Adabiyat-i-Delhi, 1991), p. 330.

14. Salim al-Din Quraishi (ed. and comp.), *Cry for Freedom: Proclamations of Muslim Revolutionaries of 1857* (Lahore: Sang-e-Meel, 1997), p. viii.

15. Malleson, *The Indian Mutiny of 1857,* pp. 17–18.

16. T. R. E. Holmes, *History of the Indian Mutiny,* as cited in Ashraf, *Muslim Attitudes towards British Rule,* p. 172.

17. Ashraf, *Muslim Attitudes towards British Rule,* p. 171.

18. See Mohammad Saeed-ur-Rahman Alvi (ed.), *Allamah Fazl-i Haq Khairabadi aur Jihad-i Azadi* (Lahore: Sunni Publishers, 1987).

19. Afzal Haq Kurshi, "Allamah Fazl-i-Haq Khairabadi," ibid., p. 61; Mushirul Haq, *Shah Abdul Aziz: His Life and Times* (Lahore: Institute of Islamic Culture, 1995), p. 59.

20. Kurshi, in Alvi, *Allamah Fazl-i Haq Khairabadi aur Jihad-i Azadi,* pp. 64–69.

21. S. Moinul Haqq, "The Story of the War of Independence, 1857–58 by Allamah Fadl-i-Haqq of Khayrabad," *Journal of the Pakistan Historical Society* 5, no. 1 (January 1957): 51–52.

22. Manazir Ahsan Gilani, *Sawanih-i-Qasimi* (Lahore: Maktaba Rahmaniya, n.d.), 2:26.

23. Ibid., pp. 90–115; Maulana Syed Muhammad Mian, *Ulema-i-Hind ka Shandar Maazi* (Karachi: Maktab-i-Rashidiya, n.d.), 4:276–81.

24. Gilani, *Sawanih-i-Qasimi*, 2:122–129, 173–200.

25. See Quraishi, *Cry for Freedom*.

26. "Advice to the Royal Army of Delhi," ibid., pp. 137–138n5.

27. Ibid., pp. 3, 22, 47.

28. Khan, *The Causes of the Indian Revolt*, p. 151.

29. "Proclamations Issued by Firoz Shah," Quraishi, *Cry for Freedom*, p. 81.

30. Ibid., pp. 8–9, 28, 75, 89.

31. Ibid., p. 134 (my emphasis).

32. Ibid., pp. 135–136.

33. Kaye, *The History of Indian Mutiny*, p. 348.

34. Quraishi, *Cry for Freedom*, pp. 32–34.

35. Proclamation by Hindus and Muslims of Delhi, ibid., pp. 107–108.

36. "The King of Delhi's Circular Letter to the Princes and People of India," ibid., pp. 61–62.

37. "Advice to the Royal Army of Delhi," ibid., p. 14.

38. "Notice Issued by Nana Sahib," ibid., pp. 74–76.

39. "Proclamation Issued by Firoz Shah," ibid., pp. 80–82.

40. Ghalib, *Nawa-i-Saroosh*, Ghulam Rasul Mehr (comp.) (Lahore: Sheikh Ghulam Ali and Sons, n.d.), p. 337.

41. Ibid., p. 308.

42. Ralph Russell and Khurshidul Islam (eds.), *Ghalib, 1797–1869: Life and Letters* (Delhi, Oxford University Press, 1994), chap. 6.

43. C. F. Andrews, *Zaka Ullah of Delhi, with an introductory memoir by the Late Maulvi Nazir Ahmad*, reprint (Lahore, Universal Books, 1976), pp. 19–20, 68, 109.

44. Pyaam Shahjahanpuri (ed.), "1857 ka jehad," in *Taqazaah* (Lahore, n.d.), pp. 40–41.

45. Ibid., p. 45.

46. Khan, *The Causes of the Indian Revolt*, pp. 39–40.

47. J. M. S. Baljon, *The Reforms and Religious Ideas of Sir Sayyid Ahmad Khan* (Leiden: Brill, 1949), p. 25.

48. Khan, *The Causes of the Indian Revolt*; and *An Account of the Loyal Mohomedans of India*, in Malik, *Political Profile of Sir Sayyid Ahmad Khan*.

49. Khan, *The Causes of the Indian Revolt*, pp. 138–139.

50. Ibid., pp. 140–141.

51. Khan, *Loyal Mohomedans of India,* pp. 193, 230–231, 239–240.

52. Ibid., pp. 233–234, 237.

53. Cited in Dar, *Religious Thought of Sayyid Ahmad Khan,* p. 79.

54. Freeland Abbott, "The Transformation of the Jihad Movement," *Muslim World* 52, no. 4 (October 1962): 289.

55. Khan, *Loyal Mohomedans of India,* p. 241.

56. Dar, *Religious Thought of Sayyid Ahmad Khan,* p. 79.

57. Rizvi, *Shah Abdul Aziz,* pp. 537–538, 540–541; and *Selections from the Records of the Bengal Government, no. 42—Papers Connected with the Trial of Moulvie Ahmedoolah of Patna and Others for Consipiracy and Treason* (Calcutta: Alipore Jail Press, 1866), p. 141.

58. Hunter, *The Indian Musalmans,* pp. 149–151.

59. Ibid., p. 138.

60. Ibid., pp. 67–68.

61. Ibid., pp. 111, 113, 121.

62. Ibid., pp. 124–127.

63. Ibid., pp. 67, 71, 147.

64. Sayyid Ahmad Khan, "Review on Dr. Hunter's Indian Musalmans: Are They Bound in Conscience to Rebel against the Queen?" in Malik, *Political Profile of Sir Sayyid Ahmad Khan,* p. 272.

65. Ibid., p. 273.

66. Ibid., pp. 279–82.

67. Ibid., pp. 282–283, 295.

68. Sayyid Ahmad Khan, "Jihad," published in the editorial columns of *Pioneer* (23 November 1871), reprinted in Malik, *Political Profile of Sir Sayyid Ahmad Khan,* p. 320.

69. Rudolph Peters, *Islam and Colonialism: The Doctrine of Jihad in Modern History* (The Hague: Mouton, 1979), p. 125; Mustansir Mir, "Jihad in Islam," in Hadia Dajani-Shakeel and Ronald A. Messier (eds.), *The Jihad and Its Times: Dedicated to Andrew Stefan Ehrenkreutz* (Ann Arbor: University of Michigan Center for Middle Eastern and North African Studies, 1991), p. 117.

70. Khan, "Review on Dr. Hunter's Indian Musalmans," pp. 285, 295–296.

71. For corroboration of this point, see Muhammad Qasim Zaman, *The*

Ulama in Contemporary Islam: Custodians of Change (Princeton, N.J.: Princeton University Press, 2002), chap. 1.

72. *Panjabi Akhbar,* 29 January 1887, pp. 81–82, in Selections from the Vernacular Newspapers, L\R\5\64, 1887, IOL.

73. For a detailed account of the Deobandis, see Barbara Daly Metcalf, *Islamic Revival in British India: Deoband, 1860–1900* (Princeton, N.J.: Princeton University Press, 1982), chap. 3.

74. Sheikh Muhammad Ikram, *Mauj-i-Kausar* (Lahore: Islamic Cultural Centre, 2000), p. 72.

75. Usha Sanyal, *Devotional Islam and Politics in British India: Ahmad Riz Khan Barelwi and His Movement, 1870–1920* (Delhi: Oxford University Press, 1996), pp. 40–41n.

76. See Metcalf, *Islamic Revival in British India,* pp. 296–314.

77. Maulana Ahmad Raza Khan Barelvi, *Malfuzat,* reprint (Jhelum: Book Corner, n.d.), p. 96.

78. Sanyal, *Devotional Islam and Politics in British India,* pp. 273–274.

79. Metcalf, *Islamic Revival in British India,* pp. 269, 274–275.

80. Ibid., pp. 281–295.

81. Nawab Muhammad Siddiq Hasan Khan, *Tarjuman-i-Wahabiya* (Agra: n.p., 1884), pp. 7, 15, 17.

82. Ikram, *Mauj-i-Kausar,* pp. 68–71.

83. Metcalf, *Islamic Revival in British India,* p. 270.

84. *Sahih Muslim,* 1, and *Sahih al-Bukhari,* 1.8, both on *Alim* (compact disk).

85. Sayyid Ahmad Khan's address at Patna College, 26 May 1873, in *Sir Sayyid Ka Aiana Khana-i-Afkar: Muqalat, Khutbat, Muktubat aur Manzumat ka Intikhab,* Sayyid Abul Khair Kashfi (comp.) (Karachi: Fazli Sons, n.d.), p. 131.

86. Cited in Baljon, *The Reforms and Religious Ideas of Sir Sayyid Ahmad Khan,* p. 14.

87. Sir William Muir, *The Life of Mahomet, with Introductory Chapters on the Original Sources for the Biography of Mahomet, and on the Pre-Islamite History of Arabia,* 4 vols. (London: Smith, Elder, 1861), 4:318, 321–323.

88. Christian W. Troll, *Sayyid Ahmad Khan: A Reinterpretation of Muslim Theology* (New Delhi: Vikas, 1978), p. 102.

89. Sayyid Ahmad Khan, *Essays on the Life of Mohammed and Subjects Subsidiary Thereto* (London: Trubner, 1870). The Urdu version was published as *Khutabat-i-Ahmadiyyah,* and the English was reprinted as *Essay on the Question Whether Islam Has Been Beneficial or Injurious to Human Society in General and to the Mosaic and Christian Dispensations* (Lahore: Orientalia, 1954), which I have used for my references.

90. Khan, *Essay on the Question,* pp. 30–32.

91. The evolution of Sayyid Ahmad Khan's religious thought is analyzed in Troll, *Sayyid Ahmad Khan,* chaps. 3 and 4, and Dar, *Religious Thought of Sayyid Ahmad Khan,* especially chaps. 5 and 6. His ethical ideas are discussed in Sheila McDonough, *Muslim Ethics and Modernity: A Comparative Study of the Ethical Thought of Sayyid Ahmad Khan and Mawlana Mawdudi* (Ontario: Canadian Corporation for the Study of Religion, 1984), pp. 3–53.

92. Sayyid Ahmad Khan, *Essay on the Question,* pp. 32–34, 39–40.

93. Sayyid Ahmad Khan, *Tafsir-ul-Quran,* comp. Rafiuddin Shahab (Lahore; Dost, 1998), pp. 309–315.

94. Syed Ameer Ali, *A Critical Examination of the Life and Teachings of Muhammad* (Edinburgh: William and Norgate, 1873); Ameer Ali, *The Spirit of Islam: A History of the Evolution and Ideals of Islam with a Life of the Prophet* (London: Christophers, 1922; reprint, Lahore: Islamic Book Service, 1989). Citations here are to the reprint edition.

95. Ibid., pp. 178–179, 207, and chap. 8 for his defense of Ali's right to succeed the Prophet.

96. Ibid., pp. 209–211, 213–215, 218–221.

97. Maulvi Chiragh Ali, *A Critical Exposition of the Popular Jihad, Showing That All the Wars of Mohammad Were Defensive; and That Aggressive War, or Compulsory Conversion, Is Not Allowed in the Koran. With Appendices Proving That the Word "Jihad" Does Not Exegetically Mean "Warfare" and That Slavery Is Not Sanctioned by the Prophet of Islam* (Karachi: Karimsons, 1977 [1885]), pp. i–ii, lxi–lxii, xc.

98. Ibid., pp. xc–xcii.

99. Surah 6:120, cited ibid., p. lxiii.

100. Ibid., pp. xc–xciii, cii–civ.

101. Ibid., pp. xciv–cii.

102. Ibid., pp. 114–116, 158.

103. Ibid., pp. 120–122, 129, 159.

104. Mir, "Jihad in Islam," pp. 117–118.

105. Khan, *Tafsir-ul-Quran*, pp. 316–317.

106. Abu Said Mohammad Husain, *Treatise on Jihad* (Lahore: Islamia, 1893), call no. 4503.C.25, British Library, Catalogue: Humanities 1, pp. 3–4, 13, 34–36. I am grateful to Shruti Kapila for providing me with a copy of this tract.

107. Troll, *Sayyid Ahmad Khan*, pp. 91–92.

108. G. W. Leitner, "Jihad," *Asiatic Quarterly Review* 2, no. 4 (1886)—reprinted in M. Ikram Chaghatai, *Writings of Dr Leitner* (Lahore: Government College Research and Publication Society and Sang-e-Meel, 2002), pp. 35–37.

109. Ibid., pp. 40–44.

110. Pandit Lekh Ram, *Risala-yi jihad ya'ni din-i muhammadi ki bunyad* (Lahore: n.p., 1892), cited in Yohanan Friedmann, *Prophecy Continuous: Aspects of Ahmadi Religious Thought and Its Medieval Background* (New Delhi: Oxford University Press, 2003), p. 9.

111. See preface to Mirza Ghulam Ahmad, *The British Government and Jehad* (Qadian: Mutba Zia-ul-Islam, 1900). The treatise was originally published in Urdu as *Government Angrez aur jihad* (Qadian: Mutba Zia-ul-Islam, 1900). My references are to the English version.

112. Ibid., pp. 2–3.

113. Ibid., pp. 4–5.

114. Emir Abdur Rahman, *Kalimat amir al-balad fi al-taghrib ila al-jihad* is mentioned ibid., p. 27; Ahmad, *The British Government and Jehad*, pp. 7–8, 12.

115. Ibid., pp. 14–15.

116. Speech by Sayyid Ahmad Khan at the Muhammadan Literary Society, 6 October 1863, in Malik, *Political Profile of Sir Sayyid Ahmad Khan*, pp. 330–331, 335.

117. Sayyid Ahmad Khan, *Khud Nawisth, Hayat-i-Sur Sayyid*, Ziauddin Lahori (comp.), 2nd ed. (Karachi: Fazli Sons, 1998), p. 155.

118. Ibid., pp. 312–313.

119. G. F. I. Graham, *The Life and Work of Sir Syed Ahmed Khan* (Karachi: Oxford University Press, 1974), pp. 125–127.

120. For a discussion of how his ethical ideals were in accordance with earlier rational Islamic thought, see McDonough, *Muslim Ethics and Modernity,* chap. 2.

121. Sayyid Ahmad Khan, *Mazamein-e-Sir Sayyid, Muntakhib Tehzib-ul-Akhlaq,* comp. Ghulam Husain Zulfikar (Lahore: Sang-e-Meel, 1993), pp. 8–15.

122. Khan, *Khud Nawisth,* pp. 299–303.

123. Ibid., pp. 304–305.

124. Sayyid Ahmad Khan "Tahsab," *Tehzib ul-Akhlaq,* in *Sir Sayyid Ka Aiana Khana-i-Afkar,* pp. 86–87.

125. Maulana Shibli Numani and Maulana Sayyid Sulaiman Nadvi, *Sirat-ul-Nabi,* 7 vols. (Lahore: Al-Faisal, n.d.), 5:8–14.

126. Ibid., pp. 217–224.

127. Sayyid Ahmad to Maulana Altaf Husain Hali, 10 June 1879, in *Sir Sayyid Ka Aiana Khana-i-Afkar,* pp. 191–192.

128. Altaf Husain Hali, *Musadas-i-Hali* (Lahore: Ferozesons, n.d., p. 50).

5. Jihad as Anticolonial Nationalism

1. The activities of the mujahideen in the first five decades of the twentieth century are documented in Fazal Ilahi Vazirabadi, *Kavaf-i-Yaghistan: Yani, Mujahidin-i-Yaghistan ki Sad Salah Dairy* (Gujranwala, Pakistan: Idarah-i-Ihya-al-Sunnat, 1981).

2. Aziz Ahmad, *Studies in Islamic Culture in the Indian Environment,* reprint (Delhi: Oxford University Press, 1999), p. 59.

3. *Aligarh Institute Gazette,* 19 June 1877, Selections from Vernacular Newspapers, L\R\5\54, 1877, p. 424.

4. *Nusrat-ul-Islam* (Urdu trimonthly, Delhi), 1 July 1877, ibid., p. 461.

5. Cited in Nikki R. Keddie, "Jamal Al-Din Al-Afghani in Afghanistan," in M. Ikram Chaghatai (comp.), *Jamal Al-Din Al-Afghani: An Apostle of Islamic Resurgence* (Lahore: Sang-e-Meel, 2005), pp. 215–216.

6. Jamaluddin al-Afghani, "The Benefits of Philosophy," in Nikki R. Keddie, *An Islamic Response to Imperialism: Political and Religious Writings of Sayyid Jamal ad-Din al-Afghani* (Berkeley: University of California Press, 1983), p. 111.

7. Aziz Ahmad, "Afghani's Indian Contacts," *Journal of the American Oriental Society* 89, no. 3 (1969): 476–504, reprinted in Chaghatai, *Jamal Al-Din Al-Afghani,* pp. 173–198.

8. Ibid., p. 182.

9. Nikki Keddie has emphasized the political nature of the difference, whereas Aziz Ahmad traces it to their differing views of Islam. For a selection of their writings on Afghani, see Chaghatai, *Jamal Al-Din Al-Afghani.*

10. Cited in Aziz Ahmad, "Sayyid Ahmad Khan, Jamal al-Din al-Afghani and Muslim India," in *Studia Islamica* (Paris) 13 (1960), reprinted in Chaghatai, *Jamal Al-Din Al-Afghani,* p. 266.

11. Jamaluddin al-Afghani, "The Materialists in India," in Keddie, *An Islamic Response to Imperialism,* pp. 178–179.

12. Jamaluddin al-Afghani, "Lecture on Teaching and Learning," ibid., p. 107.

13. Albert Hourani, *Arabic Thought in the Liberal Age, 1798–1939* (Cambridge: Cambridge University Press), pp. 124–126.

14. Ali Baksh, *Hadiyat al-Haramain,* April 1874 (Lucknow: Munshi Nawal Kishore), Vernacular Transcripts, VT 530, IOL.

15. Ahmad, "Afghani's Indian Contacts," in Chaghatai, *Jamal Al-Din Al-Afghani,* pp. 190–192.

16. Ibid., p. 190.

17. Cited in Sylvia G. Haim, "Al-Afghani and the Crisis of Islam," in Sylvia G. Haim (ed.), *Arab Nationalism: An Anthology* (Berkeley: University of California, 1962), reprinted in Chaghatai, *Jamal Al-Din Al-Afghani,* p. 500.

18. *Paisa Akhbar* (Lahore), 9 August 1897, pp. 691, 694, Punjab Native Newspaper Reports, L\R\5\181, 1897, IOL, pp. 718–719.

19. Ibid., 30 July and 5 August 1897.

20. W. C. Smith, "Afghani," in Chaghatai, *Jamal Al-Din Al-Afghani,* p. 491.

21. Syeda Saiyidian Hameed, *Islamic Seal on India's Independence: Abul Kalam Azad—a Fresh Look* (Karachi: Oxford University Press, 1998), pp. 42–43.

22. Abul Kalam Azad, *Sada-i-Haq* (compilation of selected writings from *Al-Hilal*) (Lahore: Maktaba Jamal, n.d.), pp. 86–89.

23. Ibid., pp. 31–33.

24. Ibid., pp. 34–39.

25. Ibid., pp. 20, 44–50.

26. Hameed, *Islamic Seal on India's Independence,* pp. 45–51.

27. Azad, *Sada-i-Haq,* pp. 57–58, 61–62.

28. Ibid., pp. 88–89.

29. Ian Douglas Henderson, *Abul Kalam Azad: An Intellectual and Religious Biography,* Gail Minault and Christian W. Troll (eds.) (Delhi: Oxford University Press, 1988), pp. 111–112, 138–139.

30. Hameed, *Islamic Seal on India's Independence,* pp. 61–62.

31. Abul Kalam Azad, *Majmua-i-Azad* (Mirpur: Arsalan, n.d.), p. 49.

32. Ibid., pp. 51–54.

33. Hameed, *Islamic Seal on India's Independence,* p. 73.

34. Abul Kalam Azad, *Khutbat-i-Azad* (Lahore: Maktaba Jamal, 2004), pp. 14–15.

35. Smith, "Afghani," p. 492.

36. Azad, *Khutbat-i-Azad,* p. 22.

37. Ibid., pp. 17–19.

38. Ibid., pp. 19–23, 28.

39. Azad, *Majmua-i-Azad,* pp. 87–88.

40. Abul Kalam Azad, *Islam ka Nazirya-i-Jang,* Ibn Raai (comp.) (Lahore: Basat-i-Adab, 1965), pp. 7, 143–145, 152–160.

41. Ibid., pp. 12–17, 42–45.

42. Azad, *Majmua-i-Azad,* pp. 49–50.

43. Hameed, *Islamic Seal on India's Independence,* pp. 73–74.

44. Peters, *Islam and Colonialism,* pp. 90–94.

45. Hameed, *Islamic Seal on India's Independence,* pp. 73–74.

46. Azad's letter to Maulvi Zahir al-Haq, written after India gained independence, cited in Muhammad Hajjan Sheikh, *Maulana Ubaid Allah Sindhi: A Revolutionary Scholar* (Islamabad: National Institute of Historical and Cultural Research, 1986), p. 261.

47. Obaidullah Sindhi, *Shah Waliullah aur unki Siyasi Tehrik, Yani Haji Waliullah Dehalwi ki Ijmaii Tehrik ka Muqaddimah,* 2nd ed. (Lahore: Sind Sagar Academy, 1952).

48. Hajjan Sheikh, *Maulana Ubaid Allah Sindhi,* p. 18.

49. Cited ibid., p. 21.

50. *Secret Punjab Police Abstract of Intelligence* (henceforth *SPPAI*), vol. 36, no. 11 (27 November, 1915): 680; *SPPAI*, vol. 37, no 47 (4 December 1915): 694, National Commission on Historical and Cultural Research, Islamabad (henceforth NCHCR).

51. Sayyid Mahbood Rizvi, *Tarikh Dar-ul-Ulum Deoband* (Lahore: Al-Mezan, 2005), 2:184–185.

52. See Muhammad Shafi Sabir, *Tazkara Sarfaroshan-i-Sarhad* (Peshawar: University Book Agency, 1990).

53. Zafar Husain Aybek, *Khatrat: Aap Beeti* (Lahore: Sang-e-Meel, 1990), p. 36.

54. Hameed, *Islamic Seal on Indian Independence*, p. 76.

55. Hajjan Sheikh, *Maulana Ubaid Allah Sindhi*, p. 44.

56. Aybek, *Khatrat*, pp. 112–113.

57. Hajjan Sheikh, *Maulana Ubaid Allah Sindhi*, pp. 48–51.

58. Rizvi, *Tarikh Dar-ul-Ulum Deoband*, pp. 187–188.

59. Hajjan Sheikh, *Maulana Ubaid Allah Sindhi*, pp. 71–79.

60. Ibid., p. 62.

61. *SPPAI*, vol. 41, no. 16 (19 April 1919): 166, NCHCR.

62. *SPPAI*, vol. 41, no. 26 (5 July 1919): 294, NCHCR.

63. Aybek, *Khatrat*, pp. 137–138.

64. Ibid., pp. 154–156.

65. *SPPAI*, vol. 41, no. 26 (5 July 1919): 294, NCHCR.

66. *SPPAI*, vol. 41, no. 5 (31 January 1920): 67, NCHCR.

67. *SPPAI*, vol. 41, no. 2 (11 January 1919): 20, NCHCR.

68. *SPPAI*, vol. 41, no. 20 (17 May 1919): 208, NCHCR.

69. *SPPAI*, vol. 41, no. 49 (20 December 1919): 719, NCHCR.

70. *SPPAI*, vol. 41, no. 22 (31 May 1919): 211–212, NCHCR.

71. Abul Kalam Azad, Presidential address to the Khilafat Conference at Agra, 25 August 1921, in Azad, *Khutbat-i-Azad*, pp. 36–39.

72. Abul Kalam Azad, *Jama-ul-Shuhud: Dawakhil Ghair Muslim Fil Masjid*, reprint, Masih-ul-Hasan (comp.) (Lahore: Maktaba Akuwat, 1996).

73. Abul Kalam Azad, *Islam Mein Azadi ka Tasawar* (Lahore: Maktaba Jamal, 2004).

74. Abul Kalam Azad, *Qaul-i-Faisal*, reprint (Lahore: Maktaba Jamal, 2004), pp. 95–96.

75. For an analysis of the *hijrat* movement, see Ayesha Jalal, *Self and Sov-*

ereignty: Individual and Community in South Asian Islam since 1850 (London: Routledge, 2000), pp. 214–224.

76. Aybek, *Khatrat,* pp. 260–261.

77. Ibid., pp. 287–288.

78. Swami Shradhanand, "Hindu Muslim Itihad and Congress ka aik Tarikhi Warq," in *Ali Baradaran ke Khutbah-e-Sadarat par aik Tanqidi Nazar,* comp. L. Gyan Chandra Arya (Delhi: Tej, 1924), Urdu D 435, IOL, pp. 10–13.

79. Note on the Punjab Press for the Week Ending 24 May 1924, 28 May 1924, Islamabad: NCHCR, p. 191.

80. Aybek, *Khatrat,* pp. 241–246.

81. In northwestern India, the Eastern Punjab, Western Punjab, NWFP, Kashmir, Sind, Baluchistan, and Gujarat would become independent democratic countries. Similar countries would be formed in eastern and southern India. Aybek, *Khatrat,* p. 298.

82. Ibid.

83. Hajjan Sheikh, *Maulana Ubaid Allah Sindhi,* pp. 159–160.

84. Ibid., pp. 160–161.

85. Ibid., pp. 162–163.

86. Aybek, *Khatrat,* pp. 295–298.

87. Hajjan Sheikh, *Maulana Ubaid Allah Sindhi,* pp. 166, 173–174.

88. Ibid., p. 189.

89. Sindhi, *Shah Waliullah aur unki Siyasi Tehrik,* p. 119.

90. Hajjan Sheikh, *Maulana Ubaid Allah Sindhi,* pp. 224, 235–236.

91. Ibid, pp. 200–210, 224.

92. "The Programme of the Jamna, Narbada, Sind Sagar Party," ibid., app. 2, pp. 268–269.

93. Sindhi, *Shah Waliullah aur unki Siyasi Tehrik,* pp. 119–121.

94. In a number of essays, Sindhi extolled the principles of a universal human ethics, fellow feeling, and the oneness of mankind. See *Shaur-i-Agahi: Afadiyat-i-Maulana Obaidullah Sindhi,* comp. Sayyid Matlub Ali Zaidi (Lahore: Makki Dar-ul-Kitab, 1994), especially pp. 13–34.

95. Azad, Presidential address to the Khilafat Conference at Agra, pp. 38–39.

96. Muhammad Iqbal, *Javidnama,* Urdu trans., Mian Abdur Rashid (Lahore: Sheikh Ghulam Ali and Sons, 1992), pp. 70–71.

97. Ibid.

98. Iqbal's letter to Sayyid Sulaiman Nadvi, cited in Abul Kalam Azad, *Tazkirah* (Lahore: Maktaba Jamal, 1999), p. 13.

99. For an analysis of Iqbal's politics, see Jalal, *Self and Sovereignty*, pp. 166–179, 277–284, 295–296, 323–334.

100. V. G. Kiernan, *Poems from Iqbal*, reprint (Lahore: Iqbal Academy, 2003 [1947]), p. 170.

101. Muhammad Iqbal, *The Reconstruction of Religious Thought in Islam* (Lahore: Sang-e-Meel, 1996), p. 156.

102. Muhammad Iqbal, *Kulliyat-i-Iqbal* (Lahore: Sheikh Muhammad Bashir and Sons, n.d.), pp. 272, 289, 294.

103. For the suggestion that Iqbal gave the word new meaning, see Sheila McDonough, *The Flame of Sinai: Hope and Vision in Iqbal* (Lahore: Iqbal Academy, 2002), p. 231.

104. Iqbal, *Kulliyat-i-Iqbal*, pp. 619, 332, 301, 344, 662.

105. Ibid., p. 687.

106. Ibid., p. 319.

107. Iqbal, *The Reconstruction of Religious Thought in Islam*, p. 89.

108. Ibid.

109. Iqbal, *Kulliyat-i-Iqbal*, p. 631.

110. Ibid., pp. 260–261.

111. Iqbal, *Javidnama*, p. 10.

112. Iqbal, *Kulliyat-i-Iqbal*, pp. 304–308.

113. Ibid., p. 636.

114. Iqbal, *Javidnama*, p. 142.

115. Ibid., p. 235.

116. Ibid., pp. 232–235, 241–245. The Battle of the Khyber was one of the early campaigns of the Prophet in which Ali excelled as a warrior of faith.

117. Ibid., pp. 246–247, 256–257.

118. Iqbal, *Kulliyat-i-Iqbal*, pp. 626, 630.

119. Ibid., pp. 637, 645, 650.

120. Ibid., p. 659.

121. Naim Siddiqui, *Iqbal: Baal-i-Jibreel—a Verse Translation* (Fremont, Calif.: Alhamra Publications, 1996), p. 30.

122. Ibid., pp. 37.

123. Iqbal, *Kulliyat-i-Iqbal,* pp. 347–348.

124. Iqbal, *The Reconstruction of Religious Thought in Islam,* p. 130.

125. Iqbal, *Kulliyat-i-Islam,* p. 616.

6. Jihad as Terrorism

1. In view of the problems associated with the concept of Muslim fundamentalism, in this chapter I examine Mawdudi's thought on its own terms.

2. Faisal Devji, *Landscapes of the Jihad: Militancy, Morality, Modernity* (New Delhi: Foundation Books, 2005), p. 65.

3. David Cook, *Understanding Jihad* (Berkeley: University of California Press, 2005), p. 2.

4. See Talal Asad, *Formations of the Secular: Christianity, Islam and Modernity* (Stanford, Calif.: Stanford University Press), 2003, pp. 187–201.

5. Samuel Huntington, *The Clash of Civilizations and the Remaking of World Order* (New York: Simon and Schuster, 1998).

6. Rafiuddin Hashmi and Salim Mansur Khalid (eds.), *Khutut-i-Mawdudi* (Lahore: Al-Badar, 1983), 1:15–16.

7. Abul Ala Mawdudi, *Al-Jihad fi-ul Islam,* 2nd ed. (Lahore: Tarjaman-ul-Quran, 1948), pp. 10–11.

8. Cited in Hazrat Mirza Tahir Ahmad, *Murder in the Name of Allah* (Cambridge, Eng.: Lutterworth, 1989), p. 15.

9. Ibid.

10. Muhammad Iqbal, who in 1926 had been elected to the provincial council, took a leading part in the disturbances. For a discussion of his role, see Ayesha Jalal, *Self and Sovereignty: Individual and Community in South Asian Islam since 1850* (London: Routledge, 2000), pp. 295–296.

11. Hashmi and Khalid, *Khutut-i-Mawdudi,* 1:17.

12. Mawdudi, *Al-Jihad fi-ul Islam,* pp. 8–10.

13. See, for instance, Cook, *Understanding Jihad,* pp. 99–102.

14. Mawdudi, *Al-Jihad fi-ul Islam,* pp. 14–16.

15. Ibid., pp. 18–24.

16. Ibid., pp. 25–38.

17. Ibid., pp. 120, 138–139.

18. Abul Ala Mawdudi, "Jihad in Islam," reprint (Lahore: Islamic Publications, 2001), pp. 5–6.

19. Ibid., pp. 6–11, 19–21.

20. Ibid., pp. 27. 31.

21. For a detailed discussion of Mawdudi's thought, see Seyyed Vali Reza Nasr, *Mawdudi and the Making of Islamic Revivalism* (New York: Oxford University Press, 1996), pp. 49–68, 72–106.

22. Abul Ala Mawdudi, *Tajdid wa Ihya-i-Din,* 9th ed. (Lahore: Islamic Publishers, 1966), pp. 30–32.

23. Ibid., pp. 36–41.

24. Ibid., pp. 42–54.

25. Ibid., pp. 77–88, 91, 109, 114–117.

26. Ibid., pp. 12–13, 128–129, 144–147.

27. Hashmi and Khalid, *Khutut-i-Mawdudi,* pp. 17–18.

28. "Zuhd taang nazar ne mujhe kafir jana / Aur kafir samajhta hai Musalman hoon main."

29. Abul Ala Mawdudi, *Haqiqat-i-Islam—Khutbat* (Lahore: Idara Tarjuman-ul-Quran, 2003), 1:64.

30. Abul Ala Mawdudi, *Khutbat* (Lahore: Din Muhammad Electric Press, n.d.), pp. 238–244.

31. Muhammad Iqbal, *Reconstruction of Religious Thought in Islam,* reprint (Lahore: Sang-e-Meel, 1996), pp. 135–138, 144, 157.

32. For an analysis of the difference in their conception of the relation between the state and religion in Islam, see Ayesha Jalal, "In the Shadows of Modernity? Theology and Sovereignty in South Asian Islam," in Charles Cohen and Leonard V. Kaplan (eds.), *Theology and the Soul of the Liberal State,* forthcoming.

33. Mawdudi, *Khutbat,* pp. 6–7.

34. Iqbal, *Reconstruction of Religious Thought in Islam,* p. 135.

35. Abul Ala Mawdudi, *Purdah and the Status of Women in Islam,* 8th ed. (Lahore: Al-Ashari, 1986), p. 211.

36. See Abul Ala Mawdudi, "Ethical Viewpoint of Islam," Khurshid Ahmad (trans. and ed.), www.witness-pioneer.org/vil/Books/M_EVI.

37. Mawdudi, "Jihad in Islam," pp. 28–29.

38. For the most detailed exposition of the rationale for the declaration

of jihad in Kashmir, see Fazal Ilahi Vazirabadi, *Maslah-i-Jihad-i-Kashmir aur us ki Mukhtasar Tarikh* (Rawalpindi: Tanzim-ud-Dawat-ul-Quran wa Sunnah, 1997 [1948]); see also the Lashkar-i-Tayyiba edition, *Jihad-i-Kashmir: Farziyat, Fazliyat aud Tarikh,* comp. Hafiz Mohammed Saeed (Lahore: Dar-ul-Andlus, 2004), henceforth *Jihad-i-Kashmir.* My references are to this last edition.

39. Abul Ala Mawdudi, *Maslah Kashmir aur us ka hal,* 2nd ed. (Lahore: Islami Jamiat-i-Talaba, 1981), pp. 73–76.

40. The Ahmadi connection with Kashmir has deep historical roots. For a discussion of its relevance in late colonial Punjab, see Jalal, *Self and Sovereignty,* pp. 356–360, 362–369.

41. Abul Ala Mawdudi, "The Problem of Qadiyanism: How the Heretical Beliefs of the Ahmadiya Sect, Who Accept Their Founder Ghulam Ahmad as a Prophet, Have Put Them outside the Fold of Islam and Left Them Designated as Non-Muslims in Pakistan"; www.islamfortoday.com/mawdudi.1.htm.

42. *Tulu-i-Islam,* May 1953, p. 64; http://aaiil.info/misconceptions/fatwas/bvsd.htm.

43. *Report of the Court of Inquiry Constituted under Punjab Act II of 1954 to Enquire into the Punjab Disturbances of 1953* (Lahore: Superintendent Government Printing Press, 1954), henceforth, *Munir Report,* pp. 124, 158, 185, 201.

44. Abul Ala Mawdudi, *Islami Nizam aur Maghribi La Dinyat,* 12th ed. (Lahore: Islamic Publishers), 1974.

45. *Munir Report,* pp. 221–222, 224, 226.

46. Nasr, *Mawdudi and the Making of Islamic Revivalism,* pp. 71, 76.

47. Cited in Ayesha Jalal, *The State of Martial Rule: The Origins of Pakistan's Political Economy of Defence* (Cambridge: Cambridge University Press, 1990), p. 285.

48. See Israr Ahmad, *Jihad sey Ghurez ki Saza Nifaq: Surah-tul-Munafiqin ki Roshani Mein* (Lahore: Markazi Anjuman Khudam-al-Quran, 2002).

49. Maulana Wahiduddin Khan, *The True Jihad: The Concept of Peace, Tolerance and Non-Violence in Islam* (New Delhi: Goodword, 2002), pp. 14, 16.

50. Nasr, *Mawdudi and the Making of Islamic Revivalism,* p. 65.

51. Barbara D. Metcalf, "Nationalism, Modernity, and Muslim Identity

in India before 1947," in Peter van der Veer and Hartmut Lehmann (eds.), *Nation and Religion: Perspectives on Europe and Asia* (Princeton, N.J.: Princeton University Press, 1999), p. 136.

52. Excerpt from Abul Hasan Ali Nadwi, *Life and Mission of Maulana Muhammad Ilyas,* at www.central-mosque.com.

53. Zia-ul-Hasan Faruqi, "The Tablighi Jamat," in V. K. Gokak (ed.), *Transactions of the Indian Institute of Advanced Studies* (Simla: n.p., 1965), p. 61.

54. Nadwi, *Life and Mission of Maulana Muhammad Ilyas.*

55. For a discussion of the Tablighi Jamaat's role in the politics of Muslim nationalism in the preindependence era, see Metcalf, "Nationalism, Modernity, and Muslim Identity."

56. Yoginder Sikand, "The Tablighi Jama'at and Politics: A Critical Reappraisal," *Qalandar,* May 2005, www.islaminterfaith.org.

57. Ibid.

58. Khaled Ahmed, "The Genius of Ghulam Ahmad Pervez," *Friday Times* (Lahore), 11 December 1999.

59. Cited in Ahmad, *Murder in the Name of Allah,* p. 56.

60. Chaudhri Ghulam Ahmad Parvez, *Islam: A Challenge to Religion* (Lahore: Idara-e-Tulu-i-Islam, 1968), pp. 8–10.

61. *Munir Report,* p. 218.

62. *Islami Mumlakat Ka Khwab (Jo Kasrat-i-Tabir sey Pareshan Ho Gaya)* (Lahore: Tulu-i-Islam, n.d.), pp. 4–6, 9–10, 28.

63. Ahmad, *Murder in the Name of Allah,* pp. 13, 37, 45–60.

64. Interview with Zbigniew Brzezinski, *Le Nouvel Observateur,* 15–21 January 1998, p. 76.

65. George Crile, *Charlie Wilson's War: The Extraordinary Story of the Largest Covert Operation in History* (New York: Atlantic, 2004).

66. Syed Talat Hussain, "Breeding Ground of Extremism," *Dawn* (Karachi), 3 December 2001.

67. Fazlur Rahman, *Islam and Modernity: Transformation of an Intellectual Tradition* (Chicago: University of Chicago Press, 1982), p. 42.

68. Hussain, "Breeding Ground of Extremism."

69. Muhammad Amar Rana, *Jihad Kashmir wa Afghanistan: Jihadi Tanzimeen aur Mazhabi Jamatoon ka Aik Jyiza* (Lahore: Mashal, 2002),

pp. 18–19. The book has been translated into English as *A to Z of Jihad Organizations in Pakistan* (Lahore: Mashal, 2004). My references are to the original Urdu edition.

70. Rana, *Jihad Kashmir wa Afghanistan,* pp. 122–123.

71. Khaled Ahmed, "The Grand Deobandi Consensus," *Friday Times* (Lahore), 4 February 2000.

72. Ibid.

73. Rana, *Jihad Kashmir wa Afghanistan,* pp. 19–20.

74. Khaled Ahmed, "The Grand Deobandi Consensus."

75. For the statement that not all members are jihadis, see Alex Alexiev, "Tablighi Jamaat: The Stealthy Legions of Jihad," *Middle East Quarterly* 12, no. 1 (January 2005).

76. Rana, *Jihad Kashmir wa Afghanistan,* pp. 17, 49.

77. Khaled Ahmed, "Re-Assertion of the Barelvis in Pakistan," *Friday Times* (Lahore), 8 September 2000.

78. Corroboration can be found in newspaper reports from mid-1999 to the summer of 2001.

79. Syed Talat Hussain, "Breeding Ground of Extremism," *Dawn* (Karachi), 3 December 2001.

80. Ansar Abbasi, "Anti-Arms Campaign a Failure So Far: Musharraf," *News* (Lahore), 26 August 2001.

81. For an interesting analysis of the dilemma, see Khaled Ahmed, "Is There Life after Kashmir?" *Friday Times* (Lahore), 27 August 2001.

82. Rana, *Jihad Kashmir wa Afghanistan,* p. 51.

83. Ahmed, "Is There Life after Kashmir?"

84. Mubashir Zaidi, "ISI Still Playing a Double Game as Talks Become Imminent," *South Asia Tribune,* 18–24 May 2003.

85. See, for instance, the letters written to Masood Azhar by young women pining to participate in jihad, in *Jaish-i-Muhammad* (Karachi), July 2000, pp. 35–36.

86. Rana, *Jihad Kashmir wa Afghanistan,* pp. 30, 34–37.

87. Ibid., pp. 22–28.

88. Ibid., p. 54.

89. *Voice of Islam,* September 2000, n.p.

90. Editorial by Hafiz Mohammed Saeed, *Voice of Islam,* November 2000.

91. Ibid.

92. Mawdudi, *Maslah Kashmir aur us ka hal,* p. 75.

93. In addition to the two considered here, see the voluminous book by Mufti Abdur Rahman Al-Rahmani, *Al-Jihad Al-Islami,* comp. Abu Yusuf Ijaz Ahmad Tanvir (Lahore: Al-Andlus, 2004). *Gulistan-i-Jihad* (The Garden of Jihad) (Lahore: Al-Andlus, 2004) is a short pamphlet consisting of Al-Rahmani's sermons. Other titles include Obaidur Rahman Mohammadi, *Difa-i-Jihad* (Lahore: Al-Andlus, 2003); and two pamphlets: Maulana Emir Hamza, *Insaniyat ka Qatil: Hindu Dharam* (Killer of Humanity: The Hindu Religion) (Lahore: Al-Andlus, n.d.), and Hamza, *Kashmiri Aurat aur America* (The Kashmiri Woman and America) (Lahore: Al-Andlus, n.d.).

94. Vazirabadi, *Maslah-i-Jihad-i-Kashmir.*

95. Ibid., pp. 109, 116.

96. Ibid., pp. 19–22.

97. Ibid., pp. 66–67.

98. Ibid., pp. 137–140.

99. Abdus Salam Bin Muhammad, *Jehad in the Present Times,* trans., Khalid Mahmood (Lahore: Dar-ul-Andlus, n.d.), pp. 10–22.

100. Ibid., p. 61.

101. Ibid.

102. Ibid., pp. 62–65.

103. *Weekly Ghazvah Time,* 22–28 March 2002.

104. *Voice of Islam,* November 2000, p. 15.

105. *News,* 21 November 2002.

106. The denial was made to me in person by Hafiz Mohammed Saeed, whom I interviewed in Lahore in November 2005. This contradicts his statement in an interview with Mohammad Shehzad published in the *Friday Times* (Lahore), 17 April 2003.

107. Interview with Hafiz Mohammed Saeed, November 2005.

108. For the condemnation, see Mohammed Hanif Ramay, *Islam ki Rohani Qadreen: Maut Nahin Zindagi* (Islam's Spiritual Vision: Life Not Death) (Lahore: Sang-e-Meel, 2005); and Abu Sulaiman Shahjahanpuri (comp.), *Jihad-Islami aur Daur-i-Hazar ki Jang* (Lahore: Jamiat, 2002).

109. Yoginder Sikand, "Ahl-i Hadith Scholar Denounces Lashkar-i

Tayyeba Terrorism," at http://groups.yahoo.com/group/indiathinkersnet/ message/8600?viscount=100.

Conclusion

1. Jalaluddin Rumi, *Mystical Poems of Rumi,* trans. A. J. Arberry (Chicago: Chicago University Press, 1968), p. 70, poem no. 80

2. Abu Abdullah Shaban Ali's Last Will and Testament, photocopy in my possession.

3. Larry Witham, "Muslims See Wordplay as Swordplay in Terrorism War," *Washington Post,* 24 July 2002.

4. Muhammad Hedayetullah, *Sayyid Ahmad: A Study of the Religious Reform Movement of Sayyid Ahmad of Ra'e Bareli* (Lahore: Sheikh Muhammad Ashraf, 1970), p. 103.

5. Fazlur Rahman, *Islam* (New York: Anchor, 1966), pp. 250–254.

6. Muhammad Iqbal, *Kulliyat-i-Iqbal* (Lahore: Sheikh Muhammad Bashir and Sons, n.d.), pp. 824–825.

7. *Sahih al-Bukhari,* 9.64, on *Alim* (compact disk).

Index

Index